Basic Verbal Skills

for the

Middle School

Basic Verbal Skills

for the

Middle School

Philip Burnham

Richard Lederer

St. Paul's School
Concord, New Hampshire

Independent School Press

Wellesley Hills   Massachusetts

The authors and publishers thank Scott, Foresman & Company for permission to use some material originally in their copyright. Such material has been revised and brought up to date by the authors.

CONTENTS

A Word to Teachers. ix
A Word to Students. xv
Unit 1   Verbs and Subjects of Verbs 1
    Verbs 1; Nouns as subjects of verbs 3; **Improving sentences #1** 4;
    Pronouns 5; Subjects not directly before their verbs 6; **Improving
    sentences #2** 8; **Composition:** How oral compositions should sound 8;
    Telling what happened 9.
Unit 2   Modifiers. 13
    Adjectives 13; **Improving sentences #3** 15; Predicate adjectives 16;
    Adverbs 17; **Improving sentences #4** 19; **Composition:** How written
    compositions should look 21; Telling what happened 23.
Unit 3   Joiners. 27
    Prepositions 27; **Improving sentences #5** 29; Ways you have
    learned 31; Conjunctions 32; Compound subjects 34; Compound
    verbs 35; **Improving sentences #6** 36; **Composition:** Keeping a straight
    line 38; Telling how to do or make something 39.
Unit 4   Other Uses of Nouns and Pronouns. 45
    Predicate nominatives 45; **Improving sentences #7** 47; Direct
    objects 49; **Improving sentences #8** 51; Indirect objects 53; Objective
    predicates 54; Adverbial nouns 54; Active and passive verbs 56;
    Improving sentences #9 57; Appositives 58; **Improving sentences
    #10** 60; **Composition:** Telling how something looks 62.
Unit 5   Verbals and Verbal Phrases 69
    Active participles 69; **Improving sentences #11** 72; Ways you have
    learned 74; Passive participles 75; **Improving sentences #12** 77;
    Gerunds 79; **Improving sentences #13** 82; Infinitives 84; **Improving
    sentences #14** 87; **Composition:** Telling about others 89; **Improving
    sentences #15** 95; Ways you have learned 97.
Unit 6   Clauses 99
    What a subordinate clause is 99; Adjective clauses 100; Uses of
    relative pronouns 102; Omitted relative pronouns 103; **Improving
    sentences #16** 105; Noun clauses 107; **Improving sentences #17** 110;
    Indirect questions 112; Adverb clauses 114; Adverb clauses at the
    beginning of sentences 117; Adverb clauses of comparison 118;
    Improving sentences #18 120; **Composition:** Expressing a prefer-
    ence 123.
Unit 7   Review of Grammar: The Kinds of Sentences. 129
    What a simple sentence is 129; Parts of the simple sentence 130;
    Compound sentences with conjunctions 133; Compound sentences
    without conjunctions 135; Independent adverbs 136; What a complex
    sentence is 138; **Improving sentences #19** 140; Parts of complex and
    compound sentences 142; **Improving sentences #20** 145; Ways you
    have learned 150; **Composition:** Telling what something means 154.

Unit 8   Ending Sentences and Using Commas **159**

Punctuating sentences accurately 159; Commas for series 161; Setting off words with commas 163; Commas for addresses and dates 165; Commas for parenthetical words 166; Setting off appositives 168; Appositives that are not set off 168; Setting off nonrestrictive participial phrases 170; Setting off nonrestrictive adjective clauses 171; Setting off introductory adverb clauses 173; Commas with coordinating conjunctions 175; Commas for clearness 177; **Composition**: Expressing an opinion 179.

Unit 9   Other Marks of Punctuation **185**

The "half-period" semicolon 185; The "double comma" semicolon 187; Colons that introduce 189; Parentheses 191; Dashes that interrupt 193; Direct quotations 195; More uses for quotation marks 198; Summary review of all marks 199; **Composition**: Persuading others 202.

Unit 10   Standard English Usage **207**

Improving usage #1 207; Singular and plural nouns 207; Pronoun subjects 208; Pronouns as objects of prepositions 208; Pronouns as objects of verbs 209; Pronouns as appositives 210; *We* or *us* 210; Pronouns with gerunds 211; Pronouns in adverb clauses of comparison 211; *Them* and *those* 212; Pronouns that end in *self* and *selves* 212; *Who, which,* and *that* 213; *Who, whom,* and *whose* 214; *Who* and *whoever; Whom* and *whomever* 215; **Improving usage #2** 216; Pronoun reference 216; **Improving usage #3** 218; Adjectives and adverbs 218; Singular adjectives 220; Comparison of adjectives and adverbs 221; Adverbs that end in *where* 223; **Improving usage #4** 224; Agreement of subject and verb 224; Plural verbs with *there* 225; Agreement of relative and verb 226; Avoiding shifts in time 227; Forms of *be, have,* and *do* 228; **Improving usage #5** 231; Prepositions 231; **Composition**: Telling about books and magazines 232.

Unit 11   Working with Sentences **235**

Parallel forms 235; **Improving sentences #21** 237; **Improving sentences #22** 240; Careless repetition 243; Wordiness 244; **Improving sentences #23** 247; **Improving sentences #24** 249; Verbals cannot make sentences 250; Adjective clauses are not sentences 252; Noun clauses are not sentences 253; Adverb clauses are not sentences 254; **Improving sentences #25** 255; Sentence errors caused by adverbs 255; Sentence errors caused by prepositions 257; Comma splices with clauses 257; Twenty-five ways you have learned 259; **Composition**: Telling a secret ambition 260.

Unit 12   Working with Paragraphs **263**

What makes a good paragraph 263; Selecting details 265; Developing the idea 269; Explaining details adequately 271; Telling how details are related 271; General statement 276; Clinching the point 278; Summary sentence 287; Trying paragraphs together 283; Linking expressions 286; Paragroups 288; Grouping details effectively 291;

Allocating space 294; Using space wisely 297; A good start 298; Introductory paragraph 301; Summarizing important ideas 305; A Summarizing paragraph 306; Bridging the gaps 308; Keeping the reader in mind 310; **Composition**: Telling about interesting jobs 312.

Unit 13   Seven Basic Spelling Rules. 315

Dropping the final *e* 315; Doubling a final consonant 318; Changing *y* to *i* 320; *ie* and *ei* 321; Possessives 326; Contractions 330; Using capital letters 331; Adding suffixes 335; **Composition**: Telling about our community 337.

Unit 14   Spelling Demons and Other Creatures. 339

The demons 339; Similar forms together 343; The *dis* words; Second-grade words; Solid words 345; Words ending with *ful* and *ous* 346; Words with *con, ad, re, ness* 347; Words with *ly* 348; Words with *i* and *le* 349; Words with *al;* One *s* and two *s*'s; Soft *c* and *g* 350; Words with *o, u,* and *ou* 352; Words with *a; Does* and *goes* 353; Words with *e* 354; Words with *el;* Single letter 355; Three groups and six marvels 356; **Composition**: Telling about interesting people 357.

Unit 15   A Glossary of Troublesome Words 359

Affect and *effect* 359; *All right* 359; *Allusion* and *illusion* 360; *Almost* and *most* 360; *Amount* and *number* 361; *Anyone else,* etc. 361; *Beside* and *besides* 361; *Between* and *among* 362; *Borrow* and *lend* 363; *Bring* and *take* 363; *Childish* and *childlike* 363; *Discover* and *invent* 364; *Formerly* and *formally* 364; *Hardly* and *scarcely* 365; *Healthy* and *healthful* 365; *Human* and *humane* 366; *Imply* and *infer* 366; *Learn* and *teach* 366; *Leave* and *let* 367; *Less* and *fewer* 367; *Lie* and *lay* 368; *Like* and *as* 369; *No* and *any* 369; *Precede* and *proceed* 370; *Since, as,* and *because* 370; *Sit* and *set* 371; *Them* and *those* 371; *Uninterested* and *disinterested* 372; *Where* and *how* 372; **Composition**: Expressing opinions by mail 373.

A Word to Teachers

BASIC VERBAL SKILLS FOR THE MIDDLE SCHOOL, like its predecessor, BASIC VERBAL SKILLS, has been designed especially for the classes of those teachers who believe that success in language teaching can best be achieved through a return to the fundamentals of grammar, punctuation, usage, composition, and spelling.

The book is a return with a difference. It is a return conditioned by experience and investigation and much thought as to why fundamentals are worth teaching and how they can best be taught to modern middle schools students.

Mere mastery of "the basics" for their own sake has, we know, little value for students, since it has no appreciable effect on improving skill in using language. The teacher must approach the fundamentals (as effective teachers have always done), not as ends in themselves, but as a source from which direct applications are made to the challenges of sentence, paragraph, and composition improvements. Only then do the basics become truly functional, truly valuable.

As the outline below indicates, the unremitting goal of this book is *language growth through a program of systematic application to real speaking and writing situations.* To this end each lesson in grammar culminates in an extensive application to *Improving Sentences* (twenty-five in number). In addition, "Standard English Usage" (Unit 10) is organized around five concepts of *Improving Usage,* and "Working with Paragraphs" (Unit 12) contains ten specific applications for *Improving Paragraphs.*

One more word about BASIC VERBAL SKILLS FOR THE MIDDLE SCHOOL. The format, the organization of the material into work units, and the semi-inductive approach — all of which have drawn a positive response from users of BASIC VERBAL SKILLS — are similar in this book. But the differences between the two texts are everywhere apparent: a simplification in approach, in point of view, in allotment of time, in level of achievement. The addition of the sequence of oral and written composition lessons, which come at the end of each Unit, and the addition of an extensive unit on paragraphing (Unit 12) means that BASIC VERBAL SKILLS FOR THE MIDDLE SCHOOL offers a complete program in speaking and writing skills.

Available, in addition to the present book, is BASIC VERBAL SKILLS FOR THE MIDDLE SCHOOL: GRAMMAR WORKBOOK. Its first purpose is to supplement the exercises and practices available in the grammar and punctuation Units of this text. Since pages of the *Workbook* are perforated, the materials serve as convenient and helpful additional exercises under varying circumstances. As a further help to the burdens of teachers, the publisher has available a "Teacher's Key" for both the textbook and the WORKBOOK.

The Basic Types of Composition. The special concern of BASIC VERBAL SKILLS FOR THE MIDDLE SCHOOL is the teaching of composition skills—primarily those skills that middle school students will find most useful in their everyday lives. Eight basic types of composition are taught in Units 1-9: narration (Telling What Happened), exposition (Telling How to Make or Do Something), description (Telling How Something Looks), character study (Telling about Others), statement of a preference based on a comparison (Expressing a Preference), explanation of an abstract term (Telling What Something Means), statement of an opinion based on reasons (Expressing an Opinion), and persuasive exposition (Persuading Others).

Two closely integrated lessons in each Unit present a step-by-step explanation of each of these eight basic types. The first lesson—concerned with thinking and planning—helps the student select a suitable topic, choose and arrange details effectively, determine good beginning and ending sentences, and prepare useful notes for an oral composition. The second lesson—on writing and revising—shows the student how to convert his or her notes into first-draft paragraphs, and then how to revise, title, and proofread his or her written composition. In both lessons specific examples are used to show exactly what the problems are and how they might be solved. And in each assignment the examples used and the suggestions made are designed to encourage students to talk and write about subjects of greatest interest to them—their own experiences, interests, observations, ambitions, opinions, and work.

Outlining and Paragraph Development. Students are seldom at a loss for things to say about themselves and their personal interests. Their weakness, revealed in so many oral talks and written compositions, is often not lack of ideas, but lack of skill in organizing. By teaching outlining (a simple two-level grouping) as an integral part of the composition process, BASIC VERBAL SKILLS helps the students organize their ideas effectively. And by means of specific examples illustrating the grouping of details in time, space, and logical orders, the book creates in the student an awareness of how paragraphs are developed. Without mentioning the abstract terms *unity* and *coherence,* the lessons show how unity and coherence are achieved through careful planning and the use of topic sentences, indications of point of view, and transitional expressions.

Applications of Composition Skills. Once the basic composition skills are mastered, there is no further need for the two-part lessons. Thus, the oral and written lessons in the latter part of BASIC VERBAL SKILLS are each an entity. Each assignment is designed to give the student an opportunity to apply the composition skills to a new situation.

Grammar for Sentence Improvement. Even if all the students in a typical English class had had uniform instruction in grammar, their understanding of grammatical concepts would very likely be far from uniform. For that reason alone, a complete reteaching of grammar would seem desirable to most teachers. This reteaching is doubly desirable—in fact, it is imperative—in BASIC VERBAL SKILLS, where grammar is presented not for its own sake but to show the student the ways in which words can be put together in sentences for more effective communication. As soon as each grammatical concept is learned—or relearned—it is immediately applied to some phase of sentence improvement; its value in effective communication is immediately demonstrated. A minimum number of constructions are covered, and standard terminology is used throughout. The emphasis is not on the classifications, but on the way the constructions can be used in revising sentences to make them clearer, more forceful, more interesting: In other words, grammar is taught because it has a direct bearing on effective expression.

Punctuation for Meaning. The punctuation lessons, which work hand in hand with the grammar lessons, emphasize the need for observing the standard conventions of written expression. Rules are given, but they are presented as generalizations growing out of a discussion of examples. Students are shown the importance of using punctuation marks to make clear to the reader exactly what meaning is intended.

Spelling for Acceptable Form. The carefully planned spelling lessons are based on recent studies of the most efficient ways to handle the problems. Since the "demons" account for an overwhelming percentage of all misspellings, the lessons focus attention on these common sources of error. Various methods of attack are used: grouping words of similar spelling; using phonetic clues, mnemonic devices, distorted pronunciations, careful pronunciations; making generalizations to cover certain groups; observing prefixes and suffixes; visualizing the forms.

Levels of Usage. For the correction of persistent errors in word usage and for the development of an awareness of what constitutes "good English" BASIC VERBAL SKILLS follows the modern trend of concentrating attention and drill on a relatively small number of carefully selected language forms. The usage lessons, together with their associated oral drill, provide a means for helping students acquire ear-patterns based on forms generally accepted at each of three levels. Usages ordinarily considered substandard English (and as such requiring remedial treatment in high school) are designated by the label "We." Usages normally expected in standard cultivated English are designated by "Educated people." Usages limited mostly to formal or literary English are designated by "Careful speakers and writers." The designations indicate roughly the relative importance of the items; which ones should receive greatest stress in a particular classroom situation can best be determined by the teacher, who knows the background and ability of the students. Explanation of usages in terms of what is done at each of the three levels rather than in terms of logic or grammar emphasizes the need for practicing the acceptable forms until they become habitual and "sound right" to the student.

Paragraph Study. Unit 12 moves beyond the concern with sentences into a discussion of paragraphs, the next "unity" beyond that of sentences. The student is shown a number of selections from magazines to see how modern writers write. By observing the various functions sentences may have in a paragraph, the ways in which the paragraphs in a composition are linked together, the importance of using space wisely, the uses of special paragraphs (introductory, summarizing, transitional), he or she learns—from concrete examples instead of from abstract discussion—just what unity and coherence and emphasis mean. And in the "improving paragraphs" sections the student is given specific suggestions for using what he or she has learned in revising his or her own paragraphs for greater effectiveness.

Philip Burnham
Richard Lederer

A Word to Students

All of us—boys and girls, men and women—want people to understand what we say. We are alike in our desire to express our thoughts so that others will not misunderstand our meaning. Have you ever said something that was misunderstood, and then thought, "Oh, how I wish I could say what I mean!" Or have you ever listened carefully to someone who was speaking, or tried hard to read something that someone else had written, and then been forced to say, "But I don't understand what it's all about"?

The ability to make people understand what you say is not always a natural gift. It usually takes practice. Do you know someone who is a good storyteller? Do you admire persons who talk well? Such people were not necessarily born with the gift of making themselves understood. They simply wanted others to understand—and wanted this badly enough to keep trying again and again until they found ways of making their meaning clear. Good speakers and good writers—and, after all, writing is just talk put down on paper—have worked long and hard to develop the ability to interest you and make you understand what they mean.

You have, of course, already done much talking and some writing. As you grow up and leave school, you will have to do more and more. Almost every adult occupation requires to some extent the ability to express ideas orally, and many require also the ability to express ideas in writing. The purpose of this book is to help you in the kinds of everyday talking and writing that all of us must learn to do in this modern age of much talking and writing.

You do not need exceptional talent to become a good talker or writer. The truth is that most people—even professional speakers and writers—have to *learn* how to talk and write well. Some may seem to be more talented than others, but this is usually the result of their being more interested and so more willing to work at improvement. And you must never think, because writing perhaps seems difficult for you now, that you are doomed to be an awkward, clumsy writer all your life. Any intelligent person *who sincerely wants to* can greatly improve his writing ability in one short year.

As with many arts and trades and hobbies, learning to talk and write well requires much practice. But that practice does not have to be difficult or dull. The easiest things to talk and write about are those most familiar to you—things you have seen or done or thought about. In this book are many suggestions to help you decide which of these things will be likely to interest your classmates. With a little thought, you should have no trouble in choosing topics that you will enjoy talking and writing about.

Here is something that may surprise you. Famous authors, skillful and experienced as they are, often write parts of their books over and over again before sending their manuscripts to a publisher—just as high-school students must often rewrite sentences and even whole paragraphs before handing their compositions to the teacher.

There is a great deal about sentences in this book, and for a good reason. Clear, forceful, interesting sentences are the building blocks of all good composition. But they are only building blocks. If you put them together in haphazard ways, without a plan, others may not be able to understand what you mean. When you carelessly jump back and forth from one idea to another, it is very difficult for any-one else to follow your thoughts. But when you put your sentences together according to a plan and move smoothly from one idea to the next, it is easy to follow your thoughts and to know what you mean. So there are also many suggestions about planning what you want to say *before* you start to talk and write.

The quickest and easiest way to plan a composition is to outline what you want to say. Making an outline of your ideas helps you arrange them in an order that can be easily followed as you talk.

Using an outline when you write helps you group sentences into paragraphs that show your reader what your main points are—and help him understand better what you have written.

Learning to talk and write well is not easy. It takes long study and hard work and much patience. But each time you plan a good composition, each time you succeed in making others understand something you want them to know, you gain confidence in your ability to express your thoughts. Step by step you move nearer the goal we all desire—the ability to make others understand what we say. Even if you do not expect to become a famous author or speaker or radio commentator or reporter, you will find this ability invaluable in the school years just ahead. And, later, you will find it important in making a living and in enjoying the companionship of others.

Writing, by the way, can be a very good hobby, even if you are not expert at it. You do not have to be a concert pianist to have fun playing the piano, or a champion figure skater to enjoy skating. Nor do you have to be a Shakespeare or a Dickens to have fun writing. And who knows what might happen? You yourself might turn out to be a famous writer. At one time or another the famous writers of today were in school—as you are now—struggling with a composition book and quite unaware that someday they would become successful authors. Could it not happen to you?

Basic Verbal Skills

for the

Middle School

GRAMMAR AT A GLANCE

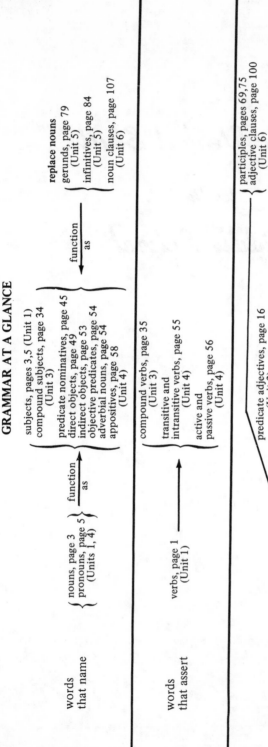
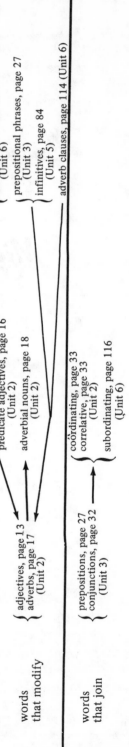

words that name

nouns, page 3
pronouns, page 5
(Units 1, 4)

function as →

subjects, pages 3,5 (Unit 1)
compound subjects, page 34 (Unit 3)
predicate nominatives, page 45
direct objects, page 49
indirect objects, page 53
objective predicates, page 54
adverbial nouns, page 54
appositives, page 58 (Unit 4)

function as →

replace nouns

gerunds, page 79 (Unit 5)
infinitives, page 84 (Unit 5)
noun clauses, page 107 (Unit 6)

words that assert

verbs, page 1 (Unit 1) →

compound verbs, page 35 (Unit 3)
transitive and intransitive verbs, page 55 (Unit 4)
active and passive verbs, page 56 (Unit 4)

words that modify

adjectives, page 13
adverbs, page 17 (Unit 2) →

predicate adjectives, page 16 (Unit 2)
adverbial nouns, page 18 (Unit 2)

participles, pages 69,75
adjective clauses, page 100 (Unit 6)
prepositional phrases, page 27 (Unit 3)
infinitives, page 84 (Unit 5)
adverb clauses, page 114 (Unit 6)

words that join

prepositions, page 27
conjunctions, page 32 (Unit 3) →

coördinating, page 33
correlative, page 33 (Unit 2)
subordinating, page 116 (Unit 6)

Verbs and Subjects of Verbs

Verbs: The foundation of sentence mastery

The foundation of "sentence sense" is a knowledge of verbs. Until you can quickly find all the verbs in a long paragraph from a newspaper or from literature, you have not begun to learn what a sentence is. But once you have mastered verbs, you will find it easy to recognize sentences and avoid serious errors.

The verbs are italicized in the following six sentences:

> Madrid *is* a large city.
> He *could* not *see*.
> The word *had* often *been* incorrectly *spelled*.
> They *might have been caught*.
> *Don't* you *like* it?
> *Stand* farther away.

In the second sentence the verb does not include the word *not*. In the fifth sentence the verb does not include the contraction *n't*. The word *not* (or its contraction *n't*) is never a part of the verb. Such words as *down, at,* and *over* are not parts of verbs; neither are words like *good, sick, angry,* and *sure*. Notice carefully what the verbs are in the next seven sentences:

> We *looked* down the avenue.
> He *had been gazing* at the clouds.
> She *was* now *hurrying* over the bridge.
> It *does*n't *taste* good.
> He *had* long *been* sick.
> Dan *may be* angry at us.
> Perhaps he *was* not sure.

The verbs are *looked, had been gazing, was hurrying, does taste, had been, may be,* and *was*.

A verb is a word or group of words that makes a statement or asks a question or gives a command. It may consist of one, two, three, or four words, and these words may be separated from each other.

You can see the ways in which verbs of more than one word are made if you study the examples below. There is nothing new or hard about these five ways, because you use all the forms in your own speech. Verbs of more than one word are made:

1) With *do, does,* and *did,* usually in questions or with *not:* Do you like it? It does not suit me. They didn't hear us.

2) With *have, has,* and *had:* have seen, has gone, had felt.

3) With *am, is, are, was,* and *were:* am asking, am asked; is doing, is done; are watching, are watched; was telegraphing, was telegraphed; were sending, were sent.

4) With *have been, has been,* and *had been:* have been seeing, have been seen; has been sinking, has been sunk; had been writing, had been written.

5) With *may, can, must, might, could, shall, should, will, would:* may have seen, can be doing, must have been done, might go, might have gone, might have been going, could tell, could have driven, could have been driven, shall know, shall be elected, should have seen, will arrive, will have arrived, will be forgotten, would have skidded, would have been skidding.

Your work in the following exercise is to find the whole of every verb, and nothing but the verb. This is the first step on the road to sentence recognition. It is worth your best effort.

EXERCISE 1. Each of the sentences contains one verb. Find the verb and write it on a sheet of paper, numbering it with the number of the sentence. Each verb in the first four sentences is only one word. For the first sentence you should write: *1. heard*

1. About an hour after dinner we heard a loud ring at the door.
2. Through the door came a whirling mass of snowflakes.
3. Sergeant Wade's head stuck up suddenly from the stairway.
4. Miss Fenn's clear, tireless voice was the only sound in the room.

Each verb in the next six sentences consists of two or more words:

5. Don't you ever take off your diamond ring at night?
6. There may not be any firewood in the cellar.
7. For an hour he had been idly watching the fountain in Grant Park.
8. The packages will now be inspected by the woman at the counter.
9. Can your absence from class be explained in any other way?
10. The ornamental tower may have been put on for a different purpose.

2

Nouns as subjects of verbs

Every grammar lesson in this book has a purpose—to show you how to make good sentences. In the first part of this lesson you learned about the foundation of every sentence, the *verb*. The rest of the lesson will tell you about nouns—one of the two kinds of words that may be "subjects" of verbs. A sentence is made by combining a verb and its subject. Because thousands of young people do not understand that simple fact, they make serious mistakes in their writing. If you study this lesson carefully, you will learn *what a sentence is*.

A word of caution: Just as a student cannot have a complete understanding of biology or chemistry until he has made a thorough study, so a student cannot have complete understanding of what a sentence is until he has made a thorough study. For example, a verb and its subject do not form a sentence if they are preceded by what is called a subordinating conjunction ("*while* the gas was escaping") or a relative pronoun ("*which* Tom had been reading"). But these are matters you need not be concerned about now. Simply recognize that you are taking the first great step and that complete knowledge of what a sentence is lies further along the way.

If a word is the special name of a person or animal or place or thing and begins with a capital letter, it is called a "proper noun"—for example, *Lucy, Mr. Hayne, Fido, Havana, New Mexico, Niagara Falls, Empire State Building*. Ordinary names of objects are called "common nouns"—for example, *pencil, lake, country, airplane, dog*. Names of conditions or qualities are called "abstract nouns"—for example, *darkness, speed, height, courtesy, cowardice*.

A word used as a name is called a noun.

A common noun is the sort of word that could naturally be used with *a, an,* or *the:* a *chill,* an *act,* the *ink*. But you cannot tell whether these words are nouns unless you see them in a sentence: "I felt a *chill*." "We left after the first *act*." "He spilled some *ink*." In other sentences the same words might be verbs: "I *chill* the melons before serving them." "We *act* our parts naturally." "They *ink* the roller." If a word like *act* is used to make a statement, it is a verb. If it is used as a name, it is a noun.

When you find a verb in a sentence and ask "Who or what?" the right answer is the **subject** of the verb. For instance, suppose that the sentence is "A man in a long fur overcoat opened the door." You ask, "Who or what opened?" The *man* opened. The subject of the verb *opened* is *man*. What is the subject of *is* in the following sentence? "The screeching of brakes is unpleasant." The word *screeching* is. The subject of the verb is *screeching*.

The surest and easiest way to find the subject in a question is to put the question into the form of a statement. Suppose the question is "Was the thief never caught?" When put into the form of a statement, this becomes "The thief was never caught." The verb is *was caught*. Who or what was caught? *Thief* is the subject.

EXERCISE 2. In each of the groups of words there are two verbs. Find each one and find the subject of each by asking "Who or what?" Write the subjects and verbs on a sheet of paper, numbering them to correspond with the numbers of the groups. Begin each subject with a capital letter and put a period after each verb. For the first sentence you should write: *1. Car is. Father gave.*

1. The car is my property. Father gave it to me.
2. Many weird stories of witchcraft are still told by the peasants. Can a grown-up person believe them?
3. The water is hot already. The new heater must be a good one.
4. Mr. Pierce was a grocer. His business had once been very successful.
5. Jennings, as a boy, collected coins. Now his taste runs to rare stamps.
6. Is your mother feeling better today? I hope so.
7. The clock has stopped! Did Malcolm wind it last night?
8. Archie hesitated. His eyes felt queer.
9. The lesson is too long. Did Miss Baker count the pages?
10. Has something gone wrong? Didn't Alec telephone?

Improving sentences
1. Ask a question

In this lesson you have seen that a sentence has a subject and a verb and that usually the subject comes before the verb. But you saw one kind of sentence—a question—in which part of the verb came before the subject: "Was the thief never caught?" One of the simplest and easiest ways of improving sentences in a composition is to vary the monotony of subject-verb, subject-verb, subject-verb by occasionally

4

asking a question. For example, compare these two paragraphs:

<table>
<tr><td>The day had been very hot. Clouds were piling up in the afternoon sky. The wind was changing to the east. The rain might come before evening. Our hopes for a picnic supper were slowly dwindling.</td><td>The day had been very hot. Clouds were piling up in the afternoon sky. The wind was changing to the east. Would the rain come before evening? Our hopes for a picnic supper were slowly dwindling.</td></tr>
</table>

Did you notice that the paragraph on the right seemed less monotonous than the one on the left? Changing the fourth sentence to a question provides a "change of pace" that breaks the monotony of too many subject-verb sentences in a row. You should not overwork this trick. It is only the first of many ways of improving sentences that you will learn in this book. But remember it. Use it whenever you can naturally and easily. Only an *occasional* question is needed to add interest to your sentences.

Pronouns as subjects

Instead of saying "Arthur heard a whisper. Arthur listened intently," we say "Arthur heard a whisper. *He* listened intently."

A word used in place of a noun is called a pronoun.

The pronouns that can be used as subjects of independent sentences are of four sorts:

1) The personals: I, we, you, he, she, it, they
2) The demonstratives: this, that, these, those
3) The indefinites: all, another, both, each, either, neither, few, many, none, one, others, several, some, etc.
4) The interrogatives: who, which, what

You find pronoun subjects in the same way that you find noun subjects—by asking "Who or what?" In a question, change the sentence to the form of a statement. For instance, change "Where have you been living?" to "You have been living where." The verb is *have been living*. Who or what have been living? The subject is *you*. If the sentence is "Where in the world was it?" change it to "It was where in the world," in which *it* is the subject of the verb *was*. Notice that subjects in questions may come between parts of the verb or after the verb.

The subject of a command—like "Run to the drug store"—is seldom used. If you ask who or what is to run, you will see that it is some person who is being spoken to. Therefore we say that the subject of a command is an "understood" *you.*

In the following exercise you will find pairs of independent sentences separated by periods or question marks. Notice each pair carefully as you do the work. Notice in each pair that a noun or pronoun and its verb form the first sentence, that a pronoun and its verb form the second sentence. Each of the two sentences is grammatically complete and should stand as a separate sentence. In *meaning* they may be closely related, but as a matter of *grammar* they are independent.

EXERCISE **3.** Find each verb in the sentences. Find each subject by asking "Who or what?" and carefully looking for the right answer. On a sheet of paper, write each verb and its subject. Begin each subject with a capital letter. Put a period after each verb. If the sentence is a command, write the understood subject *you* in parentheses. For the first group you should write: *1. (You) hurry. We can walk.*

1. Hurry! Can't we walk faster?
2. Some people are born rich. Others must earn every dollar.
3. Shall I call a doctor? Do you want Dr. Moore?
4. Leslie had never heard of Arabia. He had not studied geography.
5. Wait a minute. Is she calling us?
6. Don't complain about the sandwiches. That is my advice.
7. Do these cantaloupes cost more? Those look larger and fresher.
8. They must be wrong. This is not my handwriting.
9. Many were wilting. Some had already died.
10. Where have you been? I have been waiting two hours.

Subjects not directly before their verbs

The most common way of putting a subject after its verb is to begin with *there.* Ask "Who or what are?" in the following sentences:

> There are eight thousand *pupils* in that school.
> There are only two *windows* in the room.

The subjects are *pupils* and *windows.*

Ask "Who or what?" about each verb in the next three sentences:

> In the yard were some worn-out *tires.*
> Near the courthouse is a *statue* of Lee.
> Beyond the bridge are some splendid *homes.*

The subjects are *tires, statue,* and *homes.*

You have already learned that a subject may come between parts of the verb in a question: "Where have *you* been living?" And you saw one form of question in which the subject came after the verb: "Where in the world is *it?*" Some questions beginning with *who, whom, which,* or *what* are in the form of statements; the subjects are before the verb: "*Who* called me?" "*What* will happen?" But in the following questions the subjects are after the verb: "Who is *he?*" "Which is the shortest *road?*" "What is that *noise?*" In the form of statements these sentences are: "*He* is who." "The shortest *road* is which." "That *noise* is what." The subjects are *he, road,* and *noise.* If you wish to be sure about the subject of a question, always take time to put it into the form of a statement.

What do you think is the subject of the verb in the next sentence?

One side of the room had been painted black.

The sentence does not say that the *room* had been painted. It tells us that one *side* had been painted. The word *side* is the subject. Beware of any noun with *of* that comes between a subject and its verb. "Of the room" could not be a subject.

Never grab blindly at a noun or pronoun before the verb. Always take time to ask the "Who or what?" question. Always take time to find the right answer. Otherwise, even the brightest student may make a foolish mistake. Any student is almost sure to name the subject correctly if he takes time to ask the "Who or what?" question and looks for the answer that makes sense.

EXERCISE 4. Each numbered group contains two sentences. Write each subject and its verb as you did in Exercise 1, using capital letters and periods. For the first group you should write: *1. (You) study. It will keep.*

1. Study your map. It will keep you straight.
2. There are twenty-nine days in February. It is leap year.
3. Many of us got a perfect mark on the test. It was altogether too easy.
4. What is wrong? All of the committee are present.
5. We watched the clouds above the mountain. They made shadows on it.
6. Neither of the women would move out of line. Each was very angry.
7. Under the clamshells was a knife. Both of the boys jumped for it.
8. Who is he? What is he talking about?
9. Isn't either of them for sale? That seems ridiculous.
10. Where is it? Doesn't anybody know?

Improving sentences
2. Use a command

Too many statements, each beginning with a subject followed by a verb, make our talking and writing monotonous. You have seen how an occasional question can be used to vary your sentences and make them more interesting to others. Now you will see that an occasional command can also be used to break the monotony of subject-verb, subject-verb, subject-verb. Compare these two paragraphs:

Neither team had scored. The last quarter was almost over. People were beginning to leave. The visitors tried a long, long pass. One of our players intercepted it. He streaked down the sideline for a touchdown. There was a lot of noise from our side of the field.

Neither team had scored. The last quarter was almost over. People were beginning to leave. The visitors tried a long, long pass. One of our players intercepted it. He streaked down the sideline for a touchdown. Imagine the noise from our side of the field!

Notice how changing the last sentence to a command makes the paragraph on the right more interesting. The "change of pace" caused by beginning with a verb breaks the monotony of too many subject-verb sentences. Keep your ears and eyes open for sentences that can be improved by changing them to commands, but do not overwork this trick. Only an occasional command is needed to add interesting variety to your sentences.

Composition

How oral compositions should sound

Much of the composition with which you will be concerned in this book and for the rest of your life is oral composition. You will be telling incidents from your own experience. You will be making reports on your activities or reading. You will be giving informal talks or formal speeches. And you will be taking part in conversations and discussions of all kinds. For all of these, you will need to know how to talk clearly and effectively.

Have you ever heard a talk that was full of "and, and, and-uh, and, and-uh, and-uh"? It is painful to listen to "and" for two minutes. Why, then, do most of us overuse the wearisome word? The explanation seems to be that as soon as we have finished a sentence, we are afraid of an awkward pause, but have not decided just what is to come next. It seems that we want to make some sounds to kill time while deciding about the real words, and the handy noise is "and-uh." Once you learn how disagreeable this trick of speech is, you grow to dislike it more and more.

Nearly all of us—old and young alike—use *and* too much when we speak before an audience. If we are a little flustered, or at a loss for what to say next, we support ourselves with "and-uh, and-uh." All of us ought to get along without the vocal crutches. We can succeed, if we really care to, by a simple rule: "When you have finished a sentence, don't make any noise." Your listeners are not in a hurry. They will be glad to have you pause for a second or two. Take your time. Wait. Decide what real words are going to come next. Do not say *and*. Say some real word that begins a real sentence.

It is not wrong to use *and* or *so* or *why* or *well* occasionally; public speakers use these words now and then. These words are wrong in school only because they are used constantly as aids in crippled speech. In school there is only one safe remedy for invalids: "Throw away your crutches altogether." It is often necessary to put an absolute ban on the useless *and, so, why,* or *well* at the beginning of a sentence.

Telling What Happened PART ONE: ORAL

For your first composition assignment you are to prepare a short talk in which you tell about something that happened—an amusing incident, an unusual occurrence, an exciting adventure, a narrow escape. You should, of course, tell about something that happened to you or about something that you saw happen.

This is nothing new for you. For years you have been telling others what happened to you, and you have listened many times to others tell about what happened to them. You may have noticed that sometimes your listeners seemed interested in your account of what happened, while at other times they were inattentive. You yourself have probably listened to others with varying degrees of interest. You may even have wished occasionally that you could tell about your experiences as well as certain of your friends told about theirs.

What makes a personal incident interesting? First, of course, is the experience itself. If Joe accompanies his father to Africa to hunt big game and shoots a lion all by himself, his account of the adventure will be interesting because it is so unusual. Second is how well you know the person who had the experience. If you know Joe, the account of his adventure will be extremely interesting to you. If you do not know him, you may be more interested in hearing Ted tell about killing a snake in the back yard. Third is how well the person tells what happened. Margaret may be able to tell about the time she found her baby brother crawling around on the porch roof and make it as exciting as Ted's killing of the snake. All three—the incident, the person, the telling—work together to make an interesting account of a personal experience.

The incident you choose to tell about is therefore important. But if you are alive, you have had many experiences that will be interesting to your classmates. What funny things have happened to you? What odd things have you seen happen to others? Have you had a strange adventure or a narrow escape that others might enjoy hearing about? Choose an incident that you think is amusing or exciting or unusual in some way. Remember that it does not have to be something big, just so long as it is something that actually happened to you or something that you personally saw happen.

Next make a plan for telling about the incident. Where did the incident take place? What were you doing just before it took place? What happened first? What happened next, and next, and finally? How did you feel about the incident then, or how do you feel about it now? If you were going to tell about the time your cat had the whole neighborhood in an uproar, your plan might look like this:

10

1. Home alone one hot afternoon last summer
2. Lying on porch swing, half asleep
3. Heard neighbor's dog bark excitedly
4. Saw Dusty, our cat, race by and climb tree
5. More dogs started barking. Dusty climbed higher
6. Neighbors called off dogs, but Dusty stayed in tree
7. Tried coaxing. Tried rattling saucer against milk bottle. Tried everything
8. Finally called fire department
9. Sirens brought out all the neighbors
10. Firemen rescued a badly scared cat
11. Was thanking firemen when our car raced up the street and slid to a stop
12. Father jumped out shouting, "Where's the fire? Anybody hurt? What's going on here?"

A plan like this helps you in several ways. It helps you remember the important details. It helps you arrange them in the order in which they happened. It helps you save the most important detail until last. But do not make your list too long. Put only the important details in your plan. Keep the rest of your talk in your head until you are ready to give it.

Finally, think of a good opening sentence to catch the attention of your audience. You might start with a statement: "I still like cats, but my father doesn't." You might begin with a question: "Have you ever seen a little cat scare a grown-up man?" You might even use a command: "Don't buy a cat if your father has a weak heart." A good opening sentence arouses the interest of your listeners and makes them want to hear the rest of your talk.

Sometimes a special closing sentence helps end an account of a personal incident with a snap. Here again you might end with a short statement: "I had some explaining to do." Or you might close with a question: "What would you have said?" Or you might use a command: "Don't ever argue with a frightened parent." But if you have trouble thinking up a brief closing sentence, simply end with the final detail of the incident. A long, rambling closing sentence will weaken the effect of your last—and most important—detail.

What is the opening sentence you plan to use for the incident you are going to tell about? Write it on a card or a small piece of paper. Under it write your plan, being sure to include only the important details and to put the most important one last. Then write out your special closing sentence, if you decide to use one. With this card or paper in your hand you have nothing to be nervous about when you stand up to give your talk: You know exactly how to start. You know what details you are going to give and in what order. You know how to end —with the last detail or with a special closing sentence. And you know what to do with one of your hands while talking.

Practice your talk at least once, timing it to see that you can give it in three minutes or less. If you are asked to give your talk in class, be sure to speak slowly and distinctly. Try to avoid "and-uh," "and so," "why-uh," and "well" at the beginning of sentences.

Keep your notes. You will need them for the composition assignment in Unit 2. Your teacher may ask you to turn in a copy of them.

Modifiers

Adjectives

When nouns and pronouns do not make our meaning as clear as we want, we can make them more exact by using additional words that we call **adjectives**. Notice the words that are printed in italics in the following sentences:

> *A small* boy ran through *an open* doorway and down *the front* steps.
> *No* one spoke to *the two* strangers.
> *What* reasons can you give for *this* request?

In the first sentence the words *small* and *open* tell what kind of boy and what kind of doorway are meant. The word *front* tells which steps are meant. Most of the adjectives we use answer the question "What kind?" or "Which one?" The words *a* and *an* mean "one" or "any" and are sometimes called **indefinite articles.** The word *the* shows that a certain one or ones are meant and is sometimes called the **definite article.** These articles are usually thought of as adjectives. In the second sentence the word *no* changes the meaning of the pronoun *one* so that "no one" means about the same as "nobody" or "not a single person." The word *two* makes the meaning of the noun *strangers* more exact by telling the number meant. In the third sentence the use of the word *what* is easier to understand if you change the question to the form of a statement: "You can give *what* reasons for this request." The word *this* tells which request is meant. Because these added words affect the meanings of nouns and pronouns, we sometimes call them **modifiers,** and we say that they "modify" the nouns and pronouns.

An adjective is a word that modifies a noun or a pronoun.

Adjectives usually come before the word they modify, but sometimes they follow the noun or pronoun. Notice the italicized adjectives in these sentences:

> Can he spare the time *necessary* for answering these questions?
> Has she money *enough* to buy both of the sweaters?

According to the best information *available* at this time, he is one *worthy* of trust.

In Unit 1 you learned that some words may be either nouns or verbs, depending on their use in sentences. Similarly, many words may be either nouns or adjectives, depending on their use. In the following pairs of sentences, the italicized words are used first as nouns and second as adjectives:

Miss Jones teaches *school*.   The boys played in the *snow*.
Miss Jones is a *school* teacher.   They made a *snow* man.

Nouns and pronouns that show possession are frequently used like adjectives to tell exactly which person or thing is meant. Notice the italicized words in the following sentences:

Mr. Wagner's car was stolen yesterday.
My brother enters college next fall.
The little *boy's* coat was badly torn.

Because nouns and pronouns used in this way may themselves be modified by adjectives, as in the last example, we say that they are possessive nouns and pronouns "used like adjectives."

EXERCISE 1. Find the adjectives modifying the noun or pronoun that is the subject of the verb in each of the sentences. Ignore any other adjectives. Write the number of the sentence and, after it, the adjectives modifying the subject. Then write the subject and put parentheses around it. Keep the words in the same order as in the sentences. For the first sentence you should write: *1. a man's black (umbrella)*

1. Near the front door was a man's black umbrella.
2. Four new players have recently been added to the football squad.
3. What is his first name?
4. Few high schools offer courses in psychology.
5. Is your algebra paper on the teacher's desk?
6. On top of the old car were tied a half-dozen long, flexible bamboo poles.
7. No special reference books are required for this course.
8. What did your pesky little Irish terrier do with my newspaper?
9. There are many excellent reasons for not buying a car that old.
10. Where will the final basketball game of the season be played?

Improving sentences
3. Choose exact modifiers

Another way of improving your sentences is to use exact adjectives that make your meaning clear. You can, of course, write sentences without using adjectives other than the articles *a, an,* and *the,* but such sentences are flat. They lack flavor. They are like food without seasoning. For example:

> John lives in a house. It has a yard with trees and a fence around it. There is a garage at the rear.

Sentences like these can be improved by using adjectives—if the adjectives are chosen for exactness. It is easy enough to use adjectives like *swell, nice, grand, cute, awful,* and *terrible.* In fact, you may use such words frequently. But they are not exact. They are "lazy" adjectives. They merely express approval or disapproval, without telling what caused it. Notice the lazy adjectives in the following:

> John lives in a *swell* house. It has a *nice* yard with *grand* trees and a *cute* fence around it. There is an *awful* garage at the rear.

These sentences have too much flavor. They are like overseasoned food. You know only that the writer liked the house and yard and that he did not like the garage. But what kind of house was it? What kind of yard was it? What was wrong with the garage? Notice how exact adjectives add to the meaning:

> John lives in a *large red brick* house. It has a *beautiful big* yard with *tall elm* trees and a *low white picket* fence around it. There is an *ugly ramshackle frame* garage at the rear.

When you want your meaning to be clear to others, avoid lazy adjectives that tell only your feelings. Choose *exact* adjectives that tell also what you saw or heard.

EXERCISE 2. In each of the sentences is a lazy adjective in italic type. Revise the sentences, substituting for the lazy adjectives one or two modifiers that would make the meaning of the sentence more exact. For the first sentence you might say: *Isn't it a pleasant, sunny day?*

1. Isn't it a *grand* day?
2. Wasn't it a *grand* movie?
3. Isn't he a *grand* swimmer?
4. Hasn't it been a *grand* experience?
5. Isn't she a *grand* person?
6. Hasn't he a *swell* voice?
7. Wasn't it a *great* party?
8. Isn't that a *cute* dress?
9. Hasn't she a *nice* personality?
10. Aren't they *swell* people?
11. It was an *awful* day.
12. We saw an *awful* movie.
13. He is an *awful* dancer.
14. That place serves *awful* food.
15. It was an *awful* experience.
16. We had a *lousy* trip.
17. She wears *frightful* clothes.
18. He has *horrible* manners.
19. It was a *bum* game.
20. She is a *terrible* gossip.

Predicate adjectives

Adjectives are often used after verbs to modify a subject:

She may be *timid*.
The road was *rough*.
The old bridge is considered *unsafe*.

The verb and the words used with it to tell about the subject of a sentence are called the **predicate** of that sentence. And adjectives used after verbs to modify a subject are called **predicate adjectives.**

After such verbs as *look, taste, smell, feel,* and *sound* there is often a predicate adjective that modifies the subject. Notice the italicized words in the following sentences:

Miss Allison doesn't look *happy*.
The wilted berries didn't taste *good*.
Does the milk smell *sweet*?
The cool air felt *pleasant* to us.
His voice sounded *hoarse*.

Many students find it hard to realize that a predicate adjective modifies the subject. Make sure that you understand this now, for it is the important idea in the lesson. If we say "She tasted it carefully," *carefully* tells in what way she did the tasting; it modifies the verb. But if we say "The berries tasted good," *good* tells about the berries; it is an adjective modifying the subject. If we say "He yelled hoarsely," we are telling the way in which he yelled; but if we say "His voice sounded hoarse," we are telling how the voice *appeared to be* by its sound. Both *good* and *hoarse* are predicate adjectives after their verbs; they modify the subjects *berries* and *voice*.

16

EXERCISE 3. Most of the sentences have one or more adjectives in the predicate. Some of the adjectives modify nouns in the predicate, and some are predicate adjectives modifying the subject. Find each predicate adjective. Then write the number of the sentence and, after it, the predicate adjective and the subject it modifies. Put parentheses around the subject. For the first sentence you should write: *1. weary (men)*

1. The five men were quite weary after the long trip.
2. The open fire was very pleasant on cool evenings.
3. At first glance your product seems too expensive for general use.
4. A number of people became ill after the picnic supper.
5. With a shift in the wind the day suddenly turned hot.
6. Both of us should probably be considered for the next job.
7. The lake may appear dangerously rough to you on a windy day.
8. Doesn't black coffee taste bitter to you after a sweet dessert?
9. Not one of the teams looked good to our football coach.
10. Many of my brother's friends may be home for the Easter holidays.

Adverbs

Notice the italicized words in the following sentences:

Close the door *carefully*.
The air is *too* cold.
He closed the door *very* carefully.

In the first sentence the word *carefully* modifies the verb *Close*. In the second sentence the word *too* modifies the adjective *cold*. In the third sentence the word *very* modifies *carefully*. Words such as *carefully, too*, and *very* are called **adverbs**.

An adverb is a word that modifies a verb, an adjective, or another adverb.

This lesson is mostly about adverbs that modify verbs. Notice the meanings the italicized words add to the verbs in these sentences:

Come *here*.   He works *hard*.
This happened *yesterday*.   The speed increased *rapidly*.

The adverb *here* modifies the verb *Come* by telling where to come; *yesterday* tells when; *hard* and *rapidly* tell how. Most adverbs that modify verbs tell *where, when,* or *how*.

Some adverbs tell to what extent a statement is true. Notice how the italicized adverbs in the following sentences affect the meaning:

He will *surely* enjoy the show.   He will *perhaps* enjoy the show.
He will *probably* enjoy the show.   He will *not* enjoy the show.

The adverb in each sentence modifies the verb *will enjoy*. The adverb
not is sometimes shortened to *n't* and joined to the verb:

isn't = is not	don't = do not	won't = will not
haven't = have not	can't = can not	shan't = shall not

Many adverbs end in *ly*, but so do adjectives such as *lonely, lively,
cowardly*. Other words, such as *hard, straight, early, fast,* may be used
as adjectives or adverbs. And any of these may follow verbs:

The big fellow's actions were cowardly.
Some grammar lessons are hard.
His home is a lonely cabin.
The shortest distance between two points is a straight line.

These four sentences have no adverbs. The words *cowardly* and *hard*
are predicate adjectives modifying the subjects *actions* and *lessons*.
The words *lonely* and *straight* are adjectives modifying the predicate
nominatives *cabin* and *line*. When you know what word is modified,
you can tell the difference between an adverb and an adjective.

Earlier you learned that some words may be used as nouns or
adjectives. Now look at the italicized words in these sentences:

Last *Sunday* was cold and rainy.
Sunday dinner is a big meal at our house.
We had visitors last *Sunday*.

In the first sentence *Sunday* is a noun used as the subject of the verb
was. In the second sentence *Sunday* is used as an adjective modifying
the noun *dinner*. In the third sentence *Sunday* modifies the verb *had*
by telling when. Because nouns that modify verbs in this way are
sometimes themselves modified by adjectives, as in the third sentence,
we say that they are nouns "used like adverbs." They are also called
adverbial nouns. Remember that you must always know what work
a word does in a sentence before you can say what it is.

EXERCISE 4. Find the adverbs; and find the verbs, adjectives, and adverbs they modify. Write the numbers of the sentences and, after them, the
adverbs and the words they modify. Use a separate line for each adverb, and

put parentheses around the word modified. For the first one you should write: *1. Earlier (was)*
              quite (faint)

1. Earlier the sound of the thunder was quite faint.
2. Now the sound is almost continuous and much louder.
3. Practically no one has ever seen these extremely shy animals.
4. Nearly always our friends have been quite loyal to us.
5. Fortunately such poisons are now practically unobtainable.
6. Some of his obviously rude remarks were quietly relayed to his friends.
7. We are very sorry to hear of your extremely unhappy plight.
8. I am also writing to some of our less fortunate friends.
9. Seldom have so many prominent students been suddenly expelled.
10. Too often these old jalopies are driven dangerously fast.

Improving sentences
4. Begin with an adverb

Notice the adverbs that come first in the following sentences:

Often I have wondered about such things.
Swiftly the water poured through the opening.
Already the rain had started.
Soon we came to a small brook.

The adverbs beginning these four sentences could also be placed before or after the verbs. That is what students usually do with adverbs of this sort. Yet one or two sentences beginning with adverbs like *slowly* or *later* or *quietly* may make a whole paragraph sound better by breaking the monotony of subject-verb, subject-verb, subject-verb. Compare these two paragraphs:

The fire engine came to a sudden stop. Flames shot out from under the hood. Two firemen leaped quickly from the back. They turned streams of chemicals on the blazing motor. Clouds of smoke rolled upward. The fire was soon extinguished. A group of embarrassed firemen gazed sadly at the smoking wreck. What would the chief say?

The fire engine came to a sudden stop. Flames shot out from under the hood. Quickly two firemen leaped from the back. They turned streams of chemicals on the blazing motor. Clouds of smoke rolled upward. Soon the fire was extinguished. A group of embarrassed firemen gazed sadly at the smoking wreck. What would the chief say?

The paragraph at the right is more interesting to read because two of the sentences begin with adverbs that might ordinarily be put after a verb. Moving these adverbs first in their sentences helps in avoiding too many subject-first sentences.

Sentences beginning with adverbs are not "better" than other sentences. In fact, too many sentences beginning with *then* or *so* or *still* or *also* can become as tiresome as too many subject-first sentences. But beginning an occasional sentence with an adverb like *suddenly* or *softly* or *clumsily* is a good way of varying your sentences and making them more interesting to read.

A few cautions: Some adverbs cannot be put first without making the sentence sound ridiculous. Sentences like "Awkwardly he handled the bat" or "Here come at once" do not sound much like English. The adverbs in sentences like the following are better left where they are:

> He handled the bat *awkwardly*.
> Come *here* at once.

If you remember that the purpose of any change is to improve a sentence, you will not move adverbs in such sentences.

Some adverbs are so broad in meaning that they mean little more than "very." Notice the "lazy adverbs" in these sentences:

> The food was *awfully* good.
> Her parents are *mighty* rich.
> He is *terribly* handsome.

You can avoid such meaningless adverbs by using words like *extremely, quite,* and *unusually*. When you use adverbs, try to choose those that express your meaning exactly.

Some adverbs are not needed. For example, *again* means "once more," and *return* means "turn back." You can see that in "Will you sing it *once more* again?" or "Is it time to return the book *back* to the library?" the italicized adverbs are not needed. When you revise first drafts of your written compositions, eliminate unnecessary adverbs that make you appear ignorant of the meanings of simple words.

20

EXERCISE 5. In each of the sentences are two or three adverbs printed in italics. Decide which adverbs could be put first and which are unnecessary or meaningless. Then revise the sentences, beginning with an adverb wherever you can do so without making the sentence sound awkward. Drop the unnecessary adverbs. Substitute a word like *quite, unusually,* or *extremely* for the meaningless adverbs. For the first sentence you might say: *Ordinarily mail service from the city is extremely slow at this time of the year.*

1. Mail service from the city is *ordinarily awfully* slow at this time of the year.
2. She *probably* wants me to return just this one book *back* to the library.
3. Harris seemed *mighty* glad to be home once more *again*.
4. He is *apparently* just *awfully* tall for his age.
5. A *terribly* old man rose *up clumsily* from his chair to greet us.
6. You will *perhaps* need to repeat the long names *again* for him.
7. The big wheels of the locomotive *slowly* began to revolve *around*.
8. It will *fortunately* be possible for the members of the committee to meet *later* in the week.
9. The police *eventually* returned the car *back* to its rightful owner.
10. You *doubtless* already know the details of his *terribly* daring escape.

Composition

How written compositions should look

The first page of an ordinary composition should look something like the example shown on the next page.

The title is well above the first line, in the middle of the page. The first word, the last word, and all the principal words are capitalized. Other words—such as *a, an, the; of, to, at; and, but, or, if*—begin with small letters.

There is a margin on the left about one inch wide. On the right there are no large "holes" that make a wavy appearance, but there need not be a wide margin unless your teacher requests it.

In order to give the right side of the page the proper appearance, words must often be divided at the end of some syllable. A syllable is a part of a word that can be pronounced separately; it must always contain a vowel sound, and may contain one or more consonants.

Little Boy Blues

Lion taming may be exciting, but it isn't as nerve-racking as baby sitting. I know. Last Saturday afternoon Mother went downtown to shop, leaving me in charge of my baby brother, a fat, chunky one-year-old, whose big blue eyes and sweet smile held no hint of the horrible moments he was to give me. For an hour or so I had no trouble — no trouble at all. Baby was safe in his crib, taking a nap! But then he woke up.

I spent the next hour trying to entertain Baby. I was, in turn, an elephant, a lion, a train, an airplane. Finally I hit upon a trick that pleased him — piling up blocks and knocking them down. This was so simple a game that I got him to try it for himself, while I flopped on Mother's bed for a rest. A minute later I heard a shout and ran to the window. Two of my friends wanted me to come down to hear some exciting news. With a hurried glance at Baby to see that he was all right, I

The following words are divided by hyphens into syllables:

math-e-mat-ics	dis-ap-pear-ance	oc-ca-sion-al-ly
knowl-edge	nev-er-the-less	un-for-giv-ing
hu-mor-ous-ly	trans-la-tion	ac-ci-den-tal-ly
re-plied	ar-range-ment	def-i-nite-ly

The following must not be divided, for each has only one syllable:

thought   meant   straight   stretch   through   rolls   played

When a word is divided, the hyphen must be put at the right-hand end of the line, not at the beginning of the next line.

A thorough study of all the rules for dividing words is too long and complicated for this lesson; but if you are always careful to divide in such a way that you can pronounce each part separately, you will seldom make bad blunders. When in doubt, consult a dictionary.

Always read a composition through carefully before handing it in. A student who is not learning to find his own errors is learning hardly anything.

Telling What Happened PART TWO: WRITTEN

For the composition assignment in Unit 1 you prepared a short talk in which you told about something that happened to you or about something that you saw happen. Now you are to write about this same incident, using the notes you made for your talk. Since these notes show you how to begin, what details to give, and how to end, you can concentrate on the special problems of written composition. These are (1) paragraphing, (2) revising, (3) titling, and (4) copying and proofreading your paper before handing it in.

A paragraph usually consists of two or more sentences that are related in some way. Because the first word of a paragraph is indented —that is, set in a short distance from the left-hand margin—paragraphs help the reader recognize groups of related sentences. In writing about what happened, you have only to group related details from the notes you made for your talk, since the details are already in the order of what happened first, next, next, and so on.

You know that your first paragraph will begin with the opening sentence you planned for your talk. Now look at your list of details. How many details give the setting or background for what happened? Usually the first paragraph tells where the incident happened and what you were doing just before it happened. What details will you include in your first paragraph?

Your second paragraph will probably begin with the first detail of what actually happened. If your list has only a few details about what happened, this paragraph may end with the last detail or the closing sentence you planned for your talk. If there are many details, you may want to end the second paragraph just before the most important detail. Look again at the list of details that you have made, and decide whether you will need a third paragraph in your composition.

The third paragraph, if you use one, will probably be short. It should begin with the most important detail—the climax of your account of the incident—and end with a special closing sentence or a brief statement telling how you felt about the incident. Do not let your final paragraph ramble on and on. Bring your account to an end quickly—and stop. Do you need a third paragraph? How short can you make it?

If you were writing about the cat that would not come down from the tree, your plan might look like this:

FIRST PARAGRAPH

OPENING SENTENCE: I still like cats, but my father doesn't.
1. Home alone one hot afternoon last summer
2. Lying on porch swing, half asleep
3. Heard neighbor's dog bark excitedly
4. Saw Dusty, our cat, race by and climb tree

SECOND PARAGRAPH

5. More dogs started barking. Dusty climbed higher
6. Neighbors called off dogs, but Dusty stayed in tree
7. Tried coaxing. Tried rattling saucer against milk bottle. Tried everything
8. Finally called fire department
9. Sirens brought out all the neighbors
10. Firemen rescued a badly scared cat

THIRD PARAGRAPH

11. Was thanking firemen when our car raced up the street and slid to a stop
12. Father jumped out shouting, "Where's the fire? Anybody hurt? What's going on here?"
CLOSING SENTENCE: I had some explaining to do.

Now mark your list of details so that you will know where each paragraph begins and ends. Then write your account of the incident just as you planned to tell it in class. Use pencil and scratch paper for your first attempt—or draft—so that you can make corrections and

24

changes easily before copying it to hand in. While you are writing, remember that you may be asked to read your composition aloud to your classmates. Keep them in mind as you write. Try to *hear* the sentences before you put them on paper.

When your first draft is completed, you are ready for the next step—revision—in which you begin to use what you have been learning about improving sentences. Read over your first draft carefully. Does each sentence have a subject and a verb? Does each sentence begin with a capital letter and end with a period, a question mark, or an exclamation mark? Have you used verb forms correctly? Is every sentence a statement? If so, can you change one to a question or a command? Are there any lazy adjectives in your sentences? If so, can you change them to more exact words? Do you need additional modifiers to make your sentences clearer? Does every sentence say exactly what you mean?

Revision is the most important step in learning to write better. The more interest you take in it, the more improvement you will make during this year. At first, revision may seem tedious and mechanical to you. Later, as you learn more about the various ways in which you can express your ideas in sentences, it may seem more like a game—a game that is different each time you write, a game that constantly challenges the skill of experienced writers.

After revising your first draft, you are ready for the third problem—selecting a suitable title. In writing about what happened, this can be fun; for you want a title that will arouse the interest of the reader. The title may be clever or amusing—but it should not be just a statement of what happened. If you were writing about the cat in the tree, you would not want a title like "The Day I Scared My Father Half to Death by Calling the Firemen to Get Our Cat out of the Tree." A title should be brief and should not tell too much.

You might start by playing around with the word *cat,* writing down each title that could be used. For example, you might think of titles like these:

Firemen Save My Cat	Cats as Cats Can
Cat's in Our Elm Tree	The Cat Hangs High

The idea of "high" in the last title might lead to titles like:

On the Up and Up   All That Goes Up—

Or the name of the cat, Dusty, might suggest titles like these:

It's Dusty in the Treetop   Dusty Does Me Dirt
Dusty Does Everything—Wrong

Now think of possible titles for your own composition. Then choose one that you think will interest or amuse your classmates and make them want to hear your story.

The final step is to copy your first draft in a form suitable for handing in. The first part of this lesson explained how written compositions should look. Your teacher may have added other suggestions. Write neatly and as legibly as you can, keeping margins even and spacing words carefully. Then proofread the entire composition, reading it over carefully to make sure that you have not omitted any words, that you have not left off any final letters or misspelled any words, and that you have put in all necessary punctuation marks. Make corrections as neatly as possible.

Your teacher may ask you to read your composition to your classmates before handing it in. If so, read slowly and distinctly. Be sure that everyone can hear what you say. When a classmate is reading his composition, listen carefully so that you can tell what you like about it and what you think might be improved.

Joiners

Prepositions

Notice the italicized words in these sentences:

He walked *over* the bridge.   He walked *around* the bridge.
He walked *under* the bridge.   He walked *past* the bridge.
He walked *toward* the bridge.   He walked *off* the bridge.

The italicized words in these sentences express different relationships between the noun *bridge* and the verb *walked*. Because the relationships are different, the sentences have different meanings. Such words are called **prepositions.**

Now notice the italicized words in the following sentences:

The book on the *table* is mine.   The book on the *floor* is mine.
The book on the *desk* is mine.   The book on the *chair* is mine.

The italicized words in these sentences complete the meaning of the preposition *on*. Because these words are names of different things, the sentences have different meanings. Each of the words is called the **object** of the preposition *on*.

A preposition and its object form a **phrase** that almost always modifies some word in the sentence. In the first set of sentences the phrases *over the bridge, under the bridge,* and so on, modify the verb by telling where he walked. Because such phrases do the work of adverbs, they are called "adverb" phrases. In the second set of sentences the phrases *on the table, on the desk,* and so on, modify the noun *book* by telling which book is meant. Because such phrases do the work of adjectives, they are called "adjective" phrases.

A preposition is a word that together with a noun or pronoun called its object forms a modifying phrase.

A prepositional phrase may modify a noun that is the object of another preposition. Two or more phrases may modify the same word. The prepositions in the sentence at the top of the next page are italicized. What do the phrases modify?

The letter *from* my friend *in* Mexico arrived *at* the hotel *on* Monday. *From* has an object, *friend;* the phrase *from my friend* modifies *letter.* *In* has an object, *Mexico;* the phrase *in Mexico* modifies *friend.* *At* has an object, *hotel;* the phrase *at the hotel* modifies *arrived* by telling where the letter *arrived.* *On* has an object, *Monday;* the phrase *on Monday* modifies *arrived* by telling when the letter arrived.

An adverb is a modifying word, but a preposition does not, by itself, modify. An adverb never has an object, but a preposition always does. The combination of a preposition and its object makes a phrase. It is the whole phrase that modifies.

The way to find out what word a phrase modifies is to ask questions like "What *from my friend*?" "What *at the hotel*?" Ask the questions about the italicized phrases in this sentence:

We learn *from a newspaper* which has just come *to our attention* that a society *for the prevention of gossip* has been formed.

What *from a newspaper*? The right answer is *learn;* the phrase modifies *learn.* What *to our attention*? The phrase modifies *has come.* You can easily find out what *for the prevention* and *of gossip* modify.

EXERCISE 1. In each of the sentences there are two prepositions. Find them and their objects. Then decide what words the phrases modify. Divide a sheet of paper into three columns. In the first column, write the words modified by the phrases. In the second column, write the prepositions. In the third column, write the objects. Use a separate line for each preposition. Number your answers with the numbers of the sentences. For the first sentence you should write:

1. man	on	corner
was looking	at	her and me

1. The man on the corner was looking severely at her and me.
2. A man in a heavy coat stood near me.
3. We looked around the back yard and through the alley.
4. There was no one there except her and me till noon.
5. She walked into the room and sat down quietly by the window.
6. A vase of chrysanthemums stood just inside the door.
7. The boy behind Alfred once lived among the Navajo Indians.
8. The car was coming toward Janet and me from Howard Avenue.
9. An iron bar ran along the edge and was fastened below the corners.
10. We put Rex in the back seat between Mother and me.

Improving sentences
5. Begin with a preposition

Prepositional phrases ordinarily follow the words they modify:

> The house *on* the corner burned *to* the ground.
> Yesterday a box *of* candy arrived *by* mail.

Sometimes, however, phrases tend to pile up at the end of a sentence:

> Bill's family moved *from* the country *to* the city *at* the time *of* his enlistment *in* the Air Force.

Sentences like these are usually clearer and more interesting to read if some of the phrases modifying the verb are put first:

> *At* the time *of* his enlistment *in* the Air Force, Bill's family moved *from* the country *to* the city.

Even in shorter sentences phrases that modify verbs are sometimes put first to break the monotony of too many subject-first sentences. Compare the sentences in the following paragraphs:

I always listen to the latest song hits. The new tunes are most interesting to me. But my parents do not share this enthusiasm. The old songs seem good enough to them.	I always listen to the latest song hits. To me the new tunes are most interesting. But my parents do not share this enthusiasm. To them the old songs seem good enough.

The paragraph on the right is more interesting to read because two of the sentences begin with something besides the subject. Furthermore, beginning the second sentence with *To me* and the last sentence with *To them* makes clearer the contrast between what the writer likes and what his parents like.

There is, however, no special charm about beginning a great many sentences with prepositions. Only an occasional sentence need be changed to avoid the monotony of too many subject-first sentences. And a change should never be made if the sentence then sounds clumsy or unnatural. For example, changing the first sentence in the paragraphs above to "To the latest song hits I always listen" would be foolish. Do not make changes recklessly.

The only preposition that students regularly put first in sentences is *with*. They use it in an endless variety of meaningless ways: "*With* all these people subscribing liberally, success seems assured." "*With* so

many things happening at once, I acted *with* haste *without* thinking."
The preposition *with* often makes sentences sound absurd. Be afraid
of it. Do not tack it on at the end of a sentence where it seems to modify a wrong word in a ridiculous way: "New textbooks were given to
some of the older students with bright red backs." Put the *with* phrase
earlier in the sentence, next to the word it modifies, *textbooks*:

> New textbooks with bright red backs were given to some of the
> older students.

As you revise the first drafts of your written compositions, watch
for opportunities to improve your sentences by moving phrases. Put
them first occasionally to make your sentences more interesting to
read. Put them closer to the words they modify to make your sentences
clearer and more forceful. But never make changes that cause your
sentences to sound silly or artificial. The goal is always clearer, more
interesting sentences.

EXERCISE 2. At the end of each of the sentences you will find a phrase or
a group of phrases that is clumsily placed. Revise each sentence, putting the
awkwardly placed group of words at the beginning of the sentence or nearer
the word it modifies. Be ready to read your revised sentences aloud. For
the first sentence you might say: *For a long time he raged against the burly
detective who had arrested him in his uncle's office.*

1. He raged against the burly detective who had arrested him in his
   uncle's office for a long time.
2. This policeman is able to make his rounds in the villages that were an-
   nexed to Los Angeles some time ago by means of a police car.
3. We were shown to a hayloft full of timothy that was hardly dry after
   a substantial supper in the farmhouse.
4. We were getting far down on Broadway, where the wholesale houses
   have their showrooms, by this time.
5. I wondered how the men knew when to quit driving the piles for the
   first hour or so.
6. Submarines can be tested frequently without doing them any injury
   by means of a device patented in Brazil.
7. Wilson opened the door of his room, which was on a long, narrow
   corridor, with his overcoat still on his arm.
8. Martin had been lucky enough to fall in with an official who had a
   generous sense of humor on that occasion.
9. I saw an advertisement telling how a bright young man could easily
   earn a hundred dollars a week in a magazine.
10. Hot water was allowed to run continuously upon this special paraffin
    coating that he was selling for twenty-four hours.

30

Improving sentences: Ways you have learned

1. **Ask a question**   4. **Begin with an adverb**
2. **Use a command**   5. **Begin with a preposition**
3. **Choose exact modifiers**

Perhaps you would like to see how these five ways of improving sentences can be used to make a composition more interesting to read. Printed below in two columns is an account of a boy's experience at a camp. In the left-hand column the experience is told in twenty-one sentences, each of which begins with the subject and verb. In the right-hand column the same experience is told in the same number of sentences, but seventeen of the sentences have been varied in the ways you have learned. The italics show what changes were made. As you read and compare the two accounts of the experience, notice how these simple changes improve the sentences in the second one.

You may have heard about a "practical joker." We had one, named Pete Dorman, in our camp on the Blue Fork. He was simply cracked about making people uncomfortable and ridiculous. He would fill up the sugar bowls with salt sometimes. He put a tack on Mr. Walker's chair once. He thought it was very funny to tie knots in overalls and put frogs in shoes.

Several tame and friendly bears lived near our camp. We didn't see them often during the day, but they would come nosing and "whoofing" around the tents at night. They were always mighty hungry animals. One of them smelled a box of chocolates under Jack Crawford's pillow one night. He stuck his paw under the wall of the tent and tried to drag the pillow out to get at the swell food.

Did you ever hear about a "practical joker"? *In our camp on the Blue Fork* we had one, named Pete Dorman. He was simply *daft* about making people uncomfortable and ridiculous. *Sometimes* he would *fill* the sugar bowls with salt. *Once* he put a tack on Mr. Walker's chair. *Imagine a boy who* thought it was very funny to tie knots in overalls and put frogs in shoes!

Near our camp lived several tame and friendly bears. *During the day* we didn't see them often, but *at night* they would come nosing and "whoofing" around the tents. They were always *very hungry*. *One night* one of them smelled a box of chocolates under Jack Crawford's pillow. He stuck his paw under the wall of the tent and tried to drag the pillow out to get at the *tempting* food.

This gave Jack an idea. He begged a large slice of ham from the cook the next afternoon. He slipped away from the mess tent during dinner early that evening. He stowed the piece of meat in the bottom of Pete's sleeping bag.

The camp was awakened about midnight by Pete's yells and screams of terror. He thought he was being eaten up alive evidently. You can guess what had happened. A bear had been made wild by the smell of the ham. He had seized the bottom of the sleeping bag in his teeth and was pulling Pete down the slope toward a gulch.

Pete Dorman never thought practical jokes were awfully funny after that.

This gave Jack an idea. *The next afternoon* he begged a large slice of ham from the cook. *Early that evening* he slipped away from the mess tent during dinner. He stowed the piece of meat in the bottom of Pete's sleeping bag.

About midnight the camp was awakened by Pete's yells and screams of terror. *Evidently* he thought he was being *eaten alive.* Guess what had happened. A bear had been made *frantic* by the smell of the ham. He had seized the bottom of the sleeping bag in his teeth and was pulling Pete down the slope toward a gulch.

After that Pete Dorman never thought practical jokes were *very* funny.

EXERCISE 3. Be ready to discuss the changes made in the sentences in the right-hand column of the account about Pete Dorman. What change is made in each sentence? In what way does the change improve the sentence? Do the changes make the right-hand account more interesting to read? Are there any changes that you think should not have been made? Are there any sentences that you would have changed in some other way? Would you have made changes in any of the sentences left unchanged? You will no doubt think of other questions that you might bring up for discussion in class.

Conjunctions

While prepositions join nouns to the rest of the sentence in which they appear, **conjunctions** join together words, phrases or clauses. Notice how the conjunctions work in the following sentences:

Her attic room was *small* but *cheerful.*
They should be here *by Monday evening* or *by Tuesday morning.*
The teacher told us *that the test would have four questions* and *that one of these would be a written composition.*

In the first sentence *but* joins two predicate adjectives. In the second sentence *or* joins two adverb phrases. In the third sentence *and* joins two noun clauses used as objects of the verb *told*. When words like *but, or,* and *and* join words, phrases, and clauses that are used in the same way, they are called **coördinating conjunctions**.

The most useful coördinating conjunctions are the following six, which can be remembered by the rhyme:

and, but, for,
yet, or nor

Or you can picture a little boy fanning a large sultan who is sitting in the sun. The little boy would be called a FANBOY:

*F*or
*A*nd
*N*or
*B*ut
*O*r
*Y*et

Notice how the sentence that introduces the FANBOY memory device above itself begins with a coördinating conjunction—*or*.

Experienced writers will occasionally begin a sentence with a coördinating conjunction to gain emphasis and enhance sentence rhythm.

Now look at the words *either* and *or* in the sentence below:

Either a streetcar or a North Street bus will take you there.

Words like either . . . *or*, used in pairs as they are above to emphasize the words they join, are called **correlative conjunctions**.

A third kind of conjunction—a subordinating conjunction— joins a clause to the word the clause modifies. Subordinating conjunctions will be discussed in Unit 6 on page 116.

Compound subjects

If a child were asked to tell about a party, he might say:

> Jimmy was at the party. And Joe was at the party. And Mary was at the party, too.

He might use a separate sentence for each person. But an older person would be more likely to say:

> *Jimmy* and *Joe* and *Mary* were at the party.

The older person would be more likely to use the three names as one subject. Two or more words used as the subject of a verb are called a **compound subject.** Notice the compound subjects in these sentences:

> Lying at anchor in the harbor were many small *sailboats* and a few power *cruisers*.
> Friday *evening* or Saturday *afternoon* is the best time for me to go to a show.
> A *locomotive*, its *tender*, and four *coaches* were derailed at this crossing last week.

In the first sentence the subject follows the verb and consists of two nouns that are joined by the word *and*. In the second sentence the two nouns that are the subject are joined by *or*. In the third sentence a series of three nouns is used as the subject, with *and* between the last two only.

Compound subjects joined by *and* usually take a plural verb:

> John and his brother *are* excellent athletes.
> There *were* a small boy and a dog playing on the lawn.

The verbs *are* and *were* are used because these compound subjects mean more than one person or thing. But compound subjects joined by *or* take a singular verb when they mean only one person or thing:

> Anne or Helen *is* usually at the head of the honor roll.
> There *was* a fireplace or a coal stove in each room.

The verbs *is* and *was* are used because these sentences mean that only one of the girls is at the head of the list and only one heating device was in each room. When a compound subject joined by *or* consists of singular and plural words, the verb agrees with the nearer word:

The carburetor or the spark plugs *were* defective.

There *was* a watchman or automatic gates at each crossing.

Notice that the verb *were* and the noun *plugs* are both plural. Notice that the verb *was* and the noun *watchman* are both singular.

Compound verbs

Students often write sentences like these:

Hazel picked up a heavy rock. Then she pounded at the cabin door.

Since *Hazel* and *she* mean the same person, you can see that two sentences are not necessary:

Hazel *picked* up a heavy rock and *pounded* at the cabin door.

In this sentence the verbs *picked* and *pounded* tell what Hazel did. Two or more verbs used with one subject are called a **compound verb**. Notice the compound verbs in these sentences:

Bill *jammed* a hat on his head, *grabbed* his books, and *dashed* out of the front door.

Mary *remembered* to buy the meat, but *forgot* all about the buns.

The authorities either *planned* the riot or *allowed* it to happen.

The prisoner neither *admitted* nor *denied* his guilt.

In the first sentence a series of three verbs, with *and* between the last two, is used as a compound verb. In the second sentence the two verbs are joined by the conjunction *but*. In the third sentence the first verb is preceded by *either* and the second one by *or*. Likewise, in the fourth sentence *neither* precedes the first verb, and *nor* precedes the second one. These correlative conjunctions emphasize the words they precede.

Occasionally both the subject and the verb are compound:

The *radiator* in the corner and the *one* under the window *are connected* by a pipe and *are heated* by the same boiler.

EXERCISE 4. Each of the sentences contains a compound subject or a compound verb or both. Find the subject and verb of each sentence. Then divide a sheet of paper into two columns. In the first column, write the subjects. In the second column, write the verbs. If the subject or verb is compound, write the conjunction that connects the parts, putting parentheses around it. Number your answers with the numbers of the sentences. For the first sentence you should write: *1. Monica | drew straightened (and) walked*

1. Monica drew a deep breath, straightened her shoulders, and walked bravely to the center of the stage.
2. Neither the saleswoman nor the shipping clerk could explain the error.
3. Mr. Barnhill hated criticism of any kind, yet always encouraged it.
4. Along the sides of the flimsy bandstand were festooned yards and yards of blue and yellow cambric.
5. Don swaggered over to the mirror, peered at his eye, and scowled.
6. To approach Ed now and to confront him with this new evidence of Bert's dishonesty will make him furious, but will convince him.
7. From a large tent in the center of the clearing came the squeak of a violin and the wail of a trumpet.
8. The silly chatter of the women, the stupid jokes of the men, and the affected airs of his hostess amused, yet annoyed him.
9. Will one of the diagrams mounted on these boards or one of those in Dick's office be used as a model?
10. In this movie Frankie Van Haymes, the idol of millions of fans and the despair of his many rivals, neither sings nor dances.

Improving sentences
6. Use a compound verb

Some students seldom think of using two or more verbs with one subject. Instead, they write sentences like these:

The empty truck bounced noisily over the rails. Then it came to a stop in front of the shed.

Without another word the old woman turned away from the door. She picked up the battered suitcase by its broken handle. Then she walked slowly down the hall toward the elevator.

The boys probably had a flat tire. Maybe they ran out of gas.

Betty accidentally discovered our hiding place. However, she promised not to tell the others about it.

Bob dislikes school intensely. Nevertheless, he somehow manages to make fairly good grades.

The boys did not help prepare the food for the party. Also they did not offer to clean up afterwards.

You can see that the sentences in each group are about the same person or thing and are related in meaning. Using compound verbs instead of separate sentences shows the relationships more clearly:

36

The empty truck *bounced* noisily over the rails and *came* to a stop in front of the shed.

Without another word the old woman *turned* away from the door, *picked* up the battered suitcase by its broken handle, and *walked* slowly down the hall toward the elevator.

The boys probably *had* a flat tire or *ran* out of gas.

Betty accidentally *discovered* our hiding place, but *promised* not to tell the others about it.

Bob *dislikes* school intensely, yet somehow *manages* to make fairly good grades.

The boys neither *helped* prepare the food for the party nor *offered* to clean up afterwards.

This simple trick of using compound verbs to combine sentences having subjects that mean the same person or thing is easy to learn and do. Exercise 5 will give you practice. As you revise first drafts of your written compositions, look for opportunities to use compound verbs.

EXERCISE 5. Each of the numbered groups consists of two or more sentences that are about the same person or thing. Read each group of sentences and decide how they can be combined by using a compound verb. Be prepared to read the improved sentences aloud. For the first group you might say: *Dixon had coached winning teams for three years and did not want to fail now.*

1. Dixon had coached winning teams for three years. He did not want to fail now.
2. Dad gave me a five-dollar bill. However, he told me not to spend it.
3. I despised our sarcastic, grouchy supervisor. Nevertheless, I always pretended to like him.
4. My aunt took one startled look at our grimy, tear-stained faces. Then she screeched for her maid.
5. With a determined look Leslie stepped over to the desk. She pulled out a checkbook. Then she filled out a check for the entire amount.
6. Ross did not look like a movie star. Also he did not act like one.
7. Anne skillfully cut along the edges of the pattern. She basted the pieces of material together. Then she stitched them carefully on the machine.
8. The ball sailed through the air. It slammed against the limb of a tree. Then it dropped to the ground just two inches outside the foul line.
9. Betty had promised to help me with my Latin. However, she broke her promise in order to go to the movies with Dave.
10. The favor is a slight one. It wouldn't cause you any trouble.

Keeping a straight line

Suppose that Joan were telling you about a queer happening of the day before:

> Yesterday in Father's office I thought the information girl looked at me as if she knew about Clara's message, but I paid no attention. Well, I got interested in two women who were pacing up and down, looking very peevish. You see, Clara had told me she would surely be waiting for me at a quarter of three. So I had to amuse myself somehow. The girl was watching those women, too. She didn't seem to have anything to do for a while. You see, I didn't get there till ten minutes of three, and I thought maybe Clara had left. Finally one of the women I told you about rushed toward the door. Clara had told me she would wait, but I didn't know she had forgotten that her message didn't reach me till nine o'clock. So I . . .

About this point you would lose patience; you would want Joan to go back to the beginning and tell in a straight line of time what had happened. The account of the incident is all snarled up. It begins at three o'clock (the time in the first line must be about three); then in the second line ("Clara's message") it loops back to nine; later it swings forward to ten minutes before three, and then swoops back to nine. It should begin at nine, when the message came from Clara, and from that moment should move straight forward to ten minutes of three, and then to three, and so forward to the climax at ten minutes past three.

If Joan had made a plan, as you did in Unit 1, she could have kept the details in order. She should have asked herself, "What happened first? What next? What next? What happened last?" Then she could have told the details in a **time order**—in the order in which they happened, from the first detail to the last.

Time order is also frequently used to keep details in order in other kinds of writing. For example, when you are explaining how to make or do something, you will find it helpful to ask yourself, "What do I do first? What do I do next? What next? What do I do last?" In this way you can keep the various steps in a straight line, so that your explanation will be clear to others. And if your explanation is clear, you will find it easy to hold the interest of your audience.

Telling How to Make or Do Something 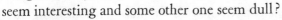 PART ONE: ORAL

In Units 1 and 2 you prepared oral and written compositions in which you told about something that happened. In this Unit you are to prepare another kind of composition—a short talk in which you tell how to make or do something. Of course you should tell about something that you know how to make or do yourself.

Almost everyone likes to tell others about things that he has learned to make or do. And almost everyone likes to hear about such things—if they are well told. What is it that makes one explanation seem interesting and some other one seem dull?

First, of course, is how much you know about the subject itself. If you are interested in airplanes, you will very likely be interested in hearing Jim tell how to make a flying model. If you know nothing about airplanes, you will probably be bored. Second is the use of complicated details without explanation. If Jim rattles on and on about ailerons, elevators, dihedral angles, and stressed-skin construction without explaining these technical terms, you will not know what he is talking about. Or if Sue's talk about making a skirt is full of details like basting a placket, stitching a gusset, and pinking a seam, you may lose interest simply because you do not know what she means. Third is the arrangement of the details in a straight line, from the first step to the last. Sally may choose a subject that you may know something about and use details that you understand. But if she does not follow a straight line in telling what to do, you may become hopelessly confused and may even lose interest in what she is trying to tell you.

Selecting a suitable subject for your talk requires some thought. You may know how to build a television receiver, but could you explain it so that your classmates would know how to build one, too? Unless they are experienced builders of radios, you would probably make a better talk on a less complicated subject, such as how to tune a television receiver. Think of your classmates—your audience.

Hobbies and sports offer many possibilities—organizing a coin collection, restringing a tennis racket, laying out a baseball diamond. So do household duties—sharpening a lawn mower, baking bread, repairing a leaky faucet. Do not pick too broad a subject. In a three-minute talk you can probably tell how to repair a leaky faucet, but you would certainly not be able to tell about all kinds of plumbing repairs. Do not pick a complicated or technical subject. Your classmates will probably be more interested in a simple subject that is fully explained, step by step. Now decide what you are going to talk about.

The plan for an explanation usually follows a time order. What is the first step? What next? What next? What is the last step? If you were telling how you start a fire in your fireplace without using any kindling, your plan for arranging the details might look like this:

1. Select three split logs that are dry.
2. Get an old newspaper or two.
3. Be sure you have also a few matches and a little patience.
4. Put two large logs on andirons.
5. Have split sides facing each other about one-half inch apart.
6. Put third log on top.
7. Open the damper in fireplace.
8. Roll several sheets of newspaper tightly and light with a match.
9. Shove lighted paper under logs.
10. Repeat two or three times until logs start burning.

Now make a plan for the talk you are going to give. When you have finished, ask yourself these questions: Have I included all the necessary steps? Have I given only those steps that are necessary? Have I arranged the steps in a straight line? Be sure that the answer to each of these questions is "Yes."

You may begin your talk in various ways. You may simply start with the first detail: "The first step in repairing a leaky faucet is to turn off the water supply. . . . " You may state what you are going to talk about: "There are four important steps in making bread: mixing the dough, allowing it to rise, shaping it into loaves, and baking the loaves. The dough is mixed by. . . . " You may use an introductory sentence: "Satisfactory reception of television signals often depends on knowing exactly how to use the knobs on the front of the set. The first knob. . . . " Occasionally you may want to use a sentence that arouses the interest of your listeners: "Do you still rub two sticks together when you start a fire? You won't need them for kindling, either, if you will follow these instructions. First, select. . . . " The first way of beginning is usually most satisfactory for a short talk. If you use any of the other ways, limit yourself to one or two sentences.

Decide how you will begin your talk. Then write your first sentence on a card or a small piece of paper. Under it write the plan for your talk, keeping the details in a time order.

Special closing sentences are rarely needed in telling how to make or do something. You simply stop with the last detail: "Now turn on the water supply. If the new washer has been put in properly, there should be no more dripping." Or: "When the crust is a golden brown, take the loaves out of the oven and set them on a rack to cool." This is usually the best way to end an explanation. But sometimes you may want to add a summary sentence: "Knowing how the controls work enables you to tune in various programs and adjust the picture for greatest brilliance and sharpness." And occasionally you may even want to end with a little twist that will help your listeners remember your talk: "When the blaze catches, I usually stand back, look surprised, and say, 'Well, what do you know!'" If you use either of the last two ways, limit yourself to a single sentence. Do not spoil the straight line by introducing a new idea in the closing sentence.

How will you end your talk? Write your closing sentence on your card or paper. The notes for your talk are now complete. Have them in your hand when you practice your talk and when you give it. They show you exactly how to begin, what details to give, and how to end.

Practice your talk at least once, timing it to make sure that it does not take longer than three minutes. If you are asked to give your talk in class, be sure to speak clearly so that all can hear.

Keep your notes. You will need them for the next assignment. Your teacher may ask you to hand in a copy of your notes.

Telling How to Make or Do Something

Now that you have prepared a short talk telling about something you know how to make or do, you are to prepare a written explanation, using the notes you made for your talk. Since these notes show you how to begin, what details to give, and how to end, you can concentrate on the problems of writing.

The first problem is deciding how many paragraphs you will need. This is done, not by picking a number from one to ten, but by studying the notes you made for your talk. If the details are listed in a time order and follow a straight line from beginning to end, your problem is easily solved by merely grouping details that are closely related.

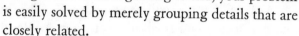

An easy way to organize paragraphs from a list of details is simply to mark the groups of related details with a line or bracket. Label the first group "A," the second "B," and so on. After each letter, write a few words telling how the details are related. For example, if you were writing about building a fire in your fireplace without using any kindling, your paragraphs might look like this:

A.
Getting
the
materials

OPENING SENTENCES: Do you still rub two sticks together when you start a fire? You won't need them for kindling, either, if you will follow these instructions.
1. Select three split logs that are dry.
2. Get an old newspaper or two.
3. Be sure you have also a few matches and a little patience.

B.
Laying
the
fire

4. Put two large logs on andirons.
5. Have split sides facing each other about one-half inch apart.
6. Put third log on top.

C.
Lighting
the
fire

7. Open the damper in fireplace.
8. Roll several sheets of newspaper tightly and light with a match.
9. Shove lighted paper under logs.
10. Repeat two or three times until logs start burning.
CLOSING SENTENCE: When the blaze catches, I usually stand back, look surprised, and say, "Well, what do you know!"

There are many ways of organizing paragraphs in written explanations. If you were telling how to repair a leaky faucet or tune a television receiver, your paragraphs might be:

A. Taking the faucet apart   A. Tuning in a station
B. Changing the washer   B. Adjusting the sound
C. Putting the faucet together   C. Adjusting the picture

If you were telling about making bread, your paragraphs might be:

A. Mixing the dough   OR   A. Mixing the batter
B. Letting the dough rise   for brown bread
C. Shaping the loaves   B. Preparing the molds
D. Baking the loaves   C. Steaming the molds

Now mark your list of details, so that you will know where each paragraph begins and ends. Your first paragraph will begin with the opening sentence you prepared for your talk. The last paragraph will end with your closing sentence. You will not need an "introductory" paragraph or a "concluding" paragraph.

Then write your explanation just as you planned to tell it in class, following your list of paragraphs to keep details in a straight line. Use pencil and scratch paper for this first draft so that you can make corrections and changes easily. Keep your classmates in mind as you write. You may be asked to read your composition to them.

The second problem is revising your first draft to make your sentences clear, forceful, and interesting. Read over your first draft carefully, sentence by sentence. Does each sentence say exactly what you mean? Can you make the meaning of any sentence more forceful by beginning with an adverb? Can you make your paragraphs more interesting by beginning an occasional sentence with something besides the subject? Are there any series of words that need commas? Does each sentence begin with a capital letter and end with a period or a question mark or an exclamation mark? Are you sure of the spelling of each word? This is the time for making corrections, too.

The third problem is selecting a suitable title. In writing about something you know how to make or do, the title should ordinarily be brief and clear. You may simply state what the explanation is about, or you may want to use a title that merely suggests what your explanation is about. Such titles are often effective in arousing the interest of the reader. For instance, compare these two sets of titles:

Repairing a Leaky Faucet	Stop That Drip!
Making Bread	It Takes Dough
Tuning a Television Receiver	Know Your Knobs!
Building a Fire Without Kindling	Fire Without Fuss

Now think about the title that you will use for your composition. When you have one that satisfies you, copy your first draft in a form suitable for handing in. Write neatly and legibly. Keep margins even. Space words carefully.

The final problem is proofreading your composition, word by word, to make sure that you have not omitted any words or final letters, copied the same word twice, misspelled any words, or omitted necessary punctuation marks. Make corrections as neatly as possible.

Your teacher may ask you to read your composition to the class before turning it in. If so, read slowly and distinctly and loudly enough for all to hear what you have to say. When a classmate is reading his composition, listen carefully so that you can tell what you like about it and what you think might be improved.

Other Uses of Nouns and Pronouns

Unit 4

In previous Units you learned some of the ways in which nouns and pronouns function—as subjects of verbs (Unit 1) and as objects of prepositions (Unit 3). This Unit will explain four more common uses of nouns and pronouns—as predicate nominatives, direct objects, indirect objects, and as appositives—and two occasional uses —as objective predicates and as adverbial nouns.

Predicate nominatives

In Unit 1 you learned to recognize a noun or pronoun that is used as the subject of a verb. Now you will see that nouns and pronouns are sometimes used after verbs to explain a subject. A noun or pronoun used in this way is called a **predicate nominative.** A predicate nominative means the same thing as the subject. It explains the subject by telling what it is, or was, or might be, or becomes, or seems to be:

> This is *Joe Davis.*
> The report was a *mistake.*
> The new boy is considered a skillful *player.*
> The caterpillars will be *moths* in a few weeks.
> That would have been a queer *reason* for your absence.

The great majority of predicate nominatives are used after forms of the verb *be.* But sometimes predicate nominatives are used after verbs like *was elected, has been appointed, should have been made:*

> Max Roberts was elected *secretary* of the class.
> Mary has been appointed *chairman* of the committee.
> Tom should have been made a *member* of the committee also.

Notice that in each of the sentences the subject and the predicate nominative refer to the same person. *Max Roberts* and *secretary* are the same person. *Mary* and *chairman* are the same person. *Tom* and *member* are the same person. When a noun after a verb is another name for the subject of the verb, the noun may be a predicate nominative.

After forms of the verb *be* and verbs like *become, turn, seem,* and *is considered,* either a predicate nominative or a predicate adjective may be used. Notice the following pairs of sentences:

Today he is a *hero.*   Today he is *brave.*
He became *president.*   He became *famous.*
This is considered an *error.*   This is considered *false.*

Now look at the following sentence:

This was considered a poor report.

In this last sentence, there is an adjective in the predicate, but it is not a predicate adjective, because it does not modify the subject *This.* It modifies the predicate nominative *report.* Of course the subject *This* and the predicate nominative *report* refer to the same thing; but as a matter of grammar the adjective *poor* modifies only the predicate nominative *report.*

EXERCISE 1. Some of the sentences have predicate adjectives. Some have predicate nominatives. Some have neither. Find each predicate adjective and each predicate nominative. Write the number of the sentence and, after it, the predicate adjective or the predicate nominative and the word it modifies or explains. Put parentheses around this word. For the first sentence you should write: *1. device (micrometer)*
1. A micrometer is a device used for measuring small distances with great accuracy.
2. The old red barn was considered quite ugly in spite of its new roof.
3. Did the coach appear angry after the first half?
4. Arthur always turned pale at the sight of blood.
5. Dale appeared that evening with his left arm in a sling.
6. Does she become nervous at the sound of the siren?
7. The manager has been a good friend of mine for many years.
8. Was this explanation of the incident considered adequate?
9. Perhaps some member of the senior class should have been appointed chairman of the nominating committee.
10. Over this door was a huge poster of blue paper with red lettering.

46

Improving sentences
7. Avoid unnecessary words

We sometimes use a predicate nominative where a predicate adjective would make a shorter, clearer sentence. Without thinking about meanings, we carelessly write sentences like these:

> This report was considered a poor *one*.
> My father is a very strong *man*.

The predicate nominatives in such sentences add nothing new or important. Everyone knows that a report is a report or that a father is a man. Such sentences are usually more forceful if predicate adjectives are used, as in the following:

> This report was considered *poor*.
> My father is very *strong*.

This does not mean that you should avoid using words like *one* and *man* as predicate nominatives when other words follow to make the meaning more exact. Sentences like the next two are examples of useful predicate nominatives:

> A casement window is *one* with hinges along the side.
> The doctor was considered a *man* of great skill and understanding.

It is only the *unnecessary* predicate nominatives that you should try to eliminate. Only when a shorter, clearer sentence is the result, should you make a change. The goal is always better sentences.

In using predicate adjectives, we sometimes add unnecessary words that seem ridiculous when we stop to think about them. For example, we may write sentences like these:

> The sheet of paper was rectangular *in shape*.
> The walls are bright yellow *in color*.

How could a sheet of paper be rectangular except in shape? How else could walls be bright yellow except in color? The two sentences can be improved by eliminating the unnecessary words "in shape" and "in color":

The sheet of paper was rectangular.
The walls are a bright yellow.

In a similar way, we sometimes carelessly use unnecessary adjectives before nouns:

The *two* twins wear identical clothes.
With a compass he drew a *round* circle.
She wore a crimson *red* rose in her *black* ebony hair.

Everybody knows that twins come in pairs and that circles are round. And since crimson is deep red and ebony is black, the words *red* and *black* are not needed:

The twins wear identical clothes.
With a compass he drew a circle.
She wore a crimson rose in her ebony hair.

Questions beginning with *where* and sentences using the verb *ought* sometimes cause us to use unnecessary words:

Where are you living *at* now?
Where are they going *to* this afternoon?
He *had* ought to spend more time on his lessons.

Since *where* means "at which place" or "to which place," the words *at* and *to* are not needed. And you can see that the unnecessary word *had* adds nothing to the meaning of *ought*:

Where are you living now?
Where are they going this afternoon?
He ought to spend more time on his lessons.

When you are revising your sentences, always watch for words that add nothing to the meaning. Avoiding these unnecessary words is another way of making your sentences clearer, more forceful, and more interesting.

EXERCISE 2. Each of the sentences contains one or more unnecessary words. Revise the sentences, eliminating the word or words that are not needed. Be ready to read your revised sentences aloud. For the first sentence you might say: *Your sister has become very pretty in the last few years.*

1. Your sister has become a very pretty girl in the last few years.
2. Some of the players are over six feet in height.

3. The twins are both alike.
4. Mr. Towne seems a much happier man since his vacation.
5. Someone had ought to tell her about coming to meetings on time.
6. The new office building is simply huge in size.
7. Where was he at during football practice?
8. Motorcycles are considered highly dangerous vehicles by some people.
9. Objections to the committee's plan have been few in number.
10. Where has she worn that scarlet red hat before?

Direct Objects

In many sentences the action expressed by the verb passes to a word
that means something different from the subject. Notice the italicized
words in the following sentences:

>Mother baked *cookies*.
>Did anyone help *her*?
>We saw *Martha* at the concert.
>The first batter hit a foul *ball* into the stands.

The noun *cookies* tells what Mother baked. The pronoun *her* tells
who might have been helped. The noun *Martha* tells who was seen.
Did the batter hit anything? He hit the ball. The noun *ball* receives
the action expressed by the verb *hit*.

**A noun or pronoun that tells what or who receives the action
expressed by the verb is called the object of the verb.**

The object of a verb is a word that means something different
from the subject. The only exception is the group of pronouns ending
in *self* or *selves*, such as *himself* and *themselves* and so on. Compare
the two sentences that follow:

>I cut the *cake* with a knife.
>I cut *myself* with a knife.

In these sentences the verb *cut* expresses an action performed by the
subject. The words *cake* and *myself* receive that action and are objects
of the verb.

Verbs may express an action that is not passed to an object. You
can see this clearly in sentences like these:

>My dog ran away.
>The team fought hard.

The verbs *ran* and *fought* express actions, but there are no nouns or pronouns to receive the actions. When verbs like these are modified by prepositional phrases, the objects of the prepositions may be carelessly mistaken for objects of the verbs. For example, notice the italicized words in the following sentences:

> Tom sent for the *doctor*.
> In case of fire, walk to the nearest *exit*.

The verbs in these sentences may seem to have objects; but if you ask "Did Tom send anything?" you will see that the word *doctor* is not the object of the verb. Tom did not send the doctor. Tom sent *for* the doctor. The word *doctor* is the object of the preposition *for*. And nobody can "walk" an exit. The word *exit* is the object of the preposition *to*. The verbs *sent* and *walk* do not have objects. Nouns and pronouns that are objects of prepositions cannot also be objects of verbs.

Nouns and pronouns that are predicate nominatives cannot be objects of verbs either. Those that are used with forms of the verb *be* are not confusing, but you must remember that predicate nominatives are sometimes used with other verbs:

> George Washington became our first president.
> Benedict Arnold turned traitor.
> This was considered a poor excuse.
> Max Roberts was elected secretary.

If you ask "Did George Washington become anything?" you may answer "He became president." But if you stop to think, you will see that *became* does not express any action performed by George Washington; in fact, the verb means about the same thing as *was*. The word *president* means the same person as *George Washington* and is a predicate nominative. Examine carefully the remaining sentences, and you will see that in each sentence the noun following the verb means the same as the subject and is a predicate nominative.

You can recognize the object of a verb most easily by asking yourself the following questions:

1) Does the verb express an action performed by the subject?
2) Does this action pass to a noun or pronoun that (except for a word like *himself* or *themselves*) means something different from the subject?

EXERCISE **3.** Each sentence contains one subject and one verb. In five of the sentences the verb has an object; in five others the verb is followed by a predicate nominative. Divide a sheet of paper into four columns. In the first column, write the subjects. In the second column, write the verbs. In the third column, write the objects of the verbs. In the fourth column, write the predicate nominatives. Number your answers with the numbers of the sentences. For the first sentence you should write:

> *1. most* | *do provide* | *service* |

1. Don't most of the dealers in this city provide guaranteed service for their automobiles?
2. Everybody at one time or another wants a home of his own.
3. For many years Tony had been a waiter in this little restaurant.
4. The most popular play of that season was *Life with Father*.
5. Several of the children ran across the street.
6. Your model airplane was one of the best in the contest.
7. Very few of those used cars are really bargains.
8. In all his thirty years of running the store he had never knowingly cheated a customer.
9. Has anyone in the class seen my notebook?
10. All week I have been hoping for a reply to my letter.
11. In spite of this mistake he is expecting a high mark on the examination.
12. Some senior will be appointed chairman of the refreshment committee.

Improving sentences
8. Begin with an object

In questions the object of the verb frequently comes before the subject and verb. Notice the italicized words in the following sentences:

> *What* do you know about trigonometry?
> Which *players* has the coach dropped from the squad?

Putting an object first in a statement calls attention to the word that receives the action of the verb and often makes the sentence more forceful. Compare the following pairs of sentences:

> I know that *song*.   Anyone would appreciate a *gift* like this.
> That *song* I know.   A *gift* like this anyone would appreciate.

This trick is not difficult to learn and is particularly effective when the objects in two sentences receive different actions. Putting the object first in one or both sentences emphasizes the contrast:

> I seem to have forgotten his *face*. The *name,* however, I remember extremely well.
> We simply threw the *books* into old boxes. But the *china* and *glasses* we carefully packed in barrels.
> The *pineapples* we gave to our friends. The *tangerines* we kept for ourselves.

In Unit 3 you learned about prepositional phrases. Objects of prepositions, like objects of verbs, often come before the subject and verb in questions:

> *What* is this substance made of?
> How many *samples* have you sent for?

Occasionally a sentence can be made more forceful by putting the object of a preposition first in a statement. Compare the following pairs of sentences:

> We have known about this *escapade* for some time.
> This *escapade* we have known about for some time.
> He had not heard from *some* of his friends for years.
> *Some* of his friends he had not heard from for years.

As with objects of verbs, a contrast between two sentences can sometimes be made more emphatic by putting the object of a preposition first in one or both sentences:

> Many of Edison's discoveries were the result of deliberate study. *Others* he came across accidentally.
> Our *advice* they would not listen to. Our *fears* they laughed at.

Try putting an object first occasionally, especially when you wish to emphasize a contrast between two sentences. But do not overuse this trick, and do not use it at all if it makes the sentence sound awkward or unnatural to you. Never make changes in the usual order of words unless the final sentence sounds more forceful or more interesting than the one with which you started.

EXERCISE 4. The sentences in each numbered group contain objects. Revise each group, making the meaning more forceful by putting an object first in one or both of the sentences. Make no change if putting an object

52

first causes the sentence to sound awkward or unnatural. Be ready to read your revised sentences aloud. For the first group you might say: *The good ones we sold to our friends. But the bad ones we had to dispose of promptly.*

1. We sold the good ones to our friends. But we had to dispose of the bad ones promptly.
2. First check the figures in each column for accuracy. You can check the totals later.
3. Grandfather stayed angry with Norman for weeks. But he forgave the twins the very next day.
4. Inspector Holmes found Ellis's fingerprints on the doorknobs. He did not look for more evidence after that.
5. Miss Crandall didn't object to our working together. But she would not tolerate cheating.
6. First I sent for Dr. Grayson. Then I called the police.
7. Slyly he slipped two of the letters under the blotter. He gave the rest to Mrs. Parrish.
8. I don't care for his poetry. But I like his short stories.
9. Keith put his own suitcases on the rack. He left my luggage in the aisle.
10. We can define carelessness as lack of interest in one's work. We can remedy this by using more interesting material.

Indirect objects

You often see sentences in which the verb seems to have two objects that mean different persons or things. But the words are not joined by *and* or *or*, and only one of the words actually receives the action expressed by the verb. Can you find the object of the verb in each of the following sentences?

> Mr. Swanson sent a book.
> Mr. Swanson sent a book to John.
> Mr. Swanson sent John a book.

In the first two sentences you know that *book* is the object of the verb. And in the second sentence you know that *John* is the object of the preposition *to*. In the third sentence the verb seems to have two objects; yet the sentence means about the same thing as the second one. Look again at that third sentence. Did Mr. Swanson send anything? He sent a book. The word *book* is the object of the verb *sent*. The answer to the question makes it clear that Mr. Swanson did not send

John. The word *John* tells to whom the book was sent. In sentences like the third one the word *John* is called the **indirect object,** and the word *book* is called the **direct object.**

Now look at these three sentences:

Father built a doll house.
Father built a doll house for my little sister.
Father built my little sister a doll house.

Did Father build anything? He built a house. He built it for the little sister. In the third sentence the word *sister* tells for whom the house was built and is the indirect object. The word *house* is the direct object. Notice that the indirect object always precedes the direct object.

Objective predicates

Occasionally you will come across sentences in which the verb seems to have two objects that mean the same person or thing. But the words cannot be joined by *and* or *or,* and only one of the words actually receives the action expressed by the verb. Can you find the object of the verb in each of the following sentences?

The class elected Virginia president.
This made her very happy.

Whom did the class elect? The class elected Virginia. The word *Virginia* is the object of the verb. The word *president* tells what she was elected to be. It is another name for the object of the verb and is called an **objective predicate.** Now look at the second sentence. Was anyone made happy? The pronoun *her* is the object of the verb. The adjective *happy* tells how the object was made to feel. Adjectives also may be objective predicates; but they are seldom confusing, since you know that a modifying word cannot be an object.

Adverbial nouns

The only other nouns that might be confused with the object of the verb are those used like adverbs to tell where or when or how far. In Unit 2 you learned that these nouns are called adverbial nouns. Can you find the object of the verb in each of the following sentences?

54

The teacher sent Bill home Friday.

The boys ran the car twenty miles on one gallon of gasoline.

Will you call me the first thing in the morning?

I received your letter Sunday morning.

Did the teacher send anything? The teacher sent Bill. The word *Bill* is the object of the verb. The teacher did not send a "home" or a "Friday"; these words are adverbial nouns that tell where and when. Did the boys run anything? They ran the car. Will you call anything? You will call me. Did I receive anything? I received a letter. Always ask questions like these to help you decide which words are the objects of the verbs.

A word of caution: Sentences that contain indirect objects also contain direct objects. Sentences that have objective predicates also have objects of the verb. But a sentence may have adverbial nouns without having an object of the verb. Compare these two sentences:

The teacher sent Bill home Friday.

The teacher went home Friday.

In both sentences the words *home* and *Friday* are adverbial nouns. In the first sentence *Bill* is the object of the verb. Because the action expressed by the verb passes to an object, we say that the verb in the sentence is a **transitive** verb. In the second sentence there is no object of the verb. Because the action expressed by the word does not pass to an object, we say that the verb in the sentence is an **intransitive** verb. Adverbial nouns often follow intransitive verbs. When you are looking for the object of the verb, do not grab blindly at any noun or pronoun in the predicate. Only a noun or pronoun that receives the action expressed by the verb can be an object of that verb.

EXERCISE 5. Find the verbs in the sentences, and decide which are followed by indirect objects, which are followed by objective predicates, and which are modified by adverbial nouns. Divide a sheet of paper into five columns. In the first column, write the verbs. In the second column, write the indirect objects. In the third column, write the objects of the verbs. In the fourth column, write the objective predicates. And in the fifth column, write the adverbial nouns. Number your answers. For the first one you should write: *1. bought | me | hat | | Tuesday*

1. Mother bought me a new hat last Tuesday.

2. Your talk gave Louise an unusual idea.

3. Their combined efforts made the party a huge success.
4. Uncle Jim usually sends me ten dollars for Christmas.
5. Skeptical observers named the strange craft "Fulton's Folly."
6. All work and no play surely make this Jack a dull boy.
7. Will you give us some help tomorrow before the game?
8. Why did our team lose Saturday?
9. Why did Mr. Allen send you home early Tuesday afternoon?
10. The coach taught us several new plays last week.

Active and passive verbs

In the preceding section on objective predicates you saw these two sentences:

> The class elected Virginia president.
> This made her very happy.

In both sentences the action expressed by the verb passes to an object. Who elected Virginia president? The class elected her. The subject *class* tells who is the doer of the action that passes to the object *Virginia*. What made her happy? The pronoun *This* is the subject of the second sentence and tells what is the doer of the action that passes to the object *her*. When the subject tells who or what is the doer of the action expressed by a transitive verb, we say that the verb is **active**.

Now look at these two sentences:

> Virginia was elected president of the class.
> She was made very happy by this.

Who was elected president? Virginia was. The noun *Virginia* is the subject of the sentence, but it does not tell who is the doer of the action expressed by the verb. The class did the electing, and Virginia became president as a result of that action. The subject tells who is affected by the action of the verb. Who was made very happy? The pronoun *She* is the subject of the second sentence and tells who is affected by the action of the verb. When the subject tells who or what is affected by the action of the verb, we say that the verb is **passive**.

A passive verb can be changed to an active verb by making the doer of the action the subject of the verb:

> The books were taken back to the library by two boys.
> Two boys took the books back to the library.

56

In the sentences at the bottom of the preceding page you can see that *books,* the subject of the passive verb *were taken,* becomes the object of the active verb *took.*

Passive verbs are useful wherever the doer of the action expressed by the verb is obvious, unknown, or unimportant:

> Virginia was elected president of her class.
> Only one window was broken on Halloween.
> During hot weather the grass should be cut every other week.

In the first sentence it is obvious that the class elected Virginia to be president. In the second sentence it is not known who broke the window. And in the third sentence it makes no difference who cuts the grass. Except for sentences like these, however, active verbs are generally preferred because they call attention to the doer of the action expressed by the verb.

Improving sentences
9. Use an active verb

Students often use too many passive verbs. They tend to write sentences like these:

> From the top of the cliff many ships were seen by us at anchor in the quiet bay below.
> Christmas was looked forward to with great eagerness by my niece.
> John was sent a book by Mr. Swanson.

Sentences like these are almost always awkward and sometimes confusing. For example, in the last one you cannot tell whether the book was written by Mr. Swanson or was sent by him. You have learned that passive verbs are useful when the doer of the action is obvious, unknown, or unimportant. But in each of the examples above, the doer of the action has been expressed in a phrase beginning with *by.* Such sentences are more forceful when active verbs are used:

> From the top of the cliff we saw many ships at anchor in the quiet bay below.
> My niece looked forward to Christmas with great eagerness.
> Mr. Swanson sent John a book.

As you revise the first drafts of your written compositions, watch for awkward sentences in which the doer of the action expressed by a passive verb is in a phrase beginning with *by*. If the doer of the action is obvious or unimportant, cross out the phrase. Otherwise, use an active verb, making the doer of the action the subject.

EXERCISE 6. Each of the sentences contains a passive verb. Revise the sentences that you think might be improved by changing passive verbs to active verbs. Be ready to read your revised sentences aloud. For the first sentence you might say: *Everybody at the party had a good time.*

1. A good time was had by everybody at the party.
2. The umpire was booed vigorously by a few of the students.
3. An accordion is always called a "squeeze box" by Tom.
4. One night last week our front steps were daubed with red paint.
5. An effort to repair the damage before Dad's return was made by my little brother.
6. Betty was appointed chairman of the committee on outside reading by the teacher.
7. Some of the men in the orchestra were asked for autographs by Ed.
8. The doctor had been called right after the accident by a patrolman.
9. Then the heavy box was lifted by two big fellows from the gutter.
10. All the guests were questioned after the robbery by the sheriff.

Appositives

Earlier you learned that predicate nominatives are nouns and pronouns used after verbs to explain subjects by giving other names for the subjects. Sometimes nouns and pronouns are merely set alongside other words in a sentence to explain these words by giving other names for them, no verb being used. Notice the italicized words in the following sentences:

My closest friend, *Ed Mayfield,* has one of the leading parts in this year's play.

One of the tools, a *micrometer,* measures differences of a thousandth of an inch with great accuracy.

We spent a week in his charming home, a colonial *farmhouse* with all modern conveniences.

This next man, *one* always aware of his civic responsibility, served on the school board.

58

In the first sentence the proper noun *Ed Mayfield* explains the word *friend*. In the second sentence the common noun *micrometer* explains the word *One*. In the third sentence the noun *farmhouse* with its modifiers adds to the meaning of *home* by explaining what kind of building it is. And in the fourth sentence the pronoun *one* with its modifiers adds to the meaning of *man* by explaining what kind of person he is. Notice that each sentence has only one subject and verb.

A noun or pronoun that is set alongside another word or group of words to explain or add to its meaning is called an appositive.

An appositive is said to be "in apposition with" the word it explains. And as you have just seen, it usually comes right after the word.

Sometimes appositives are preceded by *or, like, such as, namely, that is, for example,* or other introductory expressions:

> The timpani, or *kettledrums*, are tuned by means of pedals.
> A few of these organizations, like the *American Red Cross* and the *Boy Scouts*, ask for contributions annually.

An appositive may sum up the meaning of a group of words:

> Grandpa always got up at five o'clock in the morning—a *habit* the rest of the family considered absurd.

EXERCISE 7. Each sentence contains one or more appositives. Find each appositive and decide what it is in apposition with. Then divide a sheet of paper into two columns. In the left-hand column, write the words that are explained by the appositives. In the right-hand column, write the appositives. Number your answers with the numbers of the sentences. For the first sentence you should write:

1. clock	*gift*
repairs	*mainspring, hands, glass*

1. The mahogany clock on the mantel, a Christmas gift from the five grandchildren, needed extensive repairs—a new mainspring, new hands, and a new glass to protect the dial.
2. Finally he saw his old friend, William Jerome, standing in the doorway.
3. Argentina, Brazil, and Chile—the "A B C" states—are becoming wealthier and more progressive every year.
4. One important product is native to this hemisphere—cocoa.
5. They had on woolen trousers of all colors—brown, drab, and gray.
6. The most productive region of Polynesia, the Hawaiian Islands, is now one of the fifty states.

7. Robert Bailey, the only son of a well-known banker, has been missing from his home for several days.
8. Even I, a salesman, cannot afford to buy one of the new cars, a real necessity for me.
9. There are three zones—the frigid, the torrid, and the temperate.
10. Nearly all the very valuable spices—such as pepper, ginger, cloves, and nutmeg—come from islands on the other side of the globe.

Improving sentences
10. Use an appositive

Untrained writers seldom use an appositive. When they want to give more than one fact about a person or thing, they use a separate sentence for each fact. They write sentences like these:

> Pete Jenkins made the winning touchdown. He is captain of our team.

> Miss Rodman is my music teacher. She is going to broadcast over a nation-wide network next Sunday evening.

If you look carefully at the two sentences in the first example, you will see that the first sentence gives a fact that is important, while the second sentence merely gives additional information about Pete Jenkins. In the second example, the first sentence merely explains something about Miss Rodman, while the second sentence gives important information. Trained writers avoid weak explanatory sentences by using appositives to give added information. They write sentences like these:

> Pete Jenkins, captain of our team, made the winning touchdown.

> Miss Rodman, my music teacher, is going to broadcast over a nation-wide network next Sunday evening.

The purpose of this lesson is not to teach you that a long sentence containing an appositive is better than two short sentences. Instead, the purpose is to show you how appositives can sometimes be used to avoid *weak* sentences that merely explain words used in other, more important, sentences. Short sentences can be just as effective as long sentences. But weak sentences, regardless of their length, are never effective. They distract the reader and make it difficult for him to know

60

which sentences are important. Every time you use an appositive in place of a weak explanatory sentence, you make the important sentences stand out more clearly.

EXERCISE 8. Each of the numbered groups consists of two sentences. Read each pair of sentences, and decide which sentence is merely explanatory. Then change each group into one good sentence, using an appositive in place of the explanatory sentence. Be ready to read your revised sentences aloud. For the first group you might say: *Two sophomores signed up for chemistry, a course usually open only to seniors.*

1. Two sophomores signed up for chemistry. This is a course usually open only to seniors.
2. Three groups were represented at the meeting. These were the firemen, the engineers, and the switchmen.
3. The war led to many acts of violence. There were such acts as burning homes, destroying bridges, and tearing up railroads.
4. Last Saturday afternoon Mike took me for an exciting ride in his "hot rod." It is an old car with a powerful engine and high-speed gearing.
5. In flight the position of the plane is governed by three movable surfaces. These are the rudder, the elevators, and the ailerons.
6. Two officers of the club do most of the work and get none of the glory. They are the secretary and the treasurer.
7. Three of the driving controls are the accelerator, the clutch, and the brake. They are operated by the driver's feet.
8. Jim Flint was old Mrs. Sweezy's chauffeur. He was color-blind, partly deaf, and utterly reckless with an automobile.
9. Dorothy Clark is the daughter of our principal. She plans to study medicine and become a doctor.
10. In Mrs. Wolf's yard were a dozen fat gobblers. These were to be the food for a dozen families on Thanksgiving.

Telling How Something Looks

If you like to visit new places and see new things, you know how much fun it is to talk about your trip when you come back home. You probably also like to hear others tell about interesting things they have seen. Perhaps you know a Bill or a Betty who can tell about such things in a way that is almost as interesting as seeing them for yourself.

Why are people like Bill and Betty successful in telling how something looked? First, of course, is their choice of an interesting subject. If you live in a big city, Bill may decide you would be interested in hearing about a small mountain lake where he camped last summer. If you live in a small town, Betty may choose to tell you how Times Square looked at night. They tell about things that are unusual or different in some way from your everyday surroundings. Second is their ability to make you feel as though you were actually standing beside them. When Bill is sitting in a canoe and looking at the white cottages nestling among the dark green pine trees on the shore, so are you. When Betty is looking over the city from a skyscraper window, you are there with her. They never let you forget their point of view. Third is their care in keeping a straight line. You know when Bill's eyes move from left to right along the wooded shore, and your eyes move with his. You follow Betty's gaze as it moves from the distance to the street directly below and off to the distance again in the opposite direction. They never confuse you by jumping back and forth from one detail to another. They follow a straight line.

In preparing a short talk in which you tell how something looked, the first step is to select a subject that will be interesting to your listeners. What have you seen that they have not seen? If you have been away from home on a visit or a vacation, you have probably seen many new and different things that would interest your classmates—a snow-covered mountain range or a beautiful bay, a log cabin or a granite memorial, a great bridge or dam or tunnel. You have merely to select one that you remember most about. If you have not been away from home, you still have many possible subjects. You might, for instance, tell about a walk to school on the morning after a heavy snow or a bad storm or Halloween, about Main Street the week before Christmas, about church on Easter morning, about a spectacular fire at night. Familiar things under unusual circumstances are often as interesting as unfamiliar things. Or you might tell about the strangest vehicle you ever saw, about a building or store or theater or house that you consider unusual for some reason, about something that you yourself made—a dress, a tree house, a birthday cake, a motor scooter. Even the most ordinary things can be interesting when you make them seem personal.

Now decide what you are going to tell about. Try to select some *one* thing that you remember enough about to make it seem real to your classmates. You want them to be as interested as you in what you have seen.

In telling how something looked you must have a **point of view** so that your listeners can visualize the details you give. The point of view may change, as, for example, in telling about a walk to school on the morning after a bad storm. First you might tell what you saw as you stepped out of the front door and looked down the street. Then you might tell about the wreckage along the way. Finally you might tell what you saw as you approached the school building itself. Or the point of view may remain fixed, as, for instance, in telling about Main Street before Christmas. You might stand at the center of the shopping district and tell, first, what you saw by looking north and, then, what you saw by looking south. Remember that your talk will be more interesting if you make clear to your listeners where you were when you saw the things you tell them. What will be the best point of view for the details of your talk?

The plan you use for telling how something looked may follow a **time order**. In telling about a trip through a tunnel, for example, you might describe the approach to the tunnel, what you saw inside the tunnel, and your exit from the tunnel. More often, however, you will need to follow a **space order**. In describing a mountain or a tall building, you might begin by telling what you saw at the bottom, and end by telling about the snow-capped peak or the flag waving from the tower. In describing a bay, you might tell what you saw at the extreme left, then straight ahead, and finally at the extreme right. In describing a view from a high place, you might start with the things near at hand and move to those in the distance.

Your plan should give the important details in a time order, a space order, or some combination of the two. In addition, it should also give the original point of view and any changes in the point of view. If you were telling about an old abandoned house on the outskirts of town, your plan might look like this, with the words in italics showing the various points of view:

1. First saw the house *as I came out of the woods* late one gray afternoon in November.
2. Noticed that the house was big and stood alone in a fenced-in clearing.
3. *Coming closer,* I looked for signs of life but found none.
4. Noticed the tumble-down chimney and holes in the roof, the weather-beaten walls with blank windows and broken shutters, the rickety fence and the yard overgrown with weeds.
5. *Approaching the front of the house,* I saw that front steps were falling in and that the door was partly open.
6. *Stood at foot of steps,* wondering whether to have a look inside the old house.
7. Just then a gust of wind swung the door open, and hinges creaked, shutters banged, windows rattled.
8. Suddenly decided it was getting late and *turned to go.*
9. *Looking back as I reached the road,* I thought I saw a dim light in one of the upstairs windows.
10. May have been a reflection or just my imagination.

Now write out the plan for the talk you are going to give. Put only important details in your plan. Be sure the plan shows the original point of view and any changes in the point of view.

The beginning sentence of your talk should make your listeners want to hear what follows. It may be a question: "Have you ever stopped to notice the Christmas decorations along Main Street? One snowy night last week . . ." It may be a statement: "I'll never forget how the streets looked the morning after the hurricane. The first thing I saw as I came out of the house was . . . " It may challenge your listeners: "Imagine a mountain so high that the snow on its peak never melts! Last summer . . . " Or it may arouse the curiosity of your listeners: "I'm not sure the house was haunted, but it certainly should have been. I saw it first as I . . . " Notice that only one beginning sentence is used. Notice that it is followed immediately by the first detail.

Decide how you will begin your talk. Then write your beginning sentence on a card or a small piece of paper. Under it write the plan for your talk, keeping the details in order. Underline words that show your point of view so that you will remember to tell your audience when you change from one point of view to another.

Your closing sentence may be simply your last detail: "Even the red and green traffic lights along Main Street seemed somehow to be part of the Christmas decorations." This is usually the best way of ending a short description. Sometimes, however, you may want to comment briefly on what you saw: "How could wind alone have caused so much damage?" Or you may want to emphasize your feelings: "This was not the only mountain I saw, but it was surely the most beautiful one." Or you may want to end in a way that will help your listeners remember your talk: "I have never known whether it was caused by a reflection or by my imagination. Could it, perhaps, have been a ghost?"

How will you end your talk? Will you end with the last detail? Will you use a special closing sentence? Write the last sentence of your talk on your card or paper. The notes for your talk are now complete. Have them in your hand when you practice your talk and when you give it. They show exactly how to begin, what details to give and in what order, and how to end. Your notes will help you give a good talk.

Now that you have prepared a short talk in which you told how something looked, you are to prepare a written description, using the notes you made for your talk.

The first problem is deciding how many paragraphs to have. In a description this can best be solved by considering the point of view. If, for example, you were telling about a walk to school on the morning after a bad storm, your point of view would change as you left home, walked down the street, and approached the school. The details in your talk could then be arranged into groups in a time order—what you saw first, what you saw next, what you saw last:

A. What I saw as I stepped out on the porch
B. What I saw along the way to school
C. What I saw as I approached the school building

But if you were telling how Main Street looked one night before Christmas, your point of view might not change at all. You would simply tell first what you saw by looking in one direction and then what you saw by looking in the other direction:

A. What I saw looking north on Main Street
B. What I saw looking south on Main Street

Of course, if you were describing a tall building or a bay, you might need three or four paragraphs to group the details you want to tell about. The number of paragraphs is unimportant so long as each paragraph groups all the details seen at one time. The reader usually expects that the details in each paragraph will be related in either time or place. For a short written composition, you will probably use from two to four paragraphs.

If the details in your notes are in a time or space order, you will find it easy to group related details by means of lines or brackets. Label the first group "A" and the second group "B" and so on. After each letter, write a few words telling how the details are related. For example, if you were telling about the old abandoned house on the outskirts of town, your paragraphs might look like this:

A.
My first
view of
the house

OPENING SENTENCE: I'm not sure the house was haunted, but it certainly should have been.

1. First saw the house as I came out of the woods late one gray afternoon in November.
2. Noticed that the house was big and stood alone in a fenced-in clearing.

B.
A
closer
view

3. Coming closer, I looked for signs of life but found none.
4. Noticed the tumble-down chimney and holes in the roof, the weather-beaten walls with blank windows and broken shutters, the rickety fence and the yard overgrown with weeds.
5. Approaching the front of the house, I saw that front steps were falling in and that the door was partly open.

C.
Strange
sights
and sounds

6. Stood at foot of steps, wondering whether to have a look inside the old house.
7. Just then a gust of wind swung the door open, and hinges creaked, shutters banged, windows rattled.
8. Suddenly decided it was getting late and turned to go.

D.
My last
look at
the house

9. Looking back as I reached the road, I thought I saw a dim light in one of the upstairs windows.
10. May have been a reflection or just my imagination.

CLOSING SENTENCE: Could it, perhaps, have been a ghost?

Now mark your list of details, so that you will know where each paragraph begins and ends. Begin your first paragraph with your opening sentence. End your last paragraph with your closing sentence. Do not use special introductory or concluding paragraphs.

Then write your description just as you planned to tell it in class, following your list of paragraphs to keep the details in order. Use pencil and scratch paper for your first draft so that you can make corrections and changes easily. Keep your classmates in mind as you write.

Revise your first draft carefully, making corrections in spelling and punctuation, changing the order of the words, crossing out unnecessary words or adding better ones until the sentences in your composition are as good as you can make them. Each written composition is an opportunity to show how much you have learned.

Selecting a suitable title for your composition is the third problem. The simplest title for a description is the name of the place or thing you are writing about: Times Square, Miami Bay, Washington Monument, Mount Rainier, Grand Canyon, and so on. Occasionally you may want to use a title that is more specific or that will arouse the interest of your reader. Compare these two sets of titles:

Broadway at Night	Manhattan Midnight
Chicago by Day	Love That Loop!
After the Storm	The Big Blow
Christmas on Main Street	St. Nick in Neon
Mystery Manor	Haunting a House?

What title will you use for your composition? Will you use a title that clearly names what your description is about, or will you use one that merely suggests what it is about? When you have selected a title, copy your revised first draft in a form suitable for handing in. Write neatly and legibly. Keep margins even. Space words carefully.

The final problem is proofreading your composition to catch any errors you may have made in copying. Go over the final draft word by word. If you have omitted any words or final letters, copied the same word twice, misspelled any words, or omitted any punctuation marks, make corrections as neatly as you can.

Your teacher may ask you to read your composition to the class before turning it in. If so, read slowly and distinctly.

Verbals and Verbal Phrases

This Unit deals with verbals—forms of verbs that are used as adjectives, adverbs, and nouns. When these verbals are joined with certain other words, the resulting word group forms a phrase—a group of closely related words that do the same work as single words.

Active participles

We often use words ending in *ing* to modify nouns and pronouns. Notice the italicized words in the following sentences:

> Mother smiled at the *trembling* child.
> The one *laughing* is my sister.
> This change seemed *encouraging*.

The word *trembling* modifies the noun *child*, describing the child Mother smiled at. The word *laughing* modifies the pronoun *one*, telling which person is my sister. The word *encouraging* modifies the subject *change*, telling what kind of change this appeared to be. You know that *trembling, laughing,* and *encouraging* are forms of verbs; and you can see that these *ing* forms are used as adjectives in the examples above. Notice that the *ing* form may come before or after the word it modifies, or may follow the verb as a predicate adjective.

A verb form that ends in *ing* and is used as an adjective is called an active participle.

An active participle is not a verb. It does not have a subject, and it cannot make a statement. But it usually suggests that the word modified is performing an action. If we say "The child trembles," the word *trembles* states an action and is a verb. If we say "the trembling child," the word *trembling* suggests an action without stating it, and *trembling* is an active participle.

Participles resemble verbs in other ways. Notice the italicized words following the participles in the following sentences:

Hearing a *cry*, Mike rushed out to investigate.

Being a *bully*, Tom hit me and ran away.

Mr. Smith, growing *angry*, began to shout.

At the news of her brother's failure to pass the examination, Alice hurried from the principal's office, sobbing *bitterly*.

The boys in the Sportsman's Club spent last Saturday afternoon at the range, firing *at clay pigeons*.

In the first sentence *cry* is the object of *Hearing*. In the second, *bully* is a predicate nominative after *Being*. In the third, *angry* is a predicate adjective after *growing*. In the fourth, *bitterly* is an adverb modifying *sobbing*. In the fifth, *at clay pigeons* is an adverb phrase modifying *firing*. In each sentence the participle, together with these other words, forms a **participial phrase.**

In the preceding examples you have seen participial phrases that modify subjects. Now look at the phrases in the following sentences:

We heard Sarah *laughing loudly at his silly jokes.*

She was met by a group of reporters *waving pencils and notebooks.*

Mr. Loomis is the delegate *representing Coe College.*

Her best work, a novel *glorifying country life,* was never published.

A good way to find what word an active participle modifies is to ask "Who or what is _____?" putting the participle in place of the blank. Who or what is laughing? Sarah is. The phrase modifies *Sarah,* which is the object of the verb *heard.* Who or what is waving? The reporters are. The phrase modifies *reporters,* the object of the preposition *of.* Who or what is representing? The phrase modifies the predicate nominative *delegate.* Who or what is glorifying? The phrase modifies *novel,* an appositive.

Participles sometimes modify a word in the phrase itself. Compare the phrases in the following sentences:

Being weary, Sally lay down to rest.

Mother being weary, Sally offered to wash the dishes.

In the first sentence the participle, like the others you have seen, modifies a word outside the phrase—*Sally.* But in the second sentence the participle modifies a word that is in the phrase itself—*Mother.* Such a phrase, consisting of a participle and the word it modifies, is called a

nominative absolute. A nominative absolute does not modify anything. It simply gives a bit of added information.

You learned in Unit 1 that a verb may be one, two, three, or four words. Since an active participle is a form of a verb, it also may be more than one word:

>*Having finished* his work, Henry left the office.
>
>Sue was quite proud of the dress, *having made* it without any help.

Two-word participles that begin with *having* make it clear that the action suggested by the participle has been completed. Henry had finished his work *before* he left the office. Sue felt proud *after* she had made the dress.

EXERCISE 1. Each of the sentences contains one or more active participles. List each active participle, and after it, in parentheses, write the noun or pronoun it modifies. Use a separate line for each active participle. Number your answers with the numbers of the sentences. For the first sentence you should write: *1. carrying (rowboats)*

1. The ship was soon surrounded by rowboats carrying rival salesmen.
2. There was a dazzling light on the wet pavement.
3. Wishing to be sure of the facts, I looked in a *World Almanac*.
4. There had been an appalling earthquake in Chile.
5. Mr. Morton, fearing to seem impolite, raised his hat and smiled.
6. Having worked all day, Dad was too tired to go to the movies.
7. Dick spent a glorious hour among the side shows, wandering happily from one gaudy display to another.
8. Taking it for granted that she didn't care to see me, and not wishing to intrude on her, I left her entirely alone.
9. Noticing a police car up ahead and wanting to avoid trouble, Philip slowed down to twenty miles an hour.
10. Once in five or six weeks a small schooner visits the lonely island, bringing a bag of mail and supplying us with fresh meat and vegetables.

Improving sentences
11. Use an active participle

Too often students depend on the word *so* to show the relationship between two sentences, one of which gives a reason for what happens in the other. They write sentences like this:

> Joan wished to surprise Ed. *So* she said nothing about buying the dog.

The second sentence expresses the important idea, the first one merely giving the reason for not mentioning the purchase. Better sentences can be made by using a participial phrase to give the reason:

> Joan, *wishing to surprise Ed,* said nothing about buying the dog.
> *Wishing to surprise Ed,* Joan said nothing about buying the dog.
> Joan said nothing about buying the dog, *wishing to surprise Ed.*

The first sentence treats the reason as a mere explanatory detail. The second one stresses the reason somewhat more, and the third stresses it somewhat less. But in each of the sentences Joan's behavior is of greater importance than the reason for it.

Sometimes sentences that are related have subjects that mean different persons or things. For example:

> The *time* was short. So *we* skipped lunch.
> *Tommy* ran back and forth. The *dog* yelped at his heels.

Such sentences can be combined by using nominative absolutes:

> *The time being short,* we skipped lunch.
> Tommy ran back and forth, *the dog yelping at his heels.*

Nominative absolutes do not modify anything and may come either first or last in a sentence.

A word of caution: Readers expect a participial phrase at the beginning of a sentence to modify the subject. If you omit the word you intended the participle to modify or fail to make it the subject, you may write sentences as ridiculous as these:

> Strolling down the lane, a glorious sunset was seen.
> Wallowing in the mud, we saw our prize pig.

You know that a sunset, however glorious it may be, does not go strolling down a lane; and you know that the writer probably meant that the pig was wallowing. But the writer of the first sentence carelessly omitted the word he intended the participle to modify; and the writer of the second sentence carelessly put the phrase first, where it seems to modify the subject *we*. The participle in each sentence is said to be a **dangling** participle because it either has no word to modify or seems to modify a wrong word. The remedy is obvious:

> Strolling down the lane, *I* saw a glorious sunset.
> *We* saw our prize pig wallowing in the mud.

Either make the word modified by the participle the subject of the sentence, or move the phrase closer to the word actually modified by the participle. Dangling participles are not always amusing, but they are almost always puzzling to the reader. When you use participial phrases, always be sure that the participle modifies a word in the sentence and that it is the word you intended the participle to modify.

EXERCISE 2. Read each of the pairs of sentences, and decide which sentence is the more important. Then revise the sentences, using participial phrases in place of the less important sentences. Be ready to read your revised sentences aloud. For the first sentence you might say: *Howling at the sparks, the wolves ran away.*

1. The wolves ran away. They were howling at the sparks.
2. The seal swam round and round the pool. He frequently ducked his head under water.
3. She ran to the door. She cried out in amazement, "It's my Sammy!"
4. The picture crashed to the floor. It made a terrifying noise.
5. The man stopped his car suddenly. He seemed to suspect that something was wrong with me.
6. Allison looked at his compass. He announced that we must take a course more to the northward.
7. A high hedge runs across the back of our yard. It cuts off the view of an untidy house.
8. The little train climbs four thousand feet in three hours. It winds back and forth on the face of the mountain.
9. Eileen ran from the room. Tears were streaming down her cheeks.
10. General Porter felt suspicious. So he questioned the man closely.

Improving sentences: Ways you have learned

1. **Ask a question**
2. **Use a command**
3. **Choose exact modifiers**
4. **Begin with an adverb**
5. **Begin with a preposition**

6. **Use a compound verb**
7. **Avoid unnecessary words**
8. **Begin with an object**
9. **Use an active verb**
10. **Use an appositive**

11. Use an active participle

EXERCISE **3.** The following paragraphs tell of an unusual experience that a bus driver had early one cold, foggy morning. There was only one passenger, who appeared to be a minister. The driver was expecting to collect his fare when he left the bus. Every sentence begins with the subject and verb. Rewrite the story, improving the sentences whenever there is a natural and easy opportunity to do so. Use any of the ways you have learned, but do not try to use them all. Be sure that every change you make is a *natural* one. If a sentence sounds all right to you, let it stand as it is.

(1) The bus driver was always ahead of schedule on this early morning trip. (2) He had to drive awfully slowly in order not to arrive at Lake Street ahead of time. (3) Passengers complained about the slow speed sometimes. (4) The minister said not a word, however.

(5) The driver began to wonder at the minister's silence. (6) He wondered how far the minister was going also. (7) He would be getting off at the far side of the airport perhaps. (8) It was horribly muddy along the road near the edge of the field. (9) The driver began to look for a dry spot accordingly.

(10) He turned in his seat to ask the minister where he wanted to stop. (11) But no passenger was left in the seats. (12) The minister had stepped out somewhere. (13) The driver stopped the bus. (14) He climbed down from the seat and stared back along the road. (15) The minister was nowhere in sight.

(16) The driver climbed slowly back to his place at the wheel. (17) He twisted around to stare at the empty seat once more. (18) Something caught his eye. (19) It was a crumpled piece of greenish paper. (20) He held a five-dollar bill in his fingers ten seconds later.

(21) The driver remembered the policemen at Black Falls now. (22) So he began to put two and two together. (23) The passenger was not a minister at all probably. (24) He was the escaped criminal maybe! (25) The driver started the bus, back at the wheel again. (26) He said to himself, "This is one trip I won't forget."

74

Passive participles

You know that active participles are verb forms that end in *ing* and are used as adjectives. Now look at the italicized words in the following sentences:

> Harriet threw away the *cracked* cup with the *broken* handle.
> To her great surprise Mother found all the beds *made* and the rugs *swept*.
> The spoon in that glass of water looks *bent*.

You know that the italicized words are forms of verbs, and you can see that they are used to modify nouns. But these participles, unlike the participles that end in *ing*, suggest that the words they modify have received or are receiving an action. The cup had been cracked, and the handle had been broken. The beds had been made, and the rugs had been swept. The spoon has the appearance of having been bent. But from the sentences you cannot tell who or what performed these actions. Notice that these modifying verb forms may come before or after the words they modify, or may follow the verb as predicate adjectives.

A participle which shows that the word it modifies has received or is receiving an action is called a passive participle.

Passive participles are like active participles in other ways. They form modifying phrases and nominative absolutes, and they may be more than one word. A participial phrase consisting of a passive participle and its modifiers may come before or after the word it modifies:

> *Thoroughly frightened by the noise,* the boys ran away.
> The sailors replaced the sail *torn by the wind.*

To find what word a passive participle modifies, ask "Who or what was _____?" putting the passive participle in place of the blank. Who or what was frightened? The boys were. The phrase modifies the subject *boys*. Who or what was torn? The sail was. The phrase modifies the object *sail*.

Passive participles may also be more than one word. The two-word forms are useful in telling about an action going on at the time expressed by the verb in the sentence:

The work *done* in Miss Hale's class is always good. The work *being done* in her class this year is excellent.

By using the two-word participle *being done* in the second sentence, the writer stresses the fact that the work is still in progress, that it is not yet completed. In contrast, the three-word forms are useful in telling about an action that has been completed before the time expressed by the verb in the sentence:

Having been warned by the police, we set a trap for the thieves.

The use of the three-word participle *Having been warned* emphasizes the completion of the action suggested by the participle. Where this emphasis is not necessary, the one-word form is more often used:

Warned by the police, we set a trap for the thieves.

EXERCISE 4. Each of the sentences contains one or more passive participles. List each passive participle and, after it in parentheses, write the noun or pronoun it modifies. Use a separate line for each passive participle. Number your answers with the numbers of the sentences. For the first sentence you should write: *1. delighted (I)*

1. Delighted by his nonsense, I invited him to lunch.
2. The rotted timbers gave way under his weight.
3. Shocked by her cruelty to the child, Allan interfered.
4. The waitress, accused of the theft, broke into tears.
5. The letter, torn into small pieces, had been thrown into the waste basket.
6. I pretended not to notice her lifted eyebrows.
7. The frightened king gave orders for the execution of all the officers suspected of the plot against his life.
8. Clarence, goaded by their laughter, determined to spend a night in the haunted house.
9. In the drawer he found a torn photograph, evidently taken years before.
10. Louise, aided by her father, repaired the broken toys for the children.

Improving sentences
12. Use a passive participle

Students who do not know about passive participles may write sentences like the following:

> These big radio towers can be seen from a distance. Then they look even higher.

The two sentences have subjects that mean the same thing, and the word *Then* shows that they are related in meaning. But the two sentences are not of equal importance. The first one merely explains the condition under which the statement in the second one is true. Better sentences can be made by using a participial phrase to give this explanatory detail:

> These big radio towers, *seen from a distance,* look even higher.
> *Seen from a distance,* these big radio towers look even higher.
> These big radio towers look even higher, *seen from a distance.*

The first sentence treats the condition as a mere explanatory detail. The second one stresses the condition somewhat more, and the third one stresses it somewhat less. Notice that the position of the phrase in the first and second sentences shows that the phrases are useful also for avoiding the monotony of too many subject-verb sentences.

Some students rely entirely on the word *so* to show the relationship between two sentences, one of which merely gives a reason for what happens in the other. They write sentences like these:

> My old pocketknife had been rusted by the damp weather. *So* it could not be used to cut up the meat for the stew.
> The bridge had been weakened by the high waters. *So* it had to be reinforced with heavy steel beams.

By expressing the reasons in participial phrases instead of in separate sentences, the writer can direct attention to the important ideas:

> My old pocketknife, *rusted by the damp weather,* could not be used to cut up the meat for the stew.
> The bridge, *weakened by the high waters,* had to be reinforced with heavy steel beams.

Sometimes sentences that are related have subjects that mean different persons or things:

> *Joe* limped off the field. His *face* was twisted with pain.
>
> *Silas* was leaning against the picket fence. His *eyes* were shaded by an old straw hat.

Such sentences can be combined by using a nominative absolute—a phrase consisting of a participle and the word it modifies:

> *His face twisted with pain,* Joe limped off the field.
>
> Silas was leaning against the picket fence, *his eyes shaded by an old straw hat.*

Nominative absolutes do not modify anything and may come first or last in the sentence.

A word of caution: Readers expect a participial phrase at the beginning of a sentence to modify the subject. If you omit the word you intended the participle to modify or fail to make it the subject, you may write sentences as ridiculous as these:

> Wrapped in heavy blankets, the stadium was comfortable in spite of the cold wind.
>
> Wedged between two small boxes in the bottom drawer, the detective discovered the missing will.

You know that it would take unusually large blankets to wrap up a stadium; and you know that the writer probably meant the will was wedged between two small boxes in the bottom drawer. But the writer of the first sentence carelessly omitted the word he intended the participle to modify; and the writer of the second sentence carelessly put the phrase first, where it seems to modify the subject *detective*. The remedy is obvious:

> Wrapped in heavy blankets, we found the stadium comfortable in spite of the cold wind.
>
> The detective discovered the missing will wedged between two small boxes in the bottom drawer.

Either make the word modified by the participle the subject of the sentence, or move the phrase closer to the word actually modified by the participle. When you use participial phrases to combine sentences, always be sure that the participle modifies a word in the sentence and that it is the word you intended it to modify.

EXERCISE 5. Read each of the pairs of sentences, and decide which sentence in each pair should stand out. Then revise the sentences, using phrases with passive participles in place of the less important sentences. Be sure that each participle modifies the word you want it to. Be ready to read your revised sentences aloud. For the first sentence you might say: *Not having been told of the change, Peter was very much astonished.*

1. Peter had not been told of the change. He was very much astonished.
2. Mrs. Kilpatrick had not been consulted. So she refused to help the committee with the work.
3. The curtain in front of the shower had been used constantly for three years. It was now dotted with a rust-colored mold.
4. Bram was blinded by the whirling snow. He ran plump into Jim Ferguson's mother.
5. The article was written by a woman doctor. It was informative as well as entertaining.
6. The ax head was fastened to the handle by three thongs. It must have been a little wobbly.
7. Jim had been fired twice before because of his impudence. He determined this time to keep his temper in check.
8. Arthur was embarrassed by their loud quarreling. So he tried to change the subject.
9. A stick of charred wood had been fanned into flame by the breeze. So it set fire to the tent.
10. Mr. Fries had been very much impressed by the clever sales talk. He wanted to buy one of the lots himself.

Gerunds

Verb forms that end in *ing* are often used as nouns. Notice the italicized words in the following sentences:

> *Seeing* is *believing.*
> Do they enjoy *swimming?*
> He hates so many hours of *studying.*
> This one defect in her character—*gossiping*—has cost Madelyn many
> friendships.
> The papers gave his poor *pitching* only brief notice.

You can see that *Seeing* is a subject; *believing* is a predicate nominative; *swimming* is the object of a verb; *studying* is the object of a preposition; *gossiping* is in apposition with *defect;* and *pitching* is an indirect object, the direct object being *notice*. In the last sentence the word *pitching* is modified by the adjective *poor* and the possessive pronoun *his,* just as a noun might be.

A verb form that ends in *ing* and that is used as a noun is called a gerund.

Gerunds almost always are names of actions. But gerunds do not have subjects, and they cannot make statements. Like participles, gerunds may take an object, may be followed by a predicate nominative or a predicate adjective, may have adverbial modifiers—forming phrases with these words:

> *Riding a surfboard* is the greatest thrill in the world.
> She is thinking of *becoming an airline hostess*.
> By *having remained calm,* we can now give an accurate and detailed report of the accident.
> He resents *having been seated so far back*.
> *Being ducked in cold water* is not my idea of fun.

In the first sentence *surfboard* is the object of *Riding;* in the second, *hostess* is a predicate nominative after *becoming;* in the third, *calm* is a predicate adjective after *having remained;* in the fourth, *having been seated* is modified by the adverb *back;* and in the fifth, *Being ducked* is modified by the adverb phrase *in cold water*. Notice that the gerunds in the last three sentences are more than one word. In each sentence the italicized words form a **gerund phrase** that is used as a noun. In the first and last sentences the gerund phrases are used as subjects. In the other sentences the phrases are used as objects.

Active participles and gerunds both end in *ing*. But you know that participles are used as adjectives, while gerunds are used as nouns:

> A *ticking* clock keeps me awake.
> The *ticking* of my alarm clock kept me awake last night.

In the first sentence who or what is ticking? The clock is. The word *ticking* modifies the noun *clock* and is an active participle. In the second sentence who or what kept me awake? The ticking did. The word *ticking* is the subject of the verb *kept* and is a gerund. Now look at these two sentences:

80

Opening the door, he invited us to come in.

After *opening the door,* he invited us to come in.

In the first sentence *Opening the door* modifies the pronoun *he* and is a participial phrase. In the second sentence *opening the door* is the object of the preposition *After* and is a gerund phrase.

For some strange reason the word "participle" rushes to the lips of many students whenever they see an *ing* word. Yet gerunds are very common, and an *ing* word is just as likely to be a gerund as a participle. Always be sure that you know how an *ing* word is used before saying what it is. If it is used as a noun, it is a gerund.

EXERCISE 6. Each of the sentences contains one or more gerunds. Find each gerund, and decide how it is used in the sentence. Then divide a sheet of paper into two columns. In the first column, write each gerund. In the second column, tell how the gerund is used. Number your answers with the numbers of the sentences. For the first sentence you should write:

1. complaining | *object of "enjoys"*

1. Phil enjoys complaining about the bus service.
2. His interest in the dancing mice set us to wondering about him.
3. Refusing to answer was the best thing for him to do.
4. His first job—ushering at the Bijou Theater—paid very little.
5. I don't like going to work without breakfast.
6. She could not see a tiny mouse without shrieking.
7. The next morning Dad scolded us for getting home so late.
8. I resented his asking me so many impertinent questions.
9. I have a good reason for disliking Bill—his being so utterly selfish.
10. Our pounding finally stopped the quarreling in the next apartment.

EXERCISE 7. Since gerund phrases act as nouns, they can assume most of the noun functions described in Unit 4. To see how this is true, write six sentences in which you use the gerund phrase *singing in the bathtub* as:

        a subject

        a predicate nominative

        an appositive

        an object of a preposition

        a direct object

        an indirect object

13. Use a gerund

The more ways you know for getting rid of weak explanatory sentences, the more ways you know for making your important ideas stand out clearly. Notice these three sentences:

> Soon I began to notice queer sensations in my chest. My heart was fluttering. My lungs were gasping.

You can see that the first sentence expresses an important idea. The other two sentences merely explain what the sensations were. By using gerunds to make appositives out of the two weak explanatory sentences, you can combine the three sentences into one effective sentence:

> Soon I began to notice queer sensations in my chest—a fluttering of the heart and a gasping of the lungs.

In the revised sentence the gerunds *fluttering* and *gasping* are in apposition with the noun *sensations*.

Sometimes two sentences are used to express one important idea—the first one telling what is done, and the second one telling why:

> The sketches are sprayed with a fixative. *This* keeps them from smudging.

Untrained writers frequently use two sentences in this way and rely on a word like *This* to show the relationship between the two sentences. But you can see that the subject of the second sentence—*This*—means the same thing as the whole sentence preceding it. By using a gerund phrase instead of the first sentence, trained writers express the one important idea in a single sentence:

> *Spraying the sketches with a fixative* keeps them from smudging.

The gerund phrase is the subject of the verb *keeps*.

Now notice how the relationship between the two sentences in each of the following examples is shown:

> Ted washed all the windows. *Then* he put on the screens.
> Dad was going to bed pretty soon. *So* he locked the door.
> Mary reviewed every spelling lesson in the book. *Thus* she was well prepared for the final test.

82

The relationship between the two sentences in each example is shown by the word *Then, So,* or *Thus* at the beginning of the second sentence. By using a gerund phrase in place of the first sentence in each example and making it the object of a preposition, you can combine each pair of sentences into one sentence that is more interesting:

> After *washing all the windows,* Ted put on the screens.
> Before *going to bed,* Dad locked the door.
> By *reviewing every spelling lesson in the book,* Mary was well prepared for the final test.

Notice that the subject of each sentence is also the doer of the action named by the gerund. Who put on the screens? Ted did. Who did the washing? Ted did. Who was going to bed? Dad was, and it was he who locked the door. Mary did the reviewing, and as a result she was well prepared.

A word of caution: In prepositional phrases of this kind, readers expect the doer of the action named by the gerund to be the same person or thing as the subject of the sentence. Otherwise the phrase will dangle, and sentences as ridiculous as these may be the result:

> After doing his homework, the radio was turned on.
> Before going into the game, the coach gave him instructions.

You know that a radio cannot do anybody's homework, and you can guess that it was not the coach who was going into the game. In either sentence the doer of the action named by the gerund is not the subject. The remedy is obvious:

> After doing his homework, *Joe* turned on the radio.
> Before going into the game, *he* was given instructions by the coach.

In these sentences the subject *Joe* shows who had been "doing" the homework, and the subject *he* shows who was "going" into the game. When you use a prepositional phrase with a gerund for its object, always be sure that the sentence shows who or what is the doer of the action named by the gerund.

EXERCISE 8. Each of the numbered groups consists of two sentences. Read each group of sentences, and decide how to combine them into one good sentence by using a gerund phrase or a gerund. Be ready to read your revised sentences aloud. For the first pair of sentences you might say: *After taking one quick look at my swollen hand, the doctor said, "You'll stay in the hospital tonight."*

1. The doctor took one quick look at my swollen hand. Then he said, "You'll stay in the hospital tonight."
2. We watched the magician carefully. So we learned where the pigeon came from.
3. The brass lamps and brackets are coated with lacquer. This prevents them from tarnishing.
4. Grant set up an easel and arranged several tubes of paint on the table. Then he finally started to work.
5. He fed the birds every day. That was his only recreation.
6. Henry helped Mr. Fitzmaurice put up the storm windows. For this he was given a dollar.
7. Curtis offered himself to the doctors as a human guinea pig. Thus he hoped to be of service to humanity.
8. Jack worked in a cannery for three long, hard weeks. In that way he earned enough money for a trip to Washington, D. C.
9. She rides horseback every day. This is her favorite form of exercise.
10. Myrtle has one annoying habit. She pokes people to get their attention.

Infinitives

The simple form of a verb, usually preceded by *to,* is often used as a noun. Compare the italicized words in the following sentences:

> *Algebra* was not easy for him.
> *To decide* was not easy for him.

> My father likes *hunting.*
> My father likes *to hunt.*

> Her plan was a *mystery.*
> Her plan was *to escape.*

> I have only one goal, *success.*
> I have only one ambition, *to succeed.*

You can see that in each pair of sentences the italicized words have the same use. *To decide* is the subject of the verb *was,* just as *Algebra* is the subject of its verb. *To hunt* and *hunting* are both objects of the verb *likes. To escape* and *mystery* are both predicate nominatives. *To succeed* and *success* are both appositives.

The simple form of the verb, usually preceded by *to* and used as a noun, adjective, or adverb, is called an infinitive.

The *to* is ordinarily not used after certain verbs:

I dared not *complain* about the noise.   I heard you *come* in.
She helped *paint* our fence.   They made us *work*.
She saw us *leave* the building.   Watch him *run*!

When two or more infinitives are used in the same way in a sentence, the *to* is often not repeated:

He likes *to meet* people, *talk* with them, and *learn* their views on matters of the day.

Infinitives—like gerunds and participles—may take objects, may be followed by predicate nominatives or predicate adjectives, may have adverbial modifiers:

They want *to buy a larger house in the spring*.
His goal is *to become rich quickly*.

In the first sentence the infinitive *to buy* takes the object *house* and is modified by the adverb phrase *in the spring*. In the second sentence the infinitive *to become* is followed by the predicate adjective *rich* and is modified by the adverb *quickly*. In either sentence the italicized group of words is called an **infinitive phrase**.

A common way of using an infinitive phrase for a subject is to begin the sentence with *It* and put the phrase after the verb:

It then became necessary *to get a job in a factory*.

If you ask "Who or what became necessary?" you will see that the real subject is the infinitive phrase *to get a job in a factory*. The word *It* does not refer to anything. Like the word *There* in "There were two men in the car," the word *It* is merely a dummy subject. An *it* or a *there* used in this way is called an **expletive**.

Infinitives, like other verbals, may consist of more than one word. The infinitives of more than one word are italicized in the following sentences:

To be seen with the hero made him proud.
To have seen so many things in such a short time was very confusing to all of us.
To have been seen in shabby clothes was humiliating.

Infinitives may also be used as adjectives to modify nouns:

> His ability *to entertain* was remarkable.
> She will have some books *to sell* next week.

In the last two sentences the infinitive *to entertain* modifies the noun *ability* by telling which ability of his was remarkable. It means about the same as his ability "for entertaining." The infinitive *to sell* modifies the noun *books* by telling what kind of books she will have. It means about the same as books "for selling."

Infinitives may also be used as adverbs to modify not only verbs, but adjectives and adverbs as well:

> The girls were soon ready *to start.*
> One of the survivors was too weak *to walk.*
> Many of the spectators stood up *to cheer.*

The infinitive *to start* modifies the adjective *ready* by telling how ready the girls were. It means about the same thing as ready "for starting." In the second sentence the infinitive *to walk* modifies the adverb *too* by telling how much too weak the survivor was. It means about the same thing as too weak "for walking." In the third sentence the infinitive *to cheer* modifies the verb *stood* by telling why. It means about the same thing as "for cheering."

EXERCISE 9. Each of the sentences contains one or two infinitives. Find each infinitive, and decide how it is used in the sentence. Then divide a sheet of paper into two columns. In the first column, write each infinitive. In the second column, tell how the infinitive is used. Number your answers with the numbers of the sentences. For the first sentence you should write:

1. to have | *predicate nominative*

1. His next move was to have an interview with the distracted parents.
2. Bob's first impulse was to turn down their offer to buy his farm.
3. Dad was too tired to help with the painting.
4. To wear so much jewelry to class is not good taste.
5. It is embarrassing to be scolded in public.
6. I tried to suggest one other way—to look through all the *N*'s in the telephone directory.
7. They were too late to see the first number.
8. It was easy to guess Mrs. Clarkson's yearning—to have the new grand-child in her home.
9. For weeks we tried to find an apartment to rent.
10. Richard wanted to prove his ability to act various kinds of parts

86

Improving sentences
14. Use an infinitive

Like the other verbals you have studied, infinitives are useful in combining sentences that are related in meaning. Students who do not know about using infinitives for this purpose are likely to write sentences like the following:

> You shouldn't read other people's mail without permission. It is extremely rude.

You can see that the second sentence gives a reason for what is said in the first sentence. Using an infinitive phrase in place of *It* makes the relationship clearer:

> *To read other people's mail without permission* is extremely rude.

Sometimes the second sentence makes an important comment about what is said in the first sentence:

> Joe went swimming right after lunch. This was very foolish.

Using an infinitive phrase in place of *This* shows the relationship more forcefully:

> For Joe *to go swimming right after lunch* was very foolish.

On page 85 you saw a sentence beginning with *It* in which the infinitive phrase comes after the verb: "It then became necessary to get a job in a factory." The same arrangement can be used for either of the examples shown above:

> It is extremely rude *to read other people's mail without permission.*
> It was very foolish for Joe *to go swimming right after lunch.*

The sentences are equally good. In your own sentences you should use whichever way sounds better.

Students also write sentences like these:

> Mr. Brown made a plan. He would leave secretly on the early morning train.
> Ellery had an idea. It was to weather-strip the doors and windows.

In either example the second sentence explains a word in the first sentence. By the use of infinitive phrases, the sentences may be combined to make this relationship clear:

> Mr. Brown planned *to leave secretly on the early morning train.*
> Ellery's idea was *to weather-strip the doors and windows.*

In the first sentence the infinitive phrase is used as the object of the verb *planned*. In the second sentence the infinitive phrase is used as a predicate nominative.

Occasionally students may write three or more sentences that are related in meaning:

> Mr. Brown made a plan. He would leave secretly on the early morning train. This plan was successfully carried out.
> Ellery had an idea. The doors could be weather-stripped. Storm sash could be put on the windows. This would save on heating costs.

Better sentences can be made by using infinitive phrases in place of the weak explanatory sentences:

> Mr. Brown's plan, *to leave secretly on the early morning train,* was successfully carried out.
> Ellery's idea, *to weather-strip the doors and put storm sash on the windows,* would save on heating costs.

The infinitive phrases are in apposition with *plan* and *idea*.

EXERCISE 10. Each of the numbered groups consists of two sentences. Read each pair of sentences, and decide how they can be combined by using an infinitive phrase. Be prepared to read the improved sentences aloud. For the first group you might say: *Mr. Sorenson's suggestion, to ask businessmen to write letters of protest, was the best of the lot.*

1. Mr. Sorenson's suggestion was the best of the lot. He suggested asking businessmen to write letters of protest.
2. Late that afternoon Slim Perkins made a decision. He would give himself up to the police.
3. Mrs. Gard told the ladies of another possibility. They might sell their clubhouse and move to a suburb.
4. Dora screams loudly at the mere sight of a spider. This is ridiculous.
5. Aunt Clara had an idea. It was to appeal to his sense of humor.
6. Amy wanted only one thing more. She wanted to be elected president of the class.

7. Bud took the books without asking permission. This was an extremely serious offense.
8. Jim's dream was never realized. He dreamed of staging a revival of *The Witching Hour*.
9. He worked constantly toward one goal. His goal was to clear the slum areas in Plainford.
10. You should not spread malicious rumors without knowing the facts. It is unfair.

Composition

Telling about Others PART ONE: ORAL

In Units 1 and 2 you told about a personal experience—something that happened to you or something that you saw happen. In this Unit you are to tell an **anecdote**—a brief story about an interesting incident in the life of some person.

Anecdotes about famous men and women are quite common. You probably remember the anecdote about George Washington and the cherry tree or others about Abraham Lincoln or Thomas Edison or other well-known persons. Almost as common are anecdotes about the wise remarks or humorous sayings of ordinary men and women and children. For all good anecdotes have a "point"—a serious or amusing comment that is remembered because of the way it is said.

If you were writing a biography of a famous man or woman, you would very likely search far and wide for anecdotes about that person. But for a classroom talk you need not go to all that trouble. An anecdote about some member of your family or a friend will probably be just as interesting to your classmates, particularly since they know you personally. Think carefully about the members of your family and your friends. Have you a brother or sister who has made remarks that you and your parents like to laugh about and repeat? Have you an uncle or an aunt who has made serious or thoughtful comments that are often remembered and told at family gatherings? Have you been with friends who made you laugh or think by what they said in certain situations? Almost anyone who is willing to try can remember inci-dents that would make good anecdotes about people he knows. Choose an incident that you think will interest your classmates.

When you have selected an incident for your anecdote, you are ready to make a plan for telling it effectively. Since the point of an anecdote is what somebody said in a certain situation, you must explain that situation as briefly as you can without omitting a single important fact. Start with a list of important details. If you make *Who? When?* and *Where?* the headings for the first three items, you will have the important details you need to explain the setting of your anecdote. Then write down what happened first, what happened next, and next, and so on, being careful to keep the important details of the incident in a time order. Last of all, write the remark or comment that is the point of your anecdote. For example, if you were telling about something your young brother said, your list might look like this:

Who? Bobby, my little brother
When? One morning not long ago
Where? At the breakfast table
Bobby entertained us with a long, rambling account of a dream he had had the night before.
After he had finished his story, Mother asked him if he knew what dreams are.
Bobby nodded his head and said that he knew all right.
Wondering whether he really did know, I asked him to tell me just what dreams are.
He said they're moving pictures you see when you're asleep.

After you have made your list, examine it carefully. Do the items that give the setting tell whom your anecdote is about and when and where the incident occurred? Are the items that tell what happened arranged in a time order? Are additional items needed to explain clearly what happened? Are there any unimportant items that should be crossed off? Does the last item give the remark or comment that is the point of your anecdote? Try to keep your list of details brief.

Because it gives the setting of your anecdote, the opening sentence is almost as important as the closing remark. Your first sentence should tell whom the anecdote is about, when and where the incident occurred, and, if possible, what happened first. This usually means a fairly long sentence; but it should not be one word longer than necessary, and it must not be about other things. By telling who, when, where, and what happened first, your opening sentence arouses the interest of your listeners and makes them want to hear more.

Now look at the list of details you made for your anecdote. Think of a good opening sentence that will give the setting and, if possible, the first detail of the incident. Then copy this sentence on a card or a small piece of paper and, under it, write the important details of the incident, ending with the remark or comment that is the point of your anecdote. Keep these notes in your hand as you practice your talk and as you give it, so that you need not worry about forgetting what your opening sentence is, what the important details of the incident are, or exactly how you want to word the last sentence.

Practice telling your anecdote at least once before going to class. If the opening sentence is fairly long, try giving it in several ways, pausing at different places, saying with somewhat different force the words that tell who, when, and where, until you know exactly how you will begin your talk. Then move right into your story without wasting words. Give only important details that are needed to make clear exactly what happened. Practice the last sentence of your talk as you did the first one, saying it over slowly and distinctly several times until it sounds just the way you think it should. This final sentence is the whole point of your anecdote. When you have given it, do not say another word. Adding a weak explanatory sentence like "We all thought this was the best definition of dreams we had ever heard" spoils the whole effect. A good anecdote ends with the final remark or comment of the person you are telling about.

If you are asked to give your talk in class, speak slowly and distinctly so that all your classmates can hear your anecdote and enjoy it.

Now that you have prepared an anecdote about someone you know, you are to write your anecdote, using the notes you made for your talk.

If your anecdote has conversation in it—and most anecdotes do have—you can make it seem more real by giving the actual words that might have been said. By means of **dialogue**—conversation between persons in a story—you can let the persons in your anecdote tell what happened. By enclosing each person's words in quotation marks, you can let the reader know the exact words spoken by that person. To prevent confusion between what the various persons in your anecdote say, you will need to use a separate paragraph for what each person says at one time. For example, if you were writing about Bobby's explanation of dreams, your written anecdote might look like this:

At the breakfast table one morning not long ago Bobby, my little brother, entertained us with a long, rambling account of a dream he had had the night before.

After he had finished his story, Mother asked, "Bobby, do you know what dreams are?"

Bobby nodded his head and said, "Sure, I know, all right."

Wondering if he really did know, I said, "Tell me, Bobby, just what they are."

He replied, "They're moving pictures you see when you're asleep."

If you compare this with the plan on page 90, you will see that the words in quotation marks are written just as they might have been spoken. Always test a quotation by asking yourself, "Are these the words the person might actually have said?" Bobby, for example, would not be likely to say "That he knew, all right" when talking about himself. He would probably say "Sure, I know, all right." Notice, also, that what each person says at one time is in a separate paragraph.

If you are not sure how to punctuate dialogue, you should consult the punctuation section (Unit 8) of this book.

Write your anecdote, beginning with the opening sentence you prepared for your talk. As you write the dialogue, follow your plan, to keep the details of the incident in a time order. Be sure to enclose the exact words of each person in quotation marks. Be sure to make a separate paragraph for what each person says at one time. End with the remark or comment that is the point of your anecdote. Use pencil and scratch paper for this first draft so that you can make corrections and changes easily. Think of your classmates as you write. You may be asked to read your anecdote before turning it in.

Revise your first draft carefully, making corrections in spelling and punctuation, changing the order of words, crossing out unnecessary words or adding better ones until the sentences in your anecdote are as good as you know how to make them. The more care you take in revising your sentences, the more interesting your anecdote is likely to seem to others.

Because they are often used as parts of other compositions, written anecdotes seldom have titles. In biographies, anecdotes are used to show some personal quality or characteristic. In expressing an opinion, they are used to emphasize a point. In telling what something means, they are used as examples. Anecdotes are, however, sometimes grouped according to subject matter, persons, quality, or characteristic. For example, Bobby's explanation of what dreams are might be put in any one of four different groups: Dreams, Children, Imagination, or Humor.

Think carefully about your anecdote. To what group of anecdotes does it seem to you most clearly to belong? Is it an anecdote about Loyalty, Faith, Humor, Children, Uncles, Parents, School, Family, or something else? What word best names the group to which you think your anecdote belongs? Write this word as you would a title, and then copy the revised first draft of your anecdote in a form suitable for handing in. Write neatly and legibly. Indent paragraphs equally and keep margins even. Space words carefully.

Proofread the final draft of your anecdote to catch any errors you may have made in copying. Read it over carefully, word by word, watching for words or final letters that have been omitted, for words that have been copied twice, for careless misspellings or omitted punctuation marks. Make corrections neatly.

Since your teacher may ask you to read your anecdote aloud, practice reading it at least once before going to class. Give the opening sentence in a natural, matter-of-fact way. Then try to read the dialogue so that your listeners will know that different persons are speaking. You might speak in a slightly higher or faster way for one person, in a slightly lower or slower way for another person. But do not exaggerate or overdo the difference. Since you will probably tell who the persons are with words like "Mother asked" or "Then Bobby said," very little difference is needed. Remember that the final remark or comment is your closing sentence. Practice it carefully, saying it over slowly and distinctly until it sounds just the way you think it might have been said. The success of your anecdote depends largely on how well you can read the last sentence.

When a classmate is reading his anecdote, listen carefully so that you can explain what you like about it and in what ways you think it might be improved.

Improving sentences

15. Use a direct quotation

Using direct quotations is one of the ways in which you can vary sentences to make them more interesting. For example, in Units 1 and 2 you saw a plan for telling about something that happened when a scared cat climbed a tree and refused to come down. A person who was writing about this incident might end his account in either of the following ways:

As I was thanking the firemen for rescuing Dusty, our car raced up the street and slid to a stop. Father jumped out. He wanted to know where the fire was, whether anybody was hurt, and what was going on. I had some explaining to do.	As I was thanking the firemen for rescuing Dusty, our car raced up the street and slid to a stop. Father jumped out shouting, "Where's the fire? Anybody hurt? What's going on here?" I had some explaining to do.

You can see that the paragraph on the right is more interesting to read. By giving Father's excited questions, the writer makes the incident seem more real.

Direct quotations are also useful in improving sentences that are related in meaning. Students who do not know how to use quotations may write sentences like these:

John hurried to the top of the stairs. He wanted to know who had called to him.

The driver turned around in his seat. Then he announced that everybody would have to get out because he wasn't going any farther.

Clark grinned sheepishly. He told Bruce that he would have to pay for the damaged fender also.

Mother told me to go back upstairs and comb my hair. She said that it looked like a rat's nest.

These sentences can be made clearer and more forceful by using direct quotations to give the actual words of the speakers:

"Who called me?" asked John, hurrying to the top of the stairs.

The driver turned around in his seat and announced, "Everybody out! This is as far as I go."

"I'll have to pay for the damaged fender, too, Bruce," said Clark, grinning sheepishly.

"Go back upstairs and comb your hair," Mother said. "It looks like a rat's nest."

Sometimes a whole incident can be made more interesting by using direct quotations to give the actual conversation between the persons in the incident. Compare these two accounts:

Just then Louise jumped back. She screamed something about snakes. Tom ran toward her. He wanted to know where the snakes were. Louise pointed to the left of the path. She said the snakes were in some bushes there. Tom investigated. Then he began to laugh. He told Louise to take it easy. He said that it was just an old twisted branch of a tree. Louise wouldn't believe it. She said that she had seen it move. Tom explained that she had probably kicked the end of the branch as she walked past. Louise admitted that perhaps she had. But she added that it had scared her. She suggested that they go back. Tom glanced at his watch and said that it was O. K. with him. He also said that the hamburgers would probably be ready by the time they got there.

Just then Louise jumped back and screamed, "Snakes!"

"Where?" asked Tom, running toward her.

"Right there!" cried Louise, pointing to the left of the path. "In those bushes!"

Tom investigated. Then he began to laugh. "Take it easy, Lou," he said. "It's just an old twisted branch of a tree."

"I don't believe it!" Louise insisted. "I saw it move."

"You probably kicked the end of it," Tom explained, "as you walked past."

"Well, maybe I did," Louise admitted. "But it surely scared me. Let's go back."

"O. K., Lou," said Tom, glancing at his watch. "The hamburgers will probably be ready by the time we get there."

You can see that the account at the right seems easier and more interesting to read. By using direct quotations, the writer lets the persons in the incident tell what happened.

EXERCISE 11. Read each numbered pair of sentences, and decide how to improve the sentences by using direct quotations. Then rewrite the sentences, punctuating them correctly. Remember that each direct quotation begins with a capital letter. Number your answers. For the first one you might write: 1.*"I have won," said Melissa, with triumph in her voice.*

1. Melissa said that she had won. There was triumph in her voice.
2. The conductor scowled at me. He said that I was too big to ride on a half-fare ticket.
3. Audrey told Helen that her essay had won first prize in the Booster Club contest. She jumped up and down in her excitement.
4. Anne asked me to call her later. She said that she wasn't through with her homework yet.
5. Bruce pointed to a strange address on the package. He inquired if I knew where the place was.
6. Mr. Griffith wanted to know who had broken his basement window. He sounded quite angry.
7. Ted refused to believe a word of what I said. He insisted that the coach wasn't even there at the time.
8. The waitress wiped off the counter in front of me. Then she asked me what I wanted to eat.
9. The principal told me not to go away just yet. He said there were some other things he wanted to talk over with me.
10. Mrs. Wilson exclaimed that she had never seen anything like it before. She showed considerable amazement.

Improving sentences: Ways you have learned

1. Ask a question
2. Use a command
3. Choose exact modifiers
4. Begin with an adverb
5. Begin with a preposition
6. Use a compound verb
7. Avoid unnecessary words

8. Begin with an object
9. Use an active verb
10. Use an appositive
11. Use an active participle
12. Use a passive participle
13. Use a gerund
14. Use an infinitive

15. Use a direct quotation

EXERCISE 12. The following paragraphs tell about an incident in a factory. Each sentence begins with the subject and verb, and there are many weak explanatory sentences. Rewrite the story, improving the sentences whenever there is an opportunity to do so easily and naturally. Use any of the ways you have learned, but do not try to use them all. Be sure that every change you make is a natural one. Try to make the sentences as clear, forceful, and interesting as you can.

(1) Dan Reardon had been working in a factory for over a year. (2) It was operated entirely by water power. (3) A big paddle wheel was turned by the water. (4) The water passed out through a large outlet pipe after being used. (5) The pipe had to be open at all times. (6) This was necessary to keep the great wheel turning and the factory running.

(7) Dan came running to the Superintendent in the middle of the afternoon. (8) This was the busiest time of day in the factory. (9) He burst into the office without knocking.

(10) The Superintendent looked up from his desk. (11) He said hello to Dan. (12) He asked Dan what was wrong.

(13) Dan told him that the outlet pipe was stopped up.

(14) The Superintendent jumped up from his chair. (15) He hurried out of the office. (16) He blew a shrill blast on his whistle. (17) He called the men together. (18) He ordered the great wheel shut down. (19) He explained that the outlet pipe was stopped up. (20) He asked for a volunteer. (21) He wanted a man to climb down into the pit below the wheel and open up the pipe.

(22) The men were not prepared for such a call. (23) The request came so suddenly. (24) It startled them. (25) No one responded.

(26) Dan saw a chance for promotion then. (27) He stepped forward. (28) He told the Superintendent to let him try to open the pipe.

(29) His small body slipped easily down past the paddles of the great wheel. (30) He soon found the trouble at the bottom of the pit. (31) It was a pile of broken sticks and leaves. (32) They had become wedged into the opening of the pipe. (33) He pried the sticks loose with a crowbar quickly. (34) He clambered out of the pit then. (35) He was soaking wet.

(36) The Superintendent said that Dan had done good work. (37) He told Dan to see him first thing the next morning. (38) He added that he thought there might be a better job for Dan around the factory.

Clauses

What a subordinate clause is

We often use a group of words that contains a subject and a verb to do the work of a single word in a sentence. Notice the italicized words in the following pairs of sentences:

> A *cautious* man never takes chances.
> A man *who is cautious* never takes chances.

> We didn't believe his *story*.
> We didn't believe *what he said*.

> I was sorry *later*.
> I was sorry *after I had spoken*.

You can see that in each pair of sentences the italicized words have the same use. In the first pair the group of words *who is cautious* describes the noun *man* just as the single adjective *cautious* does. In the second pair *what he said* is the object of the verb *did believe* just as the noun *story* is. In the third pair *after I had spoken* modifies the verb *was* just as the adverb *later* does; both tell *when*. Notice that each of the italicized groups of words contains a subject and verb of its own. The group of words *who is cautious* has a verb *is* and a subject *who*. In *what he said* the verb is *said*, and its subject is *he*. In *after I had spoken* the verb is *had spoken*, and its subject is *I*.

A group of words that contains a subject and a verb and that is used as a single word in a sentence is called a subordinate clause.

A subordinate clause used as an adjective is an **adjective clause.** One used as a noun is a **noun clause.** One used as an adverb is an **adverb clause.** All subordinate clauses are used in one of these three ways —as adjectives, as nouns, or as adverbs.

Adjective clauses

Adjective clauses are most commonly formed with the pronouns *who, whose, whom, which,* and *that.* Notice how these pronouns are used to attach a clause to the noun or pronoun it modifies:

> We want a boy *who keeps his nails clean.*
> Mr. Morgan is one man *whose word you can trust.*
> He is a person *whom I would hate to anger.*
> We had a parrot *which we trained to speak several languages.*
> I bought one *that had not been run more than three thousand miles.*

Adjective clauses are also formed with the adverbs *when* and *where.* Notice how these adverbs are used to attach a clause to the noun it modifies:

> He remembered a time *when actors were scorned by most people.*
> We lived in a town *where everyone knew everyone else's business.*

Since these five pronouns—*who, whose, whom, which,* and *that*—and these two adverbs—*when* and *where*—refer, or "relate," to some noun or pronoun, they are called **relative pronouns** and **relative adverbs.** A subordinate clause formed with a relative pronoun or adverb is also called a **relative clause.** It is always used as an adjective.

The noun or pronoun to which a relative pronoun or a relative adverb refers is called its **antecedent.** In the seven example sentences above the antecedents are *boy, man, person, parrot, one, time,* and *town;* and the adjective clauses come right after the antecedents. But a clause is not always placed close to the antecedent:

> Pierre told us about a house in Rochester *that has no windows.*
> There is a boy in our class at Penn High *who was born in Asia.*

The antecedent of the pronoun *that* is *house.* The antecedent of *who* is *boy.* If you take time to find the antecedent, you will know the noun or pronoun that is actually modified by the clause.

A sentence may have more than one adjective clause. For example:

> Anyone *who likes automobiles* will enjoy a show *where all the cars have been selected for their appearance and speed.*

In this sentence the two adjective clauses are italicized. The words not in italics can stand alone as a sentence and are called the **main clause.**

100

Notice that the first clause modifies *Anyone,* the subject of the main clause. Notice that the second clause modifies *show,* the object of the verb in the main clause. Now let us add two more adjective clauses:

> Anyone who likes automobiles *that are sleek and powerful* will enjoy a show where all the cars *that are on display* have been selected for their appearance and speed.

The two additional adjective clauses are in italics. Notice that the first italicized clause modifies *automobiles,* the object of the verb in another subordinate clause. Notice that the second italicized clause modifies *cars,* the subject of another subordinate clause. An adjective clause may modify a noun or pronoun in the main clause, or it may modify a noun or pronoun in another subordinate clause.

EXERCISE 1. Each of the sentences contains one or more adjective clauses formed with the pronouns *who, whose, whom, which, that* or the adverbs *when* or *where.* Find each clause, and decide what the antecedent of each relative pronoun or relative adverb is. Write the number of each sentence and, after it, put the antecedent, followed by the first and last words of the clause. Enclose the antecedent in parentheses. Use a separate line for each clause. For the first sentence you should write:

> 1. *(teacher) who complete*
> *(sentences) that complete*

1. I need a teacher who will make me answer in sentences that are grammatically complete.
2. He told us of a rich duke in Spain whose tenants refused to pay rent.
3. She always calls on me to answer at a time when I am not prepared.
4. There was a man behind us who kept talking all during the show.
5. The article that you wrote is not the one that Mrs. Cory meant.
6. The man whom I admire most is the one whose mind works fastest in time of danger.
7. Miss East told about a magician whom she had seen swallow a flaming sword that was fourteen inches long.
8. From the place where he sat he could see anyone who entered the gate.
9. Mr. Foran started a new business at an age when most men retire.
10. In the old plush case which you will find at the back of the drawer is a photograph of the boy whom Mr. Crane befriended.

Uses of relative pronouns

You have learned what relative pronouns are, and you have seen how they attach an adjective clause to the noun or pronoun it modifies. Being pronouns, they also have a use in the clause. Can you tell how the relative pronoun *that* is used in the following sentence?

The price that Tim paid was over five dollars.

If you think about "how much Tim paid" or "the price that Tim paid," you will be lost. You must find the adjective clause and separate it from all other parts of the sentence before you can decide how the relative pronoun is used.

First, find the main clause in the sentence. The verb is *was*. Who or what was? The price was. The noun *price* is the subject, and the main clause is *The price was over five dollars*. Now you can lift the adjective clause *that Tim paid* out of the sentence and have a look at it.

Fix your attention on the clause *that Tim paid*. You must stay inside this clause in order to find out how the relative pronoun *that* is used. You can see that the verb in the clause is *paid*. Who or what paid? Tim paid. *Tim* is the subject. Did Tim pay anything? He paid *that*. The relative pronoun *that*, which means the same thing as its antecedent *price*, is the object of the verb.

You may wonder why it is important to know the use of a relative pronoun. What difference does it make if *that* is the subject or object of the verb? It ordinarily makes no difference in using *that* or *which*, but it does make a difference if you are using *who, whose, whom*. The one you choose depends on its use in the clause. In the following sentences the adjective clauses are italicized:

I know the girl *who won the scholarship*.
The man *whose watch I found* gave me a reward.
A ruler *whom the people despised* occupied the throne.
The actress *for whom he wrote the play* was a great success in the leading part.

In the first sentence *who* is used as the subject of the verb *won*. In the second sentence *whose* shows possession and is used as a modifier of *watch*, telling which one. In the third sentence, *whom* is used as the object of the verb *despised*. In the last sentence *whom* is the object of the preposition *for.* Notice that the preposition comes before its object.

You will seldom make a mistake in using *who, whose, whom* if you take time to see how the relative pronoun is used within its own clause. First, lift the clause out of the sentence. Then see how the pronoun is used. If it is used as a subject, choose *who.* If it is used as a possessive modifier, choose *whose.* If it is used as an object, choose *whom.*

A word of caution: A relative pronoun is sometimes separated from the rest of the clause by such expressions as *we supposed, they thought, I had imagined.* These "inserted" expressions have no effect on the use of the relative pronoun in the clause; but they may be confusing, since they are seldom set off by commas. In the following sentences the adjective clauses are italicized:

> We hired a man *who* we supposed *could do the work.*
> The girl *whom* I had imagined *the judges would choose* did not win.

If there were commas around *we supposed,* in the first sentence, you would know that it is an inserted expression and that *who* is the subject of the verb *could do.* Without commas it may appear that the relative pronoun is the object of the verb *supposed;* but if it were, there would be no subject for the verb *could do.* In the second sentence *I had imagined* is inserted, and *whom* is the object of the verb *would choose.*

Do not let an inserted expression trick you into using a wrong relative pronoun. If an adjective clause seems to have two verbs, look carefully to see if one of them may not be part of an inserted expression.

Omitted relative pronouns

We often omit relative pronouns that are used as objects. Notice the italicized adjective clauses in the following sentences:

> The knife *that you are using* was my grandfather's.
> The knife *you are using* was my grandfather's.

> We got the same advice from all the doctors *whom we consulted.*
> We got the same advice from all the doctors *we consulted.*

Each pair of the above sentences has the same meaning. In the second sentence of each pair a relative pronoun used as an object of the verb has been omitted. Now look at the italicized adjective clauses in these sentences:

The second company *that I wrote to* sent me several pamphlets.

The second company *I wrote to* sent me several pamphlets.

My mother received a booklet of wallpaper samples from the company *to which she wrote.*

My mother received a booklet of wallpaper samples from the company *she wrote to.*

You are not the only person *about whom we were talking.*

You are not the only person *we were talking about.*

In the first sentence *that* is the object of the preposition *to.* In the second sentence the relative pronoun is omitted. When the clause comes at the end of the sentence, as in the third sentence, some writers prefer to put the preposition before the relative pronoun, using *which* instead of *that.* But if the relative pronoun is omitted, as in the fourth sentence, the preposition follows the verb, just as it does in the first two sentences. In the last two sentences you can see that a preposition may also come before *whom,* but that the preposition follows the verb if the relative pronoun is omitted

EXERCISE 2. Each of the sentences contains one or more adjective clauses. Find each clause, and decide how the relative pronoun is used. Divide a sheet of paper into three columns. In the first column, write each relative pronoun used as a subject and after it, in parentheses, the verb. In the second column, write each relative pronoun that shows possession and after it, in parentheses, the word it modifies. In the third column, write each relative pronoun used as an object and after it, in parentheses, the verb or the verbal or the preposition. Number your answers. For the first one you should write:

1. *that (is made)* | *whose (car)* | *whom (to)*

1. The man whom we spoke to is the one whose car has a top that is made of clear plastic.
2. Keep the books that you want and send the rest to anyone who you think might enjoy them.
3. All students whose last names begin with *S* are to report to Mr. Quinlan.
4. The man whom I wanted to interview was fishing in a deep pool that whirled below a huge boulder.
5. The agency that I wrote to last week has sent me notices of several jobs which interest me.
6. Any person whose writing is so illegible ought to learn how to type.
7. In all the shops that we went to he would ask the prices of a lot of articles that he knew were too expensive for him to buy.

8. The man who substituted for Miss March asked us to write a report on the essay that she had assigned the day before.
9. All the wealth that Captain Kidd ever buried would not tempt me to go out with a girl who giggles incessantly.
10. The boy whom Dad scolded is not the one who broke the window.

Improving sentences
16. Use an adjective clause

You have learned that getting rid of weak explanatory sentences is one way of making important ideas stand out clearly. If you look carefully at the following groups of sentences, you will see that one of the sentences in each group is merely explanatory:

> Then Nora reached for the towel. It was hanging on a nail above the bench.
> Bill ripped open the large box and searched frantically through the layers of tissue paper. His aunt had sent the box for his birthday.
> Henry was one of those self-appointed critics. Such people take great pleasure in pointing out everybody else's faults.

The second sentence in each group is explanatory, telling where the towel was hanging, who had sent the box, and what kind of critics are meant. When adjective clauses are used in place of the weaker sentences, the important ideas stand out more clearly:

> Then Nora reached for the towel that was hanging on a nail above the bench.
> Bill ripped open the large box, which his aunt had sent for his birthday, and searched frantically through the layers of tissue paper.
> Henry was one of those self-appointed critics who take great pleasure in pointing out everybody else's faults.

The revised sentences are better, not because they are longer, but because they get rid of weak explanatory sentences that may confuse the reader. The sentences are now about Nora and Bill and Henry. The adjective clauses take care of explanatory details about the towel and the box and the critics.

Sometimes only the writer knows which of two sentences is more important. For example:

Two young boys came to our front door on Halloween. I didn't recognize them.

The first sentence is about two boys. The second sentence is about the writer. Because the sentences seem equally important, the reader's interest is divided. The sentences can be improved in either of two ways:

Two young boys, whom I didn't recognize, came to our front door on Halloween.

I didn't recognize the two young boys who came to our front door on Halloween.

Either sentence is better than the two separate sentences shown above, but only the writer knows which one expresses his idea clearly. As you revise sentences in your own letters and compositions, always consider the meaning *you* want to communicate to your reader.

Occasionally three or more sentences can be combined into one effective sentence. Notice this group of sentences:

Maureen had always worn drab colors. She now appeared in a bright green dress. It made her look like a cover girl.

The sentences are about Maureen appearing in a bright green dress, and this can be made clear to the reader by using adjective clauses in place of the first and third sentences:

Maureen, who had always worn drab colors, now appeared in a bright green dress that made her look like a cover girl.

These are just a few of the ways in which adjective clauses can help you write better sentences. Watch particularly for opportunities to use adjective clauses in place of weak explanatory sentences that take the reader's attention away from the important ideas you want to stand out clearly.

EXERCISE 3. Read the following groups of sentences, and decide which sentence in each group is the important one. Then change the groups into good sentences, using adjective clauses in place of weak explanatory sentences. Be ready to read your revised sentences aloud. For the first group you might say: *She hid the key to her jewel case in an ebony box that her grandfather had brought her from China.*

1. She hid the key to her jewel case in an ebony box. Her grandfather had brought her the box from China.
2. Aunt Laura returned with an armful of small parcels. She had bought them at five different shops.
3. Moving cautiously, I tiptoed to the door and peered through the crack. Mr. Overton had made this crack by banging on the door with his heavy ebony cane.
4. He was one of those stout, countrified old gentlemen. They like to talk with a sharp nasal twang.
5. I could not bear listening to them blame Helen. She was not in any way responsible for the accident.
6. In the showcase I saw a bewildering assortment of old jewelry. Desperate persons had pawned this jewelry for money to live on.
7. In one corner of our yard two boys were fighting over a dirty football. I had never seen these boys before.
8. Elmer had one special friend. He would do anything for this friend.
9. Hurrying to answer the phone, Mr. Warden stumbled over a pair of roller skates. Jimmy had thoughtlessly dropped them in the hall on his way upstairs.
10. Hilda was usually very calm. She turned on him with an angry retort. The retort made him cringe.

Noun clauses

Early in this Unit you learned that a subordinate clause used as a noun is called a noun clause, and you saw these two sentences:

> We didn't believe his *story.*
> We didn't believe *what he said.*

You know that the noun clause in the second sentence is the object of the verb *did believe,* just as the noun *story* is in the first sentence. Now look at the following pairs of sentences:

> The real *culprit* is not known.
> *Who was actually to blame* is not known.
> The only reason for going is my *curiosity* about his health.
> The only reason for going is *that I want to find out about his health.*
> Try to remember his home *address.*
> Try to remember *where he lives.*

You can see that the italicized words in each pair of sentences are used in the same ways—as subjects, as predicate nominatives, as objects. Since the clauses are used in the same ways as the italicized nouns, they are noun clauses. Notice that the words introducing the clauses— *what, who, that,* and *where*—do not have antecedents as relatives do.

A noun clause may be set alongside a noun to explain it or to add to its meaning, as an appositive. Compare these two sentences:

> This constant fear, the *possibility* of failure, kept him working.
> This constant fear, *that he might fail,* kept him working.

The noun clause in the second sentence explains the word *fear* and is in apposition with it, just as the noun *possibility* is in the first sentence.

Because adjective clauses may also begin with the word *that,* students sometimes confuse a noun clause with an adjective clause. Can you tell which of the following sentences contains a noun clause in apposition?

> Jim didn't hear the announcement *that Mr. Simpson made.*
> Jim didn't hear the announcement *that classes would be dismissed.*

The clause in the first sentence tells which announcement Jim failed to hear. The word *that* is a relative pronoun used as the object of the verb *made;* and the adjective clause modifies *announcement,* the antecedent of *that.* The clause in the second sentence is in apposition with the word *announcement* and explains it by telling what the announcement was. The word *that* merely introduces the noun clause and has no other use in the clause. An easy test for such clauses is to substitute a *which* for the *that.* If the sentence still means about the same thing, as in the first sentence, the clause is very likely an adjective clause. If the sentence no longer means the same thing, as in the second sentence, the clause is probably a noun clause.

Noun clauses do not always have an introductory word:

> He had an idea *the other fellows didn't like him.*
> Everybody hopes *the team will win the final game.*

In Unit 5 you learned that a common way of using an infinitive phrase for a subject is to begin the sentence with *It* and put the phrase after the verb. Now compare these two sentences:

It then became necessary *to get a job in a factory.*
It then became necessary *that I find a job quickly.*

You know that the subject of the first sentence is the infinitive phrase in italics. What is the subject of the second sentence? If you ask "Who or what became necessary?" you will see that the subject of the second sentence is the noun clause in italics. Notice that the word *It* does not refer to anything and is merely a dummy subject—an expletive. Here are other examples:

It is a question *whether we can spare the time.*
It is not known *how the prisoner escaped.*

Ordinarily expect a noun clause after the verb to be the real subject of a statement beginning with an *It* that does not refer to anything.

In Unit 5 you saw a sentence in which an infinitive was used as an adverb to modify the predicate adjective *ready*:

The girls were soon ready *to start.*

In a similar way noun clauses are used like adverbs to modify predicate adjectives:

He is quite certain *that we have made a mistake.*
Are you sure *that she will return the money?*
Be careful *what you say.*

If you substitute prepositional phrases such as "about our error," "concerning her honesty," and "of your words" for the italicized clauses, you will see that the noun clauses tell in what manner the adjectives *certain, sure,* and *careful* are meant.

EXERCISE 4. Each of the sentences contains one or more noun clauses. Find each noun clause, and decide how it is used in the sentence. Then divide a sheet of paper into two columns. In the first column, write the first and last words of each noun clause. In the second column, tell how the noun clause is used. Number your answers with the numbers of the sentences. Use a separate line for each clause. For the first sentence you should write:
1. which gone | object of "did know"
1. Mr. Rice did not know which way the boys had gone.
2. What is strange is that no one answers the phone.
3. Mother's suggestion, that we drop the whole matter, shows how very kind she always is.

4. Try to remember where you put the keys.
5. Her story is that Mr. Stinson broke the rake.
6. Baxter could not deny that he had made a terrible mistake.
7. Knowing this would work, he expressed the hope that we would try the experiment ourselves.
8. It seems unbelievable that such good friends would quarrel.
9. His excuse is that he slipped on the ice and injured his ankle.
10. They argued for hours about whose fault it was.

Improving sentences

17. Use a noun clause

Noun clauses are useful in combining sentences that are closely related in meaning. Students who do not know about noun clauses may write sentences like these:

> The sailor couldn't swim a stroke. This seemed queer to me.
> The game begins at two o'clock sharp. That is my only reason for hurrying you.
> Copper is an excellent conductor of electricity and heat. Almost everybody knows this.
> The man is an impostor. I am positive of that.

Notice that the second sentence in each pair contains a *this* or *that* referring to the meaning of the preceding sentence. The close relationship in meaning can be more clearly shown by using a noun clause in place of the first sentence of each pair and combining the two sentences into one good sentence:

> It seemed queer to me *that the sailor couldn't swim a stroke.*
> My only reason for hurrying you is *that the game begins at two o'clock sharp.*
> Almost everybody knows *that copper is an excellent conductor of electricity and heat.*
> I am positive *that the man is an impostor.*

In the first sentence a noun clause used as the subject makes it clear what seemed queer. In the second, a noun clause used as a predicate nominative explains the reason for hurrying. In the third, a noun clause used as the object of the verb tells what it is that almost every-

110

body knows. In the fourth, a noun clause used like an adverb to modify a predicate adjective tells in what way the writer is positive. Now look at the following sentences:

Dick wouldn't answer my letters. This fact surprised me greatly.
The burglar had ignored all the silverware. This interesting clue gave me an idea.

Notice that the first sentence in each pair explains a word in the sentence that follows. The sentences in each pair can be combined by using a noun clause in place of the first sentence:

The fact *that Dick wouldn't answer my letters* surprised me greatly.
This interesting clue, *that the burglar had ignored all the silverware,* gave me an idea.

The noun clauses are in apposition with the words *fact* and *clue.*

You have just learned some of the ways in which noun clauses can be used to make better sentences; and Exercise 2 will give you practice in using noun clauses to improve sentences written by others. The real test of their usefulness will come as you talk and write about your own ideas and experiences. If noun clauses help you combine related ideas into sentences that are clear, forceful, and interesting, you will have learned another valuable trick for improving sentences of your own.

EXERCISE 5. Each of the following groups consists of two sentences. Change each group into one effective sentence by using a noun clause. Be ready to read your revised sentences aloud. For the first group you might say: *It seems strange to me that sometimes there is no salt in ice which forms on salt water.*

1. Sometimes there is no salt in ice which forms on salt water. This seems strange to me.
2. The inspector reported an interesting coincidence. This was that Grimes had been released from prison the very day of the robbery.
3. Mr. Karnes knew more about the missing boys than he would admit. We were sure of that.
4. Diane had only one comment to make. She said that she would never again take part in a Little Theater play.
5. The railway coaches of the 1850's were heated by cast-iron stoves in the center of the cars. The conductor told us this.

6. Bob's proposal was voted down as too expensive. His proposal was that we send the fruit to Palm Springs by air.
7. Brass containing a larger percentage of zinc than of copper is not malleable. The factory guide explained this.
8. Harry suggested a more exciting plan. He suggested that we pool our money to buy a sailboat.
9. Mr. Pine failed any student he caught cheating in a test. Everyone in school knew this.
10. Leonard and Jim sneaked away from the dance at nine-thirty. This fact made us suspicious.

Indirect questions

In Unit 5 you learned that quotation marks enclose the exact words of another person, as in the following examples:

> Mary asked, "Where is the money, Bob?"
> "When did the accident happen?" asked the policeman.
> "Jim," Mother said after looking over the yard, "why haven't you cut the grass?"
> The old man stopped me in the hall and asked, "How do I find the principal's office?"
> "Have you been ill?" the teacher inquired.

You know that the questions are in the exact words used by Mary, the policeman, Mother, the old man, and the teacher. By using noun clauses, the writer can tell about these questions in his own words, as in the following examples:

> Mary asked Bob *where the money was.*
> The policeman questioned me about *when the accident happened.*
> After looking over the yard, Mother asked Jim *why he had not cut the grass.*
> The old man stopped me in the hall and inquired *how he could find the principal's office.*
> The teacher wanted to know *whether I had been ill.*

In each of these sentences the italicized clause is used as a noun and is an **indirect question.** You can see that quotation marks and question marks are not used with indirect questions. Notice, too, that there is no comma separating the noun clause from the rest of the sentence.

You have learned the difference between *that* used as a relative pronoun and *that* used to introduce a noun clause. Now look at the following sentences:

"*Who* are you?" asked the woman at the door.
"*Whose* locker is this?" the boys asked.
"*Whom* did you call?" Miss Edwards inquired the next day.
"*Which* will he choose?" we kept asking one another.
"*What* do you want?" the man asked me.

When *who, whose, whom, which,* and *what* are used to ask questions, they are called **interrogative pronouns.** You can see that they have no antecedents. Neither do they have antecedents when they are used to introduce noun clauses that are indirect questions:

The woman at the door asked *who I was.*
The boys wanted to know *whose locker this was.*
The next day Miss Edwards asked *whom we had called.*
We kept asking one another *which he would choose.*
The man questioned me about *what I wanted.*

Notice that the italicized words are noun clauses used as objects.

A word of caution: You know, of course, that the subject in a question may come after the verb or between the parts of the verb, as in the following examples:

Mother asked, "Why are *you* late?"
The stranger asked Ruth, "Where is the nearest *garage*?"
Father asked, "Will *you* run an errand for me?"
The teacher asked Bill, "Do *you* know the rule?"

Students who do not know about indirect questions may say: "Mother asked why was I late." "The stranger asked Ruth where was the nearest garage." "Father asked me would I run an errand for him." "The teacher asked Bill did he know the rule." Such sentences are awkward. If you remember that indirect questions are noun clauses that are parts of statements, you will put the subject before the verb and use *whether* or *if* when there is no interrogative word:

Mother asked why *I* was late.
The stranger asked Ruth where the nearest *garage* was.
Father asked me *whether I* would run an errand for him.
The teacher asked Bill *if he* knew the rule.

Some sentences that are perfectly clear when a direct quotation is used for a question become confusing when an indirect question is used. For example:

> Elaine asked Mildred if her father had called.
> The girls asked the boys whether they were invited to the party.

Notice that you cannot tell whose father is meant or who is invited to the party. Such sentences are clearer when direct quotations are used:

> Elaine asked, "Mildred, has my father called?"
> Elaine asked, "Mildred, has your father called?"
> "Are we invited to the party?" the girls asked.
> "Are you boys invited to the party?" the girls asked.

When you use indirect questions in your writing, always be sure that your meaning is clear to the reader.

EXERCISE 6. Rewrite each sentence, changing the direct quotation to an indirect question. Try to vary the words in the main clauses of your sentences; do not use "asked" for every sentence. For the first sentence you might write: *1. Mother wanted to know where I was going in such a hurry.*

1. "Where are you going in such a hurry?" Mother asked.
2. "Where are my skates?" Sue asked.
3. "What does Al think about it?" Mary asked.
4. "Shall I call Sam at his office?" Nancy inquired.
5. "Will Mother be very angry at us?" Bob asked.
6. "Will you lend me your raincoat and an umbrella?" inquired the girl.
7. "How can Bill do so much work in an hour?" I asked myself.
8. "When will your father be back?" asked the old man at the door.
9. "Do you want me to help you?" inquired the little fellow.
10. "Why are those girls screaming so?" everyone asked.

Adverb clauses

Earlier you learned that a subordinate clause used as an adverb is called an adverb clause, and you saw these two sentences:

> I was sorry *later.*
> I was sorry *after I had spoken.*

You know that the adverb clause in the second sentence modifies the verb *was,* just as the adverb *later* does in the first sentence. Now notice

114

how the italicized clauses are used in the following sentences:

> Margaret left *before the party was half over.*
> Can you stay *until she comes back?*
> The mixture must be poured *while it is still warm.*
> We put the keys *where you can find them easily.*
> They pitch their tents *wherever there is water near at hand.*
> Hold the saw *as you have been taught to do.*

The clauses in the first three sentences tell when. Those in the next two sentences tell where. The clause in the last sentence tells how. You know that adverbs modify verbs by telling when, where, and how; and you can see that the clauses are adverb clauses modifying the verbs in the sentences. Now look at these sentences:

> Mary must stay at home *because her mother is ill.*
> Study hard *so that you can make a good grade in the test.*
> Bob will play in tomorrow's game *if the coach lets him.*
> A good soldier obeys orders *whether he likes them or not.*
> The stores were still open, *though it was long past the closing hour.*

The italicized clauses in the first two sentences tell why. The first one gives the reason for Mary's staying at home, and the second one gives the purpose of studying hard. The clause in the third sentence tells on what condition Bob will play, and the one in the fourth sentence tells a condition under which a good soldier obeys orders. The clause in the last sentence gives an opposing or contrasting fact; the stores were open in spite of the late hour. You can see that each italicized clause modifies the verb in the main clause and is an adverb clause.

Adverb clauses may modify verbs in subordinate clauses:

> Do you know the man who spoke to us *as we came in?*
> Find out what they have been doing *since we moved away.*
> Then Bill locked the door so that no one could leave *until he did.*

In the first sentence the italicized clause modifies the verb *spoke* in the adjective clause beginning with *who.* In the second sentence the italicized clause modifies the verb *have been doing* in the noun clause introduced by *what.* In the third sentence the italicized clause modifies the verb *could leave* in the adverb clause beginning with *so that.*

Adverb clauses may modify verbals, as in the following sentences:

I plan to leave *whenever you are ready.*
No one thought of quitting *because the work was hard.*

The clause in the first sentence modifies the infinitive *to leave* and the one in the second sentence modifies the gerund *quitting.*

The words that introduce adverb clauses are called **subordinating conjunctions.** They show how the clause is related to the word it modifies. For example:

I will talk to you *after* he goes.   You may stay *until* he goes.
I will talk to you *before* he goes.   I will follow *wherever* he goes.

In each sentence the subordinating conjunction joins "he goes" to the verb in the main clause and shows how the adverb clause is related to the word it modifies. Unlike the relatives that introduce adjective clauses, subordinating conjunctions do not have antecedents.

EXERCISE 7. Each of the sentences contains one or more clauses. Find each adverb clause, and decide what it modifies. On a sheet of paper, write the first and last words of each adverb clause and, after them, the word or words modified by the clause. Use a separate line for each adverb clause. Put parentheses around the words modified. Number your answers with the numbers of the sentences. For the first sentence you should write: *1. until old (had been)*

1. Alfred had never been on a train until he was almost eleven years old.
2. A man jostled my arm while I was picking up my change.
3. Stopping all traffic as we approached, the policeman motioned us across so that we wouldn't be late.
4. Wanting to be there when Mildred's train pulled in, I left the house before the six o'clock whistle blew.
5. These pewter candlesticks will look much better after they are polished.
6. Mother frowned whenever I spoke to her, though she did not scold me while the Crandalls were there.
7. We missed the opening number because Monica walked so slowly.
8. Realizing that we would be too late if we waited for the bus, we started running down the road, waving for a ride whenever a car drove by.
9. We can't have the party unless Mr. Crane gives us permission.
10. Knowing that Ernie would tag along wherever we went, we decided to wait until he left our booth.

116

Adverb clauses at the beginning of sentences

In Unit 2 you learned that beginning an occasional sentence with an adverb is one way of avoiding the monotony of too many subject-first sentences. Adverb clauses are often used in the same way:

> *Although it was late,* the stores were still open.
> *Since the game begins at two o'clock sharp,* we must hurry.

You can see that these sentences would have the same meanings if the clauses were put last. Now look at the following pairs of sentences:

> Ask Charles about the algebra assignment *when he calls.*
> *When Charles calls,* ask him about the algebra assignment.

> I would write Joe tonight *if I knew his address.*
> *If I knew Joe's address,* I would write him tonight.

Notice that a noun and a pronoun may change places when the clause is put first in sentences like these.

Sometimes it is not clear just what word an adverb clause at the end of a sentence is intended to modify. For example:

> Edith opened a box of crackers that had been standing on the pantry shelf for a month *while Mother was preparing a pot of tea.*

This sentence seems to mean that Mother had spent a month preparing the pot of tea. Putting the adverb clause first makes the intended meaning clear:

> *While Mother was preparing a pot of tea,* Edith opened a box of crackers that had been standing on the pantry shelf for a month.

The adverb clause now clearly modifies the verb *opened,* and the sentence makes a more sensible statement.

EXERCISE 8. Each of the sentences ends with an adverb clause. Study each sentence, and decide what word the clause was probably intended to modify. Be prepared to read the sentences to the class, shifting each adverb clause to the first of the sentence or closer to the word it modifies. For the first sentence you might say: *Whenever Dan looked at this photograph of the camp, he felt ashamed of the way he had behaved.*

1. Dan felt ashamed of the way he had behaved whenever he looked at this photograph of the camp.

2. Mr. and Mrs. Edmunds want to live in a place where the climate is milder as old age comes on.
3. Shep would run under the piano that stood in the dark corner of Grandfather's living room whenever a thunderstorm came up.
4. Wallace sat down on a tombstone that had been carved a century ago while he waited for the bus.
5. He would tell us thrilling tales of the lions and tigers that he had captured whenever he had a few minutes to spare.
6. I wondered if I had turned off the gas after I had left the house.
7. I wonder how people know enough to carry umbrellas whenever I'm caught in the rain.
8. Maureen remembered the snapshot she had promised to send Bob after she dropped the letter in the mailbox.
9. Marie thought of the many exciting trips she had had while she rocked lazily back and forth in the hammock.
10. Leroy had to set his alarm clock for 5:30 in order to catch the 6:32 train before he was promoted to his new job.

Adverb clauses of comparison

You have studied adverb clauses that modify verbs. Now look at the following sentences. Can you tell what words the clauses modify?

> The weather was colder *than we had expected*.
> Aunt Mary stayed longer *than I liked*.

The clause in the first sentence modifies the predicate adjective *colder*, telling how much colder. The clause in the second sentence modifies the adverb *longer*, telling how much longer. The words *colder* and *longer* are forms of *cold* and *long* used in making comparisons. Adverb clauses that modify these comparative forms are called adverb clauses of comparison.

When the verb in a clause of comparison is the same as that in the main clause, a form of *do* is often used to avoid repetition. Compare the following pairs of sentences:

> Bill talks more than I *talk*.   Bill talked more than I *talked*.
> Bill talks more than I *do*.   Bill talked more than I *did*.

Clauses of comparison are not always grammatically complete. For example, notice the italicized words in the following sentences:

Bill talks more *than I* (talk).
Bill has always talked more *than I ever have* (talked).
Bill talks more *than* (it) *is necessary* (for him to talk).

Because the words in parentheses are not necessary to the meaning, they are usually omitted. The clauses are then said to be "elliptical." But some elliptical clauses may have two meanings. For example:

The coach encourages Sam more *than the captain.*
Denver is farther from Chicago *than New York.*

The first sentence might mean:

The coach encourages Sam more $\begin{cases} \textit{than he does the captain.} \\ \textit{than the captain does.} \end{cases}$

The second sentence might mean:

Denver is farther from Chicago $\begin{cases} \textit{than it is from New York.} \\ \textit{than New York is.} \end{cases}$

Never use an elliptical clause unless the meaning you intend is quite clear. If you are in doubt, always supply the words needed to make your meaning unmistakable.

Clauses of comparison may also be introduced by *as* and *that*:

This is as far *as we can go by automobile.*
The trailer was not so large *as an ordinary boxcar* (*is*).
They made such a racket (*that*) *I couldn't hear a word.*

The clause in the first sentence modifies the adverb *as*. The elliptical clause in the second sentence modifies the adverb *so*. The clause in the third sentence modifies the adverb *such*. Notice that the subordinating conjunction *that* may be omitted, as in the third sentence.

EXERCISE 9. Find the adverb clauses in the sentences, and decide what words they modify. Then on a sheet of paper, write the first and last words of each clause, followed by the word or words it modifies. Use a separate line for each clause, and put parentheses around the words modified. Number your answers. For the first one you should write: *1. than for (worse)*

1. The trip was much worse than I had bargained for.
2. Janet walked fast so that she would not be late.
3. Janet walked so fast that she got there ahead of time.
4. Ted ate as slowly as he dared.
5. Ted ate slowly, as there was plenty of time.

6. Though the test was hard, Bob did better than he had expected.
7. We soon discovered that there were not so many people interested as we had imagined there would be.
8. As the days became shorter, the nights grew colder.
9. Since the program had not been advertised, we were surprised that the crowd was as large as it was.
10. Airplanes that go faster than sound are not so rare as you might think.

Improving sentences
18. Use an adverb clause

Earlier you learned that adverb clauses are sometimes put first to make sentences clearer or more interesting. Now you will see how adverb clauses may be used to combine sentences that are related in meaning. Look at the following sentences:

> It was growing dark. We began to look for a place to camp.
> The sun felt warm. The temperature was below zero.
> I was hurrying through my breakfast. I heard the doorbell ring.
> Work fast. You can finish before lunch.

Although the sentences in each pair are related in meaning, the relationship is not clearly shown, and the sentences seem equally important. Now notice the ways in which the sentences can be combined by using adverb clauses:

> *Since it was growing dark,* we began to look for a place to camp.
> It was growing dark *as we began to look for a place to camp.*
> *Although the sun felt warm,* the temperature was below zero.
> The sun felt warm, *though the temperature was below zero.*
> *As I was hurrying through my breakfast,* I heard the doorbell ring.
> I was hurrying through my breakfast *when I heard the doorbell ring.*
> *If you work fast,* you can finish before lunch.
> Work fast *so that you can finish before lunch.*

When one idea is put in an adverb clause, the idea in the main clause seems more important; and the subordinating conjunction shows clearly the relationship in meaning between the two clauses.

120

Adverb clauses are also useful in combining and improving related sentences like these:

> Pretty soon we sat down. Then the telephone began to ring.
> Bert ran very fast. And so he left the others far behind.

The sentences can be made more forceful and more interesting by using adverb clauses of comparison:

> We had no sooner sat down *than the telephone began to ring.*
> Bert ran so fast *that he left the others far behind.*

A word of caution: As you use adverb clauses to combine sentences of your own, always try to put less important ideas in the modifying clauses. Otherwise you may write sentences like these:

> We were dozing by the fire, when a fearful "boom" came from across the lake.
> He was a good swimmer, though he nearly drowned that day.

The sentences seem unbalanced, as though dozing by the fire and being a good swimmer were more important than a fearful explosion and nearly drowning. They look like this:

> FIRST A LITTLE FACT, then a big one.

If you remember to put the "little fact" in the adverb clause, your sentences will be more like these:

> *While we were dozing by the fire,* a fearful "boom" came from across the lake.
> *Although he was a good swimmer,* he nearly drowned that day.

Your reader expects important ideas to be in main clauses. Try not to disappoint him.

EXERCISE 10. Read the two sentences in each group, and decide how they are related. Then change each group into one good sentence, using an adverb clause in place of the less important sentence. Be prepared to read the revised sentences aloud. For the first group you might say: *Mr. Flint was so busy cataloguing his coin collection that he did not see Joan enter.*

1. Mr. Flint did not see Joan enter. He was very busy cataloguing his coin collection.
2. The flames spread to the hayloft. Then the barn was beyond saving.

3. We always have a good time at Phil's house. His parents don't care how much noise we make.
4. I was plowing my way through the muddy field. One of my rubbers came off.
5. Michael paused before the door, fumbling for his keys. He became aware of approaching footsteps.
6. Allen had spent all of his allowance. So he could not go to the carnival with the rest of us fellows.
7. My cousin Jean had had no experience in dramatics. However, she won a movie contract.
8. Dale jumped up to answer the phone. He tripped over the rug and fell sprawling to the floor.
9. The temperature was several degrees below freezing. Still the painters continued with their work.
10. The whole family gathered in the living room. Then Dad told us that he had to sell the car and the cottage at Green Lake.

EXERCISE 11. Write a "supersentence"—a single sentence in which you include at least one of each of the grammatical units you have studied in Units 5 and 6. These are: (1) a preposition (2) a participle (3) a gerund (4) an infinitive (5) an adjective clause (6) a noun clause (7) an adverb clause. These units may occur in any order in the sentence.

Composition

Expressing a Preference PART ONE: ORAL

Which do you like better—a circus or a carnival? If you were offered two summer jobs at the same pay—one indoor work, the other outdoor—which would you take? Which subject would you sign up for —biology or chemistry? Would you rather spend your time listening to radio programs or watching television? Which would you choose for making a long pleasure trip—train or automobile? In answering questions of this sort, you express a preference. How convincing your answer is to others often depends on the reasons you give to explain your preference.

As you can see, each of the questions involves making a choice between two things of the same kind. If that choice is to be based on facts rather than on feelings alone, it is necessary to compare the two things, considering carefully the differences between them, weighing the advantages of one against the advantages of the other. A preference arrived at in this way can be explained by giving the important points of comparison.

For this assignment you are to prepare an oral report in which you express a preference and give reasons for your choice. The questions in the first paragraph should start you thinking about possible subjects that involve choosing between two similar things—sports, hobbies, clothes, automobiles, vacations, careers, and so on. Whenever you feel that some persons might prefer one choice and some another, you probably have a good subject. If it interests you personally, you will have no difficulty thinking of enough points of comparison to make it interesting to your classmates. What subject will you use?

Now think carefully about your subject. What are the points of difference? One way of keeping them in order is to list the advantages of each of the two things you are comparing. Jot them down as they come to your mind, keeping them in separate groups. Then go over your list. Are there any items that are not really points of difference? Are there duplications—two items covering one advantage? Is there any item expressed as a disadvantage that could be put in the other group as an advantage? For example, if you were explaining your preference for making a long pleasure trip by car, your list might look like this:

By car—
    Costs less if several share expenses
    Can make side trips, see more scenery
    No worry about reservations, schedules, transfers
    ~~Traffic problems are nuisance~~
    Can carry baggage more conveniently
    Can stop overnight at motels —with car handy
    ~~No worry about getting baggage to hotel~~
    Can eat in different places or buy food to take along
    Can drive right up to destination
    No porters to tip
    ~~Can meet interesting people on way~~
By train—
    Usually faster
    Meals no problem —diner or club car
    ~~Interesting people to talk to~~
    Can stand up, stretch, wander about
    Can sleep in comfort —adjustable seats or Pullman
    No worry about missing way, flat tires, gas, etc.
    No worry about traffic problems

Notice that the last item in the first group and the third in the second group have been crossed out. Neither of these items is a point of difference. The seventh item in the first group has also been crossed out because it merely duplicates the fifth item. And the fourth item in the first group has been crossed out because it is a disadvantage. The idea has been rephrased as an advantage and added to the second group. In expressing a preference, you will usually find it easier to word the points of difference as advantages.

Notice, too, that the advantages of traveling by car are all in one group, while the advantages of traveling by train are in another group. The arrangement of ideas in related groups is called a **logical**

order. A logical order is often used for details that cannot be arranged in a time order or a space order.

When you have the advantages on your list clearly separated into logical groups, look at the items in each group. Which item will you mention first? Which will you mention next and next and so on to the last—and most important—one? Then number the items in each group according to the order in which you plan to give them.

The next step, once your two groups of advantages are complete and numbered, is to think of a sentence for each group to show your listeners how the details are related. In the talk expressing a choice between a train trip and a car trip, you would first discuss the advantages of going by train, since it is usually most effective to end with the advantages of the thing you prefer. Then a sentence you might use as a **main heading** for the "By train" group could be: "Going by train has a number of advantages, of course." For the "By car" group an appropriate sentence would be: "On the other hand, the advantages of going by car far outweigh those of going by train."

Your talk should include a statement of your preference. You may want to begin by telling your classmates your decision. For example: "In spite of all the comforts of our modern railroads, I would rather make a long pleasure trip by car than by train." Or you may want to wait until the end of your talk to state your preference. For example: "Can you blame me for preferring to go by car?" Or you may do both.

Now look at the advantages you have listed. Which group will you begin with? After you have decided, think of a sentence to use as a main heading for each group. Will you express your preference in the opening sentence, in the closing sentence, or in both? Then make a final plan for your talk on a card or small piece of paper. At the top write your opening sentence. Next write the main heading for the group of advantages you will discuss first. Under it copy the details you will use, in the order in which you decided to tell them. Do the same for the second group. Then add the closing sentence.

Practice your talk at least once, timing yourself to make sure it does not take over three minutes. If called on to give your talk in class, stand well away from the desks and speak distinctly.

Expressing a Preference  PART TWO: WRITTEN

You have prepared notes for an oral report in which you expressed a preference for one of two similar things. These notes will now help you in planning a written report on the same subject. How many groups of related details are shown in your notes? If you compared the advantages of two similar things, you probably have two groups of related details. Each group will be explained in a separate paragraph. Now look at the main heading you wrote for each group. Does it explain clearly how the details in the group are related? If so, you can use it for the **topic sentence** of the paragraph.

Topic sentences are particularly important when details are arranged in a logical order. Details in a time order are usually easy to follow. When they do not come one right after the other, an expression like *That evening, The next morning,* or *Several months later* is enough to warn the reader that the next group of details will be different. And details in a space order are usually grouped according to the writer's point of view. An expression like *Ahead of me, To my left, Looking upward,* or *In the distance* shows the reader that the next paragraph is to be about a different part of the subject. But details in a logical order are grouped according to an idea in the writer's mind. Topic sentences make that idea known to the reader by explaining clearly how the details in each group are related. For example, notice the topic sentences in this plan:

FIRST PARAGRAPH

OPENING SENTENCE: In spite of all the comforts of our modern railroads, I would rather make a long pleasure trip by car than by train.

TOPIC SENTENCE: Going by train has a number of advantages, of course.

A. Usually faster
B. No worry about traffic problems
C. No worry about missing way, flat tires, gas, etc.
D. Meals no problem—diner or club car
E. Can stand up, stretch, wander about
F. Can sleep in comfort—adjustable seats or Pullman

126

SECOND
PARAGRAPH

TOPIC SENTENCE: *On the other hand*, the advantages of going by car far outweigh those of going by train.

A. Costs less if several share expenses
B. Can carry baggage more conveniently
C. Can make side trips, see more scenery
D. Can eat in different places or buy food to take along
E. Can stop overnight at motels—with car handy
F. No worry about reservations, schedules, transfers
G. No porters to tip
H. Can drive right up to destination

CLOSING SENTENCE: Can you blame me for preferring to go by car?

The topic sentence for the first paragraph explains that the details following it will be advantages of going by train. The topic sentence for the second paragraph explains that the details following it will be advantages of going by car. Notice particularly the italicized phrase *On the other hand*. It shows the reader how the second paragraph is related to the first. A topic sentence often has two purposes: It explains how the details in the paragraph are related. It shows how the paragraph is related to the one preceding it.

Now make the plan for your composition. By means of lines or brackets indicate where each paragraph is to begin and end. Then look again at the main headings in your notes to be sure they can be used as topic sentences. If necessary, add words like *But, However, Nevertheless, In spite of these* to your second topic sentence to show its relation to the first paragraph.

When your plan is ready, write your first draft. Remember to begin the first paragraph with your special opening sentence. Follow it with the topic sentence and the first group of advantages. Then begin the second paragraph with the topic sentence and end with the last detail or with a special closing sentence. Tell each advantage clearly, keeping your classmates in mind. Try to hear your sentences as you write them down.

Revise your first draft carefully. Cross out unnecessary words; substitute exact modifiers for lazy adjectives or adverbs; vary the beginnings of your sentences; get rid of weak explanatory sentences by using appositives or verbal phrases. In short, make use of every means you have learned for·improving your sentences. Then look for errors in spelling and punctuation so that you can correct them before preparing your final draft.

The title for a composition in which you express a preference for one of two similar things may be simply the names of the two things. For example:

Travel by Train and Car   Indoor and Outdoor Jobs
Biology or Chemistry?   Radio or Television

But if you want to arouse the curiosity and interest of your readers, you might use a title that merely suggests what your composition is about:

I'll Take the Highway   I'm the Outdoor Type Myself
Bugs or Bottles?   TV or Not TV, That Is the Question

When you have decided on a title for your composition, copy your revised first draft. Write as neatly as you can, and space your words so that they can be read easily. Keep margins even. Then proofread your paper for errors you may have made in copying—for words omitted or repeated, for careless misspellings and omitted punctuation marks.

Trolley car or bus?

Review of Grammar
The Kinds of Sentences

What a simple sentence is

In grammar the words "simple sentence" have a special meaning. Notice these two sentences:

> Jim pointed.
>
> Up on the very peak of the jagged mountain, standing out clearly and lighted by the glow of the evening sun, was the white flag of the advance party, a sign to all the tired and complaining workmen of the ease of the climb and the weakness of giving up now an enterprise costing such a vast sum of money.

The first sentence consists of two words, a subject *Jim* and a verb *pointed*. The second sentence consists of sixty words, including a subject *flag* and a verb *was*. Notice that each sentence has one subject and one verb, and that each sentence makes one statement.

In Unit 3 you learned that sentences may have compound subjects and compound verbs:

> *Arthur* and *Tom* and *Bob* won prizes at the hobby show.
>
> Mary *washed* the dishes and *put* them away.
>
> The *potatoes* and the *corn* then *are covered* with a thick layer of mud and *are buried* in the hot coals.

The first sentence makes a statement about one thing that three boys did at the hobby show. The second sentence makes a statement about two things that Mary did at home. The third sentence makes a statement about two things that are done to both vegetables. Notice that each sentence has a compound subject or a compound verb or both.

A sentence that has only one subject and one verb, either or both of which may be compound, is called a simple sentence.

As you have seen, a simple sentence may or may not be complicated, may or may not have modifying words and phrases, may or may not have verbals and appositives. But long or short, a sentence that has only one subject and verb is a simple sentence.

Parts of the simple sentence

In the preceding Units you have learned about verbs of one or more words, nouns and pronouns, adjectives and adverbs, prepositions and conjunctions, verbals and verbal phrases. You have seen how these are used as subjects and predicates and modifiers and appositives to make simple sentences. Now you are ready to review the ways in which words and phrases are used as parts of simple sentences.

Verbs and their subjects are the framework of simple sentences. The verb in each sentence is a word or a group of words that makes a statement or asks a question or gives a command. It may consist of one, two, three, or four words; and these words may be separated from each other. The subject of the verb may be a noun or a pronoun, a verbal or a verbal phrase; and it may be compound. In the first ten sentences the verbs are in italic type. Be prepared to tell who or what is the subject of each verb:

1. Where *have* Donald and his brother *gone?*
2. Either Bill or the other fellow *may have been working* last evening.
3. *Could* one of the girls *have known* your old address?
4. These *might* possibly *be* the better ones for our purpose.
5. There *have been* too many accidents lately.
6. Beyond the city limits *are* only a few houses and a filling station.
7. Being thrown from a horse *can be* a frightening experience.
8. It *will be* necessary to do the work more carefully the next time.
9. No talking or whispering *should have been permitted*.
10. To work harder or to fail completely *was* his only choice.

Predicate words are used in various ways to help verbs tell about their subjects: Predicate adjectives modify subjects. Predicate nominatives explain subjects. Objects of verbs tell who or what receives the actions expressed by verbs. Indirect objects tell to whom or for whom actions are done. Objective predicates modify or explain the objects of verbs. These predicate words are italicized in the next nineteen sentences. In sentences 11-15 predicate adjectives are in italics. Be prepared to tell the verb in each sentence and the word that is modified by the predicate adjective:

11. The old man across the street has appeared *unhappy* for some time.
12. Her voice and its range are considered *excellent* for a young singer.
13. Doesn't the air feel *hot* and *humid* to you today?
14. Some of the food tasted unusually *good* to us.
15. His genial manner may have seemed *encouraging* at first.

In sentences 16-19 predicate nominatives are in italics. Be prepared to tell the verb in each sentence and the word that is explained by the predicate nominative:

16. The one on the bottom of the pile will undoubtedly be a total *wreck*.
17. Either Fred or you should have been *captain* of the team this year.
18. Pete's favorite pastimes were *sailing his boat* and *swimming*.
19. At the present time his main concern is probably *to find a better job*.

In sentences 20-23 objects of verbs are italicized. Be prepared to pick out each verb and to tell its subject:

20. Only after our arrival were we given a full *account* of the incident.
21. Her mother and sister have always enjoyed *cooking* and *housekeeping*.
22. Would you mind *being my assistant for the next few weeks*?
23. Both of my little sisters like *to play with dolls*.

In sentences 24-29 indirect objects and objective predicates are italicized. Be prepared to pick out the verb and the direct object in each of the sentences:

24. Mother has just knitted *me* a new sweater.
25. Who told *you* the answers to the questions on the board?
26. They should have given *Norm* and his *brother* another chance.
27. Why do they call the tallest boy in the class *Shorty*?
28. The victory has made everybody in school very *happy*.
29. Will the class choose her or her sister program *chairman*?

Modifiers are words and phrases used to make clear the exact meaning of other words. Nouns and pronouns may be modified by adjectives and adjective phrases, possessive nouns and pronouns, and verbals. Verbs, verbals, adjectives, and their modifiers may be modified by adverbs and adverb phrases, adverbial nouns, and verbals.

Modifiers of these kinds are italicized in the next twenty-three sentences. In sentences 30-39, be prepared to tell the noun or pronoun that is modified by each word or phrase in italics:

30. Drops *of rain* began to fall on *our neighbor's new concrete* sidewalk.
31. *Several* boys and girls were playing on *our large front* lawn.
32. Can you show me *one good* way *to swim?*
33. Hand me *those old football* shoes *lying in the corner.*
34. *Three small* children, *smiling* and *laughing,* greeted *the* rest *of us.*
35. For *several* weeks he has been carrying *his broken* arm in *a dirty* sling.
36. *Being her favorite,* he escaped *severe* punishment.
37. *Having done his chores,* Ed left for *the baseball* game.
38. *All that* day he trudged along, *fighting the snow and wind at every step.*
39. *Having finished the book,* Nancy made *an elaborate* outline *of the plot.*

In sentences 40-49, be prepared to tell the verb that is modified by each word or phrase in italics:

40. *Suddenly* the ship broke *away from its moorings.*
41. These brave men have *always* fought *savagely* and *without fear.*
42. Do *not* sit *down here for a while.*
43. They have *always* spoken *to Mary and me at parties.*
44. She *almost* sent us *home yesterday at noon.*
45. *During the intermission* everybody stood *up to stretch.*
46. *Slowly* but *surely* the men pulled us *up the cliff* and *over the edge.*
47. *Perhaps* I should have waited *longer before saying anything.*
48. *Finally* the girls turned *to look* at us and *then* stopped *to talk.*
49. *With great deliberation* Grandfather *slowly* settled himself *in a chair.*

In sentences 50-52, be prepared to tell the adjective or adverb that is modified by each word or phrase in italics:

50. The weather was *entirely too* hot *to be comfortable.*
51. Open the door *very* quietly and *very* little.
52. Are you *about* ready *to leave for school?*

Appositives are set alongside other words to explain or add to the meaning of those words. Appositives do not modify anything, and they are not essential parts of sentences. In sentences 53-61, be prepared to tell what words are explained by the italicized appositives:

53. We have often visited Wilson's Landing, a little-known summer *resort.*
54. Two foods he heartily dislikes—ripe *olives* and cottage *cheese.*

55. The other people, *those* with little education, must be at a tremendous disadvantage in finding jobs.
56. Some well-known programs are regularly broadcast from transcriptions, or large *records* of special material.
57. Their coach, *Bob Austin,* was a former member of our team.
58. His favorite sports, *hunting* and *fishing,* keep him outdoors a great deal.
59. Brenda's plan, *to invite* other classes to the prom, was voted down.
60. Certain vegetables—such as *cucumbers, tomatoes,* and *lettuce*—contain large percentages of water.
61. Your original idea—*to borrow* a sprayer, *buy* a gallon of the mixture, and *do* the work ourselves—seems more economical after all.

Just knowing the parts of simple sentences is not, by itself, of much value to you. Only by putting this knowledge to work, by using it constantly to help you make better sentences, can you come to know its true worth. Every first draft you write offers opportunities for revising sentences to make them clearer, more forceful, and more interesting. As you learn to take advantage of these opportunities—moving sentence parts around to sharpen your meaning and to avoid monotony, combining sentences to make your important ideas stand out clearly—you will understand and appreciate the practical values of studying grammar for sentence improvement.

Compound sentences with conjunctions

In Unit 3 you learned what conjunctions are, and you saw how they join words to make compound subjects and compound verbs. Now look at these sentences:

> Her attic room was *small* but *cheerful.*
> They should be here *by Monday evening* or *by Tuesday morning.*
> The teacher told us *that the test would have four questions* and *that one of these would be a written composition.*

In the first sentence *but* joins two predicate adjectives. In the second sentence *or* joins two adverb phrases. In the third sentence *and* joins two noun clauses used as objects of the verb *told.* When words like *but, or,* and *and* join words, phrases, and clauses that are used in the same way, they are called **coördinating** conjunctions.

There are many books here, *yet* I can't find the one that she mentioned in class yesterday.

Run fast, *or* you may not get there before the store closes.

He won't do what the coach says, *nor* will he follow the training rules that have been set up for the team.

In the first three examples the coördinating conjunctions *and, but,* and *for* join simple sentences. In the last three examples the coördinating conjunctions *yet, or,* and *nor* join simple and complex sentences. Sentences joined by such conjunctions are called **coördinate** clauses.

A sentence that consists of two or more coördinate clauses is called a compound sentence.

EXERCISE 1. Read each pair of sentences, noticing how they are related in meaning. Then combine each pair of sentences by using *and, but, for, yet, or,* or *nor.* Be prepared to read your revised sentences aloud. For the first one you might say: *We didn't think it worth while to take a bus, for the skating rink was only a few blocks away.*

1. The skating rink was only a few blocks away. So we didn't think it worth while to take a bus.
2. I am sure that I brought home some stamps. However, they are not in the drawer where I put them.
3. Keep a close check on those boys. Otherwise they will throw away the circulars and spend the day in the park.
4. Bobby's face was covered with bruises. His shirt was torn to shreds, too.
5. We knew that Curtis had a camera in his locker. However, we hated to ask him if we could borrow it.
6. Luckily for me, Mrs. Donovan did not tell Dad about my breaking the window. She did not ask me to pay for it, either.
7. Of course Dennis thought that the boss had left the room. Otherwise he would never have called him "that old crab."
8. Five amateur magicians watched carefully while Eaton did the trick. Nevertheless, none could discover how he did it.
9. I did not want to start an argument while Helen and Bob were there. So I said nothing about inviting Randall to the party.
10. There were several cans of corn and soup on a shelf over the old oil stove. However, we could not find a can opener.

Compound sentences without conjunctions

Sentences that are clearly related in meaning may be made into a compound sentence merely by putting a semicolon between them. As you read the following sentences, notice how the sentences in each pair are related in meaning:

> You mustn't leave now. It's raining very hard.
> Joan isn't speaking to the other girls. They have offended her.
> One of the twins is friendly and cheerful. The other is self-centered and sulky.
> A cat might squeeze through that opening. A man never could.
> Each student carried a placard that had been nailed to a stick. Each was singing gaily as he marched along.
> The players fully expected to win. They were supremely confident that the game would end in victory for them.

In the first two pairs the second sentence gives a reason. In the next two pairs the second sentence expresses a contrast. In the last two pairs the second sentence adds an important idea. By using a semicolon to make a compound sentence of each pair, the writer calls attention to these relationships in meaning:

> You mustn't leave now; it's raining very hard.
> Joan isn't speaking to the other girls; they have offended her.
> One of the twins is friendly and cheerful; the other is self-centered and sulky.
> A cat might squeeze through that opening; a man never could.
> Each student carried a placard that had been nailed to a stick; each was singing gaily as he marched along.
> The players fully expected to win; they were supremely confident that the game would end in victory for them.

Because the relationship between the coördinate clauses in each compound sentence is obvious, no conjunctions are needed. Notice that each semicolon shows where one clause ends and the next begins.

Independent adverbs

When two sentences are related in meaning in a way that is not obvious, the second sentence may begin with an adverb that shows what relationship is intended. Notice the italicized adverbs in the following sentences:

> The snowfall last winter was unusually great. *Accordingly,* severe floods are expected this coming spring.
> We were fairly sure that the substitute teacher had given us the wrong assignment. *Nevertheless,* we worked all the problems.
> The piano was old and very large. *Besides,* it was priced much too high for us.
> There wasn't a scratch on the enamel or the chromium. *Indeed,* the bicycle looked almost like new.
> Soon the engine began to sputter. *Then* it stopped entirely.
> The speed limit along here used to be forty-five miles an hour. *Now* it is only thirty.

Because each of the italicized adverbs begins a separate sentence, it is called an independent adverb. You can see that these adverbs point out the relationship between the two sentences in each pair. By using a semicolon to make a compound sentence of each pair, the writer emphasizes this relationship between the sentences:

> The snowfall last winter was unusually great; *accordingly,* severe floods are expected this coming spring.
> We were fairly sure that the substitute teacher had given us the wrong assignment; *nevertheless,* we worked all the problems.
> The piano was old and very large; *besides,* it was priced much too high for us.
> There wasn't a scratch on the enamel or the chromium; *indeed,* the bicycle looked almost like new.
> Soon the engine began to sputter; *then* it stopped entirely.
> The speed limit along here used to be forty-five miles an hour; *now* it is only thirty.

Because the independent adverbs show the relationship between the coördinate clauses in each compound sentence, no conjunctions are needed. Notice that each semicolon shows clearly where one clause ends and the next one begins.

136

The relationships most commonly shown by independent adverbs fall roughly into six groups, meaning

1) "for that reason": *hence, therefore, consequently, accordingly*
2) "in spite of that": *nevertheless, however, still*
3) "in addition to that": *besides, moreover, furthermore, likewise, also, too*
4) "in fact": *indeed, really, truly*
5) "of course": *surely, certainly*
6) "after that": *then, next, later;* "at last": *finally;* "at the present time": *now*

Always be sure to use an independent adverb that expresses clearly the relationship in meaning you intend.

EXERCISE 2. Read each pair of sentences, and decide how they are related in meaning. Then select one of the following independent adverbs that shows clearly what relationship you think is intended: *therefore, consequently, however, still, moreover, furthermore, also, certainly, surely, finally, next, now.* Be prepared to read your revised sentences aloud. For the first one you might say: *Paul's old jalopy uses too much gas and oil; moreover, three of the tires are in very bad condition.*

1. Paul's old jalopy uses too much gas and oil. Three of the tires are in very bad condition.
2. I was sure that Louise had copied the answers from Hilda's paper. I said nothing.
3. Mr. Orcutt was once the wealthiest man in Carbondale. He is dependent on Ann's charity.
4. Clifford has been working on that old car all afternoon. He must be ready to give up.
5. Ozzie waited until Miss Costello turned her head. He shot the paper airplane across the room.
6. Audrey and Keith quarreled constantly. They were always together.
7. Marie had three sisters and two brothers who were older than she. She seldom had a brand-new dress or toy.
8. During the night it grew cold. The sidewalks and streets were a glare of ice the next morning.
9. The dress Ellen wanted was not at all suitable for a school party. It was much too expensive.
10. The heat in the closet grew more intense. I could stand it no longer.

What a complex sentence is

In grammar the words "complex sentence" have a special meaning. Notice these two sentences:

> Jim works *when he can.*
> *As we were leaving the hall,* the artist *whose painting had won first prize* asked us *how we had liked the exhibit.*

The first sentence consists of a main clause *Jim works* and one subordinate clause. The second sentence consists of a main clause *the artist asked us* and three subordinate clauses. Notice that each sentence has one main clause and makes one statement.

A sentence that consists of one main clause and one or more subordinate clauses is called a complex sentence.

A sentence may have five words or fifty. It may be easy to understand or very difficult. But as long as it contains a main clause and one or more subordinate clauses, it is grammatically a complex sentence.

In Unit 6 you learned about subordinate clauses that modify nouns and pronouns:

> Mr. Allen, our science teacher, wrote to somebody in Chicago *who grinds lenses for small telescopes.*
> Dad asked whether we knew the boy *whose bicycle had been stolen.*
> We waited while Mary greeted the girls *whom she had invited.*
> I know a man who lives near the place *where you want to camp.*

The italicized words are adjective clauses. They modify the words *somebody, boy, girls,* and *place.* Notice that the word modified may be part of the main clause, as in the first sentence, or part of a noun clause, an adverb clause, or another adjective clause.

You have learned about subordinate clauses that are used as nouns:

> *What we want to know* is *how he got away from us.*
> There is the man who asked *where you lived.*

> While I was wondering *what would happen next,* your letter arrived.
> Mother was sure that the stranger was not what he said *he was.*

The italicized words are noun clauses. Notice that they may be important parts of the main clause, as in the first sentence, or part of an adjective clause, an adverb clause, or another noun clause.

You have also learned about subordinate clauses that modify verbs, adjectives, and adverbs:

If you wish, I'll meet you there as soon *as the store closes.*
We all laughed at the referee, who shook his head slowly *as he climbed back into the ring.*
Mother and Dad know that Maurie studies harder *than I do.*
Try to leave before the buses are so full *that you have to stand up.*

The italicized words are adverb clauses. Notice that they may modify verbs and adverbs that are part of the main clause, as in the first sentence, or words that are part of an adjective clause, a noun clause, or another adverb clause.

The important thing for you to remember about any subordinate clause is that it does the work of a single word in a sentence..If you take time to find out what that work is, you will know that a clause is never a sentence by itself, that it is only a part of a sentence.

EXERCISE 3. Find the subordinate clauses in the sentences, and decide how each one is used. Divide a sheet of paper into three columns. In the first column, write the first and last words of each adjective clause and, in parentheses, the word modified. In the second column, do the same for adverb clauses. In the third column, write the first and last words of each noun clause and, in parentheses, a word telling how it is used. Number your answers. For the first sentence you should write:

1. *who us (man)* | *When arrived (explained)* | *what Ed (object)*
1. When Mildred and I arrived, a man who recognized us explained what had happened to Ed.
2. Although I was standing only ten feet away, I couldn't hear what Monica said to the clerk.
3. The fact that Clyde was careless about his appearance annoyed me more than it did the rest of the girls in the office.
4. The children that live in our neighborhood ride to school with Mother when it rains or snows.
5. What Steve does with his money is no mystery to the people who know of his many contributions to charity.

6. Though the men searched the house from top to bottom, no one discovered the secret place where Clark had hidden the map.
7. The instructions Keith enclosed were so complicated that we could not follow them.
8. If you see Don this evening, ask him where he put the money we collected for the party.
9. While I stood there, wondering what I should do to help, Ernest dashed down to the basement to turn off the water.
10. The girls who lived next door helped Phil with his Latin translation whenever he was stuck on a hard passage.

Improving sentences
19. Use a complex sentence

In the preceding Unit you have learned to combine related sentences by using adjective clauses, by using noun clauses, and by using adverb clauses. Now you will see how subordinate clauses of different kinds may be used to combine a group of related sentences. Here, for example, are three sentences that are related in meaning:

> A circus travels all summer. Then it has to rest during the winter. Many people don't understand this.

By means of a noun clause and an adjective clause, the relationship can be made much clearer:

> Many people don't understand that a circus which travels all summer must rest during the winter.

There is no hard and fast rule for using subordinate clauses to combine sentences. Notice this next group of three sentences:

> The boys had hidden my hat. But I found it. They will never understand how.

By subordinating different ideas, you can combine the sentences in different ways:

> The boys who hid my hat will never understand how I found it.
> How I ever found my hat is something that the boys who hid it will never understand.

Occasionally groups of four or more related sentences may be combined by using different kinds of subordinate clauses. For example, here are four sentences that are related in meaning:

> The plane was long overdue. Mary soon heard about it. Right away she called Mr. Lewis. He works at the airport.

Using three kinds of subordinate clauses, you can combine the four separate sentences into one:

> As soon as Mary heard that the plane was long overdue, she called Mr. Lewis, who works at the airport.

More often you will find that subordinate clauses may be used along with other ways of combining sentences. Here, for instance, are five related sentences:

> Finally the posse reached the crossroads. The holdup had occurred there. The men split up into small groups. They spread out in different directions. They were looking for footprints.

While these sentences could be combined by using three or four subordinate clauses, a better sentence can be made by using only one:

> Finally reaching the crossroads where the holdup had occurred, the posse split up into small groups and spread out in different directions to look for footprints.

EXERCISE 4. Read the sentences in each group, and decide how they are related. Then change the group into a good complex sentence, using one or more subordinate clauses and any of the other ways you have learned. Be prepared to read your revised sentences aloud. For the first group you might say: *When the men returned, they pitched the tents and started the campfire.*

1. The men returned later. They pitched the tents. Then they started the campfire.
2. Louis was standing near the cage. He was trying to persuade the canary to sing. At the same time Miss Ralston was watching him in the mirror. This hung over the mantel.
3. No one lived in the house. Mike had told me that. Yet I saw a face peering out of the attic window.
4. Liza heard footsteps outside her door. She quickly hid the candy bar. She had smuggled the candy bar into her room that afternoon. Then she pretended to be fast asleep.

5. Henry was lying. I was certain of this. But I didn't like to say so in front of Miss Porter. She would have fired him immediately.
6. Nora apologized to Mrs. Quinn for Bobby's rudeness. Then she stamped angrily out to the porch. Bobby was playing there with his friends. Then she ordered him to come into the house.
7. Diggens spent very little time in his room. And so he thought it unfair of Mrs. Taylor to charge him an extra dollar for the use of the radio.
8. I saw Horace open the front door. Right away I signaled the rest of the fellows. They were stationed behind the picket fence. They were armed with snowballs.
9. Smithers was being followed. He realized this. So he walked faster. He hoped to lose himself in the crowds on Broadway.
10. I was tiptoeing out of the kitchen. My arms were loaded with food. Just then Mother walked in.

Parts of complex and compound sentences

You have learned that a complex sentence consists of one main clause and one or more subordinate clauses. You have seen that a subordinate clause is a group of words that contains a subject and a verb and is used as a single word in a sentence. Now you are to review the three kinds of subordinate clauses and the ways in which they are used.

Adjective clauses are ordinarily introduced by relative pronouns (*who, whose, whom, which, that*) or relative adverbs (*when, where*) and are used like adjectives to modify nouns or pronouns, the antecedents to which the relatives refer. In the first ten sentences the adjective clauses are italicized. Be prepared to tell the noun or pronoun each modifies:

1. The Dunnigans lived in a ramshackle old house *which was badly in need of paint.*
2. Anything *Bob does* is well done, according to his mother.
3. Lisa was slender and looked rather like the models *that you see on the covers of fashion magazines.*
4. About thirty yards beyond the house was a shed painted an ugly yellow, *where Uncle Tim kept all his tools.*
5. On the days *when classes did not meet,* the children gathered in the playroom for games.

142

6. Dorothy was frantic on learning that the suitcase *in which she had packed her party dress* had been lost on the way to the Crandalls'.
7. Dick was learning to fly a plane at a time *when most boys are satisfied with bicycles and motorcycles*.
8. Uncle Andy, *whose bad temper was no joke,* bellowed his disapproval, pounding on the table with a heavy fist.
9. At that time there were only two families on our block *who had television sets*.
10. Pat Hill, *to whom we sent a last-minute invitation,* refused to come.

Noun clauses may have any of the uses that a noun has: They may be used as subjects, predicate nominatives, appositives, objects of prepositions, of verbs, or of verbals. Unlike the relatives that introduce adjective clauses, the words that introduce noun clauses (*that, whether, if, who, whom, whose, how, why, where, which, what,* etc.) do not have antecedents. In the next ten sentences the noun clauses are italicized. Be prepared to tell how each is used:

11. Why do you worry about *what Gertrude will say?*
12. If Phil had known at the time *who Mrs. Ekert was,* he wouldn't have told her about our skipping school.
13. Kermit slipped off his shoes and tiptoed up the stairs, hoping against hope *that his father wouldn't wake up*.
14. Milly sat at the desk, a scowl on her face, trying desperately to remember *where she had put the tickets*.
15. The only question in my mind was *whether we could find a house big enough for his whole family*.
16. *Why anyone would want to steal Aunt Lizzie's portrait* was a mystery to all of us.
17. Carson was busy putting up screens, but he said *he'd help us later*.
18. Though Jim tried, he could not get rid of the feeling *that his every move was being observed*.
19. Can you tell me *whose hat is on the hall table?*
20. It will be a miracle *if Terry ever speaks to me again*.

Adverb clauses are introduced by subordinating conjunctions (*after, before, unless, if, while, that, as, than, because, since, though, when,* etc.) and are used like adverbs to modify verbs, verbals, adjectives, and adverbs. In the next ten sentences the adverb clauses are italicized. Be prepared to tell what word each modifies:

21. I ran up to my room, slammed the door, and stayed there *until I saw Dr. Roberts leave.*
22. Mr. Murphy, the principal, sounded so angry *that I was afraid to explain my version of the incident.*
23. No one would have noticed Dirk's absence *if Aunt Martha hadn't suggested counting noses.*
24. *As the footsteps came closer,* Laura grew more frightened.
25. I heartily disliked Aunt Abby *because she had once called me "an ugly, skinny child."*
26. *Though Kathleen was alone in the gloomy old house,* she wasn't the least bit afraid.
27. Billy is a nuisance, causing trouble *wherever he goes.*
28. Joe grabbed a handful of cookies and scrambled away as fast *as he could.*
29. *Since she had promised to go to the game,* Jane came with me; but she grumbled all the way.
30. Before leaving the house, Mother warned me to put the matches *where the baby could not reach them.*

You have seen how two or more sentences may be made into a compound sentence. The coördinate clauses may be joined by a coördinating conjunction (*and, but, for, yet, or, nor*); or, if clearly related in meaning, they may simply have a semicolon between them. Each of the next five sentences is a compound sentence. Be prepared to tell the subject and verb of the coördinate clauses in each sentence:

31. My oldest brother, Corwin, and Bill Buxton, who was visiting in Plainview that summer, knew next to nothing about radar; yet they posed as experts, using as many big words as they could.
32. It was easy enough to make out a long list of New Year's resolutions; it was almost impossible to keep them.
33. There was a long moment of silence while we waited, wondering what would happen next: and then into the room, stooping a little as he came through the low door, walked a tall, gaunt, white-haired man, carrying a heavy case covered with steamship labels.
34. Clinton and Bud, who had ducked into one of the stalls, quickly realized that they were trapped; for Tod Evans, the hired man, had come to feed the horses and would find them as soon as he reached that end of the barn.

144

35. Whispering in class and reading comic books when you should be translating Latin or working algebra problems are not the best ways to make friends and influence teachers; but Wendell, disappointed because he hadn't made the football team, didn't seem to care.

EXERCISE 5. *A Seven-Carat Diamond:* Write a coherent paragraph that contains the following sentence order: 1. simple 2. compound 3. complex 4. compound-complex (two or more main clauses, one or more subordinate clauses) 5. complex 6. compound 7. simple. Note the diamond-like symmetry of the paragraph structure in this assignment. Your paragraph should hold together. It can even be funny or beautiful.

Improving sentences
20. Avoid the deadly "so" and the tiresome "and"

The deadly "so"

One hundred years ago the word *so* was almost always considered an independent adverb, like *therefore* and *consequently*. It began a sentence or followed a semicolon:

> Mother seemed quite satisfied with my explanation. *So* I said nothing further.
> It will be much colder before night; *so* be sure to take along plenty of warm clothing.

A *so* beginning a sentence or following a semicolon is a dignified and respectable word.

Today, however, the word *so* is commonly considered a conjunction, like *and* or *but*. It frequently joins coördinate clauses in compound sentences, as in the following examples:

> These small shells tell something about how petroleum was formed, so geologists study them very carefully.
> Jim had lived in Nicaragua a long time, so he could tell us all about banana plantations.

Modern periodicals and books provide many examples of *so* as a conjunction with the meaning of "therefore as a result." But in schools this little word has become a pest through constant overuse. It infests compositions and twists student thinking into the shape of "Something was true, *so* something else was true." It is like a microbe that causes a perpetual epidemic of *so-itis*. It is deadly.

There is, of course, nothing particularly deadly about an occasional *so* between coördinate clauses. But many students use "so" sentences constantly. They can hardly keep up a conversation without using *so* in every other sentence. Their habit produces monotony. And it is this monotony that makes *so* deadly. For example, students often write sentences like these:

> Everybody was watching him closely, *so* he had to be careful.
> The elephant has tremendous strength, *so* it can pull very heavy loads with ease.
> The price was higher than advertised, *so* Mother refused to buy the cashmere sweater.
> The plate had been badly nicked, *so* we threw it away.
> Taylor studied very hard, *so* he always made good grades.
> The winding streets confused me, *so* I soon lost my way.

A student who knows about subordinate clauses can think of many ways of avoiding monotonous "so" sentences. Here are a few of the ways he might use:

> Everybody was watching him closely, *so that he had to be careful.*
> The elephant has *such* tremendous strength *that it can pull very heavy loads with ease.*
> *When Mother learned that the price was higher than advertised,* she refused to buy the cashmere sweater.
> We threw away the plate *that had been badly nicked.*
> *Since Taylor studied very hard,* he always made good grades.
> *Because the winding streets confused me,* I soon lost my way.

A student who knows about verbals can think of other ways of avoiding monotonous "so" sentences:

> *With everybody watching him closely,* he had to be careful.
> The elephant, *having tremendous strength,* can pull very heavy loads with ease.

146

On learning that the price was higher than advertised, Mother refused to buy the cashmere sweater.

We threw away the *badly nicked* plate.

By studying very hard, Taylor always made good grades.

Confused by the winding streets, I soon lost my way.

These are some of the common ways of curing *so-itis.* You will no doubt think of still other ways as you learn to watch for deadly *so* in your own sentences. Use whichever way seems most natural to you. The important thing is to avoid the deadly monotony caused by overusing *so.*

EXERCISE 6. Read the sentences, and decide how they can be changed to get rid of *so* between coördinate clauses. Use as many different ways as you can. Be prepared to read your revised sentences aloud. For the first sentence you might say: *Wanting to learn his tricks, we watched him closely.*

1. We wanted to learn his tricks, so we watched him closely.
2. Dad was busy reading, so he didn't realize Jim had sneaked out.
3. We were told that nobody had been hurt, so the ladies began to chat about the scenery again.
4. Captain Dobbs knows more about the weather signs than anybody else in town, so you had better consult him.
5. Some of the statues in the gallery were found to be counterfeit, so the director was deeply disturbed.
6. We had called the doctor twice before during the night, so we hated to disturb him a third time.
7. A special switch controls the lights, so they cannot be turned on without the owner's key.
8. We searched in the pasture for half an hour without finding any mushrooms, so we decided that Ross had been joking.
9. The blinds will have to be painted before long anyhow, so I don't see the use of delaying.
10. Her voice sounded much cheerier when I saw her next, so I knew her son was better.

The tiresome "and"

In Unit 3 you learned that *and* often joins coördinate clauses in compound sentences. Useful as they are for showing that a pair of related sentences are of equal importance, these "and" sentences produce a tiresome singsong effect when used in sentence after sentence. In many compositions *and,* like *so,* becomes a pest—and for the same reason: it causes monotony.

A trained writer avoids monotony by using "and" sentences infrequently and consciously; but students use them constantly and thoughtlessly. Most tiresome is their habit of using *and* to join coördinate clauses that have subjects meaning the same thing or person:

> My uncle's house is a huge old-fashioned brick structure with many gables, and *it* has over twenty rooms.
>
> Mother was curious about my new teachers, and *she* asked me many questions about them.
>
> Bill and I stood by the door of the gymnasium, and *we* counted every person who entered.
>
> Tom ran all the way to the station, and *he* got there just as the train was pulling in.
>
> The raft was made of rough logs about ten feet long, and *it* had a single steering oar at one end.
>
> The boys had hiked the whole way to camp, and *they* arrived there hungry as bears.

Such sentences are monotonous to read. They can be improved by using compound verbs, omitting the italicized pronouns and dropping the comma before *and.* Or the sentences can be further improved by using appositives and participles and gerunds to get rid of the *and:*

> My uncle's house, *a huge old-fashioned brick structure with many gables,* has over twenty rooms.
>
> Mother, *curious about my new teachers,* asked me many questions about them.
>
> Bill and I stood by the door of the gymnasium, *counting every person who entered.*
>
> *By running all the way to the station,* Tom got there just as the train was pulling in.
>
> The raft, *made of rough logs about ten feet long,* had a single steering oar at one end.
>
> *Having hiked the whole way to camp,* the boys arrived there hungry as bears.

Students sometimes use *and* to join clauses that are not of equal importance. For example:

148

The manager of the store has but one ambition, and *that* is to show a profit every month.

She was always guided by one principle, and *this* was that differences of opinion could be settled by discussion.

He peered at me through thick lenses, and *these* were mounted in a heavy black frame that made him look like an owl.

Ned is working his way through school, and *I* think you might give him a helping hand.

The boat rocked gently with the waves, and its *mast* swayed to and fro like an inverted pendulum.

In these sentences the subjects of the two clauses are different, making it impossible to use compound verbs. But there are other ways of showing the relationship between the two ideas in each sentence. Here are a few:

The manager of the store has but one ambition—*to show a profit every month.*

She was always guided by the principle *that differences of opinion could be settled by discussion.*

He peered at me through thick lenses, *which were mounted in a heavy black frame that made him look like an owl.*

Since Ned is working his way through school, I think you might give him a helping hand.

The boat rocked gently with the waves, *its mast swaying to and fro like an inverted pendulum.*

These are some of the common ways of getting rid of tiresome *and.* No doubt you will think of other ways as you learn to avoid the monotony caused by using too many compound sentences in your talking and writing.

EXERCISE 7. Read the sentences, and decide how they can be changed to get rid of tiresome *and* between coördinate clauses. Use as many different ways as you can. Be prepared to read your revised sentences aloud. For the first sentence you might say: *Hogan, drawing his breath in slowly, took time to think before answering our questions.*

1. Hogan drew his breath in slowly, and he took time to think before answering our questions.
2. The roadway was cut through a grove of tall trees, and it looked exactly like a tunnel.

3. Ty Johnson was very nervous, and he failed to make a hit during the entire game.
4. Clifford had eaten no food for forty-eight hours, and he had had almost nothing to drink.
5. Dan's uncle is a wealthy real estate agent, and he offered us his cottage at Silver Lake for two weeks.
6. The opening of school has been postponed two weeks, and this is very lucky for me.
7. The workman wore a flashy diamond ring, and he had found it in an automobile he was repairing.
8. Mary had only one desire, and that was to be elected class president.
9. Ferdinand's wages had been increased, and he was now earning six dollars a day.
10. Nancy's costume was copied from a picture in *Seventeen,* and it won the first prize in the contest.

Improving sentences: Twenty ways you have learned

1. Ask a question	11 Use an active participle
2. Use a command	12. Use a passive participle
3. Choose exact modifiers	13. Use a gerund
4. Begin with an adverb	14. Use an infinitive
5. Begin with a preposition	15. Use a direct quotation
6. Use a compound verb	16. Use an adjective clause
7. Avoid unnecessary words	17. Use a noun clause
8. Begin with an object	18. Use an adverb clause
9. Use an active verb	19. Use a complex sentence
10. Use an appositive	20. Avoid the deadly "so" and the tiresome "and"

These are the twenty ways you have learned for improving sentences. Some of the ways enable you to avoid the monotony of too many subject-first sentences by varying the word order. Others make it possible for you to get rid of weak explanatory sentences by combining sentences that are related in meaning. Still others help you improve your expression by using words effectively. These three uses— the means to better sentences—are the secret of successful revision. By grouping the twenty ways under their three uses, you will find them easier to remember:

150

Ways of varying word order
    Ask a question (Unit 1)
    Use a command (Unit 1)
    Begin with an adverb (Unit 2)
    Begin with a preposition (Unit 3)
    Begin with an object (Unit 4)
Ways of combining sentences
    Use of compound verb (Unit 3)
    Use an appositive (Unit 4)
    Use an active participle (Unit 5)
    Use a passive participle (Unit 5)
    Use a gerund (Unit 5)
    Use an infinitive (Unit 5)
    Use an adjective clause (Unit 7)
    Use a noun clause (Unit 7)
    Use an abverb clause (Unit 7)
Ways of using words effectively
    Choose exact modifiers (Unit 3)
    Avoid unnecessary words (Unit 4)
    Use an active verb (Unit 4)
    Use a direct quotation (Unit 5)
    Use a complex sentence (Unit 7)
    Avoid the deadly "'so" and the tiresome "and" (Unit 7)

Whenever you revise sentences of your own—and that should be every time you have anything of importance to express in writing—you will find opportunities to apply what you have learned about improving sentences. The twenty ways are merely reminders to help you eliminate monotony and childish sentences and careless expression from your writing. You have the means to better sentences in your possession. If through constant revision you make intelligent use of the means, you will be well on your way to the goal—the writing of clear, forceful, interesting sentences that effectively communicate your thoughts to others.

EXERCISE 8. The following paragraphs tell about a cat that would not change his home. Rewrite the story, improving the sentences wherever there is an opportunity to do so easily and naturally. Use any of the ways you have learned, but do not try to use them all. Make the sentences as clear, forceful, and interesting as you can.

(1) We moved from our old home at Orange. (2) The new place was about five miles away. (3) We took Tom along in a box. (4) Tom was our cat. (5) We were afraid. (6) Tom might run away. (7) We kept him inside for a week. (8) We fed him. (9) We petted him. (10) This was to make him like his new home. (11) We let him go outside one morning. (12) He almost immediately disappeared. (13) My sister went all over the neighborhood. (14) Her name is Claire. (15) She called, "Tom, Tom!" (16) she found no sign of him. (17) I said that I bet he had gone back to Orange. (18) Claire and my mother thought this was impossible. (19) I was sure that Tom was already at Orange, however. (20) I was sure that he was now mewing around our old house. (21) Claire went to Orange. (22) She found Tom there. (23) She brought him back in a basket. (24) His paws were coated with red clay. (25) The weather was dry. (26) There was no mud. (27) Tom must have got wet crossing the river. (28) He had crossed fields of dry, red dirt. (29) His wet paws had moistened the dirt. (30) Some had stuck to his paws. (31) Tom was confined to the house again. (32) We kept him there for two weeks this time. (33) We let him go out, finally. (34) He disappeared again. (35) Twenty-four hours passed by. (36) He was back at Orange once more. (37) We accepted the fact. (38) It was useless to try to keep him. (39) I saw a former neighbor of mine at Orange sometime later. (40) He told me that he had seen Tom one day. (41) Tom was hiding behind a hedge. (42) He had a young rabbit in his mouth. (43) Tom had become a hunter. (44) He killed chickens in farmyards. (45) These yards were near our old home. (46) We never heard of him again. (47) He came to a bad end, no doubt. (48) He had become a robber. (49) He met with a robber's fate probably.

EXERCISE 9. The following paragraphs tell about the destruction of a pagoda by an enraged elephant, named Asoka. The pagoda, a towering temple, had been mounted on an old truck for a religious festival and was being driven through the streets of a fictitious town in India. Each sentence begins with subject and verb. Rewrite the story, improving the sentences whenever there is an opportunity to do so easily and naturally. You will find a number of chances to use good compound sentences, but not so many as you might think. For example, in combining the first two sentences, you would not say "was gilded, and it was"; you would use a pair of predicate adjectives after *was*. Notice the opportunities for parallel infinitives in 18-21. Remember the other verbals and the appositives. Use any of the other ways you have learned. Try to make the sentences as clear, forceful, and interesting as you can.

(1) The Hindu priest's truck was gilded. (2) It was much more enormous than any circus wagon. (3) A great pagoda teetered and trembled above the body of the truck. (4) It towered above the eaves of the little houses. (5) The priest and his assistants were concealed inside the pagoda. (6) A dozen attendants were on the outside of it. (7) They were beating gongs and drums. (8) They were ringing bells.

(9) There was no muffler on the exhaust. (10) Flame and foul smoke belched out behind. (11) They stung the sensitive membranes of Asoka's trunk. (12) Asoka determined to slay the abominable thing. (13) He rushed at it.

(14) His great head crashed against the rear end of the gilded mystery on wheels. (15) The sacred engine backfired with a noise like a rifle. (16) It scorched Asoka. (17) He screamed. (18) He tried to drive his tusks into the horrible thing. (19) He tried to crack it. (20) He tried to crush it. (21) He tried to trample on it.

(22) There was a panic. (23) Owners of booths and shops rushed to get their awnings down. (24) They rushed to get their shutters up. (25) Yelling crowds poured out of the alleys.

(26) Asoka decided to attack the pagoda on the side then. This side was close to a shop front. (27) The shop front was full of crockery and cheap glass lanterns. (28) He jammed his shoulders between the truck and the shop. (29) A wall beam splintered like a piece of kindling. (30) Half a roof came crashing through the floor above the shop. (31) The wall collapsed inward then.

(32) He drove his weight against the side of the truck with all his might. (33) He overturned it. (34) He sent the pagoda thundering against the shop across the street. (35) The pagoda was crushed like an eggshell.

(36) The engine was ruined. (37) It was coughing and spraying gasoline now. (38) This ignited. (39) A thousand voices yelled, "Fire!" (40) The pagoda vanished in a ghastly veil of flame.

Telling What Something Means PART ONE: ORAL

Most of the words we use have fairly exact meanings that almost everyone understands. We can, for example, talk about automobiles, houses, animals, hobbies, athletics, vacations, and food without much danger of being misunderstood. But there are some words and expressions that often cause misunderstanding because their meanings are rather vague. When we try to talk about loyalty, faith, sophistication, democracy, success, friendship, and patriotism, we soon discover that others frequently disagree with us about the meaning of these terms.

We call such terms "abstractions" because they are names for ideas rather than things. When two or more people see a building, they can readily agree as to whether it is a house or a barn. But when two or more people see a person behave in a certain way, they may disagree completely as to whether the action is an example of courage or cowardice, of loyalty or treachery, of friendship or enmity. Just which term best names the action often depends more upon a personal opinion of what the terms mean than upon the action itself.

In telling what something means, you express an opinion, much as you do in telling what you like or dislike. But instead of giving reasons for your opinion, as you learned to do in Unit 10, you give examples to show exactly what you think something means. If someone asks you, "What is beauty?" you can, of course, look up the word in a dictionary. But a mere definition can never tell what beauty means to you. A better way is to give examples of several kinds: beauty in people, beauty in nature, beauty in art or music, and so on.

In preparing an oral composition in which you tell what something means, you need to think carefully about a suitable subject. You probably have not thought much about the meaning of the term *beauty*. But you may well have had experiences that made you think seriously about such terms as *true friendship, real loyalty, fair play, classroom dishonesty.*

When you have decided on a term to explain to your classmates, list all the examples you can think of that will show exactly what the term means to you. If you were planning a talk on what classroom dishonesty means, your list might look like this:

1. Copying answers from others' test papers
2. Giving answers whispered by others
3. Copying another person's homework
4. Reading comic books instead of studying when the teacher is out of the room
5. Reciting from answers written in the book
6. Talking or writing notes to others while the teacher is absent from the classroom
7. Looking at book during examinations
8. Reciting from translations written in the book
9. Getting help from others
10. Using concealed notes to answer questions

You could, of course, use such a list for your talk, but your listeners might be confused by the lack of organization. By studying the list carefully and thinking a bit about which items are related and which ones should be omitted, you could make a plan that would group related examples in a logical order:

During recitations, classroom dishonesty consists of—
  A. Using translations or answers written in the book.
  B. Giving answers whispered by others.
During examinations, classroom dishonesty consists of—
  A. Looking in the book for answers.
  B. Using concealed notes to answer questions.
  C. Copying answers from others' papers.
During the teacher's absence, classroom dishonesty consists of—
  A. Talking or writing notes to others.
  B. Reading comic books instead of studying.

The plan shows that there are three groups of related examples. The main headings show how the examples in each group are related. If you compare the plan with the list above it, you will notice that two items have been omitted and two have been combined. Item 3 was omitted because it has to do with work usually done outside the classroom. Item 9 was omitted because it is not an example but a general statement covering most of the other examples. Items 5 and 8 were combined because they are identical except for one word and both have to do with dishonesty during recitations. The italicized words *During recitations, During examinations,* and *During the teacher's absence* help the listener know when a new group begins, just as words like *first, second,* and *finally* do. Notice that the three main headings are expressed in similar ways.

Now look at the list of examples you made for your talk. Study each item carefully. Are there any items that should be omitted? How will you arrange the examples so that related items can be put in separate groups? Make a plan for your talk, arranging the groups in a logical order. Write a main heading for each group, showing how the examples in each group are related. Underline the words that help your listeners know when you are beginning a new group of examples.

How will you begin your talk? Will you use a question or a statement? When you have decided, add the special opening sentence to your plan. Ordinarily you will need no special closing sentence. It is almost always better to give your last example—and stop. Copy your plan on a card or a small piece of paper so that you can keep your notes in your hand as you practice your talk and as you give it. By referring to your notes, you can remember what your opening sentence is, what the main headings are, and what examples you planned to give under each. Having your notes in your hand gives you confidence and helps you make a good talk.

Telling What Something Means

PART TWO: WRITTEN

Now that you have prepared an oral composition in which you told what something means by giving examples, you are to prepare a written composition, using the notes you made for your talk.

The plan for your talk will show you how many paragraphs you should have in your written composition. You know that each group of related examples should be in a separate paragraph. The main heading of each group in your plan becomes the topic sentence that tells what each paragraph is about. And the examples listed under each main heading are the details used to develop the paragraph.

156

If your plan consists of two or more groups of related examples, each group telling in part what something means, the topic sentences of the paragraphs stand out more clearly when expressed in similar ways. For instance, in a composition telling what fair play means, the topic sentences might be:

> In sports, fair play depends on both the spectators and the players.
> In class, fair play depends on both the teacher and the students.
> At home, fair play depends on both the parents and the children.
> On the job, fair play depends on both the employer and the employees.

The expressions *In sports, In class, At home,* and *On the job* let the reader know when you are beginning another group of examples. Details arranged in a logical order are more easily understood when your topic sentences help the reader know your plan.

Now look at the notes you prepared for your oral composition in Part One. How many paragraphs will you use in writing your composition? Remember that your special opening sentence is the first sentence of your first paragraph. You do not need an "introductory" paragraph. And in telling what something means, you probably do not need a special closing sentence. Simply end with your last example.

Write your composition just as you planned to tell it in class, following your plan in order to keep related examples in separate paragraphs. Be sure that each paragraph has a topic sentence to let the reader know how the examples in that paragraph are related. Use pencil and scratch paper for this first draft so that you can make changes and corrections easily. Try to write sentences that you think will interest your classmates, since you may be asked to read your composition aloud before turning it in.

Revise your first draft carefully, making corrections in spelling and punctuation, changing the order of words and phrases, crossing out unnecessary words or adding better ones until your sentences are as good as you can make them. Every time you revise a first draft carefully, you learn more about using words to express your own ideas effectively. Each opportunity to revise your own writing is a challenge to show how much you know about improving sentences. If you fail to meet this challenge, you are not learning how to write better compositions.

The simplest title for a composition in which you tell what something means is simply the subject of your composition. For instance, titles like the following are satisfactory:

Classroom Dishonesty   Intelligent Patriotism
Good Sportsmanship   Tolerance

Such titles are particularly suitable when your special opening sentence is a question. When it is a statement, you may want to use a title that will arouse the curiosity of your readers or attract their attention to what you have written. Titles of this sort may either ask a question or suggest what you are going to talk about. For instance, notice the following pairs of titles and compare them with the ones given above:

What Is Classroom Dishonesty?   Don't Look Now, But—
What Does Good Sportsmanship Mean?   What Price Glory?
Can Patriotism Be Intelligent?   My Country, Right or Wrong?
Tolerance for Whom?   A Day for the Underdog

What title will you use for your composition? Will you use a title that simply names the subject of your composition, or will you use one that arouses the interest of your readers? When you have selected a title that pleases you, copy your revised first draft in a form suitable for handing in. Write neatly and legibly. Indent the first word of each paragraph and keep margins even. Space words carefully.

When you have finished, proofread the final draft of your composition to catch any errors that you may have made in copying. Read it over carefully, word by word, watching carefully for words or final letters that have been omitted, for words that have been copied twice, for careless misspellings or omitted punctuation marks. Make corrections neatly.

If you are asked to read your composition to the class, read slowly and distinctly, keeping your eyes several words ahead of your voice. Try to read as naturally as you talk. When a classmate is reading his composition, listen carefully so that you can tell what you like about it and what you think might be improved.

Ending Sentences
and
Using Commas

Punctuating sentences accurately

When you write sentences, you know where they begin and end; but you cannot be sure that a person reading them will know unless you begin each sentence with a capital letter and end it with a period, a question mark, or an exclamation mark. Of course you learned to do this a long time ago, and it may seem so simple that you wonder how anyone would have trouble remembering it. The reason is that students sometimes become so interested in what they are writing about that they forget to show where one sentence ends and the next one begins.

Rule 1. **A sentence begins with a capital letter and ends with a period, a question mark, or an exclamation mark.**

> We are moving to Dallas tomorrow.
> Are you going to the game?
> What a fool he is!

The following exercise will show you how difficult it is to understand sentences that are run together without periods and capital letters. It will also give you an opportunity to show that you know the difference between one sentence and two sentences.

EXERCISE 1. Study the ten groups of words and decide whether each group is one, two, or three sentences. Show where each sentence begins and ends by writing the first and last words. Capitalize each first word. Put a period after each last word. Number your answers. For the first group you should write: *1. Father time. Prices season.*

1. Father never buys more than one basket at a time prices are too likely to drop later in the season
2. Norman had seldom been seen at parties dances bored him athletics were more to his liking
3. The cashier peered closely at the stranger that face seemed familiar
4. Mother answered the phone the call was for me
5. The drivers must have been going extremely fast the cars were both badly damaged
6. A minute before train time the agent closed his window one man at the end of the line never did get his ticket the train left without him
7. High overhead the airplanes roared past three to a group and with seemingly no end to the number of groups in the formation
8. The old books must have been taken to the attic the magazines were given to the Scouts for their wastepaper collection
9. The workbench was littered with tools of every kind and with boxes of rusty screws and nails left over from previous projects
10. During the hot weather the weeds flourished the grass was slowly dying in spite of all his hard work

EXERCISE 2. Read the paragraph and decide where the sentences begin and end, but do not put any marks in the book. Five of the sentences are questions. On a sheet of paper, write the first word and the last word of each sentence. Capitalize the first word. Put a period or a question mark after the last word. Number your answers and arrange them in a column. Your first answer should be: *1. One California.*

One sunny day I was walking along the shore of the Pacific Ocean in southern California I was on a railroad this ran along the face of a high cliff the track was fifty feet above the beach I had a clear view out over many miles of the blue sea about a mile from shore was a broad belt of brown seaweed something at the inner edge of the seaweed caught my eye it was a black object about six feet high moving rather rapidly have you ever seen a snake swimming in a pond its head swings with a quick swaying motion this animal looked like that it seemed smooth and shiny what could it have been could it have been the head of a seal it rose too high for that could it possibly have·been a pelican or a shark I had plenty of time to watch its motions closely it was absolutely unlike anything but the neck of a big snake I have never had any faith in the idea of a sea serpent what could that animal have been

Comma for series

Most punctuation is based upon a simple principle: "Separate the parts that are not closely connected in meaning." In this lesson you will see how this principle applies to a series of distinct items that are of equal importance.

Rule 2. **Words used as distinct items in a series are separated by commas.**

> One day a huge, swarthy, piratical fellow came to the door.
> We set sail on a gray, damp, chilly morning.

In the first sentence you know that the fellow was huge *and* swarthy *and* piratical. In the second sentence you know that the morning was gray *and* damp *and* chilly. In each sentence there is a series of distinct items—three adjectives modifying a noun, and all equally important. When the connecting *and*'s are omitted, commas are used to separate the items so that a reader can tell at once that the items are distinct and of equal importance. Notice that there is no comma between *piratical* and *fellow,* or between *chilly* and *morning;* commas are not needed between parts that are closely related in meaning.

When adjectives preceding a noun are closely connected in meaning, no commas are needed. Look at the following sentences:

> A queer old codger got off the train.
> Tom lives in an ugly brown shingle house.

In the first sentence you know that the old codger was queer. In the second sentence you know that the brown shingle house was ugly. If there were commas after *ugly* and *brown,* you would know that the house was ugly *and* brown *and* shingle; but this would not sound much like English unless this house was being compared with another one that was different in all three ways, as in the following sentence:

> Tom moved from an ugly, brown, shingle house to a beautiful, white, brick house.

Ordinarily the first adjective in a series is the most prominent, and receives the most emphasis. Putting a comma after it indicates to the reader that the next one is equally important and should receive the same emphasis, and so on. For example, read to yourself the following:

> a huge, swarthy, piratical fellow
> a gray, damp, chilly morning

Now read to yourself:

> a queer old codger
> an ugly brown shingle house

Can you see the difference between the following sentences?

> He wrote a thrilling short story.
> He wrote a short, thrilling story.

When you write two or more adjectives before a noun or a pronoun, use commas between them only when you want the reader to know that you consider them of equal importance. Each comma calls attention to the importance of the adjective that follows it.

The general principle of separating items of equal importance applies to words of any kind that might be joined by *and* or *or*:

> The visitors were impressed by the wide streets, the tall buildings, the many beautiful parks.
> A careful driver does not exceed the speed limit, pass on hills and curves, cut in and out of traffic lanes.

The commas separate the distinct items of equal importance in the series. Ordinarily no commas are needed when all the items of the series are connected by *and* or *or*:

> He was peevish and irritable and generally disagreeable.
> Laura doesn't like golf or tennis or bowling.

But when *and* or *or* is used between the last two items only, a comma should be used before it. Notice the sentences below:

> The coach, the players, and the spectators were thoroughly soaked by the end of the game.
> Swiftly, smoothly, and tirelessly the great plane roared on.
> You must accept the offer, reject it, or name a sum yourself.

The comma is used before the final *and* or *or* to make it clear to a reader that each item is distinct and of the same importance as the others, and that they are all used alike. If no comma is used, the series looks like $x + (y + z)$. We want it to look like $x + y + z$. While periodicals do not always follow this practice, many careful writers

162

and most schools prefer a comma before the final *and* or *or* in a series.

EXERCISE **3.** Most of the sentences below need commas to separate words in series. All need end marks. Decide what punctuation is needed for each sentence. Then write the numbers of the sentences. After each number, put the punctuation marks needed in that sentence and the word preceding each mark. For the first sentence you should write: *1. on, here, home.*

1. I don't care whether I go on stay here or return home
2. He is an author a journalist and an editor
3. It is divided into British Guiana Dutch Guiana and French Guiana
4. Jerry was a hot-headed reckless unreliable fellow
5. Can you add to your list a bottle of olives a jar of strawberry preserves and a carton of matches
6. Then Grabo returned to his chair drew in his breath deeply and filled his pipe for a smoke
7. The other day a man walked into a barber shop deposited upon a table a number of articles and arranged them with artistic care
8. Is it better to use a grindstone a whetstone or a hone
9. Books magazines bills pages of old letters and a lot of photographs were jumbled in a pile on the table
10. He was patient full of kindness and tender with the invalids

Setting off words with commas

A writer may make good sentences; but if he uses commas incorrectly in them, he spoils his work. His composition looks like a good suit of clothes that is spattered with mud. For at each place where a mistake is made, the reader is distracted by the carelessness of the writer. He feels as if he were looking at dirty spots. He is offended at the writer's lack of pride in his work. Pay attention to the punctuation lessons, and your compositions will be read with more interest.

The two rules in this lesson are easy. You have probably known them for several years. They are reviewed here to remind you that from now on you will be expected to use all your knowledge in all your written work.

Notice the italicized words and the commas in these sentences:

Do you see, *my boy*?
No, samples are given free.

In these two sentences the words at the end and at the beginning that are not closely connected in meaning are separated from the other words by commas. If there were no commas to keep those words apart from the other words, you would suppose the sentences meant "Do you see my boy?" and "No samples are given free." The italicized words separated from the other words by commas are said to be "set off."

A word at the end of a sentence may be set off by putting a comma before it. A word at the beginning of a sentence may be set off by putting a comma after it. Otherwise *two* commas are always needed—one before and one after the word—to set it off.

Rule 3. **A noun of address is set off by commas.**

> *William,* whose hat is that?
> Please come here, *Mother.*
> Do you think, my dear *sir,* that I am a beggar?

Rule 4. ***Yes*** **and** *no* **are set off by commas.**

> *Yes,* you may go to the library.
> *No,* you have too much work to do.

An exclamatory word that expresses only mild feeling is usually followed by a comma instead of an exclamation point:

> *Oh,* how I hate rainy weather.
> *Well,* I didn't expect to find you here.
> *Why,* I suppose you may.

EXERCISE 4. All punctuation marks have been omitted from the sentences below. Decide where the necessary commas, periods, question marks, and exclamation marks should go. Then write the numbers of the sentences. After each number, put the punctuation marks needed in that sentence and the word preceding each mark. Do not use any commas except for the definite reasons given in this lesson. Guessing at commas is worse than omitting them. For the first sentence you should write: *1. Why, rascal, you?*

1. Why you impudent rascal how dare you
2. No you must not go until you see the green light
3. Surely Dean this repair bill is too high
4. Yes he will do as well as Captain Holt

164

5. Isn't there some mistake General
6. What have you done you silly fool
7. I congratulate you on your fine speech Harold
8. Do you want to come along Joe and practice with us
9. Boy what a narrow escape that was for us
10. Can you hear the village clock striking Mabel

Commas for addresses and dates

Rule 5. The second and all following items in addresses and dates are set off by commas.

For the last five years she has lived at 4202 Westminster Boulevard, Seattle, Washington.
After March 12, 1977, his address will be Vancleave, Jackson Co., Mo., until further notice.
Walt Whitman was born at West Hills, Long Island, New York, in May, 1819.

There are no commas between *March* and *12* or *4202* and *Westminster Boulevard,* because the figures and the names together are thought of as single items. *Co.* and *Mo.* are abbreviations; notice that periods after them precede the commas. When the abbreviation comes at the end of the sentence only one mark is used, except in a question:

Her new address is 332 Lake St., Kankakee, Ill.
How long has he been in Washington, D. C.?

In an address at the head of a letter or on an envelope, commas are not needed at the ends of the lines and are now usually omitted:

Mr. Eli W. Custer   Mr. Hartley Ellis, Jr.
27 Carolus St.   32 Harrison Street
Rochester, N. Y.   Milwaukee, Wisconsin

EXERCISE 5. Except for periods after abbreviations all punctuation marks have been omitted from the sentences. Decide where the necessary commas, periods, and question marks should go. Then write the numbers of the sentences. After each number, put all the punctuation marks needed in that sentence and the word preceding each mark. For the first sentence you should write: *1. Detroit, Michigan, Cheyenne, Wyoming, Ogden, Utah.*

1. We set our watches back at Detroit Michigan at Cheyenne Wyoming and at Ogden Utah
2. Please address me at 17 Grove Street Wheeling West Virginia until further notice
3. He died on April 14 1948 in Libertyville Iowa after a long illness
4. On May 14 a most interesting boat race was held at Tampa Florida
5. Mrs. Ainley died at Economy Pennsylvania Dec. 25 1946
6. He was born at Brattleboro Vermont Sept. 8 1811 and died at Niagara Falls Canada April 13 1886
7. On the outskirts of Concord Massachusetts on April 19 1775 the fearless yeomanry met the British
8. Many letters directed to Bloomington Ill. are sent to Bloomington Ind.
9. On Nov. 10 1728 at Pallas Ireland Oliver Goldsmith was born
10. Does he live in Springfield Missouri or Springfield Illinois

Commas for parenthetical words

You already know that commas are used to set off words that are not closely connected in meaning with the other words in a sentence. Notice the italicized words in the following sentences:

> Nancy had to report after school, *too.*
> *For example,* the water pressure may be too low.
> The rain will continue, *it seems,* for several days.

The italicized words in these sentences are called **parenthetical** because they merely add an explanatory comment or side remark. They are set off to show the reader that they are not closely connected in meaning with the other words in the sentence.

Rule 6. **Parenthetical words are set off by commas.**

When adverbs such as *however, though, indeed, then, nevertheless, perhaps, surely* are parenthetical, they are set off:

> There is, *however,* something to be said for the other side.
> He won't care, *though,* in a case like this.
> *Indeed,* I am quite happy about the whole matter.
> He will, *perhaps,* be able to help you.

When phrases such as *of course, in the first place, in fact, after all, by the way* are parenthetical, they are set off:

John, *of course,* was late again.
In the first place, many of the statements are incorrect.
He is, *in fact,* her only cousin.

Etc., and so forth, and so on are usually parenthetical. But remember that no word is in itself parenthetical. No rule can say, for example, that the words *perhaps* and *indeed* are always set off. The rule can only say that when *perhaps* and *indeed* are used parenthetically, they are set off. When *perhaps* and *indeed* are closely connected in meaning with the words they modify, they are not set off:

Perhaps you would like to join us.
This is *indeed* a surprise.
However late you are, be sure to phone me.
Our team is no longer *in the first place.*

EXERCISE 6. All punctuation marks have been omitted from the sentences below. Decide where the necessary commas, periods, and question marks should go. Then write the numbers of the sentences. After each number, put the punctuation marks needed in that sentence and the word preceding each mark. For the first sentence you should write: *1. time, course, dance.*

1. I lost no time of course in telling Mother all about the dance
2. I managed however to turn the slippery corner without skidding
3. Bob I hope has the tickets
4. A typewritten letter to be sure is much easier to read
5. By the way have you time to look for that letter
6. Parsons strangely enough had not heard us come in
7. A beggar for example may earn thirty or forty dollars a day
8. In the second place basketball is the most important of the winter sports
9. Arrange your program however you please
10. Why by the way was he given the car

Setting off appositives

You have learned about appositives that explain or add to the meaning of some other word in a sentence. Because the appositive and the words modifying it—an **appositive phrase**—are not an essential part of the sentence, they are set off from the other words.

Rule 7. An appositive, together with its modifiers, is set off from the rest of the sentence.

Ordinarily commas are used to set off the appositive:

> Last June we spent two weeks at Highfield, *a mountain resort.*
> *A country of strange contrasts,* Yucatan has many ancient ruins and many miles of modern railroads.
> Franklin Delano Roosevelt, *the thirty-second president of the United States,* died in 1945 at Warm Springs, Georgia.

When the appositive phrase is last in the sentence, a comma precedes it. When the appositive phrase is first in the sentence, a comma follows it. Otherwise *two* commas are needed, one before the appositive phrase and one after it.

Sometimes dashes are used to set off the appositive. Because dashes are conspicuous marks, they are generally used only (1) when several appositives are separated by commas or the appositive phrase itself has commas in it or (2) when you wish to call attention to appositives that would ordinarily be set off with commas:

> Certain other exports—*grain, cotton, oil, and lumber*—become very important in time of war.
> Nearly 18,000,000 pounds of rubber—*that is, over a third of the total quantity imported*—were used for boots and shoes.

> Last week Tom read two full-length novels—*a record for him.*
> One thing I have no use for—*overshoes.*

Appositives that are not set off

The appositives you have studied have been those used to explain or add to the meaning of another word. There are other appositives that help identify another word by limiting or restricting its meaning. Notice the following:

the poet Milton	my son John
the word *bronco*	his uncle Charles
the poem "Chicago"	William the Conqueror

You can see that *Milton* tells exactly which poet is meant, *bronco* tells which word is meant, and *"Chicago"* tells exactly which poem is meant; the appositives restrict the meaning of *poet, word,* and *poem* to the only ones of their kind. In the same way, *John* tells which son and *Charles* tells which uncle are meant; the appositives limit the meaning of *son* and *uncle* to the ones whose names are John and Charles. And *Conqueror* is another name for only this one William; it restricts the meaning of *William* by telling exactly which one is meant. Appositives that help identify other words in this way are not set off by commas, because they are closely connected in meaning with the other words.

EXERCISE 7. Read each of the groups of words and decide whether it is one sentence or two sentences. Then look for appositives that need to be set off. On a sheet of paper, write the numbers of the groups and, after them, the first and last words of each sentence. Capitalize each first word. Put a period after each last word. Write the word preceding each comma or dash needed to set off an appositive. For the first group you should write: *1. There pause, anxiety. During breathe.*

1. There was a brief pause a minute of anxiety during this time we hardly dared to breathe
2. The next hour was a very anxious one a time of waiting and wondering without much hope
3. We noticed a sweetish smell in the air a scent like that of an ant hill on a hot day
4. The food served to the sailors on the *Dragon* and the *Hector* was exactly the same except for one item lemon juice every morning for the men on the *Dragon*
5. For his seventieth birthday the grandchildren gave him a beautiful and expensive gift a hand-carved mahogany screen with handsome leather panels at the top and hammered brass rings and corners
6. The table was set on the veranda it was a cheerless place on this damp, drizzly morning
7. Herman Voltz a professional photographer displayed his prize-winning photo a picture of a small boy at a window on a rainy day

Unit 8 Setting off Appositives 169

8. The most important attraction about the apartment on Fourth Street was the rental only twenty dollars per month
9. We had to take notes on the principal points in his lecture a long, rambling talk about the Caroline Islands
10. The natives offered us pieces of whalebone and bits of polished shells a practice very common in these island ports

Setting off nonrestrictive participial phrases

In the following sentence the participial phrase is very closely connected in meaning with the noun it modifies:

The car *coming around the corner* is Sidney's.

The phrase tells exactly which car is meant. Of all the cars in sight only the one "coming around the corner" is Sidney's. The participial phrase limits or restricts the meaning to one particular car and is called a **restrictive** phrase. Restrictive phrases are not set off from the words they modify. Now notice the following sentence:

Tommy, *coming around the corner,* fell off his bicycle.

Here the participial phrase is not needed to tell exactly which person fell off his bicycle. The name *Tommy* tells that. The phrase merely supplies an additional detail, explaining what Tommy was doing when he fell off. Since the phrase does not restrict the meaning of the word it modifies, it is called a **nonrestrictive** phrase. It is set off by commas to show that it merely adds an explanatory detail.

Rule 8. **Nonrestrictive participial phrases are set off from the rest of the sentence.**

Participial phrases at the beginning of sentences are always set off:

Catching sight of Mary, Jane ducked behind a post.
Flinging his arms around, Charles tried to keep from freezing.

Notice that the comma helps the reader know where the phrase ends and the main part of the sentence begins.

Because nominative absolutes are never closely connected in meaning with other words in the sentence, they are always set off:

The rain having stopped, the players returned to the field.
We soon left, the party being over.

170

EXERCISE 8. Read the groups of words, and decide whether each numbered group is one sentence or two sentences. Decide also where commas should be used to set off nonrestrictive phrases. On a sheet of paper, write the first and last words of each sentence. Capitalize each first word, and put a period after each last word. Always give the word preceding each comma. Number your answers, and arrange them in a column. For the first group you should write: *1. Nodding confidently, motor. He engines.*

1. Nodding confidently Archie started toward the motor he was pretending to know all about gasoline engines
2. A few days later Norman left Seattle slipping away without a word
3. He slammed his satchel down startling us half out of our wits
4. Bobby turned to his nurse trembling pitifully he told her of his dream
5. Tom rushed out of the attic screaming at the top of his lungs
6. David incensed by this remark refused to attend any more meetings
7. Angered by their repeated snubs Mona decided to teach them a lesson
8. Do you know the name of the song being played now
9. The stranger hidden in the shadows moved alarmed by the opening of the gate
10. Stopped at the door by two guards he walked briskly away

Setting off nonrestrictive adjective clauses

You have learned that participial phrases may be either restrictive or nonrestrictive. Now look at the italicized adjective clauses in the following sentences:

> Clancy asked the man *who was standing in the middle of the aisle* to find him a seat.
> A car *that stalls every hundred yards* is of little use.
> Boys *whose work showed promise* were given scholarships.

In the first sentence the clause tells exactly which man Clancy asked. It restricts the meaning of *man* to that particular one who was standing in the middle of the aisle. The second sentence does not say that every car is of little use, but only a particular car that stalls every hundred yards. The clause restricts the meaning of *car* by telling exactly which kind is meant. The third sentence is not about all boys, but only those whose work showed promise. The clause restricts the meaning of *Boys* to a particular group. Because the clauses in these sentences tell exactly which persons or things are meant, they are restrictive and cannot be omitted without changing the essential meaning of the sentence.

Now look at the italicized clauses in the following sentences:

> Clancy asked the head usher, *who was standing in the middle of the aisle,* to find him a seat.
> Our family car, *which stalls every hundred yards,* is of little use to us.
> Jim Nelson and Syd Shaeffer, *whose work showed promise,* were given scholarships.

In the first sentence the clause does not tell which particular usher is meant. The words *the* and *head* do that. The clause merely explains where the head usher was standing. The *who* means about the same thing as "and he." The adjectives *our* and *family* tell exactly which car is meant in the second sentence. The clause merely explains why the car is of little use. The *which* means about the same thing as "and it." The proper nouns *Jim Nelson* and *Syd Shaeffer* tell which particular boys are meant in the third sentence. The clause merely adds a bit of information about their work. The pronoun *whose* means about the same thing as "and their." In these sentences the clauses merely give explanatory information about the words they modify. Because the clauses are not needed to tell exactly which persons or things are meant, they are nonrestrictive and can be omitted without changing the essential meaning of the sentence.

Rule 9. **Nonrestrictive adjective clauses are set off from the rest of the sentence.**

By setting off a nonrestrictive adjective clause, the writer shows that the clause is intended to be merely explanatory, that he does not consider it essential to the exact meaning of his sentence. As you do the following exercise, try to put yourself in the place of the writer. Ask yourself questions like these: Is this adjective clause needed to tell exactly which person or thing is meant? Would omitting the clause make the sentence less exact or change its essential meaning? If your answers are "Yes," the clause is restrictive and must not be set off. But if the clause is not needed to tell exactly which person or thing is meant, if it merely adds a bit of explanatory information, the clause is nonrestrictive and should be set off from the rest of the sentence.

EXERCISE 9. Each of the following sentences contains one or more adjective clauses, some of which are nonrestrictive and should be set off. Find each clause and decide whether it is restrictive or nonrestrictive. On a sheet of paper, write the numbers of the sentences. After each number, write the commas you think are needed in the sentence, giving the word preceding each mark. For the first sentence you should write: *1. firm, trip,*

1. The president of our firm who was in the Adirondacks on a hunting trip had left complete instructions with Mr. Ingalls.
2. The pin that I found may not be the one that you lost.
3. Across the street is Kay's Grill which is famous for its steaks.
4. Cross-country running is safe only for those whose hearts have been thoroughly tested by a physician.
5. The 5:13 train which would bring me to Stony Grange in plenty of time does not run on Saturdays.
6. Because of this interruption Dave missed the train that would get him to Elmwood in time for dinner.
7. I can't remember a year when I had more fun.
8. The bicycles which the two racers used were made of duralumin.
9. His only answer was to hold out his hands which were stained with the juice of the walnut husks and grin.
10. His left hand which held the pointer cast a weird shadow on the screen.

Setting off introductory adverb clauses

You have learned that an adverb clause may come at the beginning of a sentence. When it does, a comma is used to set off this introductory clause from the rest of the sentence. The comma shows where the adverb clause ends and the main clause begins. Can you tell where the introductory adverb clauses end in the following sentences?

> If the second team plays the game tomorrow will probably be close.
> After the paint has dried the dishes are placed in a hot oven.
> While Mother was washing the telephone rang several times.
> Before he could turn around the bumper of the car hit him.
> Because Pauline was short and pretty boys liked to dance with her.
> Since the girls wanted to eat Ted took them to a hamburger place.

Commas after *plays, dried, washing, around, pretty,* and *eat* would show where the introductory adverb clauses end and would make the sentences much easier to read.

Rule 10. An introductory adverb clause is set off from the rest of the sentence by a comma.

Notice that the rule has to do with introductory clauses. Introductory adverb phrases are not ordinarily set off unless they contain verbals, as in the last two of the following sentences:

> *At daybreak* they saddled the ponies and started for the ranch.
> *From the top of Lookout Mountain* the view is even more beautiful.
> *In trying to hurry,* the boy ripped his shirt.
> *By helping her older sister,* Anne soon learned to cook.

Notice, too, that the rule applies only to introductory *adverb* clauses. An introductory noun clause used as the subject of the verb is not set off from the rest of the sentence. Compare the italicized clauses in the following sentences:

> *Whatever you decide to do* will be satisfactory to the principal.
> *Whatever you decide to do,* try not to offend the principal.

Notice that in the first sentence the clause is the subject of the verb *will be,* and so is not set off. In the second sentence the clause modifies the verb *try;* because it is an introductory adverb clause, it is set off.

Although some newspapers and magazines regularly omit commas after introductory adverb clauses, most schools require them for clearness. Your sentences will mean to the reader exactly what they mean to you if you use a comma after each introductory adverb clause.

EXERCISE 10. Most of the sentences contain introductory adverb clauses that should be set off. Each of the sentences needs a suitable mark at the end. On a sheet of paper, write the numbers of the sentences. After each number, write the marks you think are needed, giving the word preceding each mark. For the first sentence you should write: *1. tardiness, punctual?*

1. Since he always grumbles about other people's tardiness wouldn't you expect him to be punctual
2. After Leon took over sales boomed as they never had before
3. As Ronald reached out the window fell on his arm
4. Because Alan refused to answer Mrs. Filbey sent him to the office
5. After this mysterious warning Hazel jumped with alarm whenever she heard the least bit of noise in the hall
6. When Nora started pounding Mother rushed up to our room to see what was happening

7. While we were crawling through Marvin's sleeve caught on a nail at the side of the window frame
8. Although Mrs. Haines was sarcastic and shrewd women liked to do business with her
9. If Keith calls while I'm at the store will you tell him to call me later
10. Whenever Aunt Lizbeth came to visit Dad would find that he had an important business conference to attend in Chicago

Commas with coördinating conjunctions

When coördinating conjunctions are used to make compound sentences, a comma before each conjunction helps the reader know where one coördinate clause ends and the next one begins. For example, can you tell what the following sentence means?

Three days later he hired Black and Smith and Brown quit work.

Was Smith hired along with Black, or did he quit work along with Brown? There is no way of telling. The writer could have shown what he meant by using a comma before the *and* joining the two clauses:

Three days later he hired Black and Smith, *and* Brown quit work.
Three days later he hired Black, *and* Smith and Brown quit work.

Here are a few more examples of compound sentences that are difficult to understand without rereading:

Toward the end of the game they lost self-restraint and sportsmanship was forgotten.
Mrs. Ellis was greatly concerned for Henry was her favorite.
You had better invite Mabel or her mother will be angry.
His face betrayed no emotion but pity filled his heart.

Now notice how much easier it is to understand the sentences when a comma is used before each coördinating conjunction:

Toward the end of the game they lost self-restraint, and sportsmanship was forgotten.
Mrs. Ellis was greatly concerned, for Henry was her favorite.
You had better invite Mabel, or her mother will be angry.
His face betrayed no emotion, but pity filled his heart.

A comma before the conjunction helps the reader know where one coördinate clause ends and the next one begins.

Rule 11. A comma is ordinarily used before a conjunction joining coördinate clauses in a compound sentence.

Many newspapers and periodicals do not use the comma if the clauses are short and there is no possibility of misunderstanding the meaning. But most schools prefer a comma before each conjunction that joins coördinate clauses.

Remember that *but* and *for* are not always conjunctions. No commas are needed in the following sentences:

There is no one *but* me in the room.
It is *but* a step to where they live.
Aunt Clara enjoys knitting *for* people who appreciate her work.

EXERCISE 11. Read the sentences, and decide where commas are needed before conjunctions that join coördinate clauses. On a sheet of paper, write the numbers of the sentences. After each number, write the last word of the first coördinate clause, following it with a comma and the conjunction. For the first sentence you should write: *1. door, for*

1. He asked us to close the door for some of the guests were chilly.
2. I was sure that no one would come but Jane insisted on waiting.
3. Luckily we didn't run into Pat or Mike would have trounced him for telling Mrs. Sanders that we had broken her gate.
4. At Don's cry of alarm I looked up and down on my head came the can of red paint.
5. Without another word Louise grabbed her books and ran down the street for the bus was just turning the corner.
6. Books of every kind were stacked high on all the chairs and on the tables were piled hundreds of old magazines.
7. Doc Smithers disliked all of us fellows but Ernest was his pet aversion.
8. No one came to the committee meeting but Crandall and Ellen or we could have finished the work.
9. The next day we saw Clifford and Ernest and Bob gave them the money we had collected.
10. Lucy offered to do all the housework but the ironing proved too much.

Comma for clearness

As you have learned, the purpose of most punctuation is to separate parts not closely connected in meaning. Can you tell where commas would make the following sentences easier to read and understand?

> Inside the box is painted blue and gold.
> As a matter of safety matches should be kept away from children.
> To Paul Douglas seemed rather conceited.
> The work seemed interesting at first but soon turned out to be harder than expected.
> He wanted a regular motorcycle not an old bicycle with a second-hand engine mounted on the luggage carrier.
> I saw her getting on a crowded bus with both arms full of parcels.
> Then he asked whether any of the people we knew knew him.

The first three sentences are easier to read when commas are put after the words *Inside, safety,* and *Paul* to separate introductory words from the subjects:

> Inside, the box is painted blue and gold.
> As a matter of safety, matches should be kept away from children.
> To Paul, Douglas seemed rather conceited.

The next two sentences are easier to read when commas are used before *but* and *not* to separate the main thought from an added or contrasting idea:

> The work seemed interesting at first, but soon turned out to be more difficult than expected.
> He wanted a regular motorcycle, not an old bicycle with a second-hand engine mounted on the luggage carrier.

The last two sentences are easier to read when commas are used to separate *with* from *bus* and the first *knew* from the second *knew*:

> I saw her getting on a crowded bus, with both arms full of parcels.
> Then he asked whether any of the people we knew, knew him.

Rule 12. **A comma is used to keep the thought clear wherever parts that are not closely connected in meaning appear to join.**

This rule is useful in punctuating sentences that are perfectly clear to a listener, but may be somewhat confusing to a reader. Use it whenever a comma is needed for clearness; but do not use it to justify needless commas. And do not rely on a comma to straighten out the meaning of a sentence that is confusing when spoken. First express the idea clearly in spoken words. Then use this rule to keep the meaning clear in writing.

EXERCISE 12. Read the sentences, and decide where commas are needed for clearness. On a sheet of paper, write the numbers of the sentences and, after them, the words preceding each comma. For the first one you should write: *1. after, train,*

1. Shortly after he rushed to the railway station and made the train with minutes to spare.
2. The boys who voted voted for Irene.
3. Ever since we have bolted our doors at night before going upstairs.
4. Five minutes after I wondered why I had been so angry.
5. For Mike Clancy brought a pair of skis.
6. Outside the house looked shabby.
7. Just a week before she had accepted a job in Rosendale.
8. Mrs. Grimes felt sorry for us but refused to help us out.
9. There will be nine people not counting you and me.
10. Later I saw Helen pushing her way through the crowds in the lobby with a worried look on her face.

Composition

Expressing an Opinion

In all likelihood you started expressing opinions before you could talk. As a baby, you probably pushed away a spoon containing food you did not like. Later, you may have grabbed another child's toy with no more explanation than "Me want." Your actions expressed your opinions clearly enough. Nobody expected you to explain why you did not like the food or why the other child's toy seemed so desirable to you.

Now, of course, you express most of your opinions by means of words: "Football is the best game there is." "I detest school parties." "That was the worst movie I've ever seen." "In ten years everybody will travel by airplane." And sometimes people ask "Why?" When they do, can you give good reasons for your opinions? Or do you answer lamely, "Oh, just because"?

It is part of the American belief in freedom of speech that everyone is entitled to express his opinion. If a person gives good reasons, you are likely to pay attention to what he has to say. If he fails to give good reasons, you may start asking yourself "Why this?" "Why that?" "Why the other thing?" and finally decide that he just does not know what he is talking about. As you learn to give sensible reasons, keeping them together in related groups so that they can be easily understood, you will find other people paying more careful attention to your opinion, even when they disagree with it.

Subjects for an oral composition in which you express an opinion about something are easy to find. Think about things that you like or dislike. Do you like classical music, or baseball, or living in a small town? Do you dislike alarm clocks, or washing dishes, or final examinations? Think about things that you consider good or bad: a good hobby, why buses are better than streetcars, your favorite kind of dog, the worst program on the air. You should, naturally, choose a subject that you know something about. Otherwise you may find it difficult to form an opinion or to give enough good reasons.

When you have chosen a subject for your talk, make a list of all the sensible reasons you can think of for your opinion. For example, if you were going to explain why you like baseball, your list of reasons might look like this:

1. The game is usually exciting.
2. It develops muscle and skill.
3. Night games draw large crowds.
4. Almost everybody knows something about major leagues.
5. Intramural teams use a regulation softball.
6. The plays are easy to follow. .
7. Baseball encourages teamwork.
8. It builds respect for fair play.
9. Cheering and booing add to the spectators' fun.
10. World Series news is the important sports news of the year.
11. Baseball gives every player a chance to star.
12. A player is given credit for a sacrifice hit.
13. Talking about teams is a good way to make new friends.

When you make a list like this one, writing down reasons as they occur to you, you will often find that some of the reasons are not suitable and the rest need to be organized into groups. For example, in the list shown, the first item seems to be a reason for watching baseball games; the second, a reason for playing baseball; the third, a reason for having games at night; the fourth, a reason for talking about baseball; the fifth, a point of difference between intramural and school teams; and so on. You can make a good plan by omitting unsuitable reasons and grouping related reasons in a logical order.

In the first place, baseball is a good game to play.
    A. It develops muscle and skill.
    B. It encourages teamwork.
    C. It builds respect for fair play.
    D. It gives every player a chance to star.
In the second place, baseball is a good game to watch.
    A. The plays are easy to follow.
    B. The game is usually exciting.
    C. Cheering and booing add to the spectators' fun.

180

Finally, baseball is a good game to talk about.

    A. Almost everybody knows something about major leagues.

    B. World Series news is the important sports news of the year.

    C. Talking about teams is a good way to make new friends.

The plan shows that there are three groups of related reasons for liking baseball. The three main headings show how the reasons in each group are related. You will notice that three items in the original list have been omitted: Item 3, because it has nothing to do with liking baseball; Item 5, because it is a point of difference and not a reason; Item 12, because it is a detail explaining baseball scoring. The expressions *In the first place, In the second place,* and *Finally* introduce new groups of reasons.

    Now look at the list of reasons you made for your talk. Study each item carefully. Are there any items that should be omitted? How will you arrange your reasons so that related items can be put in separate groups? Make a plan for your talk, arranging the groups in a logical order. Write a main heading for each group, showing how the reasons in the group are related. Underline such words as *in the first place, second, next,* and *finally* so that you will remember to let your listeners know when you begin a new group of reasons.

    How will you begin and end your talk? When you have decided, add opening and closing sentences to your plan and copy it on a card or small slip of paper. Have this copy of your notes in your hand as you practice your talk and as you give it.

    Practice your talk at least once, timing yourself to make sure that it does not take over three minutes. If you are asked to give your talk in class, speak so that all your classmates can hear what you say.

Expressing an Opinion PART TWO: WRITTEN

Now that you have prepared an oral composition in which you expressed an opinion and gave reasons for your opinion, you are to prepare a written composition, using the notes you made for your talk. Since your notes show how to begin and end, what reasons to give, and in what order to give them, you can devote your attention to the special problems of written compositions.

The first problem has to do with the paragraphs you will use. If the plan for your oral composition has two or more groups of related reasons, you should explain each group in a separate paragraph. As you have learned, the main heading of each group becomes the topic sentence that tells what each paragraph is about. And the reasons under each heading are the details used to develop the paragraph.

You have already learned that details arranged in a logical order are more easily understood when there are topic sentences telling how the details in each paragraph are related. And you have also learned that expressions such as *in the first place, in the second place, third, next,* and *finally* not only let the reader know when you are beginning a new group of reasons, but also show the relation of that group to the others in your plan. By helping the reader know your plan, you help him understand better what you say.

Now look at the notes you prepared for your oral composition. How many paragraphs will you use in writing your composition? Remember that your special opening sentence is the first sentence in your first paragraph. If you have a special closing sentence, remember that it is the last sentence in your final paragraph. You do not need separate "introductory" or "concluding" paragraphs in a short written composition.

Write your composition just as you planned to tell it in class, following your plan in order to keep related reasons in separate paragraphs. Be sure that each paragraph has a topic sentence to let the reader know how the reasons in that paragraph are related. Be sure that each topic sentence contains a word like *first, second, next,* or *finally* to show the reader how that paragraph is related to the other paragraphs; but do not underline these words in your composition. Use pencil and scratch paper for this first draft so that you can make changes and corrections easily. Always keep your classmates in mind as you write, since you may be asked to read your composition to them.

Revise your first draft carefully, making corrections in spelling and punctuation, changing the order of words and phrases, crossing out unnecessary words or adding better ones until you are proud of the sentences in your composition. You learn more by revising a first draft that you yourself have written than by doing a dozen exercises. Make the best use you can of each opportunity to show what you know about writing good sentences.

Next comes the problem of selecting a suitable title for your composition. You can use a title that simply states your opinion. If you are writing about baseball or buses or photography or television, titles like the following are quite satisfactory:

Why I Like Baseball	Photography Is Fun
Buses Are Better	I Like Television

Sometimes, however, you may want to use a title that will arouse the curiosity of your readers or attract their attention to what you have written. Titles of this sort may either suggest what your opinion is or state it in an odd way. For example, notice the following pairs of titles and compare them with those given above:

Batter Up!	Take Me Out to the Ball Game
I'm a Bus Boy	Clang! Clang! Clang! Goes the Trolley
Shutterbugs	Camera Fans Are Not Crazy
Television Is Tops	The Eyes Have It

What title will you use for your composition? Will you use a title that simply states your opinion, or will you use one that arouses the interest of your readers? When you have selected a title that satisfies you, copy your revised first draft in a form suitable for handing in. Write neatly and legibly. Indent the first word of each paragraph and keep margins even. Space words carefully.

You are now ready to proofread the final draft of your composition to catch any errors that you may have made in copying. Read it over slowly, word by word, watching carefully for words or final letters that have been omitted, for words that have been copied twice, for careless misspellings or omitted punctuation marks. Make your corrections neatly.

If you are asked to read your composition to the class, read slowly and distinctly, keeping your eyes several words ahead of your voice. Try to read as clearly as you talk. When a classmate is reading his composition, listen carefully so that you can tell what you like about it and what you think might be improved.

Other Marks
of Punctuation

The "half-period" semicolon

When a compound sentence is made by putting related sentences together without a conjunction, a semicolon is used to show clearly where one coördinate clause ends and the next one begins. Compare the sentences in the following pairs:

> Some of the boys had to pay. The others had complimentary tickets.
> Some of the boys had to pay; the others had complimentary tickets.
>
> No one knows. The car hasn't been tested yet.
> No one knows; the car hasn't been tested yet.
>
> The questions were long. Also, many were unusually difficult.
> The questions were long; also, many were unusually difficult.

Just as periods are used to keep sentences from running together, so semicolons are used to separate coördinate clauses in a compound sentence. A semicolon used in this way is called a "half-period" semicolon.

Rule 13. **A semicolon is used between coördinate clauses that are not joined by a coördinating conjunction.**

Newspapers and periodicals usually use commas between three or more short coördinate clauses in a series and, sometimes, between two that are very closely connected in meaning. But many schools prefer semicolons between coördinate clauses in a series, even when the clauses are short:

The gardens blossom with flowers; cabbages and strawberries grow beside the houses; two or three trees shelter the windows; and every cottage has its trellis of vines.

A semicolon is used even before *and* in this sentence to show that the sentence is made up of four clauses of equal importance.

When adverb phrases are used to show what relationship is intended between coördinate clauses, they need semicolons before them, just as independent adverbs do:

His latest book is not bad; *in fact,* I enjoyed it greatly.
That isn't likely to happen; *of course,* you may think differently.
His strength failed; *at last* he took to his bed.

You can see that the semicolons in these sentences show clearly where one coördinate clause ends and the next one begins.

Notice that this rule is about coördinate clauses. It does not apply to subordinate clauses or to adverbs and adverb phrases used in other ways. Commas are used in sentences like these:

Since it was growing colder, he closed the window.
Can you, therefore, be at the station by seven o'clock?
He stumbled, staggered, then fell prostrate.
There is, in fact, no evidence of carelessness.

EXERCISE 13. Decide where a semicolon is needed to make a compound sentence of each group of words. On a sheet of paper, write the numbers of the word groups. After each number, write the word preceding the semicolon, then the semicolon and the word following it. For the first group you should write: *1. costs; of*

1. There is a small charge to cover mailing costs of course the pamphlets and samples are free.
2. The squire wasn't afraid he despised the captain.
3. I told him I would be ready nevertheless I was scared.
4. You cannot run away from a weakness you must either conquer it or be conquered by it.
5. A few minutes before Roland had seemed excited about the trip now he acted as if he were bored to death.
6. He walked ahead unsteadily a few steps then he paused.
7. Jimmie insists he did not break the vase however he may be lying.

186

8. Aunt Laura did all she could to make her guests comfortable still they were not satisfied.
9. Most of them realized that they had very little chance of winning nevertheless they worked with all their might.
10. She seldom spoke without being sarcastic therefore she had few friends.

The "double comma" semicolon

You have learned that a semicolon is used between coördinate clauses that are not joined by a conjunction. A semicolon used in this way is often called a "half period" semicolon because it takes the place of a period. Now notice how semicolons are used in these sentences:

> When the men returned from the search, they were dirty, weary, and hungry; and their boots were covered with red clay.
> I arrived in time to talk with Mr. Becker, the speaker from Detroit; but the other man, whose name I don't recall, had already left.
> If the frame is sound, the condition of the strings is of no importance; for the racket will be restrung before it is used.
> We expected a large crowd, since all the tickets had been sold; yet many people did not come, probably because of the bad weather.

Although the coördinate clauses in these sentences are joined by *and, but, for,* and *yet,* semicolons are used before these coördinating conjunctions. You can see that commas would not stand out clearly before the conjunctions, since commas are used for other purposes in the clauses. While commas may be used before coördinating conjunctions in such sentences, semicolons are better because they show clearly where one coördinate clause ends and the next one begins. Now look at these sentences:

> The company has set up branch offices in Atlanta, Georgia; in Dallas, Texas; in Portland, Oregon; and in Troy, New York.
> The most dramatic incidents in the book were the encounter, secretly contrived by the King; the mysterious, alarming interview with Hayraddin; and the foiling of the band of cutthroats.
> In the administration of their government there were three conditions that the people expected: first, security from foreign invasion, interference, or control; second, a force adequate to suppress internal disturbances; and third, opportunity for all to hold public office.

Commas are ordinarily used between the items of a series. But half a dozen commas—which look alike, but are doing different kinds of work—are confusing to the reader. To avoid this confusion, semicolons are used to show clearly where one item ends and the next one begins.

Rule 14. **A semicolon may be used in place of a comma before a coördinating conjunction or between items of a series to avoid confusion with other commas in the sentence.**

Perhaps it would be convenient to use a double-size comma between important sentence parts that have other commas in them. But such a comma has never been devised. We use a semicolon instead. Because a semicolon used in this way takes the place of an important comma, it is often called a "double comma" semicolon. Use it wherever it helps eliminate confusion, but use it only before a coördinate conjunction or between items of a series.

EXERCISE 14. All punctuation marks have been omitted from the sentences. Read each sentence, and decide where the necessary commas, semicolons, and periods should go. Then write the numbers of the sentences. After each number, put the punctuation marks needed in that sentence and the word preceding each mark. For the first sentence you should write: *1. big, cold, kitchen; rough, floors; sticks.*

1. A city-bred girl would dread this big cold unpainted kitchen the rough uneven boards in the floors and the windows that have to be propped open with sticks

2. When he was young he was always having fun and getting into mischief but when he grew old he frowned if he saw us even laughing

3. At the convention he met delegates from Quincy Massachusetts from Green Bay Wisconsin from Carson City Nevada and from San Antonio Texas

4. Billy lying comfortably under the shade of the old maple hated to move yet he knew that his family would be angry if he didn't finish his work before dinner time

5. Because Chris disliked the neighbors he did not encourage their visits yet when he needed their help he did not hesitate to call on them

6. When the teacher was in the room every head was bent diligently over books and papers but if she stepped out for a minute or two the uproar could be heard a block away

7. For extra credit in history Bob and I read *The Red Badge of Courage* a novel by Stephen Crane *The Copperhead* a play by Augustus Thomas and *Lafitte the Pirate* a biography by Lyle Saxon

8. If Mr. Campbell leaves which he intends to do you may have his room but if for some reason he decides to stay I cannot help you

9. Aunt Mary offered me two ugly dresses worn and faded from countless washings and when I refused them she scolded me for being proud

10. The closet has shallow drawers for shirts sweaters socks and gloves deep drawers for blankets sheets and towels two racks for shoes and a large shelf for hats

Colons that introduce

Throughout this book you have seen colons used after words that introduce examples:

> Notice the italicized words in the following sentences:
> A letter to a friend might look like this:

A colon used in this way calls the reader's attention to what follows. For example, a colon is regularly used after the salutation of a business letter:

> Gentlemen: Dear Sir: Dear Mrs. Smith:

The colon introduces the body of the letter and is more formal than the comma generally used in personal letters. Similarly, a colon is sometimes used to introduce a formal quotation, particularly one that is long or not a part of a conversation:

> The President then stepped forward and solemnly began to speak the words now known to every American: "Fourscore and seven years ago . . ."
> Over the heavy oak door someone had carved: "Abandon hope, all ye who enter here."

A colon is seldom used unless the introductory words are formal or contain expressions such as "he spoke thus" or "replied as follows." As you learned in Unit 5 , a comma is generally used before quotations that are short or are a part of a conversation.

A colon is regularly used to introduce a list of appositives that end a sentence. For example:

The heater consists of four simple parts: a *coil* of wire on a porcelain form, a large copper *reflector*, a *switch* for controlling the current, and an adjustable *stand*.

We planned the dinner party for three definite reasons: *to celebrate* Hal's birthday, *to entertain* our out-of-town guests, and *to use* up the venison steaks that Bruce had sent.

During the week he always had the same breakfast: orange *juice*, *cereal*, fried *eggs*, *toast*, and *milk*.

The marks of a successful athlete are these: excellent *coördination*, great *endurance*, and a strong competitive *spirit*.

The italicized words in the first example of this group are in apposition with the word *parts*. Those in the second are in apposition with the word *reasons;* those in the third with the word *breakfast;* and those in the fourth with the word *these*.

Rule 15. A colon is used to introduce a formal quotation or a list of appositives that ends a sentence.

Notice that the rule is about a list of appositives. Parallel forms that are not in apposition with a preceding word are not introduced by a colon. Compare the two sentences that follow:

We sent Helen a cashmere sweater, a silver bracelet, and a bottle of her favorite perfume.

We sent Helen three gifts: a cashmere sweater, a silver bracelet, and a bottle of her favorite perfume.

In the first sentence the words *sweater, bracelet,* and *bottle* are parallel objects of the verb *sent*. Because they are essential parts of the sentence, a colon is not used before them. In the second sentence, however, the words are in apposition with the object *gifts;* the colon is used to call the reader's attention to them.

EXERCISE 15. Read the sentences, and decide where the necessary colons and commas should go. Then write the numbers of the sentences. After each number, write the marks that are needed in the sentence, giving the word preceding each mark. For the first sentence you should write: *1. about: taxes, repairs,*

1. There were three items of expense that Kent had forgotten about taxes repairs and interest on his loan.

2. We found several signs that someone had been living in the cabin a stack of dirty dishes in the sink a half-used jar of peanut butter and a number of empty tins in the garbage can.
3. Kathy asked the librarian to reserve the following books *Smarter and Smoother This Is My Story Soaring Wings* and *The Yearling.*
4. On the first page of the book the author had inscribed "More things are wrought by prayer than this world dreams of."
5. Mother found several things wrong with the house its size its location and its price.
6. Aunt Harriet had included gifts for all of us a compact for Betty ice skates for Tim a chemistry set for Hank an electric clock for Mother and a pipe for Dad.
7. On her return from a winter in London Audrey was using a number of strange British words *lift* for elevator *footpath* for sidewalk *tram* for streetcar *flickers* for movies and *petrol* for gas.
8. Although Russell was a fine fellow and very popular he had two weaknesses blind confidence in everybody and a dread of disagreeing with the opinions of others.
9. When asked why he had summoned his council to an emergency meeting Mayor Van Ryn replied as follows "Since appeasement and compromise have failed we must make new plans to insure the safety of our villagers."
10. Our next issue will contain three articles that will interest the boys one on model planes one on carrier pigeons and one on professional football.

Parentheses

When we want to add an explanation or a comment inconspicuously and without changing the meaning of the sentence, we use parentheses to enclose the added material. For example:

> Taking into consideration the original cost of the material and the high shipping rate (two dollars a hundred pounds), we can see that the estimate is fair.
>
> If Carl wins today's match (the coach thinks he will), the team will go to the state finals next week.

In the first sentence the explanation in parentheses is merely a reminder. Notice that the comma marking the end of the introductory phrase comes after the parentheses. In the second sentence the comment is in the form of a statement. Notice that it begins with a small letter and is not followed by a period; the parentheses set it off clearly enough from the rest of the sentence. Although a statement in parentheses is not followed by a period, commas and semicolons are used in such a statement just as they would be in any sentence:

> The starting switch (a pushbutton or, in some models, a small pedal) controls the heavy current needed to crank the engine.
>
> Then Mike O'Connell (his teammates call him "Butch"; his mother still calls him "Michael") stepped forward to receive the award for outstanding athlete of the year.

The commas in the first sentence set off a nonrestrictive phrase inside the parentheses. The semicolon in the second separates two coördinate clauses enclosed in parentheses.

Parentheses are frequently used to enclose appositives that are merely reminders:

> Some of the Kanakas (natives of Hawaii) have names that sound strange to us.
>
> Mr. Alison's fee was four guineas (about twenty dollars).
>
> We learned that the members of the two governing bodies (the House of Bishops and the House of Deputies) are elected by the rank and file of churchgoers.

Parentheses used in these ways mean "I will explain, so that you may not misunderstand."

Rule 16. **Parentheses are used to enclose an explanation or a comment that is not closely connected with the rest of the sentence.**

Parentheses are most effective when they are used only occasionally to add a helpful reminder or a comment that may prevent misunderstanding. Used too often, they become tiresome. One particularly tiresome use is to tell about names: "(for that was his name)" or "(I forgot to say that that was the name he went by)." Avoid using parentheses to tell about names or your forgetfulness.

EXERCISE 16. Read the sentences, and decide which words should be enclosed in parentheses. Then write the numbers of the sentences and, after each number, the words that should be in parentheses. Use commas and semicolons within the parentheses or after them as needed. For the first sentence you should write: *1. (over 70 miles an hour),*

1. Fearing winds of hurricane force over 70 miles an hour we braced the tower with heavy steel cables.
2. Soft coal the scientific name is "bituminous" lights easily.
3. Mr. J. M. Wright not to be confused with the previously mentioned J. L. Wright who lives in Dallas was elected district representative.
4. My cousin in California he is really only my second cousin has invited me to go to Australia with him.
5. As long as this trunk lasts it will probably last the rest of my natural life I'll be proud of it.
6. From the Lake of Galilee to the Dead Sea a distance of about sixty miles there is a drop of six hundred feet.
7. The chief officer of the shipbuilding yard the Commandant as he is called wants to lay two new keels this year.
8. He at once moved with 6000 men 4000 of them Frenchmen who were commanded by Rochambeau from the Hudson to Chesapeake Bay.
9. Mr. Foster we had to call him "Mr." because he was now an officer before we called him "Joe" had never taken any voyages but short ones.
10. Although the large jars contain four times as much they hold two quarts the price is only twice as much.

Dashes that interrupt

On page 168 you learned that dashes are ordinarily used to set off appositives like these:

> Great quantities of the hardier grains—rye, oats, and barley—are raised in the northern countries.
> She contributed twenty dollars to the new church—an act of great generosity for one in her modest circumstances.

In the first sentence two dashes are used to set off a series of appositives that are separated by commas. In the second sentence one dash is used to call attention to an appositive that sums up the meaning of a group of words. Now look at the next two sentences:

> The whitewashed farmhouse, the massive stables, the spotless dairy, the giant haystacks—all were photographed on his memory.
> Wisdom, patience, everlasting cheerfulness—these were what endeared him to us.

In each of these sentences a dash is used before a word that sums up a preceding list of items. Dashes used in this way show clearly where the list ends.

Dashes are also used to set off explanatory remarks or comments or to call the reader's attention to an abrupt change in the thought of the sentence. For example:

> Many of them—over half, it is estimated—will remain at home.
> He is the hardest-working fellow on the football team—when the coach is looking.
> My second reason—it is really the chief one—is that some reward should be offered for good grades.
> I longed—oh, how I longed!—for a glass of water.
> She has lost that small security and gained—what?

The dashes in these sentences call attention to the explanatory remarks or comments. In the third sentence the remark is in the form of a statement. Notice that it begins with a small letter and is not followed by a period; the dashes set it off clearly enough from the rest of the sentence. Exclamation marks and question marks are used before a dash, but commas and periods are not.

Rule 17. **Dashes are used to call attention to explanations or comments that are not closely connected with the rest of the sentence.**

Because dashes are conspicuous marks and always indicate an interruption in the thought of the sentence, it is wise to use them sparingly. Parentheses are used for enclosing explanatory remarks and comments that you want to be inconspicuous; dashes are used for those you want to call to the reader's attention.

EXERCISE 17. Read the sentences, and decide where dashes should be used to set off appositives or other explanatory matter. Then copy the sentences, putting in the dashes and all other punctuation marks that are needed. Number each sentence. For the first sentence you should write: *1. Ed Jones, Gwen Simpson, and Dick Upham—the freshman committee—arranged for the entertainment and the refreshments.*

1. Ed Jones Gwen Simpson and Dick Upham the freshman committee arranged for the entertainment and the refreshments
2. This great professor's favorite books are the biographies of world-conquering warriors Alexander Caesar Charlemagne Napoleon

194

3. There were two reasons why she was so glad to meet him his big car and his football tickets
4. Heathcliff stayed to speak to Ernest and I entered the old kitchen a dingy untidy hole
5. It is only on Sundays that the lumberjacks can find time to read or what is more important for them of course to wash and mend their working clothes
6. The Bakers' Association to which Dad belongs discussed a curious question at their last meeting namely what is a cake
7. It was about half past one three bells in the sea phrase that two boats went ashore from the *Hispaniola*
8. These romances of medicine for example the fights against yellow fever and malaria have now been written up in popular style
9. The nose of every cow like the thumb of every man is traversed by innumerable little ridges and the scientists have learned how to take "nose prints" of these ridges
10. Mrs. Glennon never leaves her house but there is seldom a day when some guest often a lonely or troubled one is not seated at her table

Direct quotations

We sometimes tell what other people have said, using their own words. For example:

> Mary asked, "Where is the money, Bob?"
> "I'm afraid I have lost it," he explained.
> "You'll have to pay it back," she said, "because it belongs to the members of the club."

The writer of these sentences tells what Mary and Bob said, giving their exact words. The writer encloses the actual words of the speakers in quotation marks to show his readers that these words are not his own. The words enclosed in quotation marks are called **direct quotations.** In the first sentence the quotation comes after the verb *asked* and is set off by a comma. Mary's question begins with a capital letter and is followed by a question mark. In the second sentence the quotation comes before the subject *he* and is set off by a comma. Bob's statement begins with a capital letter and ends with a comma to show that the rest of the sentence follows it. In the third sentence part of the quotation comes before the subject *she,* and part of it comes after the verb *said.* Mary's statement begins with a capital letter and ends with a period, and the two parts of the statement are set off from the rest of the sentence. Notice that the commas and the period in these sentences come before the quotation marks.

Rule 18. **A direct quotation begins with a capital letter and is enclosed in quotation marks. When it is in a sentence, it is set off from the rest of the sentence.**

When a quotation ends with an exclamation mark or a question mark, no comma is needed to set off the quotation:

> "Get out of my house!" bellowed Mr. Thorpe.
> "Why should I go?" asked Ted.

Notice that the question mark in the second sentence comes before the final quotation marks. The question mark shows that Ted asked the question. But suppose he had said:

> Come here.

If we wished to ask him why he had said it, we would write this:

> Why did you say, "Come here"?

The question mark is now placed after the final quotation marks to show that the whole sentence—not Ted's remark—is a question.

The exclamation mark before the final quotation marks in the first sentence shows that Mr. Thorpe's words were an exclamation. But if we wanted to exclaim over a rude remark Mr. Thorpe had made, the exclamation mark would come after the final quotation mark:

> How rude it was of Mr. Thorpe to say to his hostess, "I refuse to be one of thirteen people at a dinner table"!

When you write a quotation within a quotation, use single marks to enclose the inner one, as in the following example:

> John asked in a low tone, "Didn't you hear that woman whisper, 'Take off your hat'?"

Notice that each quotation begins with a capital letter and that each one is set off by commas.

Now look at the period between these two commands:

> Go away. Don't bother me.

You know that each of these commands is a complete sentence, for each one can stand alone. Suppose that you wanted to write that a storekeeper spoke the two sentences. When you put quotation marks around them, you must make it clear that there are two quoted sentences. Notice the period after *storekeeper,* the capital *D,* and the two sets of quotation marks:

"Go away," shouted the storekeeper. "Don't bother me."

If you put both of the quoted sentences after the verb or before the subject, you need only one set of quotation marks. Notice the capital *G,* the period, and the capital *D*:

The storekeeper shouted, "Go away. Don't bother me."
"Go away. Don't bother me," the storekeeper shouted.

The first quoted sentence may be a question:

"Where are you?" called Ethel. "I can't see you."

Notice that each sentence ends with a period, even though the quotation in the first sentence ends with a question mark.

EXERCISE 18. Some of the groups of words contain a quotation of one sentence and some a quotation of two sentences. All punctuation marks and some necessary capital letters have been omitted. Read the groups and decide whether the quotations are one sentence or two sentences. Then copy the groups, putting in needed quotation marks, commas, periods, question marks, exclamation marks, capitals. For the first group you should write:
1. "Are you angry?" she asked with a smile. "Did you think I meant it?"
 1. Are you angry she asked with a smile did you think I meant it
 2. Just wait a few minutes answered Mr. Barclay I might want you
 3. We hate she added to have you leave in such a storm
 4. I'm not the least bit comfortable here growled Lucius with his customary bad temper
 5. She said bitterly but they promised to be here on time
 6. Why should he pick on me whined Jerry I've never missed a question
 7. Hit it again shouted the skipper don't be discouraged
 8. And that added Mrs. Brennan angrily is why I refused their invitation
 9. Whose package inquired the clerk is that is it yours
 10. Don't you remember she asked in a low voice that Mr. Harris said never come to me for help

More uses for quotation marks

You have learned that quotation marks are used to enclose the exact words of a speaker. Quotation marks have other uses. For example, they are used to enclose the titles of chapters of books, magazine articles, essays, short stories, short poems, songs, and plays that are not published as books. Look at the following examples:

> Ed thought "What Things Are Made Of" was the most interesting chapter in the book.
> I sent him my copy of the magazine so that he could read "Spring in Sun Valley" before he left.
> Maureen Daly's "Sixteen" won the National High School Short Story Contest in 1938.
> "The Raven" is a gloomy and depressing poem.
> Between the first and second acts a little girl sang "Jingle Bells" in a high, squeaky voice.
> After rehearsing "The Flower Shop" for weeks, Bill still stumbled over his lines.

Quotation marks are also used to call the reader's attention to a word or phrase or expression that is used in a special way, as in the following sentences:

> The teacher would not allow us to use "bunch of fellows" or "kids" in our written compositions.
> I am sure that Michael did not know what Miss Hahn meant by "the Victorian influence."

Notice that the words in quotation marks are not set off by commas. Even though the words are the exact words of a speaker, they are not introduced in these sentences as anybody's speech. You do not use commas before or after such words unless the commas are needed for some other reason, as in the following sentence:

> The teacher scolded Jim for using his favorite expression, "bunch of fellows," in a letter to the principal.

Here commas are needed because "bunch of fellows" is an appositive.

Rule 19. **Quotation marks may be used to enclose titles and to call attention to words used in special ways.**

EXERCISE 19. Study the following items, which are usually enclosed in quotation marks. Think up a good sentence for each one. Then write the sentences, using quotation marks and other punctuation marks correctly. Number the sentences. For the first one you might write something like this: *1. I thoroughly enjoyed reading "The Ancient Mariner."*

1. The poem "The Ancient Mariner"
2. The story "The Love Letters of Smith"
3. The article "And Sudden Death"
4. The song "Home on the Range"
5. The play "A Game of Chess"
6. The expression "two twins"
7. The expression "gang of kids"
8. The expression "a poor little rich girl"
9. The expressions "and-uh" and "why-uh"
10. The expression "the survival of the fittest"

Summary review of all marks

In talking, you have many ways of letting others know where your sentences begin and end, and whether they are statements, questions, or exclamations; which words are important and which are merely explanatory comments or side remarks; where clauses and phrases begin and end, and whether they are restrictive or nonrestrictive. By raising and lowering your voice, increasing its force occasionally, and pausing for varying lengths of time, you keep your listeners informed as to the meaning you intend your words to have.

In writing, you must rely on a code of signals—punctuation marks —to guide readers to your exact meaning. The twenty rules you have learned in this book are the means by which you separate items of equal importance, set off words not closely connected with the rest of the sentence, and prevent misreading in other ways. You know, of course, that a reader expects a sentence to begin with a capital letter and end with a period, a question mark, or an exclamation mark (Rule 1). To enable you to meet this expectation, fourteen lessons have dealt with what a sentence is. In addition, you have learned many uses of commas, semicolons, colons, parentheses, dashes, and quotation marks.

You have learned that commas may be used to separate certain items of equal importance (Rules 2, 5, 11), to set off words not closely connected with the rest of the sentence (Rules 3, 4, 6, 7, 8, 9), and to avoid possible misreading (Rules 10, 12). Be prepared to explain the uses of the commas in the following sentences:

1. We set sail on a gray, damp, chilly morning.
2. The coach, the players, and the spectators were thoroughly soaked by the end of the game.
3. Walt Whitman was born at West Hills, Long Island, New York, in May, 1819.
4. Toward the end of the game they lost self-restraint, and sportsmanship was forgotten.
5. Do you think, my dear sir, that I am a beggar?
6. Yes, you may go to the library.
7. Nancy had to report after school, too.
8. For example, the water pressure may be too low.
9. The rain will continue, it seems, for several days.
10. Last June we spent two weeks at Highfield, a mountain resort.
11. Before long we became aware of a strange sound in the room, a soft whirring like that of a small electric motor.
12. Mr. Brown's plan, to leave secretly on the early morning train, was successfully carried out.
13. This strange idea, that I was being watched, lasted all day.
14. Tommy, coming around the corner, fell off his bicycle.
15. His face twisted with pain, Joe limped off the field.
16. "You'll have to pay back the money," Mary said, "because it belongs to the members of the club."
17. Clancy asked the head usher, who was standing in the middle of the aisle, to find him a seat.
18. We were drenched, though the rain lasted for only a few minutes.
19. After the paint has dried, the dishes are placed in a hot oven.
20. As a matter of safety, matches should be kept away from children.

You have learned that a semicolon may be used as a kind of "half period" (Rule 13) or as a sort of "double comma" (Rule 14). You have also learned about colons that introduce (Rule 15). Be prepared to explain to the class the uses of the semicolons and colons in the next five sentences:

21. Some of the boys had to pay; the others had free tickets.
22. When the men returned from the search, they were dirty, weary, and hungry; and their boots were covered with red clay.
23. The company has set up offices in Atlanta, Georgia; in Dallas, Texas; in Portland, Oregon; and in Troy, New York.
24. Over the heavy oak door someone had carved: "Abandon hope, all ye who enter here."
25. During the week he always had the same breakfast: orange juice, cereal, fried eggs, toast, and milk.

You have learned that certain words not closely connected with the rest of the sentence may be set off by parentheses (Rule 16) or by dashes (Rule 17). Be prepared to explain the uses of the dashes and parentheses in the next five sentences:

26. The starter switch (a pushbutton or, in some models, a small pedal) controls the heavy current needed to crank the engine.
27. If Carl wins today's match (the coach thinks he will), the team will go to the state finals.
28. Great quantities of the hardier grains—rye, oats, and barley—are raised in the northern countries.
29. Patience, wisdom, everlasting cheerfulness—these were what endeared him to us.
30. I longed—oh, how I longed!—for a glass of water.

You have learned about using quotation marks in combination with other punctuation marks (Rules 18, 19). Be prepared to explain the use and placement of all punctuation marks in each of the next five sentences:

31. Mary asked, "Where is the money, Bob?"
32. Why did you say, "Come here"?
33. "Get out of my house!" bellowed Mr. Canthorpe.
34. "Where are you?" called Ethel. "I can't see you."
35. Then we heard a group of "bronco busters" singing "Roy Bean."

Merely knowing twenty rules of punctuation will no more make you a capable writer than knowing the rules of baseball will make you a star pitcher. But knowing when punctuation is needed, which marks to use, and where to place them will do much to keep your meaning clear and make your writing effective.

Composition

Persuading Others PART ONE: ORAL

There are various ways of persuading others to do something you want. You can coax or flatter or threaten them. You can appeal to their pride, their prejudices, their desire to go along with everybody else. Or you can appeal to their common sense—calling attention to a need that exists, winning them over to your way of thinking by giving good reasons, pointing out the advantages or benefits of doing what you recommend, and urging some definite action. Of these ways, the last is the one most likely to convince people who think for themselves.

Suitable subjects for a persuasive talk are those of personal interest to you and your classmates. In every school there are matters of general concern—suggested improvements in student government or the sports program, recommended changes in examinations or courses or assemblies or class parties. In every community there are conditions that might be remedied, activities that deserve greater support, individuals who ought to be elected to public office. If you choose a subject that is being widely discussed at the time, you will find your classmates interested in what you have to say about it. And if you choose one about which you have definite opinions, you will find it easy to plan and give a good talk. What will your subject be?

The first part of a talk in which you try to persuade others should not only suggest some action, but should make clear just why there is a need for that action. If, for example, you want others to adopt a plan for reorganizing the Student Council, you might start with a brief account of obvious faults in its present organization. If you are arguing for more student-produced assemblies, you might call attention to several poor programs using outside talent. Or if you want to convince others that your school should have a compulsory driver-education course, you might begin by mentioning the startling number of automobile accidents that occur every year. By beginning with what your classmates know or are willing to accept as true, you establish a common ground with them and put them in a better mood to listen to your plea for action. One of the important things you can learn about persuading others is just this: Always begin on common ground.

Once you have explained the background for the suggested action, you must convince your listeners that what you suggest is the best course to follow. You might do this in several ways—by giving reasons, by pointing out advantages or benefits, by contrasting the bad effects of not following the suggested action with the good effects of following it. In selecting details for this second part of your talk, think of your listeners. Try to foresee—and answer—their objections.

The last part of your talk should state definitely just what you hope your audience will do. For example, in a talk in which you try to convince your listeners that your plan for the reorganization of the Student Council is sound, you might ask them to vote for your plan and urge their friends to do the same. And in a talk in which you try to convince others to support the town orchestra, you might ask them to buy concert tickets, to sell tickets, and to attend the concerts.

Now make a list of all the details you will use in your talk, grouping them in three or four sections—one to give the background, one or two to explain your reasons, and one to state the action you suggest.

From your list, make the plan that you will follow in giving your talk. Arrange the details in the first section in the order that best explains the background. If there are many details in the second section, be sure to organize them in a logical order, putting related details into separate groups. If you have several details in the last section, arrange them in an effective order, perhaps placing the most important last. Your plan will have at least three groups of details—more if the second part of your talk covers more than one group of related items, as in the following plan for a talk to persuade others of the need for a compulsory driver-education course:

What is the problem?

A. Many thousands of deaths and injuries caused by autos annually

B. Bad record of teen-age drivers as compared with drivers of other age groups

C. Result of publicity about teen-age reckless-ness—parents hesitate to teach teen-agers to drive or to let them use car

D. One way of helping solve problem—institute driver-education courses in schools

What reasons are there for teaching all high-school students to drive?

A. Everyone should learn how to drive—for business, pleasure, emergencies

B. Students without family cars should be given chance to learn

C. Teens best time to learn; muscular coördination best

D. Teen-agers eligible for drivers' licenses can prepare for tests

E. Students trained in course become better pedestrians

What are the advantages of having a driver-education course as part of the curriculum?

A. Trained instructors more competent than relatives or friends

B. Special training cars better than family cars for learning

C. Movies, slides, and special equipment to show need for proper control of car

D. Hand signals, traffic laws, importance of road signs taught

E. Students also taught right attitudes—courtesy of the road, distrust of show-off and road hog, etc.

F. Less possibility of accidents on streets and highways after supervised practice in blocked-off areas

G. Tests show driver-education courses in schools cut student accidents by 50 per cent

What can we do to get such a course for our school?

A. Urge parents to talk about the idea and to get their clubs to back it

B. Sign petition asking school board to institute course

Notice that each section of this plan has a main heading that shows how the details are related. The main headings you use in your plan need not be questions. They may be statements or simply phrases. While practicing your talk, you may decide to reword the main headings. For example, if you were making a plea for a driver-education course in your school, you might begin by saying "Let's look at the record" or "Let's face some startling facts." Instead of saying "What reasons are there for teaching all high-school students to drive?" you might begin your second group of details by saying "There are a number of reasons for giving driver-education courses to all high-school students." Or you may decide to omit one or more of the main headings, feeling that your details are so well organized that your listeners can follow your plan without them. Often it is more effective to begin directly with the first detail, especially if it was chosen to catch the attention of the audience.

If you are asked to give your talk in class, hold your notes in your hand so that you can refer to them if necessary. But remember that the less you have to depend on notes, the more convincing your talk will be.

Persuading Others PART TWO: WRITTEN

Now that you have prepared an oral composition for the purpose of persuading others, you are to prepare a written composition, using the notes you made for your talk. You know that you will have as many paragraphs as there are groups of related details in your plan. And you know that the main headings of these groups will become the topic sentences that tell the reader what the paragraphs are about.

Look at the main headings in your notes. Are they statements or questions that can be used for topic sentences? If not, how will you reword them? Remember that a good topic sentence makes it easy for the reader to know how the details in a paragraph are related.

Now write the first draft of your composition, just as you planned to tell it to your classmates. If you do not intend to use a special opening sentence, begin with your first topic sentence. Then write one or more sentences about each of the details in the first group. When you have finished the first paragraph, refer to your notes to be sure that you have included all the details and that they are in the order you planned. Then write the topic sentence for the second group, and explain the details in that group, remembering to check with your notes after you have finished writing the paragraph. Do the same for each of the remaining groups. If you have a special closing sentence, be sure to make it part of your last paragraph. Write rapidly, trying to hear your sentences as you set them down. Use pencil and scratch paper to that you can make changes and corrections easily.

Allow ample time for revision. First, read your composition for sense, putting yourself in the place of the reader. Does the thought jump abruptly as you go from one sentence to another? Maybe you need to add words like *however* or *furthermore* to show how the sentences are related in meaning. Or maybe you have skimped one of the details in your notes and need to explain it further. Do certain sentences distract attention from the main idea of the paragraph? Perhaps you can combine them with other sentences by using appositives or verbal phrases or subordinate clauses. Occasionally you may find that such sentences are unnecessary and can be crossed out.

Next, read your first draft to yourself, listening to the sentences. Are they monotonously alike? If so, try varying them by combining some, by beginning others with something besides the subject, and by using fewer compound sentences. Always read your revised sentences over, to be sure that they are clear and make good sense.

When you have finished revising your first draft, you are ready to decide on a title for your composition. You may, of course, choose a title that simply tells what your composition is about:

> Should Our Student Council Be Reorganized?
> The Community Orchestra Needs Your Support
> Driver Education for Every Student

Or you may wish to choose a title that will catch the attention of your readers by arousing their curiosity:

> Let's Counsel Our Council
> Who Should Pay the Village Piper?
> Horse Sense Makes Horsepower Safer

As soon as you have selected a title, make a final copy of your composition to hand in. Copy accurately. Keep margins even, and write as legibly as you can. Proofread your work carefully.

Standard English Usage

Improving usage

1. Use nouns and pronouns accurately

Singular and plural nouns

Though words like *news, civics, mathematics, measles, mumps* are plural in form, they are singular in meaning and take a singular verb. We do not write "Mumps are a contagious disease." We write:

> Mumps *is* a contagious disease.
> Civics *is* my most interesting subject.

Foot, mile, pair, bushel, etc., are singular. When more than one of each is meant, the plural form is used. Educated people do not say "He placed the box six foot from the ground" or "Emily bought two pair of shoes." They write:

> He placed the box six *feet* from the ground.
> Emily bought two *pairs* of shoes.
> Mother ordered three *bushels* of potatoes.

Careful writers use the singular form *way* in such expressions as *a short way, a long way.* They do not write "He lives a long ways from here." They write:

> He lives a long *way* from here.
> She walked a little *way* with me.

EXERCISE 1. For the blanks in the sentences, substitute the appropriate forms. In each of the five sentences, use *is, are, has,* or *have*:

1. Mathematics _____ always been my hardest subject.
2. _____ physics harder than chemistry?
3. Economics _____ always been a popular subject with the boys.
4. Measles _____ one childhood disease that I escaped.
5. The news from Ellen and Phil _____ been more cheerful lately.

In each of the next five sentences, use *foot, feet, pair, pairs, bushel, bushels, mile, miles, way,* or *ways*:

6. The Clarks live only a short _____ down the road.
7. Uncle Jim brought us two _____ of apples from his farm.
8. Audrey owns eleven _____ of shoes and wants still more.
9. It was ten _____ to the nearest hospital.
10. The living room is twenty-four _____ long, but it is very narrow.

Pronoun subjects

Educated people do not use both a noun and a pronoun as the subject of one verb unless they mean two persons or things. They do not write "My father he sells shoes." When they are writing about one person or thing, they write:

My *father* sells shoes.	OR: *He* sells shoes.
The *stars* are like our sun.	*They* are like our sun.
Mary wrote a long letter.	*She* wrote a long letter.

When educated people are talking about two persons, they use the pronouns *I, he, she, we, they* and mention themselves second. They do not write "Me and him went to the airport." They write:

He and *I* went to the airport.
Mother and *I* enjoyed reading the book.
She and *we* almost never agree.
They and *we* had different answers.

Pronouns as objects of prepositions

Educated people are careful to use *me, him, her, us,* and *them* as objects of prepositions even when there are two objects. They write:

Give the books to John and *me*.   Make room for Mother and *her*.
Just look at George and *him*.   Jim sat between *them* and *us*.

EXERCISE **2.** Learning to use naturally the pronoun forms preferred by educated people is largely a matter of practicing these forms in sentences until they "sound right" to you. Practice using *me, him, her, us, them* in place of the blank in each of the following sentences.

1. The teacher looked at Philip and _____.
2. The letters were from Jean and _____.
3. The winning stories were written by Ted and _____.
4. The money has been sent to the teacher and _____.
5. The work will be divided between you and _____.

Pronouns as objects of verbs

Educated people are careful to use *me, him, her, us,* and *them* as objects of verbs when there are two objects. They write:

> She invited Tom and *me* to go with her.
> I saw the conductor and *him* talking together.
> Mother sent Bob and *her* to the store.
> He joined Bill and *us* on the way to the station.
> The coach will take *us* first and *them* later.

EXERCISE 3. Practice using *me, him, her, us,* and *them* in place of the blank in each of the following sentences.

1. Uncle Fred took Helen and _____ to the movies.
2. The unexpected visitor made Bill and _____ rather nervous.
3. Marie saw Father and _____ getting out of the car.
4. Miss Jones expected the chairman and _____ to do most of the work.
5. The librarian sent Fred and _____ back to study hall.

Pronouns as appositives

The pronouns *I, he, she, we,* and *they* are used as appositives of nouns and pronouns that are subjects or predicate nominatives. The pronouns *me, him, her, us,* and *them* are used as appositives of nouns and pronouns that are objects. Educated people are careful to write:

> Three boys—Ted, Harry, and *I*—took charge of buying food and cokes for the picnic.
> All purchases were made by the three of us—Ted, Harry, and *me*—working together as a committee.

Pronouns such as *himself* and *themselves* are often used as appositives for emphasis. They may come right after the word they emphasize or at the end of the sentence. They are not set off and always have the same form. We do not say "hisself" or "theirselves." We write:

> The chairman *himself* checked the names on the list.
> The chairman checked the names on the list *himself*.
> The players *themselves* protested the decision.
> The players protested the decision *themselves*.

EXERCISE 4. Write *I, me, she, her, we,* or *us* where the blanks occur:

1. Only two people—namely, the manager and _____—have keys.
2. The teacher gave three of us—Helen, Sue, and _____—permission to leave early.
3. The visitors thanked the entire class, the teacher and _____ alike, for our very interesting program of songs and dances.

We or *us*

We use *we* in expressions like *we girls, we boys, we students* when the pronoun is the subject of the verb. When the pronoun is the object of the verb or preposition, we use *us*. We do not say "Us girls will bring the sandwiches and the cake" or "Miss Evans scolded we boys for talking in class." We write:

> *We* girls will bring the sandwiches and the cake.
> Miss Evans scolded *us* boys for talking in class.
> Some of *us* students suggested a skating party.

210

EXERCISE 5. Write *we* or *us* where the blanks occur:
but do not write in the book. In each of the first five sentences, use *we* or

1. Some of _____ freshmen ought to organize a safety campaign.
2. I know that _____ girls are expected to help with the decorating and the refreshments.
3. Bing told me that Mr. Jenson's scolding was not meant for _____ boys.
4. _____ fellows left earlier than the rest.
5. Can _____ three do all the work alone?

Pronouns with gerunds

The possessive pronouns—*my, your, his, her, our, their*—are used before gerunds. We do not write "Mr. Loomis objected to him running in the halls" or "Mother doesn't like me staying out so late." We write:

> Mr. Loomis objected to *his* running in the halls.
> Mother doesn't like *my* staying out so late.
> I dislike *your* interrupting me.

EXERCISE 6. Write *my, your, his, her, our,* or *their* where the blanks occur:

1. Do you mind _____ coming with you?
2. I don't like _____ borrowing my ties without permission.
3. They seemed surprised at _____ knowing their names.
4. None of Jean's friends ever dreamed of _____ becoming such a famous actress.
5. I was angry at _____ calling me lazy.

Pronouns in adverb clauses of comparison

In elliptical clauses of comparison we use the pronouns *I, he, she, we,* and *they* when they are used as subjects of the omitted verbs. We do not write "Jack is younger than her." We write:

> Jack is younger than *she.*
> Margaret works harder than *I.*
> Donna has more money than *they.*

EXERCISE 7. Write *I, we, he, him, she, her, we, us, they,* or *them* where the blanks occur:

1. Though Pat is slower than Bob, she works more carefully than _____.
2. Gene and I are twins, but he doesn't look like _____.
3. When Al and May left, I noticed that he was shorter than _____.
4. Claire hasn't had as much practice as Kathleen or Ruth, but she types faster and more accurately than _____.
5. My little brother can ask questions faster than I can answer _____.

Them and *those*

The word *them* is a pronoun used as an object. The word *those* is used as a pronoun or as an adjective. Both words mean more than one, but only *those* is used to point out the exact ones meant. Educated people are careful not to confuse these two words. They do not write "Them on the table are mine" or "I like them roses best of all." They write:

Those on the table are mine.   I put *them* there myself.
I like *those* roses best of all.   She bought toys for *them*.

EXERCISE 8. Write *them* or *those* where the blanks occur:

1. Please hand me _____ large books with the red covers.
2. After polishing the shoes, the clerk put _____ in the window.
3. These hats are very nice, but _____ in the window are much prettier.
4. All of _____ dirty dishes on the table should be washed and put away in that cupboard.
5. Motioning the boys to follow him, he spoke to _____ in the hall.

Pronouns that end in *self* and *selves*

Pronouns that end in *self* mean one person or thing. They are *myself, yourself, himself, herself, itself,* and *oneself*. Pronouns that end in *selves* mean more than one person or thing. They are *ourselves, yourselves,* and *themselves*. When these pronouns are used as objects of prepositions or as objects of verbs, they usually refer to the subject of the sentence:

I bought a toy for my little brother and a book for *myself*.
You should see *yourself* in that costume.
Joe carelessly addressed one of the envelopes to *himself*.
This electric clock starts *itself*.
We forced *ourselves* to eat the strange food.
You will see *yourselves* and others in this next picture.
They assigned *themselves* and us to the first bus.

Caution: Other pronouns are not used with *self* and *selves*. We do not write "hisself" or "theirselves." We write:

The chairman put *himself* on the program.
The boys kept this information to *themselves*.

Educated people do not use these pronouns as objects when they mean persons or things different from the subject. They do not say "She sent invitations to Ted and myself" or "I want Gloria and yourself to go with me." Instead, they write:

> She sent invitations to Ted and *me*.
> I want Gloria and *you* to go with me.

EXERCISE 9. For the blanks in the sentences, substitute the pronoun forms used by educated people. In each of the first five sentences, use *I, me,* or *myself*.

1. Mr. Brown sent his son and _____ to the hardware store.
2. Bill, Sue, and _____ went to the class play together.
3. While canoeing I accidentally splashed Tom and _____ with the paddle.
4. At the drug store I bought an ice-cream cone for Helen and a candy bar for _____.
5. Jim and _____ were asked to introduce the guests.

In each of the next five sentences, use *he, him, himself,* or *itself*:

6. I wanted Mary and _____ to see the game.
7. Ted and _____ plan to work during the vacation.
8. Will you call Jane and _____ first thing in the morning?
9. While alone in the house, he cut _____ badly.
10. The refrigerator turns _____ on and off automatically.

Who, which, and *that*

Ordinarily we use the relative pronoun *who* when referring to persons, *which* when referring to things, and *that* when referring to persons or things. We do not write "He is the one which delivered the order." We write:

> He is the one *who* delivered the order.
> Her first novel, *which* was a failure, is her favorite.
> The boy *that* phoned this morning is in the office now.
> My cousin owns the dog *that* rescued the children.

In sentences like these we do not use *what* as a relative. We do not write "This is the only clock what runs accurately" or "The girls what came late did not get seats." We write:

> This is the only clock *that* runs accurately.
> The girls *who* came late did not get seats.

EXERCISE 10. For the blanks in the sentences, substitute the appropriate forms. In each of the ten sentences, use *who, which,* or *that.*

1. There is only one person _____ can make him laugh.
2. The Junior Prom, _____ had been scheduled for the last Friday in April, had to be postponed.
3. The woman _____ asked for Mr. Digby left without seeing him.
4. Every child _____ attended was given a toy and a candy cane.
5. The dog _____ followed at his heels was covered with fleas.
6. Any employee _____ was late more than once was fined.
7. Grandfather's clock, _____ was a real antique, nobody wanted.
8. We sent a cablegram to his youngest son, _____ was visiting his grandfather in England at the time.
9. Bassettville, _____ seemed so beautiful to Henrietta, was really an ugly village.
10. I read a story last night _____ puzzled me.

Who, whom, and *whose*

When a relative pronoun referring to a person is the subject of the adjective clause, *who* is used. We do not write "The principal always disciplined the boys whom were caught cheating." We write:

> The principal always disciplined the boys *who* were caught cheating.
> The man *who* I thought was the thief turned out to be a detective.

When the relative pronoun is the object of a verb or a preposition, *whom* is expected. Although educated people often use *who* in conversation, they try to use *whom* in writing:

> The girl *whom* I saw with Terry must have been your cousin.
> The girl *whom* I hoped they would choose didn't have a chance.
> The boy to *whom* she gave the message never delivered it.

When the relative pronoun shows possession, *whose* is used. We do not write "I know a fellow that his father is a millionaire." We write:

> I know a fellow *whose* father is a millionaire.
> The man *whose* house burned last night had no insurance.

When the antecedent is not a person but a thing, *whose* or *of which* is used.

> The magazine, *whose* circulation had been small, now boomed.
> Bill drove an old sedan, the fenders *of which* were painted red.

EXERCISE 11. Use *who, whom,* or *whose* where the blanks occur:

1. Steve is the boy with _____ Jim went to Europe.
2. Before us loomed a skyscraper _____ tower was hidden in the fog.
3. The members of the cast, all of _____ are amateurs, did very well.
4. Melissa, _____ I had been told was beautiful, seemed plain to me.
5. He is the only person _____ opinion I respect.

Who and *whoever*; *Whom* and *whomever*

When the pronoun that introduces a noun clause is the subject of the clause, *who* or *whoever* is used.

> He doesn't know *who* sent the letter.
> Give those pictures to *whoever* wants them.

When the pronoun is the object of a verb or a preposition, *who* or *whoever* is often used in everyday conversation. But careful speakers and writers try to use *whom* or *whomever*. They do not write "Do you know who he means?" or "I will hire whoever you want." They write:

> Do you know *whom* he means? Tell me *whom* she came with.
> I will hire *whomever* you want. *Whomever* I call on must answer.

EXERCISE 12. Use *whoever* or *whomever* where the blanks occur:

1. Tell _____ answers the phone that I won't be home for dinner.
2. He describes his operation to _____ will listen.
3. Mr. Stanhope will interview _____ you recommend.
4. I will have to work with _____ he assigns to this project.
5. _____ was caught cheating in a final exam was expelled immediately.

Nouns and pronouns as possessives

See Unit 13, page 326.

Improving usage

2. Use clear pronoun reference

Notice how the italicized pronouns are used in these sentences:

> After school, students must wash the blackboards; otherwise *they* begin to look smudged.
>
> Grinning broadly, Phil told Dick that *he* would get all of his money back.

In the first sentence, who or what will begin to look smudged—the students or the blackboards? In the second sentence, is it Phil or is it Dick who will be getting all of his money back? Because in each sentence the italicized pronouns can refer to either of two antecedents, the result is an **ambiguous reference.**

Every pronoun must have a single, clear antecedent. If the reference of a pronoun is not clear, the result is likely to be comic (as in the first sentence above) or puzzling (as in the second sentence). The comedy or confusion that results from ambiguous references can be cleared up by replacing the ambiguous pronoun with a noun:

> After school, students must wash the blackboards; otherwise the *blackboards* begin to look smudged.

or by recasting the sentence:

> Grinning broadly, Phil said to Dick, "I'll get all of my money back." or:
>
> Grinning broadly, Phil said, "You'll get all of your money back, Dick."

Ambiguous reference exists when a pronoun might refer to two or more antecedents. **Vague reference** exists when the antecedent of a pronoun is merely implied or is not stated at all, as in the following sentences:

> In Shakespeare's *Macbeth,* *he* creates an atmosphere of blood and blackness.
>
> People want to strengthen their language habits, *which* explains why they study grammar and usage.
>
> In the textbook *they* use too many childish pictures.

216

In the first sentence above, the pronoun *he* carelessly refers to an antecedent noun, *Shakespeare's,* that is relatively subordinate in the syntax of the sentence. The sentence should be recast:

> In *Macbeth,* Shakespeare creates an atmosphere of blood and blackness. Or:
>
> In Shakespeare's *Macbeth,* the playwright creates an atmosphere of blood and blackness.

In the second sentence, the *which* clause vaguely refers to the entire main clause rather than to a specific antecedent noun. This error can be corrected by using the expression *a fact that* or by eliminating the relative pronoun:

> People want to strengthen their language habits, a fact that explains why they study grammar and usage. Or:
>
> People study grammar and usage to strengthen their language habits.

In the third sentence the antecedent to *they* is neither implied nor stated. The sentence must be restructured:

> In the textbook the authors use too many childish pictures. Or:
> The textbook contains too many childish pictures.

EXERCISE 13. Rewrite the sentences below to eliminate ambiguous or vague reference of pronouns. For the first sentence you might say: *Walking beside the old horse, the farmer became angry and kicked him.*

1. The farmer was walking beside the old horse when he became angry and kicked him.
2. The trouble with psychology is that they think they have all the answers.
3. To be sure that her children saw her notes, Mother taped them to the refrigerator.
4. Mr. Clark was a very enthusiastic teacher, which is why I enjoyed the course.
5. An expert fisherman, Dan can do it for hours on end.
6. Joe often interrupted people in the middle of a statement, which angered everyone.
7. In the article they say that the climate is gradually becoming warmer.
8. Colorful dresses hung on the racks, but they were hidden behind a large pillar.
9. In Sally's diary she keeps her deepest secrets.
10. It says in the newspaper that they are having earth tremors out west.

Improving usage

3. Use modifiers accurately

Adjectives and adverbs

The adjective *good* is one of the most remarkable words in our language. When it is used as an adjective, it is like a harmless, colorless, rather weak plant; but when it pretends to be an adverb, it is a hardy and pestiferous weed in a garden of good speech. It is an ugly thing.

A person may do *well* or play *well* or work *well*. A car may run *well*. Some persons can write *well* or sing *well* or paint *well*. Any kind of successful operation is performed *well*. A yacht may sail *well;* a saw may cut *well;* we may hear *well* over the telephone or see *well* without glasses; some people drive *well* or swim *well* or recite *well* or dress *well* or bat *well* or live *well* on a small income.

Educated people are usually very careful to use adjectives only to modify nouns and pronouns. They do not write "He played good yesterday' or " We sure had fun at their party" or "The dentist hurt me bad." They use adverbs to modify verbs. They write:

> He played *well* yesterday. It was a *good* day for a football game.
> We *surely* had fun at their party. They can be *sure* of that.
> The dentist hurt me *badly*. I had a *bad* cavity.
> The door opens *easily* now. It was an *easy* job to fix it.

A letter to the sports editor of a well known newspaper commended Cincinnati Reds baseball manager Sparky Anderson for saying that his opponents, the Boston Red Sox, had played *well*. The letter read:

> The interviews with Sparky Anderson, as reported in your newspaper Oct. 17 show that baseball men can speak good English.
>
> This might be the time for a special plea that we all maintain the best level of English of which we are capable. It is a priceless possession of us all.
>
> To begin with, nobody ever "played good" unless he was a bad guy pretending to be a good guy. Thanks for the "played well," Sparky Anderson. You certainly did.

Educated people use *really* and *surely* before predicate adjectives. They do not write "A cold drink tastes real good on a hot day." Instead, they write:

218

A cold drink tastes *really* good on a hot day.

It was *surely* hot yesterday.

The adjectives *this, that, these,* and *those* are used to point out persons or things being talked about. The adverbs *here* and *there* mean "in or at this place" or "in or at that place." The adjectives precede a noun or pronoun; the adverbs follow it. Educated people do not write "This here table is about the right size" or "That there man is our new science teacher." They write:

This table is about the right size. The one *there* is entirely too small.

That man is our new science teacher. The one over *here* is our principal, Mr. Murphy.

These people are our friends. The ones over *there* are strangers.

Those dresses on the counter are marked down. The ones *here* are not on sale today.

In conversation with friends we sometimes use *kind* and *sort* with *of* as adverbs. Careful speakers and writers ordinarily avoid these expressions. They do not write "The plan under consideration is kind of vague" or "This experiment is sort of dangerous." They write:

The plan under consideration is *somewhat* vague.

This experiment is *rather* dangerous.

EXERCISE 14. For the blanks in the sentences, substitute the forms used by educated people. In each of the first seven sentences, use *good, well, sure, surely, bad, badly, easy, easily, special, specially, real* or *really*. Do not use any word more than once.

1. My old watch _____ keeps good time.
2. Fragile glassware is _____ broken.
3. This trick play works _____ in every game.
4. He was injured _____ in a plane crash.
5. Her voice sounded very _____ over the loudspeaker.
6. My running shoes are designed _____ for a cinder track.
7. It was _____ hot last Fourth of July.

In each of the next five sentences, use *this, that, these, those, here,* or *there*:

8. The gifts on _____ counter are too expensive.
9. Perhaps the ones over _____ are cheaper.
10. I wouldn't give a plugged nickel for any of _____ ties.

11. The ones right _____ seem much nicer.
12. I think _____ gloves will suit Bill.

In each of the next three sentences, use *rather, somewhat, kind,* or *sort*:
13. He is the _____ of boy who does well in everything.
14. The audience was _____ puzzled by the play.
15. His behavior struck us as _____ strange.

Singular adjectives

The adjectives *this* and *that* are used to point out one *kind* or *sort*. The adjectives *these* and *those* are used to point out two or more *kinds* or *sorts*. We do not write "'I like these kind of shoes." We write:

> I like *this kind* of shoes.
> We enjoy entertaining *this sort* of people.
> *These kinds* of books are found in our library.
> *Those sorts* of foolish answers are found on every set of papers.

In the same way we use *kind* or *sort* to mean one kind or sort of something that has several kinds or sorts. We do not write "We prefer a kind of a book that tells a story." We write:

> We prefer a *kind of book* that tells a story.
> He buys a *sort of apple* that is tart and juicy.
> This *sort of car* is easy to drive.
> That *kind of suit* lasts a long time.

The adjectives *each, every, either,* and *neither* also indicate one person or thing. Educated people use singular verbs and pronouns with the words these adjectives modify. They do not write "Each one of the boys are seated at their desk." They write:

> Each one of the boys *is* seated at *his* desk.
> Every girl in the class *has her* own dictionary.
> Either one of them *is* worth *its* weight in gold.
> Neither man *is* known for *his* honesty.

The same thing is true of *each, either,* and *neither* used as pronouns. When educated people use *everyone* or *everybody* to refer to each person in a class of boys and girls, or in a group of men and women, they use *his.* They do not write "Everyone has to take their own lunch to the picnic." They write:

220

Everyone *has* to take *his* own lunch to the picnic.
Everybody *is* expected to make use of *his* own ideas.
Each of them *has his* special job to do.
Either *is* able to sign *his* name.
Neither of us *has* been asked to do *his* share.

EXERCISE 15. For the blanks in the following sentences, substitute the forms used by educated people. In each of the first four sentences, use *this, these, that,* or *those.*

1. Are _____ sorts of movies ever shown in your town?
2. I have considerable difficulty in buying _____ kind of gloves.
3. She prefers _____ sort of clothes for evening wear.
4. We try to keep away from _____ kinds of people.

In each of the next four sentences, use *kind of* or *sort of*:

5. He chose a _____ bicycle that is extremely light.
6. Mother bought the _____ washing machine that is automatic.
7. What _____ person is he?
8. What _____ camera do you have?

In each of the next four sentences, use *his, her,* or *their*:

9. Did you tell each of the girls to remember _____ number?
10. Everybody may now take _____ place in the line.
11. Upon entering the room, each of the boys removed _____ hat.
12. See that all the boys turn in _____ books tonight.

For the first blank in each of the next three sentences, substitute *is, are, has,* or *have;* for the second blank, substitute *his, her,* or *their*:

13. Each of the children _____ glad to do _____ share.
14. _____ everybody dropped in _____ nickel?
15. Neither of the girls _____ given _____ answer.

Comparison of adjectives and adverbs

When we are comparing two persons or things, we may add *er* to the adjective or adverb, or we may place *more* before it; but we do not combine the forms. We do not write "Joan is more prettier than Helen" or "Dick worked more faster than Clinton." We write:

Joan is *prettier* than Helen.
Joan is *more beautiful* than Helen.
Dick worked *faster* than Clinton.
Dick worked *more efficiently* than Clinton.

Similarly, when we are comparing three or more persons or things, we may add *est* to the adjective or adverb, or we may place *most* before it; but we do not combine the forms. We do not write "Arthur is the most smartest boy in our class." We write:

> Arthur is the *smartest* boy in our class.
> Arthur is the *most intelligent* boy in our class.

We do not add *er* or *est* or use *more* or *most* with adjectives or adverbs that have irregular forms. We do not write "Harriet looks worser today than she did yesterday" or "Dave dances more better than I." Instead, we write:

> Harriet looks *worse* today than she did yesterday.
> Mike's paper is the *worst* of the lot.
> Dave dances *better* than I.
> Sam's picture is the *best* of the group.

Although the "superlative" form (*tallest, most tall*) of the adjective is commonly used in everyday speech in comparing two persons or things, many careful speakers and writers prefer the "comparative" form (*taller, more tall*). They do not write "Clara is the tallest of the Merton twins" or "Henry's suggestion is the most useful of the two." Instead, they write:

> Clara is the *taller* of the Merton twins.
> Henry's suggestion is the *more useful* of the two.

In comparing a person or thing with another or others of the same group, we use the expression *than any other* or *than the other* after the comparative form of the adjective or adverb. We do not write "Elsa is shorter than any girl in the room" or "Don sings better than any boy in the operetta." We write:

> Elsa is shorter *than any other* girl in the room.
> Don sings better *than any other* boy in the operetta.
> Claire is a better cook *than the other* girls.

After the superlative form we use the expression *of all* or *of the*. We do not write "Sue is the shorest of any girl on her team." We write:

> Sue is the shortest *of all* the girls on her team.
> Vincent is the most coöperative *of the* new members.

222

EXERCISE 16. For the blanks in the sentences, substitute the appropriate forms. In each of the first five sentences, use a form of *cold, talkative, young, long,* or *bad*:

1. Nora is the _____ of.the two sisters, though even she has little to say.
2. Sunday was the _____ day we have had in twenty years.
3. Can't you make that skirt _____ by letting down the hem?
4. Though I tried hard, my third copy was _____ than the original.
5. The _____ of the two boys is now a freshman at Notre Dame.

In each of the next five sentences, use *than any other, than the other,* or *of all*:

6. Lois moved more gracefully _____ dancer on the stage.
7. Ernest was the best player _____ the boys who reported for practice.
8. Grace is a better manager _____ girls.
9. Though Mr. Rowe was not strong, he worked harder _____ man there.
10. Dean liked "Patterns" the best _____ Amy Lowell's poems.

Adverbs that end in *where*

Notice that the adverbs *anywhere, everywhere, nowhere,* and *somewhere* end in *where*, not *wheres*. We do not write "I have looked everywheres for her gloves" or "The car was nowheres in sight." We write:

> I have looked *everywhere* for her gloves.
> The car was *nowhere* in sight.

Careful speakers and writers do not use *any place, every place, no place,* or *some place* for adverbs ending in *where*. They do not write "The letters weren't any place I looked" or "He must have put the key some place." They write:

> The letters weren't *anywhere* I looked.
> He must have put the keys *somewhere*.
> The letters weren't *in any place* I looked.
> He must have put the key *in some place*.

Use *anywhere, everywhere, nowhere, any place* or *some place* where the blanks occur:

1. Audrey never goes _____ without her little brother.
2. She always puts the key in _____ that is hard to find.
3. The boys were _____ in sight.
4. _____ I went, I got the same answer.
5. Dick has hidden the map _____ in this house.

Improving usage

4. Use verbs accurately

Agreement of subject and verb

Subjects that mean one person or thing are used with singular verbs. We do not write "One of the tables were badly damaged." We write:

> One of the tables *was* badly *damaged*.
> Don or Bob *has paid* the bill.

Subjects that mean more than one person or thing are used with plural verbs. We do not say "In the box there was a ring and a pin." We say:

> In the box there *were* a ring and a pin.
> Neither the shirts nor the ties *are* on sale.

Phrases beginning with *together with, as well as, in addition to* that come between a subject and its verb do not change the number of the subject. Careful writers do not write "The coach, together with the reporters, have left the field." They write:

> The coach, together with the reporters, *has left* the field.
> Oscar, as well as Dick, *has been expelled*.
> This error, in addition to the increase in prices, *has cost* us customers.

Nouns that are names of groups of persons or things—such as *family, jury, committee, class, team, flock, swarm, herd*—may take a singular or a plural verb. When we are thinking of the group as a whole, we use a singular verb:

224

The team *is determined* to win.

The herd *was sold* yesterday.

But when we are thinking of the individuals in the group, we use a plural verb:

The team *are driving* down in several cars.

The herd *were grazing* in every corner of the pasture.

Words like *all, some, more, half, none* may be singular or plural, depending on the meaning of the sentence. When we are thinking of one thing, we use a singular verb; when we are thinking of more than one thing, we use a plural verb:

All of the food *is ready.*	All of the apples *have spoiled.*
Some of the money *was spent.*	Some of the bills *are* Henry's.
More of the metal *has been cut.*	*Are* there more of these nails?
Half of the order *is* mine.	Half of the orders *are lost.*
None of the work *is* well *done.*	None of the jobs *are filled* yet.

EXERCISE 18. For the blanks in the sentences, substitute the appropriate forms. In each of the sentences, use *is, are, has,* or *have*:

1. The rug, as well as the drapes, _____ been cleaned.
2. None of the writing on these pages _____ legible.
3. _____ your mother or your father there?
4. Some of the plants _____ been wrapped in burlap.
5. The apples in the second bushel in this row _____ the best.
6. Mr. and Mrs. Higgins, together with their two sons, _____ taking the late train.
7. _____ none of the girls going to the track meet?
8. One pair of skates _____ Herbert's.
9. Neither my sister nor my brothers _____ ever had a plane ride.
10. The jury _____ finally reached a decision.

Plural verbs with *there*

When *there* is followed by a singular subject, we use a singular verb. But when *there* is followed by a plural subject, we use a plural verb. We do not write "There has been very few peaches this year." We write:

There *have* been very few peaches this year.
At the door there *were* two men in uniform.
There *is* one sparrow on the telegraph wire.

EXERCISE 19. For the blanks in the sentences substitute the forms used by educated people. In each of the first three sentences substitute for the blank the noun that is italicized in the question. Then be ready to use a pronoun in each answer in place of the noun.

1. What does your *father* do? _____ works in an office.
2. Is your *uncle* still visiting at your home? No, _____ left last week.
3. What does the *mainspring* do in a watch? _____ provides the power to move the hands.

In the next three sentences, use pronouns in each pair of blanks in the answers to the questions:

4. Where did you and Bill go last night? _____ and _____ went to a movie.
5. Did Sue and Mary plan the club party, or did you and Tom do it? _____ and _____ worked out the plans together.
6. Have you and your sister ever gone roller skating? _____ and _____ went last week for the first time.

In each of the next six sentences, use *is, are, was, were, has,* or *have*:

7. There _____n't been many warm days this month.
8. For a long time there _____ been no word from him.
9. There _____ a lot of noise in our room yesterday.
10. There _____ four more sentences to do after this one.
11. Yesterday there _____ several letters for me in the afternoon mail.
12. _____n't there been more visitors than usual this week?

Agreement of relative and verb

When a relative pronoun used as a subject refers to a singular antecedent, a singular verb is used in the relative clause. We do not write "Copy the list of books that are on this card." We write:

Copy the *list* of books that *is* on this card.
Martin is the only *one* of our players who *was* badly *injured*.
The *boy* or *girl* who *wins* will compete in the state contest.

When the relative pronoun refers to a plural antecedent, a plural verb is used. Careful writers do not write "She is one of those girls who screams at the sight of a spider." They write:

226

She is one of those *girls* who *scream* at the sight of a spider.
That is another of those work-saving *gadgets* that never *work*.
Make a list of the *books* that *are* on that table.
Notice the *cup* and *saucer* that *are* on the top shelf.

EXERCISE 20. For the blanks in the sentences, substitute the appropriate forms. In each of the first eight sentences, use *has* or *have*:

1. Clara is one of the most capable girls who _____ ever worked for us.
2. Make an outline of the chapters that _____ to do with the Civil War.
3. Mona is the only one of that group of girls who always _____ a kind word for everybody.
4. Isn't hers one of those coats that _____ two linings?
5. They lived in one of those tiny cottages that _____ barely enough room for one person.
6. This is one of the most encouraging letters that _____ been received.
7. Anyone who _____ as much talent as Ronald should be encouraged.
8. Wear a sweater or blouse that _____ long sleeves.

In each of the next five sentences, use *is* or *are*:
9. Crandall, Hopkins, and Flynn are on the committee that _____ in charge of the budget.
10. Bring me the hat and scarf that _____ on my dresser.
11. George is the only one of those boys who _____ willing to help.
12. I'd like to see a movie or a play that _____ really exciting.
13. Give Jane one of the books that _____ on that table.

Avoiding shifts in time

In telling about something that happened at some time in the past, we use verbs of the same form, unless there is a reason for changing the form. We do not write "Fred dodged past the two girls and tosses the note to me" or "Then she turned to Jim and tells him the same story." Instead, we write:

Fred *dodged* past the two girls and *tossed* the note to me.
Then she *turned* to Jim and *told* him the same story.

Forms of *be, have,* and *do*

The first form is one we use mostly in telling what is now so, or always so, or usually so:

> I *am* happy.
> Tom *is* my cousin.
> The trains *are* ordinarily on time.
> As a rule I *have* fun at parties.
> My father *has* gray hair.
> I *do* my studying at home.
> My mother *does* all her own housework.

The second form is one we use in telling about something in the past:

> Yesterday I *was* absent.
> They *were* in Denver last Christmas.
> I *had* an exciting experience last week.
> We *had* only fifty-two cents between us.
> She *did* nothing about the matter.
> Last summer the painters *did* our house in four days.

The third form is the one we generally use with *have, has,* and *had*:

> I have often *been* there.
> He has often *had* trouble with his watch.
> The coach had *done* his very best with the team.

The fourth form is the one we use with *am, is, are, was,* and *were* when we are telling about something that is taking place at the moment we are speaking or that was taking place at some moment in the past:

> Right now I am *being* as helpful as possible.
> Mary is *having* difficulty with her algebra.
> Today many people are *doing* their own work.
> A year ago he was *being* very careful of his health.
> Yesterday they were *having* a class party.

If we list the four forms for each verb, together with a subject for each form, we have a means of reviewing and remembering the accepted forms:

Forms of	be	have	do
As a rule he	is	has	does
Yesterday he	was	had	did
Many times he has	been	had	done
Right now he is	being	having	doing

Study the list of verb forms, making up sentences with these subjects and verbs. Then think of more sentences, using *I, you,* and *they* as subjects. Try to make good, sensible sentences. Be prepared to give orally a good sentence for each of the verb forms listed. When you are called on, be sure to speak distinctly, and loudly enough for all your classmates to hear.

Using forms of *be*

We do not use "ain't" in place of "am not," "isn't," or "aren't." We write:

> I *am* not *buying* anything more at that place.
> He *isn't making* any plans for next week.
> *Aren't* you *going* to the class picnic?

We do not use *was* with *you.* We write:

> Why *were* you late this morning?
> You *were seen* in front of the store yesterday.
> What *were* you *doing* there?
> *Were* you ever *asked* an embarrassing question?
> Where *were* you *working* last summer?

Using forms of *have*

In rapid speech *have* sometimes sounds like *of.* But we do not write *of* for *have.* We write:

> I *might have known* the answer yesterday.
> You *should have written* me sooner.
> *Could* this *have been prevented?*
> Some of the work *must have been done* previously.

We do not use "ain't" in place of "haven't," "hasn't," or "hadn't." We write:

Unit 10 Forms of *be, have,* and *do* 229

I *haven't been* there yet.
Haven't you *read* the morning papers yet?
Joe *hasn't been seen* all week.
Hadn't he ever *thought* of that before?

Using forms of *do*

We do not use "don't" with a singular noun or with *he, she,* and *it.*
We write:

Doesn't the door *stick* now?
Doesn't he *speak* French?
She *doesn't sing* very well.
Doesn't it *work?*

The form *done* is not used alone as a verb. We write:

Yesterday I *did* my studying before breakfast.
I *have* often *done* my studying early in the morning.
Mr. Smith *did* all the work himself.
Has one man ever *done* all the work before?
She *did* the entire washing by hand.
She *had* never *done* a washing before.

EXERCISE 21. For the blanks in the sentences, substitute the forms of *be,*
have, and *do* that are used by educated people. In the first five sentences,
substitute forms of *be*:
1. When _____ you invited to the party?
2. The rules _____ changed last year.
3. This __n't done very often.
4. _____n't you elected chairman last week?
5. He is _____ threatened with expulsion.

In the next five sentences, substitute forms of *have*:
6. Her parents _____n't been at all well this fall.
7. Up to that time Jim ____ never flown in an airplane.
8. ____n't Mary been at school today?
9. We have ____ trouble with the carburetor.
10. How could we ____ known about your illness?

In the next five sentences, substitute forms of *do*:
11. Why ____n't Bill plan his work ahead of time?
12. I haven't _____ my homework yet.

230

13. This time it ___n't make any difference.
14. ___n't you like football?
15. A mechanic ___ the job for us in about two hours.

Improving sentences

5. Use prepositions accurately

Educated people are careful to use prepositions accurately. For example, they do not confuse *by* and *at*. They do not write "He visited by our house last night." They write:

> He visited *at* our house last night.
> We walked *by* your house last night.

Neither do they confuse *to* and *at*. They do not say "We thought you might be to home." They say:

> We thought you might be *at* home.
> Perhaps you had already gone *to* bed.

They also avoid using *off of*. They do not say "Tom fell off of his bicycle early this morning" or "Henry borrowed two dollars off of me yesterday." They say:

> Tom fell *off* his bicycle early this morning.
> Henry borrowed two dollars *from* me yesterday.

Many careful writers use *from* with *different*. They do not write "The new model is different than the others." They write:

> The new model is different *from* the others.
> Your answer is different *from* the one in the book.

They also use *in* and *into* accurately. They do not write "Just then the teacher stepped in the room." They write:

> Just then the teacher stepped *into* the room.
> Those of us *in* the room were surprised.

EXERCISE 22. For the blanks in the sentences, substitute the appropriate prepositions. In each of the first seven sentences, use *at, by,* or *to*:

1. Were your parents _____ the game yesterday?
2. We visited _____ Grandmother's house last Christmas.
3. Was your father _____ home last Sunday?
4. Some of the family stayed _____ home.
5. The rest of them went _____ a show.
6. We drove _____ the Mitchells' house the other day.
7. Have any of my friends called _____ your house recently?

In each of the next six sentences, use *off, from, of,* or *inside*:
8. The front wheels _____ the car slipped _____ the road.
9. Mother borrowed a quarter _____ me for carfare.
10. Your bicycle is different _____ mine.
11. One _____ the bricks fell _____ the chimney.
12. The movie was different _____ any I have ever seen.
13. Everything was quiet _____ the house.

In each of the next three sentences, use *in* or *into*:
14. Don't come _____ the house with those dirty shoes on.
15. Guess what I have _____ my locker.
16. Slip your feet _____ these warm shoes.

Composition

Telling about Books and Magazines

When the books and magazines we read, the movies we see, the radio programs we hear please us, we usually want to share our pleasure with others. Telling about such things can be fun for both speaker and listener. Just how much fun depends largely on our skill in selecting interesting details and in avoiding vague, meaningless statements.

Have you ever known anyone who tried to tell you about a story in this way? "Gee, I read a swell story last night. I don't remember the name of it or who wrote it, but it's all about a real guy who helps out his pal that's invented a thingumbob that another fellow is trying to get away from him for some reason or other. Well, whosis, or whatever his name is, finds out about it in some way and tells his pal what to say when the other guy comes to see him, which he does, and so fools him into thinking that he'd given the thingamajig to his friend who'd gone to some place in South America, and this saves the day so that he can marry the girl. It's sure a swell story. You ought to read it." This speaker may have known what he was talking about, but no one else does. His efforts to interest you in the story probably ended in complete failure, for all he told you was that he had read a story and had liked it. That is hardly enough. Listeners want to know what it is that you read or saw or heard, what it is about, and why you liked it.

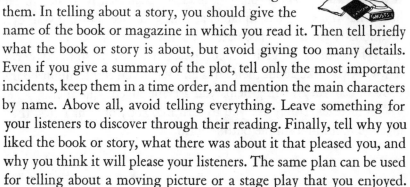

In telling about a book, for instance, you should mention the title and the author so that your listeners can find the book if it sounds interesting to them. In telling about a story, you should give the name of the book or magazine in which you read it. Then tell briefly what the book or story is about, but avoid giving too many details. Even if you give a summary of the plot, tell only the most important incidents, keep them in a time order, and mention the main characters by name. Above all, avoid telling everything. Leave something for your listeners to discover through their reading. Finally, tell why you liked the book or story, what there was about it that pleased you, and why you think it will please your listeners. The same plan can be used for telling about a moving picture or a stage play that you enjoyed. But be sure to tell where it is playing and who the leading actors are.

In telling about a magazine that you like to read, you should mention its name and whether it appears every week, every month, or at other times. Then tell briefly what kind of magazine it is and what it contains, whether it appeals to boys or to girls or to both, whether it has good stories, what kind of articles and regular features it has. If you can, mention names of some of the writers and titles of some of the recent stories and articles. Then tell why you like the magazine and why you think your listeners will like it, too. A similar plan can be used for telling about radio and television programs that you enjoy. But be sure to tell what the program is about, when it is on the air, what station carries it, and who the stars are.

Now decide what you would like to make a short talk about. Will you tell about a book or a movie or a play that entertained you? Will you tell about a magazine that you enjoy reading or a radio or television program that you like to tune in?

When you have selected one of these things that you think will be interesting to your classmates, prepare your notes carefully. Write down exact titles and names. Select interesting details and examples. List reasons for your own enjoyment and for thinking others will be entertained, too. Then add good beginning and ending sentences. With these notes in your hand as you give your talk, you will have no trouble in avoiding vague, meaningless statements.

Practice your talk at least once before coming to class, so that you know exactly what you are going to say and how you want to say it. If you are asked to give your talk in class, speak clearly so that all can hear what you say. Look squarely at your audience, shifting your eyes occasionally from one classmate to another as you talk.

When others are giving their talks, pay attention so that you can tell what you like about their talks and what you think might be improved. Careful listening helps you ask intelligent questions.

Your teacher may ask you to turn in a copy of your notes. If so, arrange them in a simple outline form.

Working with Sentences

In the last Unit you learned about correct usage when working with the parts of speech: nouns and pronouns, adjectives and adverbs, verbs, and prepositions. In this Unit you will study the structure of the whole sentence. In the process you will learn five new ways of improving sentences.

Parallel forms

In Unit 3 you learned that a single verb may have two or more subjects. You also learned that two or more verbs may have a single subject. For example:

> My *sister* and *I* are planning a party for the girl next door.
> Hearing my remark, Dad *looked* up from his paper, *closed* one eye in an elaborate wink, and *grinned* from ear to ear.

In the first sentence *sister* and *I* are used in the same way—as parallel subjects of the verb *are planning*. In the second sentence *looked, closed,* and *grinned* are used as parallel verbs, telling three equally important things that Dad did. Other parallel forms are italicized in the following sentences:

> Old Mr. Jones was extremely *rich*, notoriously *stingy*, and invariably *unpleasant* to strangers.
> Dale moved *slowly* and *cautiously* toward the cellar door.
> Mary walked *in one door* and *out the other*.
> The Safety Council has put up posters in the *stores*, the *schools*, and the *factories*.
> Only the other day we saw a *buck* and two *does* near the camp.
> Gus Wilson, *coach* of the football team and a star *athlete* in his day, spoke about the need for good sportsmanship.

Unit 11   Parallel Forms   235

In the first three sentences are parallel modifiers—parallel predicate adjectives in the first sentence, parallel adverbs in the second, and parallel adverb phrases in the third. In the next two sentences are three parallel objects of the preposition *in* and two of the verb *saw*. And in the last sentence are parallel appositives that add to the meaning of the subject *Gus Wilson*.

Verbals and verbal phrases are often used as parallel forms, as in the following examples:

> Bill's hobbies are *hunting* and *fishing*.
> Bill likes *to hunt* and *to fish* whenever he can.
> Bill finds much relaxation both *in hunting* and *in fishing*.
> Twice a year Bill takes a week off, *hunting for rabbits in the fall* and *fishing for trout in the spring*.

The italicized gerunds in the first sentence are parallel predicate nominatives, while the infinitives in the second sentence are parallel objects of the verb *likes*. The parallel adverb phrases in the third sentence have gerund objects, and the parallel participial phrases in the last sentence modify the subject *Bill*.

Subordinate clauses are sometimes used in parallel ways also:

> I know not only *where he is going* but *when he plans to leave*.
> It was feared *that the plane was down* and *that the entire crew had perished*.
> The old man, *whose snow-white hair reached almost to his shoulders* and *whose hands shook with the palsy*, called out to us.
> *After the lights were dimmed* but *before the curtain was raised*, the orchestra played a long overture to set the mood for the first act.

In the first sentence two noun clauses are used as parallel objects of the verb *knew*, and in the second, two more are used as parallel subjects of the verb *was feared*. In the third sentence two adjective clauses are used as parallel modifiers of the subject *man*, and in the fourth, two adverb clauses are used as parallel modifiers of the verb *played*.

EXERCISE 1. Read the sentences, and decide what the parallel forms are and how they are used. Then divide a sheet of paper into three columns. In the first column, write the parallel forms, one under the other. In the second column, tell what they are. In the third, tell how they are used. Number your answers. For the first sentence you should write:

| 1. *swinging her feet* | *participial* | *modifiers of* |
| *munching an apple* | *phrases* | *"Hilda"* |

1. Hilda was sitting on the porch railing, swinging her feet and munching an apple.
2. Miss Ellis told us to copy our parts and to report for a rehearsal of the first act on Friday.
3. Dick's grandfather was pleasant, charming, and extremely patient.
4. It was certainly lucky for me that Dad was out of town and that Mother was busy with plans for a bridge party.
5. At Bob's yell of alarm we scrambled out of the tree, grabbed up our bicycles, and raced for the highway.
6. After buying a corsage and paying for the tickets, Jim had only two dollars of his birthday money left.
7. We worked swiftly and efficiently, changing the tire in record time.
8. Dick Reynolds, president of our class and editor of the school paper, was voted the boy most likely to succeed.
9. Why Colonel Briggs left and where he went were questions no one could answer.
10. Before I could reach the bottle, the ink had splattered on my dress, on the rug, and on the walls.
11. Ezra, she insisted, was shiftless, dishonest, and cowardly.

Improving sentences
21. Use parallel forms

Students who do not know about using parallel forms often write sentences like these:

> Everybody in our little town knew that George was stubborn, ignorant, and a loafer.
>
> My cousin Dale liked old Mr. Crane for his generosity and because he was witty.
>
> Again and again Kenneth and Ernie tried to get the car out of the mud, but failing each time.
>
> From her mother Alice has learned to cook, how to sew, and all about managing a house efficiently.

You can see that these sentences are awkward and hard to read. They can usually be improved by using parallel forms for ideas that are of equal importance. For example:

Everybody in our little town knew that George was *stubborn, igno-rant,* and *lazy.*

My cousin Dale liked old Mr. Crane for his *generosity* and *wit.*

Again and again Kenneth and Ernie *tried* to get the car out of the mud, but *failed* each time.

From her mother Alice has learned how to *cook, sew,* and *manage* a house efficiently.

From her mother Alice has learned all about *cooking, sewing,* and *managing* a house efficiently.

The italicized words in each sentence are parallel in form and make the sentences easier to read. Notice that the last two sentences show that there may be several ways of using parallel forms to express parallel ideas. Now look at the following sentences:

We could see the crowds going through the gates, and there was a band playing somewhere inside.

You operate the clutch pedal with your left foot, and the brake pedal is worked with your right foot.

The clerk was a short, heavy blonde with round, staring eyes, and she had a crooked nose.

During the entire first period the ball was never within thirty yards of either one of the goals, and this was so during most of the second period, too.

A student who knows about parallel forms can change these awkward compound sentences to simple sentences that are more effective:

We *could see* the crowds going through the gates and *could hear* a band playing somewhere inside.

You operate the clutch *pedal* with your left foot and the brake *pedal* with your right foot.

The clerk was a short, heavy blonde with round, staring *eyes* and a crooked *nose.*

During the entire first *period* and most of the *second* the ball was never within thirty yards of either one of the goals.

Parallel forms are also useful in combining sentences like the following, which are related in meaning:

Jim Thompson made a speech of welcome to the parents. He is cap-tain of the basketball team, and he was also elected president of the Boys' Club.

238

In the window was a sleek new convertible, and it was painted yellow. The upholstery was red leather, and the wheels were equipped with white-wall tires.

Everybody turned out for the final game. It was played last Saturday, and we should have won it easily.

When the related ideas in the pairs of sentences at the bottom of the preceding page are combined by using parallel forms, the reader can see which ideas are of equal importance:

Jim Thompson, *captain* of the basketball team and *president* of the Boys' Club, made a speech of welcome to the parents.

In the window was a sleek new convertible *painted* yellow, *upholstered* in red leather, and *equipped* with white-wall tires.

Everybody turned out for the final game, *which we played last Saturday* and *which we should have won easily.*

These are some of the ways in which you can use parallel forms to make better sentences. As you revise your own sentences, watch constantly for opportunities to use parallel words, phrases, or clauses to express ideas of equal importance. As you have seen, this simple trick can often turn awkward sentences into effective ones.

EXERCISE 2. Read the sentences, and decide how they can be improved by using parallel forms. Be prepared to read your revised sentences aloud. For the first one you might say: *My chores were to cut wood for the stove and to help with the meals.*

1. My chores were cutting wood for the stove and to help with the meals.
2. Few could decide whether he was being very brave or merely a fool.
3. Last summer Bruce taught Kathleen to swim, how to dive, and sailing.
4. Bob Matthews donated the trophies that were presented to the team. He is a graduate of Parker High, and he was formerly an All-American football player.
5. As soon as Peter was well, he helped out a little by selling newspapers, and he did odd jobs for the neighbors.
6. Virginia admired the new supervisor for her patience and because she was efficient.
7. Joan's only recreations were going to the movies and to read novels.
8. From all of his workers Mr. Cunningham demanded courtesy and that they be honest.

9. Our English teacher gives us long, hard assignments, but never failing anybody who tries his best.
10. Before the end of the week Terry had learned two lessons—to speak respectfully to his aunt and that he should be on time for meals.

Improving sentences

22. Use clear modification

In your writing, make sure that any modifying phrase or clause that you use modifies a word in the sentences and that it is the word you intended it to modify. Watch especially for sentences like these:

> Mrs. Ellis paid no attention to her husband, busily measuring out flour for Pete's birthday cake.
> Suspended from the ceiling by a single hair, Damocles saw a shining sword.

Each of these sentences contains the word the participle is intended to modify. But the writer of the first sentence has carelessly put the phrase last, where it seems to modify *husband*; and the writer of the second sentence has carelessly put the phrase first, where it seems to modify *Damocles*. Such confusing and, often, amusing errors are called **misplaced modifiers.** The confusion is easily corrected. Simply move the phrases closer to the words they are intended to modify:

> Mrs. Ellis, *busily measuring out flour for Pete's birthday cake,* paid no attention to her husband.
> Damocles saw a shining sword *suspended from the ceiling by a single hair.*

Here is an example of a misplaced adjective clause:

> The tall man ducked behind the hedge that Ernie had seen prowling about the halls.

Unless you are trying to amaze your readers with a fantastic story of wandering hedges, you should place the clause right after the word it modifies:

> The tall man *that Ernie had seen prowling about the halls* ducked behind the hedge.

240

In using adverb clauses, be sure that each clause clearly modifies what you intend it to modify. Compare these two sentences:

> Mary decided to eat her breakfast at the cafeteria on the corner *before she got up*.
>
> *Before she got up*, Mary decided to eat her breakfast at the cafeteria on the corner.

The first sentence seems to mean that Mary was going to eat her breakfast before getting up. In the second sentence the clause has been put first to show the reader that it modifies the verb *decided*. Shifting an adverb clause in this way often makes the meaning clearer. And be sure to avoid elliptical clauses that may have two meanings:

> The older players taught me more *than the coach*.
> Is the sun ever closer to the moon *than the earth?*

The first sentence might mean:

> The older players taught me more $\begin{cases} \textit{than the coach did.} \\ \textit{than they taught the coach.} \end{cases}$

The second sentence might mean:

> Is the sun ever closer to the moon $\begin{cases} \textit{than the earth is?} \\ \textit{than it is to the earth?} \end{cases}$

Always supply the words necessary to make your meaning clear.

EXERCISE 3. The sentences below are confusing because modifiers have been misplaced. Revise each sentence by putting the misplaced modifier where it clearly modifies the word intended. For the first one you might say: *They used the snapshot I took of Bill standing beside the wagon.*
1. They used the snapshot of Bill standing beside the station wagon that I took.
2. Being in a rundown condition, I bought the house cheaply.
3. Backed up by a powerful army, no one could oppose the dictator.
4. Jim would lie on the sofa and daydream about running a four minute mile whenever he got tired.
5. Having broken all the laws of society, I feel the man should be punished.
6. She wore a new bonnet on her blonde head which had been bought in a bargain basement.

7. The little boy held his new dog in his arms, wearing a broad grin.
8. Jane had thrown the speech into the waste basket that Mr. Allan was to broadcast that evening.
9. After the fight Jimmy ran home to his mother with a bloody nose.
10. While sitting in the saddle, the horse threw the cowboy.

When the word a phrase is to modify is totally omitted, that phrase is said to be a **dangling modifier**, because it has no word to modify. In revising your written work, watch out for sentences like these:

Having worked all afternoon in the hot sun, the pitcher of lemonade was most welcome. (dangling participle)
To be sure of a seat, tickets must be purchased early. (dangling infinitive)
While watching the play, her headache was soon forgotten. (dangling prepositional phrase)

These sentences seem to mean that the pitcher of lemonade had been working, that the tickets are to be sure, and that the headache was watching the play. Such dangling modifiers are easily corrected by putting the missing words back into the sentences as subjects:

Having worked all afternoon in the hot sun, *we welcomed the pitcher of lemonade.*
To be sure of a good seat, *you should purchase your tickets early.*
While watching the play, *she soon forgot her headache.*

EXERCISE 4. Undangle the dangling phrases in the sentences that follow. For the first sentence you might say: *Excited at the thought of going to the party, she soon forgot her worries.*
1. Excited at the thought of going to the party, her worries were soon forgotten.
2. While sleeping in my room, two friends came to visit.
3. To become a doctor, hard work is required.
4. Having eaten dinner, the dishes were washed and dried.
5. Running through the field, Jerry's jacket caught on a bush.

242

Careless repetition

While writing, a person may be so intent upon expressing his ideas that he fails to notice how often he is carelessly repeating a word or phrase. The careless repetition of a word used in two ways can be very annoying to the reader. For example: "Only a few of the *club* members attended the first meeting of the *club*." Either of the following sentences would be better:

> Only a few of the members attended the first meeting of the club.
> Only a few of the club members attended the first meeting.

The careless repetition of two words in successive sentences is usually a sign that revision is needed. For example: "The house is surrounded by a *wide terrace*. The *terrace* is about twelve feet *wide*." Sentences like these are less wearisome to read when they are combined:

> The house is surrounded by a terrace that is about twelve feet wide.
> A terrace about twelve feet wide surrounds the house.

The careless repetition of two or three words in different forms may be not only tiresome but confusing as well. For example: "First *squeeze* the *juice* out of the *lemons* with a *lemon squeezer*. Then throw the *squeezed lemons* away and pour the *lemon juice* into a bottle." Such sentences are less confusing when they are combined:

> After squeezing the lemons, throw them away and pour the juice into a bottle.

Prepositions are often repeated intentionally in a series of parallel phrases. But when the phrases are not parallel, the careless repetition of a preposition can be unpleasant, even to the dullest ear. For example: "*On* the following morning Sue and I rode *on* the same avenue *on* horseback." The monotonous repetition can be avoided by dropping one *on* and changing another to a different preposition:

> The following morning Sue and I rode along the same avenue on horseback.

The preposition *with* has a way of making sentences awkward. When it is used several times in one sentence, the result may be absurd: "He lives in a large house *with* a red roof, white *with* green shutters, and a beautiful yard *with* two maiden aunts." Ordinarily the careless repetition of *with* can best be avoided by completely rephrasing the sentence:

> He lives with two maiden aunts in a large white house that has a red roof, green shutters, and a beautiful yard.

Repetition is not by itself bad. In fact, used intentionally for emphasis, it may be very effective. But careless, thoughtless repetition is never effective. Try to hear your words as you write your first drafts. Always watch for awkward repetition as you read over what you have written. By doing these two things, you can soon learn to avoid careless repetition in your compositions.

Wordiness

Words are so easily spoken that a person ordinarily uses more of them in talking than are actually needed to express his ideas. He may restate important points to be sure that they are understood. He may include unnecessary words that he feels make his sentences "sound" better. He may carelessly use half a dozen vague words where one specific word would be better. All these things lead to wordiness—the use of too many words—which is seldom objectionable in speaking unless carried to extremes. In writing, however, it often results in tiresome sentences.

Just how many words *are* too many is not always easy to decide. Many factors have to be considered—the difficulty of the ideas, the knowledge of the reader, the need for completeness, and so forth. But there are certain obvious kinds of wordiness that can be weeded out in revising first drafts. For example, in the first part of this lesson you learned that the careless repetition of a word can be tiresome. So also can the careless repetition of an idea be tiresome. Notice the italicized words in these two sentences:

> His big problem was what to do with the excess food *that had been left over*.
> Modern high schools *in this day and age* have professional coaches and well-kept playing fields, but *during the past* in Grandfather's day this was not so.

The italicized clause in the first sentence adds little or nothing to the meaning of *excess*. The italicized phrases in the second sentence merely repeat the ideas already expressed by *Modern* and *in Grandfather's day*. The sentences are more forceful when the unnecessary words are omitted:

> His big problem was what to do with the excess food.
> Modern high schools have professional coaches and well-kept playing fields, but in Grandfather's day this was not so.

As you know, there are usually several ways of expressing an idea. Although the longer ways may be suitable for conversation, they often make written sentences seem wordy and boring. Here are two sentences with more words in them than are needed:

> *It was* shortly after my twelfth birthday *that* I went camping for the first time *in my life*.
> It was at least a half day's journey to *the place where* the fishing lodge *was located*.

These ideas can be expressed more concisely by omitting the unnecessary words:

> Shortly after my twelfth birthday I went camping for the first time.
> It was at least a half day's journey to the fishing lodge.

Closely related to such sentences are those in which roundabout expressions cause wordiness:

> *It has seldom been the case that* a team so far behind has been able to win the pennant.
> The more care you take in sanding the wood, the better *the result will be as far as* the finish *is concerned*.

Sentences like these can be made more interesting by omitting all the italicized words but *seldom* in the first sentence and *will be* in the second:

> Seldom has a team so far behind been able to win the pennant.
> The more care you take in sanding the wood, the better the finish will be.

Notice that some changes in the order of words are required when the roundabout expressions are omitted.

A roundabout expression used in place of a single word often gives a formal tone that seems out of place in ordinary sentences:

> *Owing to the fact that* he had not eaten any lunch, Jed was nearly starved by evening.
> *An overwhelming majority* of the students *are of the opinion* that the classwork *which they do from day to day* should count as much as the examination *at the end of the year.*

The italicized words in these sentences cannot simply be omitted, but they can be replaced with single words that make the sentences less formal and more readable:

> Since he had not eaten any lunch, Jed was nearly starved by evening.
> Most of the students think that the daily classwork should count as much as the final examination.

These obvious kinds of wordiness are common and easily spotted. As you have seen, they can often be remedied by merely omitting unnecessary words or by substituting single words. If you learn to watch for wordiness as you revise your own writing, you will soon discover other ways of getting rid of unnecessary words.

Sometimes wordiness is caused by using a sentence where a clause or phrase or even a word would express the idea just as well. Notice the following sentences:

> A roof can be made of aluminum. This metal reflects the sun's rays.
> A roof can be made of aluminum, which reflects the sun's rays.
> A roof can be made of aluminum to reflect the sun's rays.
> A roof that is made of aluminum reflects the sun's rays.
> A roof made of aluminum reflects the sun's rays.
> An aluminum roof reflects the sun's rays.

As you revise your own sentences, watch for opportunities to combine related sentences by using clauses, phrases, or single words in place of one of the sentences. Rephrasing is one of the most effective ways of avoiding wordiness.

EXERCISE 5. Read the sentences, and decide how to revise them to avoid careless repetition and wordiness. Then rewrite the sentences. Number your revised sentences. For the first one you might write: *1. Because he did not enjoy associating with anyone there, he left the party early.*

1. Owing to the fact that there was no one there that he could associate with with any pleasure, he left the party early in the evening.
2. The bus went through one red light after another, and the man at the wheel of the bus didn't even blow his horn as he went through.
3. It has often been the case that the boys who do poor work in language classes do exceptionally well in science classes.
4. The modern girl of today has many careers from which she can make the choice that she wants.
5. It was fully an hour after the plumber arrived that he told me that he did not have the necessary tools that he needed.
6. By the time it was time for the curtain to go up, Muriel had memorized Jane's lines by heart.
7. In order to speed up the final checking of the orders, we arranged the cards in alphabetical order.
8. If you should happen to see him carrying a notebook like the notebook I lost, try to find out whether the notebook he is carrying could be my notebook, will you?
9. Through some friends who were passing through our town where we live, we learned that you are through school now and have gotten a job through your own efforts.
10. Because of the fact that safety devices have not been installed throughout the factory, many workers have been injured.

Improving sentences

23. Make every word count

By avoiding careless repetition and wordiness, you get rid of unnecessary words that often make sentences tiresome. But merely omitting some words does not automatically improve those that remain.

You must also seek to use words that express your ideas as clearly and forcefully as possible. You must make every word count.

Words are of many kinds. Some, such as *say* and *walk, people* and *pets,* are **general words** that apply to many kinds of saying and walking, to all sorts of persons and animals. Others, such as *mutter* and *march, students* and *spaniels,* are **specific words** that refer to particular kinds of saying and walking, to certain groups of persons and animals. One important way of making every word count is to use specific words instead of general words wherever you can. Notice the following pairs of sentences:

> The men quickly ate some food and drank a lot of hot coffee.
> The rescuers bolted hamburger sandwiches and gulped down cups of steaming hot coffee.

> A stone, thrown by an angry man, broke the windshield of the automobile.
> A stone, hurled by an angry pedestrian, shattered the windshield of the sedan.

These sentences have the same number of words; but you can see that the second sentence in each pair is more definite, more alive, more interesting because of the specific words that are used.

Repetition and wordiness can sometimes be avoided by using specific words. Notice the repetition of *board, two, pieces,* and *edge* in these three sentences:

> First William cut the board into two pieces with the saw. Then he cut a half inch off one edge of the two pieces of the board with a plane. Finally he cut two notches in the other edge of the two pieces of the board to hold the cross braces in place.

If more specific words are used, it is possible to combine the three sentences, eliminating the tiresome repetition:

> After sawing the board in two, William planed a half inch off one edge of each piece and notched the opposite edge to hold the cross braces in place.

What is important about the revised sentence is not that it is twenty-four words shorter, but that it combines three separate sentences into one clear, forceful, interesting sentence in which every word counts.

As you continue to revise your own writing, you will discover how important this twentieth and last suggestion for improving sentences really is. In a sense, it is the climax of all the ways you have learned. For your sentences are, after all, made up of words; and the more accurately these words express your ideas, the more effective your sentences will be in communicating your thoughts to others. Only by learning to make every word count can you attain the desirable goal of clear, forceful, interesting sentences in your writing.

EXERCISE 6. Read the sentences, and decide how they could be improved by using specific words in place of general words. Make at least two changes in every sentence, more if you can. Be ready to read your revised sentences aloud. For the first sentence you might say something like this: *The sailor tossed a handful of pennies to the ground and watched the native boys scramble for them.*

1. The man threw a bunch of coins to the ground and watched the children pick them up.
2. Before aid could arrive, the flames had moved through the building, burning it completely.
3. Five people were seated close together around a small table in one section of the room, talking about a number of things.
4. Grumbling with pain, the woman walked over to the window and looked out on the darkening street.
5. The men cut at the vines, trying to cut their way through to the clearing beyond.
6. The boys slowly pulled the large pieces of wood to the edge of the cliff and threw them over the edge into the water below.
7. The vehicle moved noisily over the tracks and came to a stop in front of the building.
8. The frightened boy ran up the stairs at the front of the house, a dog running at his heels.
9. While reaching for the cup on the top shelf, the woman accidentally moved the glass tray, which fell to the floor with a loud noise.
10. The girl turned just in time to see the animal moving quietly toward the injured bird.

Improving sentences

24. Avoid sentence fragments

Appositives are not sentences

You have seen how an appositive may be used in place of a sentence to give the reader additional information. But an appositive does not by itself make a statement or ask a question or give a command. No matter how many modifiers an appositive may have, it is not a sentence but a substitute expression for a word in a sentence. If you begin such an expression with a capital letter and end it with a period, you show that you do not yet know what a sentence is. Watch particularly for an appositive that comes at the end of a sentence:

Last summer we visited Hammerfest, a northern seaport in Europe. Next year he wants to learn lacrosse, a game played with a ball and long-handled rackets by two teams of twelve players each.

Such appositives must remain attached to their sentences. It is a serious error to begin them with capital letters and end them with periods. You would laugh at anyone who cut off a dog's tail and told you it was another dog. It is just as ridiculous to cut off a final appositive and punctuate it as another sentence.

EXERCISE 7. Read each of the groups of words and decide whether it is one sentence or two sentences. Then look for appositives that need to be set off. On a sheet of paper, write the numbers of the groups and, after them, the first and last words of each sentence. Capitalize each first word. Put a period after each last word. Write the word preceding each comma or dash needed to set off an appositive. For the first group you should write: *1. There pause, anxiety. During breathe.*

1. There was a brief pause a minute of anxiety during this time we hardly dared to breathe
2. The next hour was a very anxious one a time of waiting and wondering without much hope
3. We noticed a sweetish smell in the air a scent like that of an ant hill on a hot day
4. The food served to the sailors on the *Dragon* and the *Hector* was exactly the same except for one item lemon juice every morning for the men on the *Dragon*
5. For his seventieth birthday the grandchildren gave him a beautiful and expensive gift a hand-carved mahogany screen with handsome leather panels at the top and hammered brass rings and corners

Verbals cannot make sentences

In Unit 5 you learned that participles are modifiers, not verbs. They imply action; but they do not have subjects, and they cannot make statements. Neither can the gerunds that you studied in Unit 5 make statements. They are somewhat like verbs, but they cannot be the prinicpal words in sentences. Infinitives, as you have just seen, are used as nouns, not verbs. You may group dozens of words around an infinitive, but you cannot make a statement with it. No verbal is a verb. No verbal can form a sentence.

See how the participles in this group of words put on the airs of verbs and pretend to make a sentence: "On the sidewalk near the dormitory several young men, *gathering* in uneasy clusters and *talking* to one another in a nervous way." This large group of words and phrases cannot be a sentence. The participles describe the young men, but do not make a statement about them.

A gerund may put on the uniform of a verb and pose in an important group of words as if it were a commanding verb: "By *telling* everybody in the room, with a loud voice, not to pay any attention to the line of taxicabs forming at the curb." The gerund *telling,* followed by the verbals *to pay* and *forming,* looks quite imposing. It gives information and shows us an interesting picture. But it does not make a statement. The group of words is only a counterfeit sentence.

An infinitive often pretends to be·a real, live verb: "*To hear* his own son, an ensign in the navy, explaining the cause of his father's failure to be sent on this important mission." The group is built around three verbals—*to hear, explaining,* and *to be sent.* But it has no verb. It is no more a sentence than a scarecrow is a man.

If you let verbals fool you into making sentence errors, you show that you do not yet know what a sentence is. No matter how many verbals a group of words may contain, it cannot be a sentence unless it also contains a verb. Only when a group of words has a verb can it make a statement, ask a question, or give a command.

EXERCISE 8. Read each of the groups of words, and decide what other words are needed to make it a sentence. Then write the sentences on a sheet of paper. Capitalize the first word of each sentence. Put a period after each last word. Put in any commas that are necessary. For the first group of words you might write: *1. His worst fault, to think always about himself without ever spending a dollar or an hour on some friend, made him very unpopular with everyone.*

1. to think always about himself without ever spending a dollar or an hour on some friend
2. writing a letter to Don Thornton to invite him to come to the dance given by the Booster Club
3. to lift the juicy piece of pie out of the deep plate without spilling anything on the tablecloth
4. by putting thousands of billboards along all the principal highways in the state

5. after walking to the window and perching herself on the sill
6. in spite of our announcing it distinctly before opening the doors
7. standing at the rail of the bridge and looking down on a switch engine passing beneath him
8. by eating at expensive restaurants and sitting in the very best seats at the theaters
9. leaving myself without any money to pay for our cokes and hamburgers
10. by working after five o'clock and coming an hour early in the morning to make up for the lost day

Adjective clauses are not sentences

An adjective clause has a subject and a verb, but it is not a sentence. It is only a part of a sentence, a modifier of a noun or a pronoun. Just as you would not begin an adjective with a capital letter and follow it with a period, so you cannot punctuate an adjective clause as a sentence and expect it to make sense to the reader.

A restrictive clause is usually so closely connected in meaning with the rest of the sentence that there is little temptation to detach it from the sentence. But a nonrestrictive clause often merely adds an explanatory comment or an interesting detail that may not seem to have much connection with the meaning of the sentence. When such a clause comes last in the sentence, there is often a strong temptation to detach it from the sentence. But if you remember that the clause explains some word in the sentence, you will not yield to this temptation. Notice the following sentences:

> Miss Jones gave a signal to John, *who then started the projector.*
> We looked forward to meeting this famous writer, *whose name was familiar to all of us.*
> About noon the travelers reached Pittsfield, *where they stopped for a quick lunch.*
> We left the day after Christmas, *when every creature seemed to be stirring, including the mouse.*

The italicized clause in each of these sentences modifies a word in the main clause and is a part of the sentence. Notice this next sentence:

> Bob stopped to answer the phone, *which made him late for school.*

The relative pronoun in this sentence refers to the whole idea expressed by the main clause, rather than to any one word in the main clause. It was not the telephone that made Bob late for school, but his stopping to answer it. The *which* means about the same thing as "and this." Since the clause merely adds an explanatory comment, the clause is clearly nonrestrictive and must be set off with a comma.

EXERCISE 9. Read each of the groups of words and decide whether it is one sentence or two sentences. Decide also which adjective clauses are nonrestrictive. On a sheet of paper, write the numbers of the groups and, after them, the first and last words of each sentence. Capitalize each first word. Put a period or question mark after each last word. Write the word preceding each comma needed to set off a nonrestrictive adjective clause. For the first group you should write: *1. The game, season, play. That week.*

1. The Hortonville game which was the final one of the season was won in the last two minutes of play that victory made up for losing the game with River Falls last week

2. We had a hard time persuading Dad who wanted to vacation in a place where he could fish

3. She flatly refused to serve on any committee which surprised us later that day she sent us a note that explained her reasons

4. My youngest brother who likes all sorts of gadgets was fascinated by the can opener that I had bought at Crandall's for sixty-nine cents

5. Grandmother Martin who seldom spoke above a whisper ordered the agent to leave in a voice that could have been heard for blocks

Noun clauses are not sentences

A noun clause has a subject and a verb, but it is not a sentence. It is only a part of a sentence—a subject or an object, a predicate nominative or an appositive. You would never detach a noun from a sentence and punctuate it as a separate sentence. In the same way you cannot punctuate a noun clause as a separate sentence and expect it to make sense to the reader.

You know this, of course, and probably never make such a mistake when you take time to think about the work that a noun clause does in a sentence. But noun clauses at the end of the sentence, particularly those in apposition, sometimes seem almost like separate explanations and may become detached while you are thinking about something else. Notice that the noun clauses in the following sentences are necessary parts of the statements made by the sentences:

> After an interval of several weeks I again reminded him *that he had not yet paid his dues*.
>
> It was by the merest chance *that we found the lost keys*.

EXERCISE 10. Read each of the following groups of words and decide whether it is one sentence or two sentences. Decide also which noun clauses in apposition should be set off by commas or dashes. On a sheet of paper, write the numbers of the groups and, after them, the first and last words of each sentence. If there are appositive clauses that need to be set off, be sure to include the word preceding each comma or dash. Capitalize the first word of each sentence. Put a period or a question mark after each last word. For the first group you should write: *1. Even news, president, Ross. That us.*

1. Even this exciting news that he had been elected class president did not please Ross that worried us
2. I know that Jim won the tournament how he won is what puzzles me
3. Find out where Mr. Axtell is he will tell you if the pieces can be welded
4. The Department of Agriculture has reported a queer fact that people are drinking less coffee at home and more at the soda fountains
5. John's final suggestion that we eat first and then explain that we had lost our money seemed pretty dangerous to me I was sure we would be arrested or taken to the kitchen to wash mountains of dishes

Adverb clauses are not sentences

An adverb clause has a subject and a verb, but it is not a sentence. It is only a part of a sentence—a modifier of a verb, an adjective, or an adverb. You would not think of detaching an adverb from its sentence, beginning the adverb with a capital letter and following it with a period. Neither can you punctuate an adverb clause as a separate sentence and expect it to make sense to the reader.

Because an introductory adverb clause seems incomplete without the rest of the sentence, you are not likely to detach it. But a nonrestrictive adverb clause at the end of a sentence often adds an explanatory remark that may not seem to have much connection with the rest of the sentence. For example:

> We didn't go to the show last night, *because Tom had to study for a Latin test*.
>
> The team always played hard until the final whistle, *whatever the score happened to be*.

254

> Pass the ball with a short, quick motion of the arm, *as the coach showed us yesterday.*

Adverb clauses like these modify the verb in the main clause and must remain a part of the sentence. If you carelessly begin such a clause with a capital letter and end it with a period, you make a serious sentence error. By carefully going over all writing before turning it in, you can usually catch such careless sentence errors. Always take time to be sure.

EXERCISE 11. Read each of the groups of words, and decide whether it is one sentence or two sentences. Then look for adverb clauses that need to be set off. On a sheet of paper, write the numbers of the groups and, after them, the first and last words of each sentence. If the sentence has an introductory or nonrestrictive clause, be sure to include the word preceding each comma that is needed to set it off. Capitalize each first word. Put a period or a question mark after each last word. For the first group you should write: *1. Willis committee. Now well, know.*

1. Willis did an excellent job when he was chairman of the membership committee now he is not doing so well as you know
2. I felt sure that the agent would not do as he promised since I saw him wink at the other man in the office
3. Although we had no hope of finding the ring we neglected our work and searched everywhere
4. Do you think Clyde is angry because most of the critics laughed at his paintings we do
5. I urged Mother to visit Uncle Denny while the wreckers were here as she couldn't bear to see them tearing down the old home

Improving sentences

25. Avoid the comma splice

Avoiding sentence errors caused by adverbs

The most common adverb in school composition is *then*. Notice how it begins an independent sentence:

> We saw a blinding flash of lightning. *Then* came the most deafening crash of thunder I ever heard.

A sentence beginning with *then* may be very short and very closely connected in meaning with the sentence before it, but it is an independent sentence grammatically and must begin with a capital:

> For a moment the lights in the warehouse flashed up brilliantly. *Then* they went out again.

Using a comma instead of a period between these two sentences would cause a serious sentence error.

The adverbs *finally, now,* and *there* are very common. Notice how they, too, begin independent sentences:

> Paste and glue would not hold. *Finally* we tried cement.
> Classes used to be forty-five minutes long. *Now* they are only forty.
> At last I looked under the desk for it. *There* it was.

Study the three following pairs of sentences and see how short, independent sentences may begin with other adverbs:

> The screen is too tall and heavy. *Also* it is the wrong color.
> Eva was frightened by his answer. *However,* she pretended not to notice it.
> Yes, she does talk too much. *Still* I like her.

If you do the following exercises carefully, thinking all the time about the sentences in your own writing, you will have a better understanding of what a sentence is.

EXERCISE 12.   In all of the groups of words there is a serious sentence error—the use of a comma before an adverb that begins an independent sentence. Find the groups that have these comma blunders, and write the numbers on a sheet of paper. After each number, write the first and last words of the two sentences in that group. Capitalize each first word. Put a period after each last word. For the first group you should write: *1. Warren pad. Then encyclopedia.*

1. Warren jotted down several dozen notes on a big pad, then he ran to look at the encyclopedia.
2. Mr. Sexton figured carefully, still he was mistaken.
3. The dog grew more and more nervous, finally he began to yelp.
4. Icicles are hanging from the radiator, now you can see how cold it has been here.
5. The officer was entirely wrong, nevertheless Katharine and I took his scolding in silence.

256

Avoiding sentence errors caused by prepositions

In each of the following groups of words there are two sentences. You can see that in each the second sentence begins with a prepositional phrase which modifies a verb that comes after it:

> All morning it had been growing more dark and chilly. *At last* it began to snow.
> It will be very hot by noon. *At least* I think so.
> She knew very little about tennis. *In fact* she knew nothing at all.
> Skippy found a battered horn on the sidewalk. *With this* he made a din all afternoon.

In your written work, watch out for short, independent sentences that begin with a preposition. Using a comma before a preposition that begins a sentence is a serious error.

EXERCISE 13. In most of the groups of words there is a serious sentence error—the use of a comma before a preposition that begins an independent sentence. Find the groups that have these comma blunders and write the numbers on a sheet of paper. After each number, write the first and last words of the two sentences in that group. Capitalize each first word. Put a period after each last word. For the first sentence you should write: *1. All excellent. From repair.*

1. All the way to Glenview the roads were excellent, from there on they were in bad repair.
2. Early in the morning the sky was perfectly clear, after seven it began to cloud up.
3. My health is quite all right, in fact I never was better.
4. Ethel amused us by standing very stiff and still, like one of those wax models in a store window.
5. The thunderstorm was thrilling to me, to Ellen it was terrifying.

Avoiding the comma splice with clauses

In Unit 8 you learned that a comma is ordinarily used between co-ordinate clauses joined by a conjunction:

> You will find a padlock on the garage door, and here is the key to open it.
> I am very sorry, but I must disagree with your last statement.
> She had to stand the whole way, for every seat was taken.
> The forecast was for fair weather, yet it rained all afternoon.
> Step in very carefully, or the canoe may tip over.

You can see that omitting the conjunction in any of these sentences would leave only a comma between the coördinate clauses. In most schools the use of a comma alone between coördinate clauses is considered a serious error—a "comma splice."

You have learned that a semicolon is used between coördinate clauses that are not joined by a conjunction:

> Father was lost; he didn't even know what road we were on.
> We looked in the locker room; there they were.
> Don't touch that rifle; it's loaded.
> The odds were against him; nevertheless, he won the match.
> The lightning became more intense; then the rain began.
> She enjoyed the show; in fact, she went back to see it again.

You can see that using a comma in place of the semicolon between the coördinate clauses in any of these sentences would also result in a "comma splice."

The important thing for you to remember is that there are two ways of avoiding a "comma splice" in writing compound sentences. Between coördinate clauses you may use a comma and a conjunction:

> The game that would make football history was drawing rapidly to a close, and many of the spectators had already left the stands.

Or you may use a semicolon:

> The game that would make football history was drawing rapidly to a close; many of the spectators had already left the stands.

If you do not use either of these two ways, you must make separate sentences of the coördinate clauses:

> The game that would make football history was drawing rapidly to a close. Many of the spectators had already left the stands.

Otherwise you will make a "comma splice," which many schools consider the inexcusable error in punctuation; for it shows that the writer does not yet know the difference between one sentence and two sentences.

EXERCISE 14. Read the sentences, and decide how you will make a compound sentence of each pair. On a sheet of paper, write the numbers of the sentences. After each number, write the last word of the first coördinate clause, then a comma and a suitable conjunction, or a semicolon followed by the first word of the second coördinate clause. For the first pair you might write: *1. scrawl, but*

1. To me the letter was an illegible scrawl. Norman read it without any trouble at all.
2. Many of the mines are permanently closed. Others are open only part of the time.
3. Mike groaned when he saw the secretary the agency had sent. She looked as if she hadn't a brain in her head.
4. Alfred was angry. Furthermore, he didn't care who knew it.
5. He performed the trick slowly right under my eyes. I couldn't see how.
6. His pulse was normal. Nevertheless, something was wrong.
7. At the bottom of the hill there was a sharp turn in the gravel. Here I came to grief.
8. I put my nickel in the slot and heard it ring the bell. Still there was no answer from the operator.
9. At that time fingerprints were not used by the police. Now the prints of every criminal are registered.
10. There were plenty of able-bodied men in those days. However, they would not volunteer for such service.

Improving sentences: Twenty-five ways you have learned

1. Ask a question
2. Use a command
3. Choose exact modifiers
4. Begin with an adverb
5. Begin with a preposition
6. Use a compound verb
7. Avoid unnecessary words
8. Begin with an object
9. Use an active verb
10. Use an appositive
11. Use an active participle
12. Use a passive participle
13. Use a gerund
14. Use an infinitive
15. Use a direct quotation
16. Use an adjective clause
17. Use a noun clause
18. Use an adverb clause
19. Use a complex sentence
20. Avoid the deadly "so" and the tiresome "and"
21. Use parallel forms
22. Use clear modification
23. Make every word count
24. Avoid sentence fragments
25. Avoid the comma splice

Telling a Secret Ambition

Few topics of conversation are more interesting than those centering around secret ambitions we have had—and sometimes still have. Almost every small boy has at some time or other wanted to be a policeman or a fireman or a locomotive engineer. And many little girls have wanted to be nurses or teachers or ballet dancers. As we grow up, new interests may cause us to discard our earlier ambitions or may make us more determined than ever to carry them out. Whether we are afraid others will laugh at us for having these secret ambitions or whether we fail to realize how common they are, we seldom discuss them with others or even examine our own feelings about them. Yet almost everybody is interested in the secret ambitions of others, par-

ticularly when he finds out that they are not very much different from his own.

What are your secret ambitions? Have you discarded any of them as you have grown up? Have you acquired new ones that have taken the place of earlier ones? If you are a girl, you may have recently decided on a career as a social worker or a model or a skating star. If you are a boy, you may be dreaming of flying a commercial airliner or playing major-league baseball or discovering new scientific facts in a great laboratory. Whatever the ambition, you may be sure that others who know you will be interested in hearing you tell about it. Of course, it should be an ambition that you have really had or still do have. If you merely invent some outlandish ambition just to make the class laugh, your insincerity may cause others to wonder what your real ambitions are.

When you have selected a secret ambition to talk about, you are ready to plan what you are going to say. What caused you to have the ambition? How long have you had it? What do you think of it now? If you have discarded it, what were your reasons? If you still have it, how do you plan to carry it out? These questions are merely to start

you thinking of some of the things you might say about your secret ambition. You will, no doubt, think of many other things as you plan your talk.

Prepare your notes carefully, arranging the important details in a time order or a logical order. Be sure to list examples and reasons that you want to include in your talk. Then add good beginning and ending sentences.

Practice your talk at least once before coming to class, so that you will know what you are going to say and exactly how you want to say it. If you are asked to give your talk in class, speak slowly and distinctly. Hold your notes so that you can glance at them easily. If your classmates are amused by something you say, always wait for them to finish laughing before you continue. Your notes will remind you of what comes next. Stand squarely on both feet, and look at your classmates as you are speaking.

When others are giving their talks, pay close attention so that you can tell what you liked about their talks and what you think might be improved. Be alert for touches of humor, but be sure they are intentional. You do not want to hurt a classmate's feelings by laughing at something he is sincerely interested in. If you always show the same courtesy when others are speaking that you expect when it is your turn to talk, you will find that telling about secret ambitions is as interesting as a conversation among friends.

Working with Paragraphs

What makes a good paragraph

Just as words are put together in many ways to make sentences—some good and some poor—so sentences may be written in paragraph groups. By understanding the various functions that sentences have in paragraphs, you can learn what makes a good paragraph and what you can do to improve a poor one. For, as you know, writing good paragraphs is more than just starting every third or fourth sentence on a new line, indenting the first word.

In the written composition lessons you have learned that a paragraph usually consists of two or more sentences that are related in some way. And you have also learned that sometimes a topic sentence helps the reader know what that relationship is. For example, here is a simple paragraph from an article on baseball:

> The hold that baseball has on the American people is well illustrated by the testimonial rite known as the Day. During a season, on the sand lots as well as in the major and minor leagues, groups of admirers honor certain players with a Lefty Smith Day or a John Jones Day. The blushing hero is showered with money, automobiles, farm machinery, jewelry, plaques, loving cups, and speeches by civic leaders. A laborer with a large family and a small income is delighted to contribute a dollar or two to such a cause. The fact that the honored player already owns two automobiles and earns a whacking salary does not deter the committee in charge of his Day.

The first sentence tells what the paragraph is about and is a topic sentence. The remaining four state facts and opinions that tell what "the Day" is and what the writer thinks of it. These are the details used to develop the paragraph. Because the five sentences are related, they work together as a group to explain one idea.

Now look at the next example, two paragraphs from an article on new developments in the making of glass:

(1) Perhaps one of the greatest achievements of the glass scientists is "tempered glass," that has made the saying "as brittle as glass" as out of date as last week's teen-age slang. (2) Tempered glass is five times stronger than ordinary glass, being one half as strong as steel and three times more elastic, or "stretchy." (3) It can be bent and twisted without breaking, and it will not shatter when molten lead is poured onto an ice-cold slab of it. (4) Once, in a playful mood, scientists laid a piece of tempered glass between two platforms and let a full-grown elephant stand on it. (5) The glass sagged a little, but did not break.

(6) Tempered glass is made by lowering a sheet of ordinary glass into a furnace. (7) When it is so hot that it is about ready to soften, the glass is removed and rapidly cooled by blowing a stream of air across it. (8) This rapid cooling gives the glass an extremely hard "skin" on either side of the plate. (9) The rest of the glass is held in tight compression between these two skins.

The sentences have been numbered for convenience in referring to them. For example, Sentence 1 is the general statement that tells what the first paragraph is about. Sentences 2 and 3 give facts that explain how tempered glass differs from ordinary glass. Sentences 4 and 5 together are one illustration of the difference. In other words, the first paragraph consists of a general statement and three details—two sentences that give facts and two that give an illustration. Notice that the order of these details is not particularly important. If Sentences 4 and 5 —the illustration—came before 2 and 3, the paragraph would still make sense. Notice, too, that even if one of the three details were omitted, you would still have a fairly good idea of what tempered glass is.

Now look at the second paragraph. Sentence 6 tells what the paragraph is about and gives the first important step. Sentence 7 gives the second important step. Sentences 8 and 9 tell the result of the treatment described in Sentences 6 and 7. Notice that the last three sentences depend on the meaning of those preceding. If the order of the details were changed or any one of the details were omitted, the paragraph would not make sense.

Both paragraphs in the example are developed by means of details, but in different ways. The details in the first paragraph are **cumulative**. Though each has to do with tempered glass, they are practically independent of one another; and the writer might have used fewer sentences or arranged them in some other order. The details in the second paragraph are **consecutive**. Because they depend on one another, the sentences must be in a certain order, and no sentence can be omitted. These are two common ways of developing paragraphs.

As you know, a paragraph is about some one idea—one part of an incident or a description or an explanation or an expression of opinion. But there are no rules about how many details are needed to make that one idea understandable. One detail may be adequate for a simple idea. Ten may not be too many for a difficult idea. How many to use is the writer's decision. If he selects enough helpful details and arranges them wisely, he will very likely succeed in making his idea clear to the reader. When that occurs, he knows that he has written a good paragraph.

Improving paragraphs

1. Have I selected details carefully?

In the written composition lessons preceding this Unit, you have learned the importance of revising first drafts to make your sentences clearer, more forceful, more interesting to read. Now you will see some of the ways in which thoughtful revision can help you improve your paragraphs.

You know that details are used to make clear the central idea of a paragraph and that they should be related in meaning. When these related details are carefully selected, they help the reader understand the idea expressed by the paragraph. When they are not, the reader may be confused. For example, what is the central idea of the following paragraph?

(1) Among pedal-propelled vehicles the bicycle is most popular. (2) True, the one-wheeled monocycle is occasionally

seen in circus acts. (3) This strange-looking device is difficult to balance and steer, however, since there are no handle bars and you can fall in any direction. (4) Also, residential sidewalks are often made dangerous by small children on tricycles. (5) These small three-wheelers are easy to ride, since there is no problem in balancing them and little practice is needed to steer and pedal them at the same time. (6) But far more common is the bicycle, seen almost everywhere and ridden by young and old alike. (7) There are special racing models and lightweight touring models and the sturdy, brightly painted, chrome-trimmed "bike" that is the perennial favorite of the junior-high set. (8) The trick of balancing these popular two-wheelers is to turn the front wheel in the direction in which you start to fall. (9) Almost anyone can learn it.

Is the writer trying to tell about the popularity of the bicycle or to compare the difficulty of riding the various vehicles? You cannot be sure because the details in Sentences 2, 4, 6, 7 are about one idea, while those in Sentences 3, 5, 8, 9 are about another. As you can see, the details are all related in meaning, but they were not carefully selected to help the reader understand the idea expressed in the first sentence.

The writer had a plan that listed the following details for the paragraph: monocycles for circus performers; tricycles for children; bicycles for everyone; models for special purposes; most popular model. But in writing the paragraph, he somehow started thinking about riding the various vehicles and added details about this new idea. Thoughtful revision would have helped him eliminate these distracting details. It might also have enabled him to select additional details that showed his plan more clearly:

(1) Among pedal-propelled vehicles the bicycle is most popular. (2) True, the one-wheeled monocycle is occasionally seen in circus acts, and residential sidewalks are often made dangerous by small children on tricycles. (3) But far more common is the bicycle, seen almost everywhere and ridden by young and old alike. (4) For racing, there are special models with narrow tires and high sprocket ratios to give ut-

most speed. (5) For touring, there are lightweight models with ingenious gear shifts and hand-operated brakes. (6) Most popular, however, is that perennial favorite of the junior-high set—the sturdy, brightly painted, chrome-trimmed "bike" with balloon tires, coaster brake, electric light and horn. (7) So great is the popularity of these two-wheelers in some neighborhoods that long racks for parking them may be seen near schools, libraries, and movie theaters.

If you compare the revised paragraph with the first draft, you will see that many new details have been added. But notice that they help the reader understand more clearly the idea expressed in the first sentence.

The details in the paragraph about the bicycle are cumulative. As you revise paragraphs of your own containing such details, ask yourself questions like these: Have I selected the best details I know to help the reader understand the central idea of the paragraph? Are there any distracting details that should be omitted? Should I add more details to make clear what I mean? Have I arranged my sentences in the best possible order?

Paragraphs made up of consecutive details are somewhat easier to check because the details depend more closely on one another. But questions like the following may reveal weak spots that need improvement: Have I given all the important steps? Are they in the proper order? Have I selected details that will make each step clear to the reader? Have I made clear the relationship of each sentence to the one preceding?

Such questions help you criticize your own writing thoughtfully —the first step in learning to revise your paragraphs. But remember that the purpose of this revision is not to make changes, but to improve your writing so that others can more easily understand your exact meaning.

EXERCISE 1. The following selection from a letter contains ideas just as they came to the writer's mind. Read the letter. Then rewrite it, organizing the ideas into three or four paragraphs. Select details carefully, omitting any that do not belong in the paragraphs you choose. Revise sentences wherever you need to. Be sure that each paragraph is about one idea. For example, the first paragraph might be about Uncle Ed's farm. What will the others be about?

I would have written sooner, but we've been visiting at Uncle Ed's farm. He's over fifty, but full of pep and hasn't a gray hair on his head. It's a dairy farm, and there are lots of cows. I've even learned the difference between Holstein and Jersey cows! The trip out was pretty tiring. We started as early as we could every morning and drove until dark. So there just wasn't any time to write letters. I'll never forget driving through the mountains, though. The scenery was wonderful. Uncle Ed is more fun than a circus. He's always laughing and thinking up things for us to do. One afternoon we went fishing, and Dad caught two big brook trout. That made him feel pretty good, particularly since Uncle Ed had no luck at all. But he just laughed about it and kidded Dad about "beginner's luck." We eat our breakfasts on a large screened-in porch opening off the dining room. Did you know that the cream from Jersey cows is almost as yellow as butter? We have it on our cereal every morning. It's so thick Dad says you ought to spread it on instead of trying to pour it! Uncle Ed's house is as big as a barn—not his barn, of course, but the kind we see around home. His barn is about a block long, with concrete floors and fluorescent lights and everything painted white. It looks like a hospital. You ought to see the kitchen here. It's enormous, about right for a restaurant, but Aunt Nelly says it takes a lot of cooking to keep Uncle Ed filled up. He's a big man, all right, and likes a lot of space to move around in, and his house is a huge, rambling, two-story affair with wide screened-in porches, a big stone fireplace, and rooms about the size of our classrooms at school. We'll probably be staying here for at least another week or so before starting back. I'm all for it myself, since Uncle Ed promised to take me along in his plane the next time he flies to town. He says the farmers out here use planes about the same way we use cars at home. It surely must save a lot of time, and there are plenty of places to land. I'll tell you all about it when I get back home. That ought to be the latter part of August. Let's hope the return trip will be less tiresome.

Developing the idea

You have learned that a paragraph is about one idea. And you saw that sentences may either tell what the idea is or give details that help the reader understand the idea. Now you are going to see that sentences in a paragraph may have still another function, which enables the writer to develop an idea more fully.

Here is a short paragraph about research at the General Electric Company. See if you can find the sentence that tells what the paragraph is about and the sentences that give the details:

> (1) Certain men at G. E. will always be connected with certain scientific developments. (2) For instance, there is Langmuir, known for his work with electronic tubes and with cloud-seeding. (3) He was the first scientist in the United States employed by an industrial company to win a Nobel prize. (4) Guy Suits, working on electric arcs, has generated flames nearly twice as hot as the sun's surface. (5) Saul Dushman is an international authority on high vacuum, electron emission, and atomic structure. (6) Alexanderson, a young Swede, came to General Electric to study railway motors. (7) He ended by inventing a high-frequency alternator which gave America its real start in high-powered radio communication.

The paragraph consists of seven sentences. The first is a topic sentence that tells what the paragraph is about. Sentences 2, 4, 5, and 6 give examples—names of men whose accomplishments help you understand what the writer means by his general statement. The two remaining sentences neither make general statements nor give details supporting a general statement. Sentence 3 adds another fact about Langmuir, the first man mentioned. Sentence 7 adds another fact about Alexanderson, the fourth man mentioned. Sentences such as 3 and 7 give additional information about a detail—the third function that sentences may have in a paragraph.

You can see that the details in the paragraph are cumulative. The writer merely gives four examples that he thinks will make his idea understandable. Since the details do not depend on one another, he might have arranged them in some other order. But notice that he could not move Sentence 2 without also moving Sentence 3, or Sentence 6 without Sentence 7. Sentences that explain a detail belong with it, even though the details themselves do not depend on one another.

Now look at the following paragraph about gray wolves. See if you can find the general statement, the sentences that give the details, and the sentences that add information about the details:

> (1) Wolves seem to plan their hunting. (2) Led generally by a she-wolf, a pack scouts for prey; and when the deer, elk, caribou, or moose is found, one or two wolves will approach the animal from downwind until it is started up. (3) Then the long chase begins. (4) One wolf will follow directly behind the quarry; others take strategic positions and often head it off so that it runs in a wide circle. (5) The run may go on for many hours until the quarry tires and slows down. (6) Then a pursuer slashes at the animal's rear while others attack its head and throat. (7) Contrary to popular belief they do not habitually hamstring their prey, but usually bring it down by tearing at its flank and hind quarters, or throat. (8) But whether it stands or runs, the wolf's slashing teeth will eventually tear it down.

Sentence 1 is the general statement. Sentences 2, 3, and 6 give the details. Sentences 4 and 5 add information about the long chase, mentioned in Sentence 3. And the last two sentences explain Sentence 6, adding information about the way wolves bring down their prey.

You can see that the details in the paragraph are consecutive. Sentence 2 tells how wolves find their prey and start it up. *Then* Sentences 3, 4, and 5 tell about the chase. *Then* 6, 7, and 8 tell how the prey is brought down. The two *Then*'s show that the writer intended the details to be in a time order. Notice that Sentence 2 gives two details. Notice also that Sentences 3, 4, and 5 are about one detail.

Most paragraphs are developed by means of details—facts, opinions, examples, illustrations, and so forth, that a writer uses to help readers understand his ideas. If the details require little or no explanation, a writer may give one or more in a single sentence. If he feels that they are difficult, he may use two or more sentences to explain

270

each one fully. The important thing is not how many sentences a paragraph has, but how well it expresses the writer's idea.

Improving paragraphs
2. Have I explained details adequately?

Y ou know that a paragraph is a group of related sentences that work together to express one idea. And you have seen that these sentences may have different functions. For example, here is a paragraph in which the sentences have only two functions:

> The large hall in Quito, Ecuador, was filled with light and color and noise. Girl teams from the capital were playing Guayaquil teams in the basketball tournament. Downstairs the seats were filled with old and young, rich and poor. The gallery was packed with students in school uniforms, with colored caps and arm bands. Cheerleaders whipped each group into a frenzy of cheering. But the center of the gallery attracted most attention.

The first two sentences tell what the paragraph is about. The remaining four give details. As you can see, the paragraph seems sketchy and incomplete.

Earlier in this Unit you learned that sentences in a paragraph may have a third function—to explain details more fully. See how much more interesting the preceding example is when the details are adequately explained:

> (1) The large hall in Quito, Ecuador, was filled with light and color and noise. (2) Girl teams from the capital were playing Guayaquil teams in the basketball tournament. (3) Downstairs the seats were filled with old and young, rich and poor. (4) Some had hurried from their work to be there. (5) Others had come from a late afternoon party. (6) The gallery was packed with students in school uniforms, with colored caps and arm bands. (7) They called good-naturedly to the boys who worked their way up and down the stairs selling candy, bags of peanuts, and cakes. (8) They clapped and

stamped noisily when one of them lost his white cap and caught it again as it was tossed back to him. (9) Cheerleaders whipped each group into a frenzy of cheering. (10) One at a time the schools took their turns, each trying to outdo the other. (11) But the center of the gallery attracted most attention. (12) There several rows of students dressed all in blue sat together; above them were rows dressed in yellow, and below them rows dressed in red. (13) At a signal from the the cheerleader, the rows began to sway slowly, the yellow to the right, the blue to the left, and the red to the right. (14) There was an instant of silence; then the crowd recognized the waving flag of Ecuador and saluted it with deafening applause.

Sentences 4 and 5 explain more about the people mentioned in the third sentence. Sentences 7 and 8 tell what the students mentioned in Sentence 6 were doing. Sentence 10 adds information about the cheering mentioned in the ninth sentence. And Sentences 12, 13, 14 explain the statement made in Sentence 11. Notice that the explanatory sentences are closely related in meaning with the sentences they follow.

Details are not sentences. Details are facts and opinions and thoughts used to make an idea clear to the reader. How many sentences are needed to explain a detail adequately depends in part on its difficulty. It also depends on the kind of sentences used. In the preceding example, for instance, the detail expressed by Sentences 3, 4, 5 might have been given in one complex sentence: "Downstairs the seats were filled with old and young, rich and poor, some of whom had hurried from their work to be there, while others had come from a late afternoon party." And if compound sentences had not been used, the final detail might have required six or seven sentences instead of only four.

As you revise your own paragraphs, ask yourself these two questions: Have I explained the details adequately? Is there anything more I can say that will make them easier to understand? Some details will probably not need an explanatory sentence. Others may need several. How many sentences you use for each detail is not important if you remember this: Whenever two or more are used, be sure that they are closely connected in meaning, so that the reader will know that they have to do with the same detail.

EXERCISE 2. The numbered sentences tell a story about an accident at sea. As you can see, almost all the sentences begin with subject and verb. Turn back to pages 150-151, and review the various ways of improving sentences. Then rewrite the story, revising the sentences in the ways you have learned. And group related sentences into paragraphs that will help the reader know where there is a shift in time or place or action. You will probably need four or five or six paragraphs. The first one might begin in this way: *Rainsford lay in his chair on the deck of the yacht, puffing at his favorite pipe and thinking over the events of the past week.*

(1) Rainsford lay in his chair on the deck of the yacht. (2) He was puffing at his favorite pipe. (3) He was thinking over the events of the past week. (4) He grew drowsy soon. (5) A sharp sound startled him. (6) It was off to the right. (7) His ears were trained to that sort of sound. (8) They could not be mistaken. (9) He heard the sound again. (10) Someone had fired a gun twice somewhere off in the darkness of the night. (11) Rainsford sprang up. (12) He moved quickly to the rail. (13) He was mystified. (14) He strained his eyes. (15) He could not see at all through the dense blackness, however. (16) He jumped up on the rail. (17) He thought he might see better from there. (18) His pipe struck a rope. (19) It was knocked out of his mouth. (20) He lunged for it. (21) He stretched too far. (22) He lost his balance. (23) The warm waters of the Caribbean Sea closed over his head. (24) He struggled to the surface. (25) He shouted wildly. (26) The wash of the yacht slapped against his face. (27) It made him gag and strangle. (28) He struck out in desperation after the lights of the yacht. (29) They were rapidly receding. (30) He swam frantically for about fifty feet. (31) He stopped then. (32) He had to calm his excited nerves. (33) He knew this. (34) This was not the first time he had been in a tight place. (35) He regained his self-possession quickly. (36) He had to decide then what to do next. (37) He realized one thing. (38) There was a slight chance that someone on the yacht was still on deck. (39) This person might hear his cries. (40) He shouted with all his power for several minutes. (41) No one heard him. (42) The lights of the yacht grew fainter. (43) They were blotted out by the night soon.

Telling how details are related

You have seen the importance of selecting helpful details and of explaining them adequately. Now you will see some of the ways in which general statements tell the reader how details in a paragraph are related. One of these ways you know well. For example, in the following paragraph you should have no difficulty in finding the sentences that give the details and the sentence that tells how the details are related:

> (1) There is a wide disagreement among authorities as to why fish strike at artificial lures. (2) Some fishermen have the idea that fish believe the lures are good to eat. (3) More realistic fishermen are of the opinion that the fish know these offerings are merely wood or rubber or fur and feathers with hooks, and are just curious about how they taste. (4) Others hold that fish are surly and cantankerous, and resent having these monstrosities paraded before them. (5) Still other anglers feel that fish strike out of anger because their intelligence has been insulted by fishermen who think that fish believe artificial bait is food.

Sentences 2-5 give four different opinions. By telling what these opinions are about, the first sentence keeps the reader from becoming confused. Beginning with a topic sentence is a common and useful way of telling how details are related.

A topic sentence is one kind of general statement. There are other kinds that may consist of two or more sentences, as in this paragraph:

> (1) Scientists do many strange things in their search for knowledge. (2) But probably none is more odd than the recent experiments of two doctors reported in "The Yale Journal of Biology and Medicine." (3) The doctors froze the tails of mice. (4) They were not trying to be unkind to the mice. (5) They were trying to get more knowledge to help in the treatment of human beings when parts of the body are frozen. (6) After freezing the mouse tails, the doctors tried different ways of thawing them out. (7) They found that the use of snow or cold water was harmful, rather than helpful. (8) Continued mild heat was not of much value, either. (9) The best results were gotten by thawing the mouse tails rap-

idly. (10) The very best results combined rapid thawing with the use of certain drugs.

Sentences 3 and 6 give two consecutive details. Sentences 4 and 5 explain Sentence 3, and the last four sentences add information about Sentence 6. Neither of the first two sentences is clearly a topic sentence. But together they express the writer's opinion of the experiments described in the paragraph, and are a general statement.

A general statement is usually at, or near, the beginning of a paragraph, but not always. As you know, a special opening sentence often precedes the topic sentence of the first paragraph of a composition. In a similar way, one or more details may precede a general statement, as in the following paragraph:

> (1) Every once in a while you'll pick up the paper and read of a shooting accident resulting from target practice. (2) Sometimes these mishaps are caused by careless gun handling, but more often they are due to an unfortunate choice of a shooting location. (3) Of all accidents, these are the least excusable and the easiest to prevent. (4) All that is required is to transfer one's target shooting activities to a suitable range, which, besides being safer, affords much more valuable practice than does random backlot firing.

Sentences 1 and 2 give details about one kind of shooting accident and what causes it. Sentence 3 is a general statement expressing the writer's opinion. The final sentence gives a reason for that opinion.

Now look at this next example. Can you find a general statement for each paragraph?

> (1) A honeybee is not even as long as your thumbnail. (2) Its brain is hardly larger than the head of a pin. (3) Its weight is so slight it would take 750,000 bees, a single-file parade five miles long, to equal the weight of a 150-pound man. (4) Yet this midget is one of the world's most valuable animals.
>
> (5) The honey of the honeybee was Europe's chief sugar supply until after the Roman Empire. (6) Beeswax is so diversely used in industry that our native production rarely

meets the demand. (7) The value of bees as carriers of pollen on farms and in orchards is beyond calculation. (8) A hundred thousand species of flowering plants are said to depend upon bees for their existence, and orchard trees increase their yield 40-fold when they have an ample supply of bees at blooming time.

In the first paragraph, Sentences 1-3 give details about the honeybee's small size. Sentence 4 is a general statement expressing an opinion the writer has about honeybees. In the second paragraph, Sentences 5-7 give details to show three ways in which honeybees are valuable. You can see that there is no general statement in the second paragraph. But notice that the details given in the second paragraph help the reader understand the opinion expressed in Sentence 4—the general statement in the first paragraph.

As you have seen, a general statement may consist of one or more sentences, may tell what the details are about or what the writer thinks of them, may occur first or last or elsewhere in a paragraph. But always the function is the same—to tell the reader how the details are related. In some paragraphs the relationship of the details is so obvious that a general statement is clearly not needed. In all others the reader is more likely to understand the idea expressed by the paragraph when there is a general statement.

Improving paragraphs
3. Do I need a general statement?

Each paragraph you write is a signal to the reader that you consider the sentences in that group to be related in some way. The easier you make it for him to see that relationship, the more likely he is to understand your ideas. For example, here are four sentences that give details about modern phonograph records:

> Nowadays phonograph records are 7 or 10 or 12 inches in diameter. They may play at 78 or 45 or 33⅓ revolutions per minute. They may have regular grooves or much narrower "microgrooves." Even the hole in the center of the record is no longer of one standard size.

As you can see, the relationship of the details is obvious, and no topic sentence is needed. But by adding a general statement, the same four sentences might be used in a paragraph about the problem encountered in buying phonograph records today:

> If you haven't bought any phonograph records for several years, you are in for a surprise. The day has gone when a phonograph record was a phonograph record and all you needed to know was the title of the selection you wanted. Nowadays phonograph records are 7 or 10 or 12 inches in diameter. They may play at 78 or 45 or $33\frac{1}{3}$ revolutions per minute. They may have regular grooves or much narrower "microgrooves." Even the hole in the center of the record is no longer of one standard size.

With a still different general statement, the same four sentences might be used as an example of our complex—and sometimes puzzling—civilization:

> We live in a strange age. Engineers devise ways of removing the three-speed gearshift from automobiles and of putting one on phonographs. There was even a time, not many years ago, when phonograph records came in just two sizes and could be played on any machine. Nowadays phonograph records are 7 or 10 or 12 inches in diameter. They may play at 78 or 45 or $33\frac{1}{3}$ revolutions per minute. They may have regular grooves or much narrower "microgrooves." Even the hole in the center of the record is no longer of one standard size.

Notice that the general statement in this paragraph consists of three sentences. In the preceding paragraph, it consists of two sentences.

As you have seen, different general statements express different relationships of the details in a paragraph. In revising paragraphs of your own, always stop for a moment at the end of each paragraph. Ask yourself questions like these: What is this paragraph about? Do I need a general statement to make my meaning clear to the reader? Would a different general statement make my meaning easier to understand? Such questions will help you remember that it is your responsibility to show the reader how the details you have given are related. The more you accept this responsibility, the more effective your paragraphs will be.

EXERCISE 3. Each of the numbered groups of sentences might be used as supporting details in paragraphs intended for different purposes. Read each group carefully, and think of two different ways in which the sentences might be used. Then write two general statements for each group, showing the ways in which you think the relationship of the details might be expressed. For one of the general statements for the first group you might write: *1. Wisconsin, the land of lakes, is famous not only for its resorts, but also for its dairying industry and livestock production.*

1. More than half of all the cheese made in the United States is produced in Wisconsin. One tenth of the nation's butter and one fourth of its supply of condensed and evaporated milk come from the Badger state. Malted milk, invented by William Horlick in 1882, is another leading product. Wisconsin purebred dairy cattle, noted here and abroad, are sold by the thousands to farmers in other states and in foreign countries.

2. An amateur boxing match lasts for only three rounds. The boxers wear extra large, well-padded gloves, so that the damage they can inflict is minimized. A bout is stopped immediately if a boxer has an injury that seems to be at all serious or painful, and the decision is awarded to his opponent. Since the fighters are hardly ever knocked unconscious, the possibility of their becoming "punchy" from amateur competition is remote.

3. From his easy chair Mr. John Doe can view history in the making through on-the-spot news events commented on by any one of a number of excellent news analysts. He can now see the very best entertainers from stage, concert hall, movies, opera—a whole world that has in the past been restricted to small audiences. Fine young talent, which before had no place to shine in the overcrowded field of show business, is making its debut on America's TV sets.

Clinching the point

The following paragraph is about the director of a motion picture. As you read it, notice how each sentence adds to your understanding of his responsibility:

(1) Since the action for a movie is shot in short stretches, and not in the sequence it will follow in the finished production, it is obvious that someone must have the over-all picture in mind, must be responsible for the completed production,

as a conductor is responsible for the total effect all the instruments in an orchestra will make. (2) This person is the director, and it is probable that he is the one person most responsible for whether a movie will be successful or a failure. (3) The actors do only what he tells them to do, and when. (4) It is he who decides how the story is to be told, who knows what emotional effect is necessary, and guides the actors in producing that effect. (5) It is he who must figure out what the cameras must reveal, who decides whether close-ups of one person will convey an idea better, or whether the scene should show a whole group present while a speech is being made or a feeling registered. (6) He must keep in mind all the time what the total effect of the finished film will be, and work with that effect always in mind, whereas the actors need only concentrate on what they are doing at a given moment. (7) The director, to be sure, usually has a number of assistants who take care of minor details—such as getting the extras in place for a crowd scene and coaching them as to what they are expected to do—but the final assembling of all the parts into a pleasing, effective whole is up to him.

As you can see, the first two sentences make a general statement about the idea to be developed in the paragraph. And Sentences 3-6 give details in support of that statement. Now look at the final sentence. Notice that the last part of it repeats the idea expressed by the general statement, though in different words. The paragraph could have ended with Sentence 6. But by adding Sentence 7 to restate the central idea, the writer helps you remember the point of the paragraph.

This is the fourth function that a sentence may have in a paragraph—to sum up details by restating the idea they help make clear. Such a sentence is called a **summary sentence**. Because it comes last, it helps clinch the point of the paragraph.

Sometimes a summary sentence may be more explicit than the general statement itself. Notice that this is so in the following paragraph about icebergs:

(1) There are few objects in all nature as beautiful—or as dangerous—as icebergs, those floating monsters of the deep. (2) Breaking off from massive Greenland glaciers, these mountains of frozen water—frequently as long as a city block

and rising half that high out of the ocean—are carried along by the currents. (3) Some northern bergs (for there are also bergs in Antarctic regions) reach the Labrador current and are carried by it toward the heavily traveled North Atlantic steamship lanes. (4) These bergs cannot be held back, destroyed by any method now known, or even turned from their course. (5) And so the iceberg still remains a menace that science, with all of its resources, cannot control or regulate.

When you start reading, it is not clear from the general statement in the first sentence whether the paragraph is about the beauty of icebergs or about their danger. However, the details in Sentences 2 - 4 suggest the latter. And the final sentence removes all doubt by stating that the iceberg is a menace. Here the summary sentence is desirable for clearness as well as for emphasis. Because it follows the details, it can make a definite statement that might not have been fully understood earlier in the paragraph.

Occasionally a summary sentence will refer to a sentence in a preceding paragraph. This is likely to occur when the two paragraphs are closely related, as they are in this example:

(1) In speaking of a telescope, people often ask, "How much does it magnify?" (2) Actually, you can vary the magnification of a telescope by using different eyepieces; and practically all telescopes, even homemade ones, are arranged so that the eyepieces can be changed. (3) "But," you may ask, "if you can get a high magnification with a small telescope, what is the need of a large one?"

(4) There is a very good reason, you will discover, for building large telescopes. (5) For any given size, there is a practical limit to the magnification that can be used successfully. (6) As you know, the objective lens, or the concave mirror, gathers light to form the image, which is then magnified by the eyepiece. (7) The more the image is magnified, the fainter the light becomes. (8) It is like trying to spread a large piece of bread with a very small bit of butter. (9) You need more butter! (10) And to produce a high magnification in a telescope, you need more light! (11) How do you get it? (12) By using a larger objective or mirror, which will gather more light in. (13) So, you see, large telescopes are needed, after all.

As suggested by the general statement in Sentence 4, the second paragraph is an answer to the question asked in the first one. Starting with Sentence 5 and ending with Sentence 12, the writer gives a series of consecutive details explaining the "very good reason" mentioned in Sentence 4. Because the explanation is long and involved, the writer adds a summary sentence to remind you of the point of the paragraph. But notice that Sentence 13 refers more directly to Sentence 3 than to Sentence 4. In this way the writer not only sums up the details of the second paragraph, but also emphasizes its close relation to the first one.

As you have seen, summary sentences are used to call attention to the central idea of a paragraph. They may simply state this idea in a different way. They may state it in a more definite way. But they always refer to an idea that has been previously expressed. If you remember this, you will not be likely to confuse a summary sentence with a general statement placed last in the paragraph. A summary sentence always restates.

Improving paragraphs
4. Do I need a summary sentence?

You know that a general statement helps the reader understand the central idea of a paragraph. And you have just seen some of the ways in which a summary sentence helps the reader remember this idea. The more closely the general statement and the summary sentence work together, the more effective the paragraph is likely to be.

A summary sentence is sometimes more specific than the general statement, as in the following paragraph:

> A blurred image on the film may be caused in various ways. Probably the commonest cause of blurred images is movement of the camera during the exposure of the film. Another common cause is inaccurate focusing of the lens. A third cause of blurring, which occurs in photographing moving objects, is use of a shutter speed that is too slow. Only when sufficient care is given to keeping the camera steady, to focusing the lens accurately, and to selecting a shutter speed that will "stop the action" can the film record an image that is sharp and clear.

The first sentence of the paragraph tells how the details are related. The final sentence not only sums up the details, but tells what must be done to secure sharp images. A summary sentence is often used in this way to make the meaning of a paragraph more definite.

Earlier you saw that the same details might be used with different general statements to express different ideas. For example, here is a paragraph that tells how photographs depend on the quality of the negative:

> The paper print we call a photograph is made from a negative. If the image on the negative is blurred, a picture printed from it will be blurred also. Probably the commonest cause of blurred images. . . . Another common cause. . . . A third cause of blurring. . . . Thus it is apparent that if we want a sharp, clearly defined photograph, we must begin with the making of the negative.

Since the details are the same as in the first example, only the first words of each one are given. If you supply the remaining words, you will see that the details help make clear the idea expressed in the first two sentences. Notice that the summary sentence calls the reader's attention to this idea, not by summing up the details supporting it, but by stating it in another way. Notice, too, how repetition of the words *we, photograph,* and *negative* ties the first and last sentences together.

Sometimes a summary sentence calls attention to the central idea by restating it in a completely different way:

> Some people will spend sixty dollars for a good camera, yet refuse to spend sixty minutes learning to operate it properly. Then they wonder why their pictures are not always clear and sharp. Probably the commonest cause of blurred images. . . . Another common cause. . . . A third cause of blurring. . . . Violinists know that it takes more than a Stradivarius to make good music, and photographers soon discover that it takes more than an expensive camera to produce good pictures.

282

Here the comparison between violinists and photographers strengthens the idea that skill is needed to secure the best results from a fine instrument.

Summary sentences have one main function—to emphasize important ideas. And like all devices for indicating emphasis in writing, they are most effective when used with thoughtful care. As you read over paragraphs you have written, ask yourself questions like these: Which paragraphs express ideas that I particularly want the reader to remember? Will summary sentences make these ideas stand out more clearly? How can I word each summary sentence to make it work closely with the general statement of the paragraph? Have I used any summary sentences that can be improved? Such questions will help you use summary sentences intelligently—and effectively.

Tying paragraphs together

You know that a paragraph usually consists of two or more related details. And you have learned that when the details are arranged in a logical order, words such as *first, second, next, finally* and phrases such as *on the other hand, considering all the facts, to conclude* show how the paragraphs are related. Whenever such words and phrases are used to help the reader follow the thought as it moves from one paragraph to another, they are called **linking expressions**.

There are many kinds of linking expressions, but they all have one purpose—to tie paragraphs together. For example, as you read the following selection, notice how the italicized words help you follow the writer's thought from paragraph to paragraph:

> (1) New to the housing project, Mary walked uncertainly from her doorstep to the group of children. (2) At her former home she would have skipped with anticipation, and appropriate words of greeting would have formed spontaneously. (3) Here, only her father and mother remained familiar.
>
> (4) *Minutes later*, Mary again stood at the door. (5) Her mother noted the clenched fists and defiant face.
>
> (6) *Within the hour* the mothers of other children in the project had heard the new little girl was rough. (7) She had seized Judy's wagon and hit Judy.

(8) *Outcast,* Mary spent the ensuing days unhappily. (9) Increased demands upon her parents and their sympathetic attempts to help her understand how it takes time to make friends left her unsatisfied. (10) Normally a happy child, eager, affectionate, playful, and occasionally tearful, Mary had become desperately lonely.

(11) *Relief* for Mary and her concerned parents came unexpectedly. (12) A neighbor asked if Mary might accompany her and her own daughter, one of the group, for a walk in the park. (13) Mary and the little girl became friends. (14) When Mary again approached the children, she saw them in the light of her experience with her new friend and soon found a place among them.

As you can see, the five paragraphs tell about an incident, the problem it caused, and how the problem was solved. The first two linking expressions indicate lapses of time. The second two indicate shifts to other phases of the subject. Notice that each of the linking expressions is part of the general statement of the paragraph.

Sometimes a whole sentence is used as a linking expression, as in the following selection, which tells about a fruitless search for snow geese:

(1) All day we searched for snow geese. (2) Plodding along paths that wandered aimlessly across the grass marsh south of Fortesque, N. J., we flushed drake shovellers from muddy ponds and found a pair of blue-winged teal swimming in the elbow of an estuary. (3) We found black ducks, marsh hawks, snipe, and various sparrows. (4) We found, also, blind potholes by falling into them. (5) And we waded on with a hip boot full of water in search of snow geese. (6) Other birds we found, but not the geese.

(7) Sunny morning gave way to afternoon. (8) Though it was March with the snow only two weeks gone, wavering warm air made exotic the shapes of common birds. (9) In the distance gulls sunning on a black mudbank were unidentifiable, the outline of a harrier coursing over faun grass was distorted by the air, now long-necked, now long-winged, thermal waves toying with reality. (10) Every flash of a wing had to be pursued though we fell into another pothole or plowed through sucking mud. (11) In the distance one could

not be sure that flickering wing belonged to a gull. (12) We took no chances on missing the geese.

(13) Yet when evening came, hazy with pinks and yellows, turning us back toward the village, we had seen no geese. (14) That our books were filled with names and notes of other choice wild fowl, our heads filled with their vivid images, did not prevent disappointment. (15) When one looks for snow geese there is no substitute. (16) We walked back along the edge of Delaware Bay seeking the solid footing of sodded banks and hard-sand beaches, wondering why we had seen no geese.

Now look at the second paragraph. From the details you can see that Sentence 12 is the general statement. Sentence 7 merely links the second paragraph to the first. This is the fifth function that sentences may have in a paragraph—to show how the paragraph is related to a preceding one. Such a sentence is called a **transitional sentence.**

Notice that the adverbial clause *when evening came* in Sentence 13 helps tie the third paragraph to the second. Here, instead of again using a separate sentence, the writer wisely makes the linking expression part of the general statement. Variety in linking expressions is as desirable as variety in sentences.

Repetition of important words is another way of tying paragraphs together, as you can see in the following description of a coral atoll:

(1) The world contains certain patterns of beauty that impress the mind forever. (2) They might be termed the sovereign sights, and most men will agree as to what they are: the Pyramids at dawn, the Grand Tetons at dusk, the Arctic wastes. (3) The list need not be long, but to be inclusive it must contain a coral atoll with its placid lagoon, the terrifyingly brilliant sands, and the outer reef shooting great spires of spindrift a hundred feet into the air. (4) Such a sight is one of the incomparable visual images of the world.

(5) This is the wonder of an atoll—that you are safe within the lagoon while outside the tempest rages. (6) The atoll becomes a symbol to all men seeking refuge, the security of home, the warmth of love. (7) Lost in a wilderness of ocean, the atoll is a haven that captivates the mind and rests the human spirit.

(8) More than a symbol, however, the atoll is a reservoir of tangible beauty. (9) Fleecy clouds hang over it, so that in the dawn it wears a shimmering crest of gold. (10) At midday it seems to dream in the baking heat, its colors uncompromisingly brilliant. (11) At sunset the clouds once more reflect a flaming brilliance. (12) At night stars seem to hover just out of reach, and if there is a moon it does not dance upon the lagoon. (13) Its reflection lies there passively, like a silvered causeway to the opposite shore.

Repetition of the words *atoll* and *lagoon* in Sentence 5 links the second paragraph to the first. In addition, the words *safe* and *tempest rages* suggest a contrast similar to the one expressed in Sentence 3 by the words *placid* and *great spires of spindrift*. Words such as these, which suggest a previous idea without renaming it, are often called **echo words**. They, too, help tie paragraphs together.

Notice that repetition of the words *symbol* and *beauty* in Sentence 8 links the third paragraph to the preceding ones. Notice, too, that the word *passively* in Sentence 13 echoes the idea of *placid* in Sentence 3 and helps tie the three paragraphs together.

You have seen how paragraphs may be tied together by the use of linking expressions—words, phrases, clauses, even sentences, that help the reader know how a paragraph is related to a preceding one. When the relationship is obvious, no linking expression is needed. But wherever there is a lapse of time between paragraphs, a change in point of view, a sudden shift or an abrupt turn in the thought, a suitable linking expression usually helps the reader make the transition from one paragraph to another.

Improving paragraphs
5. Have I used good linking expressions?

As you drive along a well-marked main highway, your trip is made easier by the little roadside signs that show you the way. Some warn you of turns to the left or right, of junctions with other routes, of detours from the main road. Others merely give the route number, to let you know whether you are still on the right road. Together they speed your progress, mile by mile, toward your destination.

Linking expressions are also of two kinds. There are direct expressions that guide the reader as he goes from paragraph to paragraph. Because they are used to warn him of each change in time or place, each shift in thought, they are placed near the beginning of the paragraph, usually in the first sentence. There are also indirect expressions that guide the reader by repeating or echoing important ideas, thus helping to keep him on the right track. Linking expressions of this indirect sort may occur almost anywhere in a paragraph.

Here are a few examples of direct linking expressions that might be used to introduce paragraphs in a composition:

To SHOW CHANGES IN TIME. From early childhood . . . After starting to school . . . Shortly before my tenth birthday . . . Sometime later . . . When I was twelve . . . Today . . . Next year . . . Other plans for the future . . .

To SHOW STEPS IN A PROCESS. After you have checked the pattern . . . While cutting the material . . . Next . . . In fitting the garment . . . Finally . . .

To SHOW CHANGES IN SPACE. As we climbed the ladder . . . Upon reaching the top . . . Straight ahead . . . To our left . . . On our right . . . Below . . .

To SHOW SHIFTS IN THOUGHT. Upon closer examination . . . In theory . . . Practically, however, . . . Strangely enough . . . While many may disagree . . .

Notice in each example the variety of linking expressions used. As you revise first drafts of your compositions, ask yourself questions like these: Have I used linking expressions that show the relationship of each paragraph to the one preceding? Can I express these relationships more exactly by using other linking expressions? Such questions will remind you of the importance of linking expressions. If you want the reader to understand what you write, you must help him follow the turns in your thought from the first paragraph to the last.

Indirect linking expressions also help keep the reader from losing his way, but by different means. Earlier you saw two paragraphs about the need for large telescopes. Turn back to page 280, and count the number of times the word *telescope* (or *telescopes*) occurs in each paragraph. Then notice the words *magnify* and *magnification* in the first paragraph. How many times is the verb form used in the second paragraph? How many times is the noun form repeated? You can see that the writer never lets you forget what he is talking about.

Remember that you can link paragraphs together—indirectly—

in various ways: by repeating important, or "key," words (*telescope, snow geese*); by using pronouns (*this, that, these, he, they*); by using different forms (*deny, denial*); by using synonyms (*throw, toss, pitch*); and by rephrasing (*vocation, life's work, daily bread and butter, means of earning a living*).

As you revise paragraphs you have written, watch for opportunities to use linking expressions that remind the reader of important ideas. By never giving him a chance to forget what you are writing about, you help him follow your thinking closely, unerringly, to the very end.

EXERCISE 4. In a magazine you read regularly, find an interesting article that has at least ten paragraphs. Read it through carefully. Then look for direct linking expressions that helped you follow the writer's thought from paragraph to paragraph. Next see if the writer has used any indirect expressions to help link the paragraphs together. On a sheet of paper, write the name of the author, the title of the article, the name of the magazine, and its date. Then write each direct linking expression that is used. After it, in parentheses, write the indirect linking expressions—words that repeat important ideas mentioned in a preceding paragraph. Be ready to discuss your list in class.

Recognizing paragroups

Logically, a paragraph is a distinct part of a composition. And ideally, all the details having to do with that part should be in one paragraph. But practically, a paragraph is often little more than a way of showing in writing that two or more sentences are related in some way. Use of the same word for both kinds of paragraphs is sometimes confusing, particularly so when two or more written paragraphs are used to make clear one part of a composition.

You have learned that a paragraph is about one idea. Yet if you are at all observant, you must often have noticed in your reading two or more paragraphs that seemed to be about the same idea. For example, on pages 275-276 you saw two paragraphs about the honeybee, and your attention was called to the fact that the details in the second paragraph supported an opinion expressed by the general statement in the first one. It is obvious that the eight sentences are about one idea. Yet the writer grouped them into two paragraphs. Since the two paragraph groups have to do with one part of the composition, they may be called a **paragroup** to show that together they do the work of a single logical paragraph.

Here is another example of a paragroup in which the general statement is separated from the details supporting it:

> (1) The average man in the shoes of Douglas Campbell, for instance—the lad who has been shooting tigers in India and shooting pictures under the sea—would long ago have retired to a farm to spend the rest of his days protecting his nose. (2) But Campbell goes right on sticking his nose out, and getting it smashed.
>
> (3) He broke his nose first when he fell off a set of parallel bars in the gymnasium of the University of Southern California, where he went to swim and get an education. (4) He smashed it next when he fell into a tiger pit in India and was spiked by a piece of bamboo. (5) He broke it a third time against the cowl of a racing car he was driving around the track at Ascot, California. (6) He smeared it to pulp against the inside of his diving helmet when he came up fast and struck the boat off Cedros Island. (7) He put the finishing touches to it while driving a car through a house as a stunt for the movies. (8) It isn't much of a nose nowadays, but Campbell is still pushing it into trouble.

Sentences 1 and 2 express the general statement. Sentences 3-7 give the supporting details. Sentence 8 is a summary sentence, restating the idea expressed in Sentence 2. As you can see, the eight sentences are about one idea and could be in one paragraph. But the writer preferred to split them into two paragraph groups, separating the details from the general statement. The summary sentence shows that the two groups really do the work of a single logical paragraph.

A paragroup is often used for a comparison between two persons or things, as in the following example:

> (1) Wagner and Cobb are still regarded as the best all-around ballplayers America has produced. (2) They were exact opposites. (3) Wagner—a mild-mannered, ungainly, bowlegged man—had enormous hands. (4) From his position at shortstop, he could stop practically any ball hit at the left

side of the Pittsburgh infield, and from any position—on his knees or falling on his face—his throw to first base was always as straight and as fast as a rifle shot. (5) He led the National League in hitting for eight years, and he was a peerless base runner. (6) Honus always had a kind word and a smile for everybody he played against.

(7) Cobb, on the other hand, was a graceful, belligerent figure who played with a cold fury. (8) It was said that he sharpened his spikes with a razor strop. (9) Get in his way, and he'd slash you to ribbons. (10) Cobb led the American League in batting for twelve years, but he was not a slugger. (11) His hands on the bat were five or six inches apart, ready to bunt or to choke as the occasion presented itself. (12) His record of 96 stolen bases in 1915 has never been equaled.

Sentences 1 and 2 are the general statement. Sentences 3-6 give the details about Wagner. Sentences 7-12 give the details about Cobb. By splitting the details into two groups, the writer sharpens the contrast. But notice that the general statement is for the paragroup, not just the first paragraph, and both paragraphs are needed to make it clear.

Sometimes a paragroup is used to call attention to details that are more important than others. For example:

(1) Perhaps to comprehend this point fully, it is necessary to understand something of the buffalo's economic importance to the Indian, since it was primarily the buffalo which opened the bitter wedge between the two races. (2) The buffalo's hide, tanned and decorated, was used to make the lodges of the Indian. (3) Blankets and covering came from the same source. (4) The beaver, the antelope, the bear, and the wolf each contributed its small share; but these were not a dependable source, while the buffalo in its countless numbers and predictable migrations could always be relied upon. (5) Picket ropes and lariats, harness for the pony travois and dogsled; spoons and rude knives, needles and many a useful implement; horns to decorate headdresses; skulls to make masks for the medicine men—these were but some of the uses to which the buffalo was put.

(6) Most important of all, the animal meant food and sustenance, without which the Indians must perish and die. (7) Buffalo meat was the red man's principal article of diet. (8) Dried, it could be kept indefinitely; mashed into a pulp and mixed with chokeberries or wild plums and packed into parflêches (containers of buffalo hide) tight-sealed with suet, it could be kept for years on end, a reliable source of food when all others failed. (9) The marrow was used for medicine, as well as for greasing and oiling rifles. (10) The gall was a tonic. (11) In fact, there was scarcely a point in the entire scheme of Indian living where the buffalo did not play some part, great or small.

Sentence 1 is a general statement for the paragroup. Sentences 2-5 give certain details. Sentences 6-10 give other details that the writer wants to give special emphasis to. But notice that Sentence 11 sums up the details in both paragraphs and restates in part the idea expressed in Sentence 1.

You have seen three of the ways in which paragroups are used—to separate details from a general statement, to sharpen a contrast, to call attention to important details. There are other ways, some of which you will see in the Units that follow. But two things you should remember about paragroups: (1) They do not represent mere whimsy on the part of the writer. (2) They do not violate what you have learned about paragraphs; for, as you have seen, paragroups have general statements, supporting details, and summary sentences, just as logical paragraphs do.

Improving paragraphs
6. Have I grouped details effectively?

In writing from a plan, you have learned to use a separate paragraph for each group of related details. If your plan has been carefully prepared, the sentences in each paragraph will tell about one phase of your subject and so be clearly related in meaning.

As you may have discovered, however, it is often easier to arrange related details in a plan than it is to explain them in a paragraph. One group of five details may be about a simple idea that can be mad clear in a paragraph of two or three sentences. Another group of five details may be about an idea so complex that two or three sentences are needed for each detail, several more for a general statement, and possibly another for a summary sentence. Such a paragraph presents a problem, since it is difficult for the average reader to follow one thought through a dozen or more sentences. Paragroups offer a practical solution to this problem.

While writing, you should of course be concerned more with expressing your ideas clearly than with keeping track of the number of sentences you use. But in revising your first drafts, you have an opportunity to notice long paragraphs that might make your composition difficult to read. When you find such a paragraph, the first thing is to ask yourself questions like these: Have I kept to the central idea of the paragraph? Have I followed a straight line throughout the paragraph? Does each sentence help to make my meaning clear? If your answer to each of these questions is Yes, you know that all the sentences are necessary. Then the next thing is to see whether you might split the paragraph into smaller groups, making a paragroup of it.

Look at the paragraph carefully. Is the general statement long? Perhaps you can separate it from the details. This is particularly useful when the general statement is made up of several sentences or is preceded by other sentences. By putting the sentences expressing the general statement in one group and those giving the details in another, you help the reader see where the general statement ends and the details begin.

Does the paragraph express a contrast? Perhaps you can separate the two items. This is often useful when there are several points of difference. By making a separate group of the sentences that have to ˀ with each item, you help the reader keep the discussion of one item ˀrate from that of the other.

ˀoes the paragraph have many details? Perhaps you can put some into a separate group. This is usually effective when important ˀe been put last. By making a separate group of the sentences ˀdetails, you help the reader realize their importance.

ˀaragroups to make long paragraphs easier to read, try to ˀthings: (1) Effective paragroups do not just happen. ˀ grouping sentences according to their meaning

ˀ\
)\

within the paragraph. (2) The sentences are not changed in order or number. They are simply separated into smaller groups. While the sentences may be grouped in various ways, nothing is added to them, and nothing is omitted. (3) Sentences that help explain a detail belong with it. And no group should have in it explanatory sentences that belong with a detail in some other group.

Paragroups are never an excuse for slipshod paragraphing. Since the paragraphs in them look like any other paragraphs, the reader naturally expects the sentences in each group to be closely related in meaning. When they are, he can move quickly and easily from one group of sentences to the next. And this is important; for regardless of the number of groups into which they are separated, the sentences must work together to make clear the central idea of the paragroup.

EXERCISE 5. You have seen that a long paragraph is often easier to read when it is made into a paragroup. Turn to page 271, and read again the long paragraph about the large hall in Quito. How would you separate the sentences into two groups? On a sheet of paper, write "Group 1" and, after it, the numbers of the sentences you would keep in the first group. On the following line, write "Group 2" and, after it, the numbers of the sentences you would put in a second group. Then turn to page 278, and do the same for the long paragraph about the responsibility of a movie director. Be ready to discuss your reasons for dividing the paragraphs as you have.

Allocating space

In writing, space is often a measure of importance. If half of an article tells about the way in which a new automobile runs, while only a quarter of the article tells how it looks, you assume that the writer considers the performance of the car more important than its appearance. It does not matter whether the half is five hundred words out of a thousand, or fifty out of a hundred. What does matter is the proportion—that twice as much space is used to tell about one quality as about the other.

The following selection tells about the public appearances, the daily routine, and the physical appearance of a young violinist. Notice how the amount of space allocated to each idea affects your impression of its relative importance:

(1) The young violinist made his first public appearance when his teacher, Galamian, presented his pupils in a recital at Town Hall, May 19, 1947. (2) Late in 1948, when only twelve, Michael was soloist with the Rhode Island Philharmonic symphony orchestra for five concerts in Rhode Island cities.

(3) In January, 1949, Michael gave a concert at Plateau Hall, Montreal, Canada, and shortly afterwards won the Edgar Stillman Kelley scholarship of $250 yearly for three years in competition with other young musicians representing eleven northeastern states. (4) Later on Michael appeared as soloist under the baton of Leon Barzin for the Carnegie Hall children's concert that featured 146 young musicians from New York schools. (5) And soon after, he played in Cuba with the Havana Philharmonic symphony under the direction of Artur Rodzinski.

(6) Michael begins his day at 7 a.m. and spends from fifteen to thirty minutes practicing scales before breakfast. (7) Despite the many hours he practices, he finds time to play ping-pong and collect stamps. (8) He is a good swimmer and enjoys this sport and bicycle riding.

(9) Michael has jet black hair and dark brown eyes. (10) His height and weight are debatable because he outgrows his suits between concerts.

By devoting almost two thirds of the space to the public appearances, the writer shows which idea he considers of greatest importance. By using approximately one eighth of the space to tell about Michael's appearance, he shows which idea he considers of least importance.

The principle of allocating a larger proportion of space to a more important idea applies also to details, as in the following selection:

(1) Most Australians—figuratively speaking—live off the backs of sheep. (2) Australia is the greatest wool-producing (and wool-exporting) country in the world. (3) One sixth of all the sheep in the world are in Australia. (4) She has no fewer than 115,000,000 sheep—nearly 14 sheep per inhabitant!

(5) And lucky it is for Australia. (6) For today there is a record-breaking boom in wool. (7) Wool prices have shot up to an all-time high. (8) The reason is the expanding size of armies throughout the world. (9) The armed forces require large quantities of wool for uniforms and blankets.

(10) Second in importance to wool is wheat. (11) Australia is a leading wheat-growing country. (12) Other crops are oats, barley, corn, potatoes.

(13) Industrially, Australia has made remarkable progress. (14) Its manufacturing output tripled from 1915 to 1940. (15) During World War II, the country served as the "arsenal" for the Allies in the South Pacific theater.

(16) And since the end of the war, the pace has been kept up. (17) Industry has been operating in high gear. (18) Employment generally is at peak levels. (19) About 3,250,000 people are gainfully employed—which is a huge percentage of the total population.

By using ten lines to tell about wool and only three lines to tell about the other products, the writer leaves you in no doubt as to which of the agricultural products he thinks is most important. And by giving nine lines to industry, he indicates roughly his opinion of its importance as compared with agriculture. Notice that space is here a guide to the relative importance not only of two main parts, but also of the details in one of those parts.

You know that after an idea has been explained once, there is less need for explaining it fully each time it is repeated. As you read the next selection, notice the decreasing emphasis given to the idea of turning a dream into reality:

(1) In Missouri, a man stood looking over the ugly expanse of a city dump. (2) But he didn't see the rusting cans, the heaps of rubbish. (3) What he saw, instead, was a city of incomparable beauty where people would live in gardened houses along sweeping drives.

(4) It was a wild dream, yet amazingly he made it come true. (5) Today, on the site of that dump, there is a city where 50,000 people live in a parklike atmosphere.

(6) In California, another man walked through a sun-baked barley patch and looked down a dusty country road. (7) "Here," he said, "is the place for the most beautiful shopping street in the world." (8) Another dream, but it, too, came true. (9) That dirt road is now a fabulous stretch of boulevard, the "Fifth Avenue of the West."

(10) In New York City, a third man studied the monotonous piles of brick and stone that rose above the paving. (11) "Do city apartments have to be like that?" he asked himself. (12) "Why can't we have trees and lawns and children's playgrounds right here in Manhattan?" (13) Though he was old and ready to retire, he rolled up his sleeves and turned another dream into reality.

(14) These men were called crazy idealists, yet they lived to see their visions show the way to better living for everyone in America. (15) Some were real-estate men who saw beyond mere subdivisions; some were builders who found better ways to build homes; others were businessmen who dared to invest huge sums in a new kind of enterprise.

To explain that the first man made his dream come true, the writer uses two sentences (4 and 5) and sets them off as a separate paragraph. To explain that the second man realized his dream, the writer again uses two sentences (8 and 9) but this time keeps them a part of the paragraph. To explain that the third man turned a dream into reality, the writer uses only part of Sentence 13.

Notice that the first two paragraphs are a paragroup. A beginning writer would very likely be timid about using four paragraphs to give three examples. Yet the second paragraph helps call attention to an idea that runs through the next two paragraphs and is echoed by the word *visions* in Sentence 14.

You have seen various ways of emphasizing important ideas—by using summary sentences, linking expressions, paragroups, and space. Experienced writers use these ways in any combination that gives the desired emphasis to their ideas. In general, they follow the principle of saying the most about the things they consider of most importance.

Improving paragraphs
7. Have I used space wisely?

A reader judges to some extent the relative importance of your ideas by the amount of space you allocate to each of them. Once you realize this, you have a basis for deciding whether you have used space wisely. While the proportion of space allocated to each part of a composition is often only a rough guide, there are certain principles that may be helpful: (1) Paragraphs of approximately the same length may be used to express ideas of equal importance. (2) Short paragraphs may be used for unimportant ideas or those you think the reader already knows. (3) Long paragraphs or paragroups may be used for important ideas, those you particularly want the reader to understand and remember.

In revising first drafts of your compositions, always take time to ask yourself questions like these: Have I given enough space to important ideas? Have I used too much space for ideas that are unimportant or obvious? Such questions may suggest changes to make your composition more effective.

Remember that it is the proportion of space allocated to the various ideas that indicates their relative importance. For example, if you have told all you know about an important idea, you can hardly be expected to give it more space. But you can make it seem more prominent by using less space for other ideas. Explaining unimportant ideas briefly helps direct the reader's attention to those ideas you particularly want him to understand and remember.

Getting off to a good start

As you know, an introductory paragraph is rarely used in a short composition of fifteen to twenty sentences. But in compositions of fifteen to twenty paragraphs, or longer, an introductory paragraph is not out of proportion and often helps the writer get off to a good start. While the purpose is the same as with an opening sentence—to arouse the reader's interest—two problems are always present. If the introduction is not closely related in thought with the rest of the composition, the reader will feel that he has been tricked. If it is not closely linked with the following paragraph, the reader will have trouble making the transition. Notice how both of these problems have been met in the following example:

(1) It is not always easy in these days of rapid advance to distinguish what has already been achieved from what is yet to come. (2) Sometimes the newspapers herald almost as an accomplished fact a giant electronic brain that has only passed from being a gleam in an enthusiastic worker's eye to being a chronic pain in a discouraged worker's neck. (3) What predictions can be made about future developments in electronics?

(4) Some things we can see rather clearly in a general way. . . .

Sentences 1 and 2 provide a background for the important question in Sentence 3. Sentence 4 echoes this question by partly answering it and so links the introduction to the next paragraph. (The dots following Sentence 4 indicate that the rest of the paragraph has been omitted.) Sometimes an unusual incident makes a good beginning:

(1) Not long ago a Connecticut baker of specialty bread received a letter from a customer in Arizona. (2) There was nothing so very unusual about the distance of the customer.

(3) Like many specialty bakers this one regularly sends orders to faraway enthusiasts who can afford such whims, and he frequently receives glowing testimonials from them. (4) But this particular letter struck a brand-new note.

(5) The customer—a lady naturalist—reported that she had made a pet of a red-winged blackbird. (6) One day she fed him crumbs of the baker's special bread. (7) The following day she spread before him crumbs of another type of bread.

(8) "He flatly refused to touch them," she concluded, "and scolded me angrily until I gave him your bread."

(9) This is the first indication that any of our furred or feathered friends of the animal kingdom have joined us in our more and more choosy attitude toward the staff of life. . . .

By telling about the fussy blackbird, the writer leads the reader into an article about bread. Notice that Sentences 1-8, explaining the incident, are a paragroup which is closely linked to the next paragraph by the pronoun *This* and the echo words *furred or feathered friends of the animal kingdom, choosy attitude,* and *the staff of life.*

Another common way of beginning is to give a striking fact that is likely to attract the reader's attention. For example:

(1) Try to imagine eight hundred guests trooping into your home every day and thoroughly inspecting each corner of it. (2) Then try to imagine having only two hours—from eight to ten in the morning—to ready the house for that day's visitors. (3) This is what faces Mrs. Joseph N. van Buren, head housekeeper of the Governor's Palace and other exhibition buildings at Colonial Williamsburg, Virginia, where it's open house every day of the year except Christmas.

(4) All the rooms in the buildings we visited had a calmly poised air—as though confidently expecting the arrival of guests—and we wondered how this effect had been achieved in two hours. (5) Then we wondered if the same methods might be used to keep a home as neat.

Here the first paragraph states the fact, while the second leads the reader directly into the article. Repetition of the words *buildings, guests, home,* and *two hours* also helps link the paragraphs.

Occasionally the whole first paragraph may be used just to arouse the reader's curiosity, as in this next example:

> (1) Barbed wire and staples, spikes and bits of chicken wire—gulp!—an old axe head and a half-dozen metal syrup spiles—in they go! (2) How would you like to watch a scythe blade or a broken piece of crosscut saw being eaten? (3) You can; it's going on every day. (4) It sounds sensational, doesn't it?
>
> (5) For the last fourteen years I've been watching a sugar maple swallow a porcelain insulator, and sometime, about 1975, it should finish it! (6) That's the trouble with trees; they don't swallow things fast enough to make it really exciting.

The strange diet suggested in the opening paragraph is frankly intended to lead the reader into the second paragraph. Notice that the two paragraphs are also tied together by the use of the words *watch* and *watching, being eaten* and *swallow.*

An unusual or exciting incident often makes a good beginning:

> (1) The hunter dismounted from his horse and proceeded cautiously on foot through the dense brush. (2) For thirty minutes he stalked his prey, circling until he sighted it in heavy underbrush and mesquite. (3) He took careful aim and fired.
>
> (4) His horse dropped dead.
>
> (5) It is careless and tragic enough to lose a fine horse, but how about the hunter in western New York who killed three hunters with one bullet last year?

As you can see, the first two paragraphs are a paragroup. By setting Sentence 4 off as a separate paragraph, the writer gives it added emphasis. Notice that Sentence 5 echoes the idea expressed in Sentence 4 and links it with tragic accidents involving hunters.

When space permits, an incident reported all or in part by dialogue almost always attracts the reader's attention:

(1) "I wonder if it's cool enough for a jacket?" inquired a young woman at an evening lawn party last summer.

(2) "Just a minute," I volunteered, "and I'll give you the temperature."

(3) I gazed at my watch a few seconds, then advised her. (4) "The temperature is 72 degrees. (5) Hardly cool enough for a jacket—or is it?"

(6) She thought I had a tiny thermometer on my watch and wanted to see it. (7) But I had merely timed a tree cricket that was chirping in the nearby shrubbery. (8) I had counted his chirps for 7 seconds, doubled the number, and added 16, which gave me the air temperature.

(9) The crickets are the best known of all insects in respect to their response to temperature and temperature changes. (10) Indeed, one cricket has come to be known as the Temperature Cricket. . . .

While the main part of the article actually begins with Sentence 9, the introduction is so closely linked to it by repetition of the word *temperature* that the reader is scarcely aware of the transition.

You have seen some of the ways in which writers use introductory paragraphs to arouse the reader's interest. When such paragraphs are carefully chosen, kept in proportion to the rest of the composition, and closely linked with it, they frequently entice the reader into looking over an article he might otherwise have ignored.

Improving paragraphs
8. Do I need an introductory paragraph?

Good salesmen try to win the attention of their customers before pointing out the merits of the product. Skilled speakers usually tell a joke or two before plunging into a serious talk. And experienced writers often use an introductory paragraph to arouse the reader's interest in what they have written. All realize the value of whetting a person's appetite before serving the main course.

A sense of proportion is, of course, necessary. A salesman cannot spend half of his interview winning attention and still do justice to his product. Nor can a speaker spend most of his time telling jokes and still do justice to his subject. When you use an introductory paragraph, always ask yourself: Do I really need a paragraph to arouse the reader's interest? Would an opening sentence perhaps be adequate? Is the paragraph in proportion to the rest of my composition?

Necessary, too, is a sense of fitness. Any salesman can win attention by being rude and quarrelsome, but he is not likely to make a sale. And unless a speaker's jokes have some connection with his subject, you feel that he is more interested in making you laugh than in expressing his ideas. Always test an introductory paragraph by asking yourself: Will the reader see the connection between my opening paragraph and the rest of my composition? How well does it prepare him for what I am going to say?

A sense of responsibility also helps. Having won favorable attention, salesman and speaker alike try to get down to business promptly. Always ask yourself: Have I linked my introductory paragraph closely to the following paragraphs? Have I been careful to lead the reader into the next part of my composition?

As you have seen, introductory paragraphs are of many kinds—some explaining or describing a situation, others giving interesting facts or statistics, still others relating an anecdote or an unusual incident. Whatever kind you choose, be sure that it is in keeping with the rest of your composition and leads naturally into it. Though sometimes written last, or even added during revision, a good introductory paragraph gives the impression of being an essential part of the whole composition.

EXERCISE 6. In a magazine you read regularly, find an interesting article that has a good introduction of one or more paragraphs. Read through the article carefully. On a sheet of paper, write the name of the author, the title of the article, the name of the magazine, and its date. Then copy the introduction. Below it, write a few sentences telling briefly what the article is about and why you think the introduction is good. Be ready to read the introduction to your classmates and to discuss your opinion of it with them.

Summarizing important ideas

When we look at the skyline of a large city, we are inclined to notice certain buildings of distinctive size or shape. Because they stand out clearly from the rest, such buildings are landmarks that often help identify the city and plainly distinguish its skyline from those of other cities.

In almost every composition certain ideas are more important than others. When these important ideas are made to stand out clearly, they help the reader grasp the central thought of the composition and remember it accurately. A summarizing paragraph is one way of giving prominence to such ideas.

Earlier you learned that a summary sentence may be used to restate the central idea of a paragraph. In a similar way, a single sentence may be used to sum up the important ideas in a whole composition. Here, for example, is the final paragraph from an article recommending winter travel in Switzerland:

> So whether it's for the wonders of winter scenery, for elfin nostalgia, for robust snow sports, or for the sheer creature comforts of a nation which has learned how to cater to tourists, we give you Switzerland for January.

Each of the phrases beginning with *for* refers to an important idea expressed in one of the four preceding paragraphs, while the main clause sums up "in a nutshell" the central thought of the article. The sentence is set off as a separate paragraph to show that it summarizes important ideas from all the paragraphs, not just the fourth.

While final paragraphs of one sentence are fairly common, most summarizing paragraphs consist of two or more sentences. Here, for example, is one of four sentences from an eighteen-paragraph article on ways of controlling hatred and directing it to useful ends:

> Can you afford to hate? Certainly you cannot afford to hate unwisely. Whenever you are tempted to hate your fellow human beings, remember, "Let him who is without sin cast the first stone." Then get busy and hate the evils in the world that need correcting—and hate them enough to help correct them.

By repeating the title of his article, the writer emphasizes the problem. By suggesting two solutions, he makes his important ideas stand out clearly without itemizing them in detail.

The number of sentences in a summarizing paragraph is determined more by the writer's ideas and what he wishes to say about them than by the length of his composition. For example, here are four sentences used to sum up a long article of thirty-six paragraphs about famine conditions in India:

> For at least two centuries the world's production of food has increased faster than its population; but within the last few years the situation appears to have been reversed, and the population of the world has increased faster than its food supply. The world is moving toward the condition that India has already reached. India has many lessons for us. It would be well to help and to study India.

In the first two sentences of this summarizing paragraph the writer restates important ideas explained in his article. In the last two he points out their significance to his readers.

Summarizing paragraphs are not always at the end of a composition. They may also be used after any part of it to call attention to important ideas. For example, here are four paragraphs from a long article on the migration of birds. Notice that the fourth is a summarizing paragraph:

> How do birds find their way, particularly when traveling by night—yes, even through dense fogs—or when crossing great bodies of water? Many return to the same nesting ground every year. The greater shearwater moves unerringly from the North Atlantic to its only breeding place, a small island in the South Atlantic about midway between Africa and South America.
>
> Undoubtedly birds depend somewhat upon their eyesight, many theorists believing that birds fly "contact" as do aviators, by following known objects upon the ground. According to these thinkers, the old birds lead the young ones over the route to be followed, and this guided trip is sufficient to fix its pattern in their minds. But this is certainly not true in the case of the western sandpipers, at least, for the young birds do not migrate until a month after their parents.

304

Sense of sight, however, cannot function when flying through dense fogs, or over a vast stretch of water. Even if a bird's eyesight were infinite in reach, it still would not serve in some cases. When the ruby throat sets out to fly the Gulf of Mexico, even if this dauntless little aviator started at an altitude of five miles it still could not see over the earth's curvature between itself and Mexico.

Thus, in spite of research, scientists still face the facts of migration with a sense of frustration, mingled with hope. Birds must carry in their heads, in addition to their other special senses, that which for want of a better term we may call a sense of direction.

The writer might have ended this part of his composition with the third paragraph, which makes it clear that sense of sight alone does not explain the mystery of migration. But by summing up the result of the conflict in viewpoints, the writer makes it easier for readers to agree with the explanation he suggests.

Sometimes a summarizing paragraph is used to make quite clear what the writer means, as in these three paragraphs at the beginning of an article on the relationship of discipline and freedom:

The good driver brings his car to a full halt at the boulevard stop sign. He does this because he is properly disciplined. He is disciplined by *know-how*, by *know-why*, and by *want-right*. He knows how to handle his car. He knows why the stop sign is needed. He wants to obey the stop regulation because he believes it is right. His driving discipline supports and extends his freedom and the freedom of other drivers and of pedestrians to travel more safely than would be possible without discipline.

The poor driver may fail to obey the stop sign. He does so because he lacks one or more of the elements of good discipline in the situation. He does not know how to bring his car to a halt correctly. For example, he may step on the accelerator instead of the brake. He may not know why he should stop. Or he may know very well how and why to stop but just lacks the desire to do what he knows is the right thing to do. He is undisciplined, and his own freedom, as well as the freedom of others to move safely, is thereby curtailed.

This view of discipline as essential to freedom can be similarly illustrated in any activity of men in groups. To get a job done as smartly and smoothly as possible, the group develops patterns of action. The individual's freedom to act with the group is not restricted but enhanced by acquiring the discipline of those patterns.

Without the third paragraph you might think that the writer was telling about good and poor drivers. But with it you know that the first two paragraphs are intended merely as specific examples illustrating an abstract idea. Notice that the summarizing paragraph states this idea in a general way and shows how it applies to other groups.

Summarizing paragraphs may consist of one sentence or more. They may occur at the end of a composition or after any part of it. And as you have seen, they are often an effective way of giving special emphasis to ideas that the writer considers of particular importance.

Improving paragraphs
9. Do I need a summarizing paragraph?

Whether or not you use an introductory paragraph often depends on the length of your composition. Whether or not you use a summarizing paragraph is more likely to depend on the content. If you are telling about something that happened or something you have seen, a closing sentence may be adequate, no matter how many paragraphs there are. But if you are expressing an opinion or telling what something means, a summarizing paragraph may improve your composition, even though it is short. When you are trying to decide, ask yourself: Will a summarizing paragraph help the reader understand my meaning? Do I want to call his attention to the important ideas? If the answers are Yes, you probably need a summarizing paragraph.

Most of the paragraphs you have studied tend to advance the thought of a composition. Each new paragraph is another step along the way, taking up another phase of the subject, adding more facts or opinions or examples. Even introductory paragraphs, whose main purpose is to attract the attention of the reader, ordinarily lead him into the paragraphs that follow.

A summarizing paragraph is different. It has the effect of saying to the reader, "The ideas expressed in the preceding paragraphs are important. Let's stop for a moment to make certain that we understand their meaning." By bringing the reader to a halt in this way, you encourage him to think over what he has just read. You also direct his attention emphatically to whatever you wish to say about it. For this reason, only important ideas belong in a summarizing paragraph.

There are many ways of summing up such ideas so that the reader will realize their importance. You may simply restate them to show "in a nutshell" what you mean. You may analyze them, evaluate them, point out their significance, make a general comment about them, or tie them up with the opening paragraph to emphasize the central thought of your composition. Whatever your choice, you will do well to refer only to ideas that have been previously explained. A "new" idea is out of place in a summarizing paragraph. No matter how clear its relationship with the others may be in your mind, it is likely to confuse or distract the reader.

As you revise a composition containing a summarizing paragraph, ask yourself questions like these: Have I included in the summarizing paragraph the ideas that I particularly want the reader to remember? Have I shown why they are important? Have I been careful to exclude ideas that have not been previously explained? Such questions will remind you that the purpose of a summarizing paragraph is to call the reader's attention to important ideas in preceding paragraphs.

EXERCISE 7. In a magazine you read regularly, find an interesting article that has an effective summarizing paragraph. Read through the article carefully. On a sheet of paper, write the name of the author, the title of the article, the name of the magazine, and its date. Then copy the summarizing paragraph. Below it, write a few sentences telling briefly what the article is about and why you think the summarizing paragraph effective. Be ready to read the paragraph to your classmates and to discuss it with them.

Bridging the gaps

You have learned that linking expressions are useful in helping readers follow the writer's thought as it moves from paragraph to paragraph. When the paragraphs are closely related, as they usually are in a short composition, the gap in thought is narrow; and a few words are sufficient to help the reader across it. But if the gap is wide, as it sometimes is in going from one part of a long composition to another, several sentences may be needed to help the reader make the transition. A paragraph consisting of such sentences is a **transitional paragraph**.

Here, for example, are four paragraphs from an article on the importance of staying healthy. The first paragraph ends one part of the article. The third introduces another part. As you read the selection, see if you are conscious of the wide gap in thought between the two:

> (1) How about the way you walk? (2) The right walk is free and easy—toes pointed forward, legs moving close together, knees limber, body in easy balance—with head, shoulders, and hips in line. (3) Try it and see how much more comfortable and graceful it is than a head-forward stride, a toeing-out waddle, or a stiff pavement-pounding tread.
>
> (4) So far we've been discussing health mostly in relation to personality and prettiness. (5) But that word "health" is the great common denominator, as your math teacher would say, for personality, prettiness, and patriotism as well. (6) Isn't it a happy coincidence that you can also serve your country while you are serving yourself?
>
> (7) Why is it so patriotic to be healthy?
>
> (8) We'll start with the most practical consideration. (9) You probably have read or heard about the shortage of doctors and nurses in this country. (10) Even in normal times, there just aren't enough to go around. . . .

Notice how the second paragraph bridges the gap between the first and third paragraphs. Sentence 4 sums up the preceding part of the article. Sentence 5 adds a new idea—patriotism. Sentence 6 ties this new idea in with the rest of the article, so that readers can follow the thought as it moves from personal to national aspects of the subject. As you can see, the three sentences work together as a transitional paragraph.

308

Somewhat different is the transitional paragraph that links two parts of a composition by combining the end of one part with the beginning of the next one. As you read the following selection, notice the way in which the third paragraph ties together the second and fourth ones:

(1) Young hearts ache when intimate friendships break up. (2) Boys and girls of teen age feel almost destroyed when close relationships swiftly cool and wane. (3) Perhaps young people invest so great a portion of themselves in a friendship that everything seems lost when one partner puts the other one back into circulation.

(4) Girls are more inclined than boys to show outward signs of this inner hurt. (5) But boys feel just as injured and miserable over being let down by once ardent friends. (6) Most boys learn early to cover inner feelings with an outer layer of bravado. (7) I have come to have a special respect for the girl or boy who takes the break-up of a friendship with a smile and says, "Well, there are other fish in the sea. (8) I'll just have to find a new pal. (9) Wish me luck!"

(10) That kind of spunk is good. (11) It carries you over the period of shock moderately well. (12) It gives you the needed breather while you get your emotional feet under you again. (13) The next big thing you need to do is to stop a moment and ask yourself, "Why do friends drop me?"

(14) There may be several practical answers in your own case. (15) One factor that almost certainly is mixed up in the problem is that your interests and attitudes have changed considerably in the past year. (16) The interests and attitudes of the other fellow probably have changed just as much as yours—though not necessarily in the same direction. . . .

If you look carefully at the third paragraph, you will see that Sentences 10, 11, and 12 are a sort of summary for the second paragraph, while Sentence 13 introduces the next part of the article. By combining Sentence 13 with the other three, the writer not only bridges the gap between the two parts, but also shows that they are closely related in his mind.

You have seen that transitional paragraphs, like linking expressions, are useful in helping readers follow a writer's thought. And you have learned that by summing up what has come before and by preparing readers for what comes next, such paragraphs can bridge wider gaps in thought than linking expressions can. But you should also remember that a composition may have a half-dozen parts, each of several paragraphs, and still not need a single transitional paragraph. It is not the number of parts a composition has that determines the need for a transitional paragraph, but the difficulty readers may have in going from one part to the next. Skilled writers use a transitional paragraph only when they feel it is needed to make clear the meaning they intend.

Improving paragraphs
10. Have I kept the reader in mind?

In some newspaper offices it is customary for an editorial writer to keep on his desk a snapshot of an utter stranger—a laboring man in overalls, a housewife carrying a bag of groceries, or some other person representing a typical reader of the paper. This is not done for any sentimental reason, of course, but simply to remind the writer constantly of his readers so that he will write his editorials for them, not for himself.

Keeping the reader in mind at all times is probably the most valuable habit a writer can form. Certainly it helps him greatly in planning, writing, and revising any composition with ideas in it, ideas that he wants to communicate to others. From selecting suitable details to using transitional paragraphs, he must constantly be thinking of his readers, putting himself in their place, trying in every way to help them understand what he wants them to know. Only as he learns to assume this responsibility, can he hope to acquire skill in expressing his thoughts effectively.

Particularly in revising first drafts for meaning is it important to keep the reader in mind. To help you, the suggestions for improving paragraphs have been phrased as questions. As you review them here, notice how many can be satisfactorily answered only by thinking of yourself as the reader, only by putting yourself in his place and anticipating the difficulties he might have in understanding you. In this way you have been learning to assume your share of responsibility for effective communication.

1. **Have I selected details carefully?**
2. **Have I explained details adequately?**
3. **Do I need a general statement?**
4. **Do I need a summary sentence?**
5. **Have I used good linking expressions?**
6. **Have I grouped details effectively?**
7. **Have I used space wisely?**
8. **Do I need an introductory paragraph?**
9. **Do I need a summarizing paragraph?**
10. **Have I kept the reader in mind?**

As you may recall, the first five suggestions have to do mostly with individual paragraphs, while the last five are concerned more with paragraphs as parts of the whole composition. Together with the twenty suggestions for improving sentences (pages 150-151), they point the way to the clear, forceful, effective written expression that is the goal of every writer.

EXERCISE 8. The numbered sentences tell of some of the unusual foods prized in various parts of the world. Most of the sentences begin with subject and verb. After reviewing the twenty ways of improving sentences, summarized on pages 150-151, rewrite the account, revising the sentences to make them more clear, forceful, and interesting. Be sure to group related sentences into paragraphs that show a shift from one phase of the subject to another. You will need five paragraphs.

(1) There are many strange foreign foods. (2) We consider these foods unappetizing. (3) We shudder at the thought of eating such foods. (4) They are considered rare delicacies by native connoisseurs. (5) Such exotic dishes as shark-fin soup and snails in vinegar are among these unusual foods. (6) Another is African black ants. (7) These ants are deep fried. (8) Another exotic dish is sea-slugs. (9) We are particular about one thing in America. (10) We must have our eggs fresh. (11) Fermented eggs are highly esteemed in China. (12) These eggs are buried for long periods of

time. (13) They become green then. (14) They become cheeselike. (15) The older the eggs are, the more flavorful they are considered. (16) They are considered more valuable, too. (17) There are eggs one hundred years old. (18) These might be served in the homes of the very wealthy. (19) Another Chinese luxury is bird's-nest soup. (20) This soup is made from the nests of a species of swifts. (21) These swifts build their homes high on the faces of cliffs. (22) They build their homes at the mouths of caves, also. (23) The nests are made of twigs and seaweed. (24) The birds glue the twigs and seaweed together with their saliva. (25) The twigs and seaweed are strained out and discarded. (26) The saliva is used in bird's-nest soup. (27) The nests are very hard to get. (28) The cost of them is extremely great, therefore. (29) None except the rich can afford this rare delicacy for this reason. (30) We Americans like our tea with lemon. (31) We may like cream instead. (32) The Tartars of central Asia prefer butter in their tea. (33) The Tibetans prefer this, too. (34) They are also of central Asia. (35) They use a reeking, rancid butter for this purpose. (36) It is made from yak's milk. (37) The Oriental uses this butter on his cigarettes, also. (38) This causes the cigarettes to splutter in burning. (39) It makes them emit a choking and pungent smoke, also. (40) These strange habits and these strange foods are revolting to us. (41) They disgust us. (42) Many Americans eat raw clams, rattlesnake meat, and sweetbreads, however. (43) They consider them treats. (44) Such treats would delight the palate of a gourmet. (45) Taste is just a matter of geography maybe.

Composition

Telling about Interesting Jobs

If you needed a new dress or a new suit for some special occasion, would you wait until the last minute and then dash into the store nearest your home and buy the first one the clerk showed you? Or would you start "shopping around" long before the special day so that you would have plenty of time to inspect the wares in a number of stores, compare prices and values, and decide which of several things was best for you? If you are like most people, you do not make important decisions without considering all the possibilities, comparing advantages and disadvantages, getting competent advice. One of the most important decisions you will some day have to make is the choice of a vocation. It is too early, of course, for you to make a final decision. But it is not too early for you to start "shopping around" to see what jobs there are.

For this composition assignment you are to tell your classmates about a job that you think is interesting. It may be the job of a

friend or relative—a mechanic, a receptionist, a model, a football coach, a baseball umpire, a dancing teacher, a dentist, a clerk, an airline hostess, a newspaper reporter. Or it may be a job you have been reading about—that of an FBI agent, a forest ranger, a research worker, an astronomer, a dress designer, a sandhog, a lion tamer. Your talk should cover three main points: what the job is, what advantages and disadvantages it has, and what you think about it as a possible vocation.

In describing the job, you will want to give as complete a picture as you can. Just what does the worker do? How many hours does he work? Is the work well paid? What are the qualifications necessary for getting and holding the job? Try to avoid broad, vague statements; your classmates want to know specific details. In telling about the job of a clerk in a department store, for example, you might explain that clerks have other duties besides waiting on customers. They keep shelves and counters neat and clean, arrange merchandise displays, put price marks on all articles, keep close check on the stock, unload merchandise, keep daily records of their sales, attend staff meetings, and keep records of the hours worked.

To help you get started in planning the second part of your talk, you might consider questions like these: Are working conditions pleasant or unpleasant? Is the work dangerous? Is it monotonous or varied? Is it steady or seasonal? Does the worker get such company benefits as health and accident insurance, retirement pay, discounts on merchandise, paid vacations, profit-sharing payments? Does the job have other rewards besides money? For example, does it give the worker a chance to meet interesting people, to travel, to get more education? Is there any chance of advancement? Is the job easy to get, or is the field crowded? Are the rewards worth the preparation necessary to qualify for the job?

Once you have described the job and have pointed out its advantages and disadvantages, you are ready to tell your classmates in two or three sentences your opinion of the job as a vocation. Do you think it is a job you would like to have for the rest of your life? For part of your life? Not at all? Why? Is it because of its advantages? Because of its disadvantages? Or is it in spite of its disadvantages? In spite of its advantages?

Since your talk will include many details, it is important that you prepare your plan carefully, arranging the details in a logical order. Try to think of a good beginning sentence, one that will make your classmates want to hear the rest of your talk. A special closing sentence is not needed; simply end with the statement of your opinion.

Practice your talk at least once before coming to class, to make sure that you will know exactly how to present the details if you are called on to give your talk. When others are giving their talks, pay them the same courteous attention that you would expect if you were the speaker.

Seven Basic Spelling Rules **Unit 13**

W hen an employer complains angrily that high-school graduates cannot spell, he is not thinking of strange, uncommon words like *schottische* or *Popocatepetl* or *consanguineous*. Instead, his anger is aroused by the misspelling of such "easy" words as *too* and *its* and *answer* and *planned* and *business* and *ladies'* and *doesn't* and *writing*— words that you first learned in grade school and see and use almost every day of your life. These words are the troublemakers. They are useful, common words. They do not look difficult. Yet students all over the country misspell them so often and in such similar ways that we call these words "demons."

A good speller is a person with enough sense to memorize a few hundred common words that don't follow useful rules (the "demons") and to learn and apply a relatively small number of fundamental spelling rules, each of which pertains to a large number of words. This Unit first covers seven basic spelling rules. The next Unit will offer suggestions for mastering the demons.

1. Dropping the final *e*

T here is an *e* on the end of *write;* it disappears in *writing.* Other examples are *dine, dining; come, coming.* These look like the simplest forms in the world, as if any child could observe them once, see the principle, and with no mental effort always use *writing, dining,* and *coming* for the rest of his life. Yet there are bright students in every school—yes, in every college—who have never learned to use these forms invariably. *Coming* is so common that it is worth special emphasis. If you drop the *e* of *come* and add *ing,* what have you?

Always drop the final *e* of a verb before adding *ing,* unless you know a reason for not dropping it:

hope	scare	argue	shine	use	become
hoping	scaring	arguing	shining	using	becoming

This is easy to recite, but rehearsing the rule means little. What about the habit of always observing the rule, no matter how absorbed you may be in the subject you are writing about? Until that wrong form strikes you as a monstrosity, you have not formed the habit; you do not in any true sense know how to spell *writing* and *coming*. Anyone who has ever been confused will find he can help himself best by thinking of similar words together, especially in short sentences like "I was *writing* while they were *coming* into the *dining* room."

One exception to the rule is the verb *singe* ("He singed his eyebrows"), which forms *singeing*, so as not to look like "*singing* a song"; another is *dye, dyeing;* and still another, the *oe* verbs, which keep *e*— *hoeing, toeing, canoeing, shoeing.*

EXERCISE 1. Be prepared to write the following sentences from dictation:
1. I am writing to Jane, hoping she can visit us soon.
2. The days are becoming so very short that we scarcely ever see the sun shining.
3. While they were dining with the Baxters, they made plans to go canoeing the next day.
4. Should you be dyeing all these sweaters the same color?
5. We saw them coming, arguing bitterly.
6. Within a few minutes a large crowd of children had gathered around Jake to watch him shoeing the pony.
7. There they were, eagerly toeing the mark, impatient for the signal.
8. I don't mind hoeing, but I hate spading.
9. Though he was using great care, he couldn't help singeing his arm as he reached behind the candles.
10. He broke into the room with a shout, scaring Aunt Helen almost out of her wits.

Two groups of words are exceptions, each for a special and peculiar reason: (1) the *e* is kept in *hoeing, toeing,* etc., because if we did drop *e,* the sound might seem to be the same as the sound of the vowels in *coin;* (2) the *e* is kept in words like *peaceable* and *traceable* so that they will not look as if they were pronounced "peakable" and "trak-

316

able." There are a few other exceptions (*mileage, acreage*), but the rule is "Drop the silent *e* before a suffix beginning with a vowel."

Before a suffix that begins with a consonant the final silent *e* must usually be kept:

nine + teen = nineteen   safe + ty = safety
nine + ty = ninety   arrange + ment = arrangement
use + less = useless   care + ful = careful

There are a few common exceptions, words in which the *e* is dropped before a suffix beginning with a consonant:

ninth   duly
truly   argument

The *e* before *ly* needs special attention:

sure + ly = surely   entire + ly = entirely
sincere + ly = sincerely   extreme + ly = extremely
affectionate + ly = affectionately   immense + ly = immensely
immediate + ly = immediately

The word *immediately* almost deserves a paragraph by itself, but we shall have to reserve such an honor for *definitely*. It is extremely difficult. It comes from a Latin word *finis*, with two *i*'s, meaning "an end or limit." *Finite,* with two *i*'s, means "that which can have limits put upon it"; *infinite,* with the same *i*'s, means "without any limit." When we set limits to a thing we make it, with the very same pair of *i*'s, *definite,* and when we make an adverb of it by using the suffix *ly*, we have *definite + ly = definitely.*

EXERCISE 2. Be prepared to write the following sentences from dictation:
1. On the ninth day he wrote to the distributor to ask about the delay.
2. Jim was a specially lovable child, but he could be immensely annoying.
3. We had to answer questions about the acreage of our farms.
4. They immediately made definite arrangements for hoeing the ground.
5. Since the test was extremely hard, nineteen of the ninety pupils failed.
6. Though the police are definitely interested in safety rules, the responsibility for enforcing them is not entirely theirs.
7. He is, without argument, our ablest and most forcible speaker.
8. She truly feels that spreading gossip is a grievous wrong.
9. I am sincerely fond of that peaceable community.
10. Though I entirely forgot the invitation, Jack duly sent a reply.

2. Doubling a final consonant

In the previous spelling lesson you studied a verb form in which a letter had to be dropped: "Always drop the final *e* of a verb before adding *ing*, unless you know a reason for not dropping it." In this lesson you take up the opposite kind of verb form, in which a letter has to be added. Have you ever understood why there are two *n*'s in *planned* and *planning*? If you added *ed* to *plan* without doubling the final consonant, you would change the pronunciation of the word. You would have *planed*, which rhymes with *rained*, instead of what you want—*planned*, rhyming with *sand*. If you added *ing* to *bar* without doubling the *r*, you would have *baring*, which rhymes with *wearing*, instead of *barring*, to rhyme with *marring*. These forms with double consonants are so common, and therefore so important, that they deserve special attention. A person who spells the forms of *stop* any other way than *stopped* and *stopping*—with two *p*'s—makes a careless blunder.

The same doubling is used with every one-syllable verb that ends in one consonant preceded by one vowel:

drag	dragged	dragging	slam	slammed	slamming
mop	mopped	mopping	plot	plotted	plotting
slap	slapped	slapping	tip	tipped	tipping
scrub	scrubbed	scrubbing	pin	pinned	pinning
step	stepped	stepping	tug	tugged	tugging

EXERCISE 3. Be prepared to write the following sentences from dictation:
1. They stopped him as he tried to escape and dragged him back to his cell.
2. The waiters liked him for his lavish tipping.
3. I scrubbed for a while, but soon slammed the brush down in disgust.
4. She planned wildly, pinning her hopes on winning the first prize.
5. We barred the door and plotted our revenge.
6. With a smile and a bow he tipped his hat and passed quickly by.
7. Jane felt like slamming the door to let them know that she had overheard their plotting.
8. John slapped his book down on the table and groaned.
9. Jim hurried off, stopping only to make sure that Mike was barring the back door.
10. I was angry at Willie for dragging in mud when I had just finished mopping the floor.

318

You have learned to double the final consonant of verbs like *stop* and *drag* and *plan* before adding *ed* or *ing*. Now you will see another group of verbs that double the final consonant before *ed* or *ing*. This second group consists of verbs that have more than one syllable. Notice the following examples:

occur	occurred	occurring	omit	omitted	omitting
compel	compelled	compelling	allot	allotted	allotting
prefer	preferred	preferring	control	controlled	controlling

The rule is that if a verb ends in a *single* consonant, if that consonant is preceded by a *single* vowel, and if the accent comes on the *last* syllable—that is, if all three things are true—the final consonant is doubled before *ed* and *ing*.

Why is *departed* the correct form? Because the word ends in *two* consonants, our rule does not apply to it. Why is *repeating* the correct form? Because the single consonant is preceded by *two* vowels, our rule does not apply. Why is *opened* correct? Because the accent is not on the last syllable, our rule does not apply. So—once again to make sure—the rule fits only a small number of verbs, only those of which you may say all three things: (1) single consonant, (2) single vowel, (3) accent on the last syllable.

There are a few verbs that look like exceptions, such as *equip,* which has two vowels before the *p*. But here the *u* is not really a vowel; it has the *w* sound, as if the word were spelled "ekwip." The rule applies, and we write:

equip	equipped	equipping	acquit	acquitted	acquitting

These common verbs have an accent before the last syllable:

happen	happened	happening	open	opened	opening
develop	developed	developing	offer	offered	offering
suffer	suffered	suffering	travel	traveled	traveling

EXERCISE 4. Be prepared to write the following sentences from dictation:
1. Though he has suffered, he has benefited from the experience.
2. It never occurred to me that he had purposely omitted using periods.
3. He slammed through the gates and hopped on the train as it was pulling out of the station.

4. We are hoping that the epidemic can be controlled.
5. Jimmy rebelled against coming to school Saturdays to make up his work, but after arguing for a while, he gave up.
6. For the last scene the platform had to be broadened and lengthened.
7. He referred us to a secretary who told us that he preferred to receive all complaints in writing.
8. He fell against the dining-room table, tipping the bowl of hot soup over its shining surface.
9. Though he knew he was trapped, he dragged himself painfully down the corridor, stopping several times to listen for the guard.
10. It had never occurred to me that he had been compelled to resign.

3. Changing *y* to *i*

If a verb ends in a *y* that is preceded by a consonant, the *y* is changed to *i* before the *ed* or *es* is added. The same change is made to form the plurals of nouns that end in *y* preceded by a consonant:

story	family	enemy	lady
stories	families	enemies	ladies

The same change is made with adjectives and adverbs:

easy	happy	heavy	lucky	early
easier	happier	heavier	luckier	earlier
easiest	happiest	heaviest	luckiest	earliest
easily	happily	heavily	luckily	

The same change is made when we add *ness* to form a noun:

happy	heavy	clumsy
happiness	heaviness	clumsiness

Can you spell *lonely*? *lovely*? Each has an *e* in it:

lonely	lovely
loneliness	loveliness

You know what *busy* means. If you wished to make a noun of it by adding *ness,* could you hold your mind steady enough to do just exactly what you ought to do? Could you really change *y* to *i*—not altering anything else—and add *ness*? Remember the *i* in *business.*

320

EXERCISE 5. Be prepared to write the following sentences from dictation:

1. The stories the spies told were not easily believed.
2. The loneliness and the spookiness of the room did not bother him.
3. Happily she could do the work easily.
4. The pluckiness of the prettiest girl speedily impressed them.
5. The ladies sang lullabies to soothe the cries of the babies.
6. Luckily his prophecies speedily frightened their enemies.
7. Henry has the roomiest office; John has the dirtiest.
8. Your butterflies are beauties.
9. I was mightily pleased by the jauntiness of her appearance.
10. He walked clumsily toward the daintiest of the beauties of the court.

4. *ie* and *ei*

The words that contain *ie* or *ei* would seem a hard tangle if you tried to learn all the items at once. If you take just one item at a time, for five lessons, you can gradually understand them all. When each item is clear, the whole collection can be summed up in a jingle of six short lines. After you have mastered it, you can say it in a few seconds and tell instantly whether the word you want to write should be spelled with an *ie* or an *ei*.

The one item in this lesson is that *ie* usually has the sound of "long *e*"—that is, the sound in *meet* and *feel*. Look at each word in the following list, taking time to notice the *ie* and to say mentally the sound of "long *e*":

believe	retrieve	relief	chief	series
relieve	reprieve	grief	thief	frieze
grieve	belief	brief	bier	believe

Now go through the list again; hear the sound of long *e* before the *v*'s and *f*'s. Think specially of *believe*, which begins and ends the list; it is more important than all the rest together.

There are a great many words which have an *ie* for a long *e* sound. One quartet is *field, shield, wield, yield*. Another quartet has the sound before *r*: *fierce, pierce, pier, frontier*. History teachers struggle for the *ie* in *siege* and *besiege*.

The word next in importance to *believe* is *piece*. Any student who has ever misspelled *piece* should fix the letters in his mind by means of some queer sentence like "I *believe* his *niece* stole a *piece* of pie." Such nonsense has rescued many people from difficulties.

Three other *ie* words can be remembered by putting them together: "The *fiend* gave a *shriek* when he saw the *priest*."

Look again at each of the *ie* words in this lesson, pronouncing each to yourself. When you have done this, there will surely be nothing hard about understanding and learning the first line of the jingle that we have begun to make:

I before *e* when sound is long *e*.

EXERCISE 6. Be prepared to write the following sentences from dictation:
1. One piece of the frieze was ornamented with a series of figures.
2. After the siege the victors knelt at his bier and gave way to grief.
3. My niece hopes to retrieve her purse, but I don't believe she will.
4. The priests sought a reprieve for the outlaw chief.
5. Grabbing his shield, he rushed to the field, determined not to yield.
6. In brief, it was his belief that the butler was not the thief.
7. To his great relief he never again saw the fiend.
8. They besieged the castle but could not pierce through the defenses.
9. I believe I'll wait here on the pier for you.
10. They could not stop to grieve for the dead nor to relieve the dying.

There are a few—very few—freakish words in which a long *e* sound is indicated by *ei*. One of them is *weird*, a truly uncanny word because of its outlandish spelling. It gives the name to this strange collection in today's lesson—"the *weird* words." Another is *seize*. Make your mind *seize* these *weird* words.

Two more common words, *either* and *neither*, belong with the *weird* words. Two that are less common are *leisure* and *inveigle*.

If we know these six *weird* words, we know enough for all ordinary purposes in school. They can be arranged for memorizing in two rhyming lines:

Seize, inveigle, either,
Weird, leisure, neither.

322

There are others, of course—*obeisance, weir, sheik,* and some Scottish words—but the six above are the most common. Study them carefully; remember that in these *weird* words the *e* comes before *i.*

In the first lesson about *ie* and *ei* you learned to expect *ie* in words that have a long *e* sound. That is the important part of the rule: "Expect *ie.*" But today your mind has *seized* the six *weird* exceptions, and now you can understand the first three lines of the six-line jingle that you are learning:

> *I* before *e* when sound is long *e,*
>
> Except $\left\{ \begin{array}{l} \text{Seize, inveigle, either,} \\ \text{Weird, leisure, neither.} \end{array} \right.$

Learn the lines so well that they will say themselves quickly in your mind. If you are ever in doubt, remember that you always expect *ie.* Then run over the exceptions. If the word you are writing is not among them, use *ie.*

EXERCISE 7. Be prepared to write the following sentences from dictation:
1. I am sure that Bernice will inveigle him into painting the fence and repairing the front gate.
2. On his return from Arabia he told us of his strange meeting with the sheik of an unfriendly tribe.
3. Oscar is spending his leisure time at the pier.
4. I seized the thief as he ran past the door.
5. We do not believe he uses his leisure wisely.
6. Turning quickly, Oliver seized the dying man's shield and bravely faced the terrible foe.
7. Neither John nor Henry is grieved by the tragedy.
8. I believe I know what is causing that weird moaning.
9. I did not want the piece of cake, either, but I took it.
10. Seizing the opportunity, they laid siege to the fortress.

The first two lessons about *ie* and *ei* were arranged like this:

> First lesson: When do you expect *ie?*
> Second lesson: The six weird exceptions.

The other three lessons are going to be arranged like this:

> Third and fourth lessons: When do you expect *ei?*
> Fifth lesson: The seven exceptions.

This third lesson is brief and easy: "After *c* always expect *ei*." There are not many of these *c* words, but most of them are common. The most important one is *receive*. From it is formed a noun with a peculiar spelling—*receipt*.

Another pair of *c* words is *deceive* and *deceit*. A third pair is *conceive* and *conceit*. Do you *perceive* that *c* is followed by *ei* in all these words? Do you *perceive* the *ei* in *ceiling*?

No teacher has yet found out why the *c* words should ever make trouble, for the rule is regular and simple. But they do cause trouble for many unwary students. Learn to expect "*ei* after *c*."

EXERCISE 8. Be prepared to write the following sentences from dictation:
1. I could not conceive of a thing to say to him.
2. He deceived his mother and sisters easily, but his father soon perceived his dishonesty.
3. Though she is very capable and pretty, she is so conceited that all of us greatly dislike her.
4. Hastily he looked through the desk drawers, but he could not find the receipt anywhere.
5. He told us that without some conceit we would never rise to the top of our profession.
6. Skillfully concealing her deceit, she won the first prize in the contest.
7. Though he was pleasant enough, Jane soon perceived that he would not help her brother.
8. They had received warning that he was deceitful, but they had disregarded it.
9. Hanging from the ceiling was an enormous spider.
10. If you return ten gum wrappers, you will receive a police whistle.

The rule for the fourth lesson is easy: Whenever the sound is not long *e*, expect *ei*.

When the sound is long *a*, as in *hate*, we must write *ei*:

weigh	weight	sleigh	veil
rein	reign	reindeer	vein

Perhaps you also know *deign, feint, feign, heinous, neigh, seine,* and *skein*. A somewhat similar sound is in *heir* and *their*. Notice especially *their;* the *e* comes before the *i*.

When the sound is long *i*, as in *write*, we must use *ei*:

height	seismograph	sleight of hand
eider	kaleidoscope	Meistersinger

When the sound is short *i* or short *e*, the spelling is often *ei*, as in *foreign*, which is the important word in today's lesson. Many students fail to learn it. Note the order of letters: *foreign*. Other examples are:

sovereign	counterfeit	surfeit	heifer

What we have learned in this lesson and the previous one may be expressed in one line (pronounce *e* with the long sound):

Ei after *c* or when sound is not *ē*.

EXERCISE 9. Be prepared to write the following sentences from dictation:
1. During his reign the sovereign did all he could to help his people.
2. The foreign spies did not dare use counterfeit money.
3. He weighed the heifer but refused to buy it.
4. The Meistersingers promoted a popular interest in poetry and music.
5. A surfeit of hot fudge sundaes made him sick, and he is now in bed.
6. A filmy veil covered the veins of her scrawny neck.
7. The seismograph recorded a slight tremor in our county.
8. You must check your weight to see if it is right for your height and age.
9. In the background they placed a sleigh drawn by eight reindeer.
10. The kaleidoscope bored me, and I turned again to sleight of hand.

There is only one exception to the rule that we must write *ei* after *c*—a word we took over from the French language, *financier*.

Only two important words are exceptions to the rule that we must write *ei* when the sound is not long *e*—*friend* and *view*. Make up a sentence for yourself (such as "My *friend* likes the *view* from this window"); rehearse it; remember it.

If you can spell *chief*, you can spell *mischief* and *handkerchief*. *Fiery*, which belongs with this group, is a good word to know. Once in a while you may want to write about a *sieve*.

All seven exceptions to the part of the rule given in the third and fourth lessons may be jingled in this way:

Financier, fiery, and mischief,
Friend, sieve, view, and handkerchief.

You are now ready for the full rule for spelling the *ie* and the *ei* words. It is in two parts:

I. When do you expect *ie*?
   Six exceptions.
II. When do you expect *ei*?
   Seven exceptions.

Here is the full rule. You will find it worth memorizing.

I before *e* when sound is long *e*.

Except { Seize, inveigle, either,
         Weird, leisure, neither.

Ei after *c* or when sound is not *ē*.

Except { Financier, fiery, and mischief,
         Friend, sieve, view, and handkerchief.

Any person who can rattle off the full rule and the two groups of exceptions, understanding just what they mean, is a master of the whole troublesome group of *ie* and *ei* words.

EXERCISE 10. Be prepared to write the following sentences from dictation:
1. Her niece gave her a handkerchief for a birthday gift.
2. I believe you have a better view of the lake from your window than I do.
3. When Jane received word of her aunt's death, she grieved bitterly.
4. It's strange, but as far as we can tell, the thief stole only a sieve.
5. The rumor that the financier had lost all his wealth spread rapidly.
6. With a shriek of anguish, the fiend disappeared into the fiery cave.
7. The chief made a sign to his weird comrades, who turned quickly and rushed to their tom-toms.
8. As soon as he has a moment of leisure, Sam gets into mischief.
9. Mr. Crewe will not sell either of these pieces of furniture.
10. The chief trouble with Herman is that he cannot resist mischief.

5. Possessives

A singular possessive noun is formed by adding an apostrophe and *s* to a noun:

the ship's side   Sarah's hat
a woman's way   Mr. Hill's farm

If the noun ends in *s* or in an *s* sound, an apostrophe alone may be added:

James' car	OR:	James's car
Dobbs' home run	OR:	Dobbs's home run
for goodness' sake		for conscience' sake

The rule for forming singular possessives is so simple that the mere stating of it with a few examples ought to teach it for a lifetime. But it would hardly stay taught for an hour. A large proportion of American students—probably a fourth—have difficulty in fixing their eyes on a proper name long enough to write it down completely, *and then* add an apostrophe or an apostrophe and *s* to the completed name. For example, it may be that everyone in the class has heard of the English novelist, Charles Dickens, and can pronounce the name, sounding the *s* on *Charles* distinctly and the *s* on *Dickens* distinctly. Probably everyone could go to the board and write *Charles* (ending with *s*) and *Dickens* (ending with *s*). Then, when the names are written, he could repeat the rule for forming a singular possessive. If asked to follow the rule with *Charles* and *Dickens,* he could by a strong mental effort force his hand to write:

Charles' father	OR:	Charles's father
Dickens' novels	OR:	Dickens's novels

In that same class period there may be need of writing the possessive of the names *Ross* and *Briggs*. A student can pronounce them and write them with *s*'s on the end, but can he force his hand to travel *on beyond* the names before putting down the apostrophe or the apostrophe and *s?* Yes, if he has good will power, he can write the possessives of *Ross* and *Briggs*:

Ross'	OR:	Ross's
Briggs'	OR:	Briggs's

Do not forget that these names end in *s,* and that the *s* belongs to them. Remember that your hand must travel *on beyond* the entire name before it puts down an apostrophe. Study the following examples of possessives of names that end in *s*:

Miss Wells' invitation	OR:	Miss Wells's invitation
Mr. Phelps' letter	OR:	Mr. Phelps's letter

For nouns ending in *y* our rule says nothing about making any change in form. There must be no change whatever in *lady*, any more than in *ship* or *Sarah* or *Dickens*. We must first write the complete noun. Then, and not till then, we must add the apostrophe and *s*. Fix your attention on the possessive of each noun in the following list, studying it as if it might be hard:

lady	a lady's hat
Andy	Andy's brother
penny	a penny's worth
Mary	Mary's doubts
navy	the navy's pride

If the repetition of this easy rule—"Add an apostrophe and *s* or an apostrophe alone if the noun ends in *s*"—has fixed the idea in your mind, then today's lesson will save you from errors that infest all schools and that sometimes appear in painted signs and even in books.

EXERCISE 11. Be prepared to write the following sentences from dictation:
1. I saw Ross' (*or* Ross's) aunt at Dr. Holmes' (*or* Holmes's) office.
2. Did Tom Clark's uncle paint Mrs. Wells' (*or* Wells's) house?
3. Yesterday I visited Miss Hall's class.
4. Ask Bob to stop at Mr. Finney's shop on the way home.
5. His cousin's bakery is just a stone's throw from Janice's house.
6. My father's car is larger than hers.
7. His wife's brother has never done a day's work in his life.
8. What the lady's decision will be is anybody's guess.
9. The coach's suggestions were no better than theirs.
10. Tim bought a nickel's worth of candy at Alice's booth.

The plural of a noun is the form that shows more than one: two *birds*, five *matches*, seven thousand *cars*, many *shoes*. A plural usually ends in *s*, but may end in other letters: three *men*, several *geese*, a few *sheep*, fifty *people*.

Forming the possessive of plural nouns is almost as simple as forming singular possessives.

If the plural does not end in *s*, form the possessive according to the rule for singulars, as in the following examples:

328

a man's work	the men's work
a child's work	the children's work
a deer's head	the deer's heads
a mouse's tail	the mice's tails
a woman's work	the women's club

If the plural does end in *s*—and nearly all English plurals do—add an apostrophe after the *s*. That is all. Simply put an apostrophe after the *s*.

Suppose you have been reading about old hags with supernatural powers. First get the plural:

a witch   the witches

Then calmly and deliberately add an apostrophe—nothing more, just an apostrophe:

the witches' broomsticks

Perhaps you know a family whose name is Adams or Andrews or Phelps or Jones or Cummins or Robbins or Dobyns or Straus or Dix or Knox or Hayes. There are several people in the family. Just as you would have to speak of the Smiths or the Browns or the Newtons or the Coopers or the Clarks, so you have to speak of the Adamses, the Andrewses, the Phelpses, the Joneses, or the Cumminses. Strangely enough, these plurals "don't sound right" to some people. But they must be right. What does it sound like to say "The five Smith are coming to visit us" or "There are sixteen Hall in the Baltimore directory"? It sounds like "pidgin" English. We have to say:

one Smith	five Smiths
one Hall	sixteen Halls
one Nichols	two Nicholses
one Jones	four Joneses
one Knox	five Knoxes

So first get the plural. When you have done that—not before—form the possessive by adding an apostrophe. Study the following:

Charles	the two Charleses	the Charleses' reigns
a lady	two ladies	the ladies' coats
a boy	eleven boys	the boys' club
a lily	four lilies	the lilies' stalks
King Henry	eight Henrys	the Henrys' reigns

EXERCISE 12. Be prepared to write the following sentences from dictation:

1. Nancy's father has organized several boys' clubs.
2. The woman's anger at the Frenchmen's cruelty was fearful to see.
3. Hugh's wages are now paid by Mr. Hughes' (or Hughes's) brother.
4. The witches' prophecies were all fulfilled.
5. It is nobody's business to inquire about a lady's age.
6. Nancy's love for the Squire's son was thoroughly concealed.
7. Ann's keen eyes detected the gleam of the fishes' tails among the kelp.
8. We had no room for Dad's golf clubs or the children's toys.
9. This lady's real character was disclosed at the Robbinses' ball.
10. A baby's scream proved that the women's fears were well founded.

An *s* is added to personal pronouns to form the possessives:

ours	yours	hers	theirs	its

Fix **its** in your mind. "*Its* has slaughtered *its* thousands."

6. Contractions

In ordinary talking we seldom say "did not," but contract the words to "didn't." In writing this contraction we use an apostrophe where the letter *o* is omitted. Similarly "have not" becomes "haven't." No *e* has been put into *haven't; e* is not making any sound; it is as silent as it was in *have*. No letter or sound is added in making any contraction. It is always a case of taking out letters and showing the omission by an apostrophe. The contractions of "shall not," "will not," and "can not" are irregular. Instead of "sha'n't" we write *shan't*. For "will not" we have *won't*. For "can not" we use *can't*.

do + not = don't	would + not = wouldn't
have + not = haven't	does + not = doesn't
did + not = didn't	shall + not = shan't
are + not = aren't	will + not = won't
was + not = wasn't	can + not = can't
should + not = shouldn't	must + not = mustn't

Contractions are generally used in informal speech or writing. And they are frequently used in written dialogue, especially when they are the natural expression of the kind of person the speaker is meant to be.

330

More free and easy than the forms just given are:

it + is = it's	you + are = you're	I + will = I'll
what + is = what's	we + are = we're	I + have = I've
who + is = who's	they + are = they're	you + have = you've
I + am = I'm	we + will = we'll	we + have = we've

In reporting informal conversation, we often use:

where + is = where's	I + would = I'd
I + had = I'd	you + would = you'd

EXERCISE 13. Be prepared to write the following sentences from dictation:
1. He didn't say I shouldn't buy four hats; he said he wouldn't buy four.
2. Though she doesn't like him, she won't tell him so.
3. It's the first time he's climbed that boulder, I'm sure.
4. Who's he, where's he from, and what's he doing here?
5. I've written fourteen pages, and you've written only four.
6. I'll go to meet her, and then we'll make plans.
7. If I'd asked, I'd have been refused.
8. I shan't ask, because they're so busy that they haven't time to help.
9. They're not convinced that we've been thorough in our search.
10. You mustn't say you'll take the course if you're planning to leave.

7. Using capital letters

To spell correctly you must know not only which letters to use in words but also which words to begin with capital letters. The rule is simple: **Capitalize all proper nouns and all adjectives formed from proper nouns.** A proper noun is a special name of a person or animal or place or thing. It is a name that distinguishes one certain person or thing from others of the same kind. Notice the following examples of words used as proper nouns:

Persons: Mary Esther Brooks, Spike Kremer
Animals: Fido, Spotty
Places: Albuquerque, New Zealand, United States
Races, religions, languages: Caucasian, Negro, Catholic, French
Days, months, holidays: Tuesday, August, Christmas

Special events, historical periods, documents: the Louisiana Purchase, the Reign of Terror, the Atlantic Charter
Ships, trains: the *Queen Mary,* the *Constellation,* the *Challenger*
Trade names of products: Wheaties, Frigidaire, Masonite
Buildings: the Capitol, the Louvre
Business firms: Maxwell Studios, James Brosk, Inc.
The Deity: the Almighty, God, Trust in Him.

Common nouns are not usually capitalized. Words like *park, river, mountain, street, hotel, hospital, high school, college, junior, senior, club, prom* are ordinary names, not special names:

He threw the ring into the *lake* and ambled on down the *street.*

But when such words are part of a proper noun, they begin with capital letters:

Pennoyer Park	Good Shepherd Hospital
Lake Louise	Empire State Building
Missouri River	Grover Cleveland High School
Twenty-third Street	the Camera Club
Blackstone Hotel	the Senior Prom

Words that show family relationships and titles that show rank, office, or profession are capitalized when they are used with a person's name as part of a proper noun:

Aunt Harriet	Judge Purvis
Cousin Peter	Princess Margaret Rose
Mayor Denby	Superintendent Goodrich

But:

Jane told her *grandfather* that she hated her *cousins.*
The *mayor* hired a new *superintendent* yesterday.

Sometimes words that are not ordinarily proper nouns are used in place of a person's name. Compare the italicized words in the following pairs of sentences:

Here is a package addressed to *Mr. Clinton.*
Here is a package addressed to *Dad.*
"*Judge Purvis* is out of town," she explained.
"The *Judge* is out of town," she explained.

In the second sentence of each pair the italicized word is used instead of a proper noun. Since *Dad* and *Judge* are used as special names, each clearly referring to one certain person, they are capitalized.

Adjectives that are formed from proper nouns begin with capital letters:

Parisian styles	*Alaskan* furs
Puritan influence	*Colonial* days

Notice that *styles, influence,* etc., begin with small letters. These words are not part of a special name; they are merely common nouns modified by **proper adjectives.**

In Unit 1 you learned about demons—words that cause persistent errors in spelling. Capitalization also has its demons. Among them are the words *north, south, east, west,* etc. When these words show directions, they begin with small letters:

> On reaching the corner, he turned *east.*
> Our house is on the *south* side of the street.

But when they name or refer to one certain section of our country, they are proper nouns or proper adjectives, and begin with capital letters:

> My father likes the *South* better than the *North.*
> Her grandfather now lives in the *Southwest.*
> I don't like *Western* stories.

Names of school subjects are another source of trouble. Course names that are names of languages are capitalized; other course names usually begin with small letters:

Latin	civics
English	biology

Though the names of days and months are considered proper nouns, the names of the seasons are not:

> Did you do any skiing last *winter?*

Only the first word, the last word, and important words in titles of books, magazines, newspapers, stories, articles, songs, plays, poems are capitalized:

The World We Live In	the *Indianapolis Star*
With Malice Toward Some	"That's What Happened to Me"
The Saturday Evening Post	"The Song of the Shirt"

Notice that *the* before *Indianapolis Star* begins with a small letter. It is not part of the title.

EXERCISE 14. Read the sentences, and decide which words should be capitalized. Then write the numbers of the sentences and, after them, write these words, supplying the necessary capitals. For the first sentence you should write: *1. Camera Club, Bob Shields, Don Baughman, Yellowstone National Park*

1. Two of the boys in the camera club, bob shields and don baughman, are planning a trip to yellowstone national park next summer.
2. Oliver wendell holmes, the author of *the autocrat of the breakfast table*, was dean and professor of anatomy at harvard medical school.
3. During the war of 1812 the original declaration of independence—now in the library of congress—was safely hidden from the british in leesburg, virginia.
4. Do you think I had better sign up for a second year of latin if I'm going to take french, history, algebra, and english, too?
5. This spring our high school has invited judge richter of new orleans to address the seniors.
6. Late in september, 1776, nathan hale, disguised as a dutch schoolmaster, crossed the british lines to spy on the enemy.
7. In the northwest section of washington, d. c., is ford's theatre, where president lincoln was shot.
8. The board of education meets with superintendent conway every monday night at the clara barton school.
9. Aunt polly and uncle dave are visiting their nephew in the east.
10. Mother and father have reservations for easter monday on the *super chief,* crack train of the atchison, topeka, and santa fe railroad.

Adding suffixes: a review

In this last spelling lesson you will review the rules you have studied in preceding lessons about adding suffixes to words.

The first rule has to do with words that end in silent *e*: Before a suffix beginning with a vowel the *e* is dropped:

use + able = usable	sense + ible = sensible
prove + ed = proved	write + ing = writing
hike + er = hiker	decorate + or = decorator
able + est = ablest	monotone + ous = monotonous

There are several exceptions to this rule. The *e* is kept in words like *dyeing* and *singeing* (to prevent confusion with *dying* and *singing*); in *oe* verbs, such as *hoeing* and *shoeing;* and in words like *noticeable* and *changeable* (to preserve the soft sound of the *c* and the *g*).

The second rule has to do with words that end in *y* preceded by a consonant: The *y* is changed to *i* before *ly* or *ness*:

easy + ly = easily	sloppy + ness = sloppiness
happy + ly = happily	busy + ness = business

The same change is made before adding the suffixes *er, ed, es,* or *est,* all of which begin with *e*:

try + ed = tried	deny + es = denies
heavy + er = heavier	lucky + est = luckiest

Before *ing,* however, the *y* is kept:

hurry + ing = hurrying	study + ing = studying
carry + ing = carrying	accompany + ing = accompanying

The third rule has to do with words that end in a single consonant preceded by a single vowel: In words of one syllable, the final consonant is doubled before a suffix beginning with a vowel:

scrub + ed = scrubbed	big + est = biggest
plot + er = plotter	swim + ing = swimming

In words of more than one syllable, the final consonant is doubled before a suffix beginning with a vowel only when the accent is on the last syllable, as in the following:

occur + ed = occurred   prefer + ing = preferring
transmit + er = transmitter   control + able = controllable

EXERCISE 15. Be prepared to write the following sentences from dictation:

1. It had never occurred to Joyce that she was carrying the heaviest part of the load.
2. Curtis has proved to be the ablest and most sensible worker we have in the business.
3. You may be careless when snapping the camera, but you are compelled to take pains in developing your films.
4. Dan is writing to Nora, inviting her to go canoeing, as they planned last summer.
5. Dyeing the curtains as the decorator suggested made a noticeable improvement in the room.
6. I rebelled against scrubbing the kitchen after shoveling the walks.
7. Accompanying Pat was the biggest and clumsiest man I've ever seen.
8. The boys seldom referred to the unhappiness they had suffered that summer at camp.
9. Jim denied that he had gone swimming.
10. Fortunately the men were equipped for climbing the steep slope.

Telling about Our Community

The community in which we live is all too often taken for granted. Because we have grown up in it, we seldom think to explore it for interesting facts. We open a faucet and let the water run without wondering where it comes from, how it gets into our homes, why we are able to drink it safely, or where it goes after passing down the drain. We attend the community's schools, ride on its streets, walk on its sidewalks safely at night, admire its fire engines dashing by, picnic and play ball in its parks without so much as a single thought about what makes these conveniences possible. We attend church, go to the movies, borrow books from the library, mail letters at the box on the corner, shop in the stores, ride back and forth on buses or streetcars, watch people going to work in offices or factories, and never stop to consider how these things came to be in the community.

Communities vary greatly in size, of course, from large cities to small towns and still smaller villages. Yet in almost every community there are interesting facts to discover and unusual things to talk about, if you are only willing to go exploring and to ask questions.

Have you ever thought about other schools in the community and wondered how many boys and girls attend them? Do you know how many churches there are and how many faiths are represented by them? Are there any historical points of interest? What can you tell about the fire department, the police department, the health department? Who installed the street lights and keeps them in operation?

How many parks or playgrounds are there? Where is the post office, and what services does it offer? How many banks or stores or factories are there? What things are made or grown or produced in the community? Can you tell what charity organizations or service clubs or Boy Scout troops there are? If there is a transportation system, do you know how many miles its routes cover or how many buses or streetcars it operates? Can you give the number of telephones in the community or explain how the electricity in your home is made and brought there for your use?

These questions are merely to start you thinking about the community in which you live. Look at it thoughtfully. Try to find something about it that really interests you, something that arouses your curiosity, and—if possible—something that no one else in your class wants to investigate. Do not try to tell about many things. Choose one that you think will interest your classmates and plan to tell all the details you can about it.

Once you have decided what to talk about, your next step is to get the information. Write down all the questions you can think of and the names of people who might know the answers. Then talk to your teachers and your parents, asking them what they know about the subject and where to go for more information. Follow up their suggestions. Keep at it until you have as many interesting facts as you can get in the time available.

After you have collected your information, look over your facts carefully. Which ones are new to you? Which ones do you think will interest your classmates? Unless you have very little information, it is often wise to ignore facts that everybody knows and to concentrate on the things that seem most unusual.

Prepare your notes carefully, arranging the important facts in a time or space or logical order. Include exact dates, figures, or names that you think are worth mentioning. Then add good beginning and ending sentences.

Practice your talk at least once before coming to class, so that you will know what you are going to say and how you want to say it. If you are asked to give your talk in class, speak slowly and distinctly. Hold your notes so that you can glance at them easily, but try not to wave them around or look at them more than necessary. Watch your audience as you talk, shifting your eyes from one classmate to another.

338

Spelling Demons and Other Creatures

Which word in the following sentence do you think is hardest for students to spell?

> When she asks me what "anticipatory narrative" is and which constructions are parallel, her words are too big for me.

Do you suppose the most difficult one is *anticipatory* or *parallel*? No, it is *too*. A whole chapter could be filled with stories showing how hard it is to spell *too*. One student, for example, wrote it correctly through the whole of his second year in high school, was sure he knew it, quit worrying about it; but in his final examination he misspelled it. Many studies have been conducted which have analyzed thousands of compositions by high school and college students. Every one of these studies concludes that comparatively few words cause most spelling errors. The most frequently misspelled word groups are our friend "to-too-two" and "their-they're-there."

The other words or word-groups that cause the greatest trouble are (in approximate order of peskiness); (3) receive, (4) exist-existence-existent, (5) occur-occurred-occurring-occurrence, (6) definite-definitely, (7) separate-separation, (8) believe-belief, (9) occasion, and (10) lose-losing.

The "Demons"

The word *separate* is very common; it is very commonly misspelled; and students all over the country make exactly the same mistake in it. The power that this word has to cause the same error everywhere is mysterious, almost fiendish. For this reason the word is called a "demon." There are only two or three hundred real demons, but they probably cause nine tenths of all the spelling errors in the compositions written in American schools.

Put your mind intently on each word printed in **boldface** type in the list below, noticing slowly and carefully and exactly what the letters are. Every one of the words has been a fiend for some of your classmates—unless your school is different from every other school in the United States. If the words seem easy, remember that thousands of college students are unable to spell them correctly.

They were going **too** fast.	He **shows** good **sense.**
May I go **too?**	He **asks** questions.
We met at **their** house.	He **turns** the crank.
I **know** the lesson.	He **speaks** in a **weak** voice.
He **knew** it.	I am **tired** after working.
He **threw** the ball.	We got **off** the road.
The ball was **thrown.**	He ought to **have** told us.
She **tries** to do her best.	Do you know **its** name?

Notice the letters printed in **boldface** type in the following words. If you realize that each letter causes a hundred thousand young people *to make precisely the same error*, you will agree that the words are fiendish.

sep**a**rate	again	among	Saturday	sentence
ans**w**er	against	surprise	speak	stretch
rough	marriage	every	meant	road
enough	quarter	piece	weak	toward
which	knowledge	believe	before	beautiful
straight	doesn't	friend	once	woman
perhaps	persuade	since	crowd	women
probably	across	necessary	some	grammar

At the end of the list, as a climax, is the second *a* in *grammar*. For years you have written the word. Its last vowel is *a*. Hereafter it will be inexcusable to misspell *grammar*.

Try never to think of the wrong form of a word, for that causes confusion which may last all your life. You will notice that teachers seldom mention or write the wrong letters. The way to learn spelling is to put similar forms together—for example: *know, knowledge; rough, enough; piece, believe; speak, weak.*

340

EXERCISE 1. Study the words in **boldface** type in the sentences on page 340. Be prepared to spell these words orally when the sentences are read aloud in class.

EXERCISE 2. Be prepared to write the following sentences from dictation:
1. I believe a knowledge of grammar is important, but he doesn't.
2. Once again some of the crowd grew rough.
3. We will probably never know what he meant by his answer.
4. If we stretch a piece of cord from this nail to that one, we will perhaps surprise the intruder.
5. Since one sentence is not enough to explain your answer, you will have to use two.
6. Every effort was made to persuade him to leave.
7. His voice, which at all times was weak, could scarcely be heard as he walked among the prisoners.
8. Each group is working toward separate goals.
9. Against his will he walked straight across the road and into the house.
10. I will speak to your mother before your friend gets here.

More demons

Y ou will examine the spelling of the following words in **boldface** type with some fear and respect if you realize that each one has conquered **its** thousands of victims.

Are you *sure* you can spell *sure?* Some persons are helped by remembering "I am **sure** it is **sugar.**"

The Latin word *et* means "and"; *cetera* means "all the rest." The abbreviation is always **e t** and **c.** with a period after it. "Such words as *sure, insure, assure,* **etc.,** are hard."

The word *used* has a meaning of "was accustomed to." We say "He *used to* call on us every night." "I *used to* think so." Do you think you have mastered **used to?**

"He was *quite* conceited over the victory." "It is *quite* hot in this room." This word is spelled **quite.**

"He *led* the horse onto the track." "He was *led* astray by wild companions." "Harry sprinted and *led* by two yards at the finish." The past form is **led.**

"Have we anything to eat?" "Nothing **except** some crackers." "There was no one in sight **except** an old fisherman."

The wrong form of **all right** is so thoroughly planted in many minds that only a great effort will root it out. It is **all right**, the teacher supposes after he has seen a whole class write it correctly as two words. But it is really **all wrong,** for next week it will be misspelled again.

EXERCISE 3. Be ready to write the following paragraph from dictation:

I used to be quite sure that I could find my way around in a strange place, whatever its size was. In spite of the warnings of my parents and yours that I was all wrong, I assured myself that I would be all right, no matter where my travels led me. And I always was until the day I went to Chicago with Mother and Dad and Jane to visit some friends of ours. On the way there Mother had to stop at Field's to buy a number of things she needed for a cake—citron, lemon peel, brown sugar, etc. Dad had to call on a client who wished to insure some property. Jane wanted to chat with a friend in the same office. In fact, everyone except me had something to do for an hour or so. I decided to wander around and explore. I thought that at last I could prove to my family that I could take care of myself.

... And more demons

One who decides by careful judgment whether a thing is good or bad is a *critic.* His opinion is a *criticism*—with three *i*'s and no other vowel. That *ism* is a suffix regularly added to nouns and adjectives. It sounds like two syllables, as in *prism,* but has only one vowel:

hero + ism = heroism	critic + ism = criticism
social + ism = socialism	American + ism = Americanism

There are a great many common verbs that are formed from nouns and adjectives by adding the suffix *ize*:

natural + ize = naturalize	civil + ize = civilize
penal + ize = penalize	macadam + ize = macadamize
burglar + ize = burglarize	critic + ize = criticize

Fix your attention on the double letters in the following:

supplies   approach   address   arrive   parallel

Some students are unable in two years to form the habit of always putting *e* on *before.* A man who can *foretell* (tell *before*) what is going

342

to happen is a *prophet*. If he foretells the weather, he is a *weather-prophet*. The prediction that he makes is a *prophecy*. Some of his *prophecies* about the weather never come true.

There is only one **p** in *opinion*. Fix your eyes on the syllables of fas + ci + nate = *fascinate*. And have you been seeing that syl + la + ble = *syllable*?

There are two *t*'s in *stretch* and two *r*'s in *February*. Notice the *n* in *Wednesday* and *solemn* and *government*.

EXERCISE **4.** Be prepared to write the following sentences from dictation:
1. The referee penalized the team for unnecessary roughness, and in my opinion he was right.
2. As soon as the supplies arrive, the men will macadamize the road.
3. Even a good prophet would not try to foretell the weather in our town.
4. The colors in this prism fascinate me.
5. In his address on Americanism he spoke of the heroism of our men.
6. His attempts to civilize the natives brought him nothing but criticism and prophecies of failure.
7. His parents were naturalized soon after they arrived from Denmark.
8. His weird prophecy, uttered in strange words of one and two syllables, frightened all of us.
9. Why were you so solemn last Wednesday?
10. Mr. Ames has been working in a government office since February.

Similar forms together

You know how to spell *study* and *studying*, and *hurry* and *hurrying*, but can you do as well with *accompany* and *accompanying*? Is your eye used to that *ying*? A few little *ie* verbs have the same ending: *tie, tying; lie, lying; die, dying*. Think of these verbs in sentences: "We were *lying* in the shade." "Why do you suppose he is *tying* himself in a bowknot?" *Tying, lying,* and *dying* are the only ones that often occur in compositions. Put them with *trying*: "I am *trying* to keep from *untying* the parcel that is *lying* on the table."

The change in *tie* and *lie* is unusual. The change from *y* to *i* is more common:

try	tries	tried	study	studies	studied
hurry	hurries	hurried	reply	replies	replied
cry	cries	cried	deny	denies	denied

Expect *ay* verbs to be regular:

play	plays	played	delay	delays	delayed
pray	prays	prayed	dismay	dismays	dismayed
stay	stays	stayed	decay	decays	decayed

There are three—and only three—*ay* verbs that are irregular in their past form, which is spelled with *aid*:

lay   lays   laid   pay   pays   paid   say   says   said

Learn *lay, pay,* and *say* in that order and get used to *laid, paid,* and *said.* Do not compare them with forms that keep *y,* but think of them as a group of curiosities. Remember "laid, paid, and said."

Follow this plan of "similar forms together" with any word that troubles you. Group it with other words that are like it. To remember *lose,* for example, put it with *move* and *prove.*

In a similar way group together *swear, tear,* and *wear,* putting with them for convenience *break* and the adjective *great.* "He can *bear* the *wear* and *tear* that *breaks* down some *great* athletes."

You know how to pronounce *kitten, mitten, bitten, smitten.* How, then, must you spell *written* in "I have *written* a letter"? Think of it as a "double *t*" word, with two black *t*'s—*written.*

EXERCISE 5. Be prepared to write the following sentences from dictation:
1. Mr. Williams said the boys denied having written the letter.
2. The foreman said that they wanted to be paid before the walk was laid.
3. He denies that he is studying too hard.
4. I hate the wear and tear of moving from one house to another.
5. He replied that he had already tried untying the knots.
6. Accompanying the great star were her secretary and her stand-in.
7. Helen says that the thought of failure has never dismayed her.
8. I can prove that you'll lose the game if you make that move.
9. As he lay dying, he prayed for forgiveness.
10. We delayed our work while Dave played with the kitten.

The *dis* words; Second-grade words; Solid words

Some very common words begin with *dis*. Two friends may agree or they may **dis**agree. Probably everyone in the class can spell *appear* with two *p*'s and can say, "I put *dis* before it to make **dis***appear*," but in spite of this some of your classmates may not be able to write *disappear* with one *s* and two *p*'s in a test. *Appoint* is perfectly easy, with two *p*'s; everyone can spell it and everyone can say, "I put *dis* before it to make **dis***appointed*." Yet some students fail again and again during the year to write the word with one *s* and two *p*'s. Have you ever written it the wrong way? If so, you have a fight before you. The old habit will trick you every now and then unless you train yourself by always keeping your mind on what you are doing when you write *disagree* or *disappear* or *disappoint*.

The *dis* is put directly before the verb—whatever the verb happens to begin with: *dis + satisfy =* **dis***satisfy*. So with *mis: mis + spell =* **mis***spell; mis + state =* **mis***state*.

Make sure of the following words (often taught in the second grade), thinking of *there* as a sample of all the rest. Of course you can write *there* correctly if the teacher dictates "There are twenty in the class" or "It is warmer over there in the corner." There is nothing hard about the word *there*, in itself; but have you the habit of always using t-h-e-r-e when you mean "there"? It will be helpful to remember *here* and *there* together.

Stay **there**.	Wait **until** six o'clock.
This is a **new** rule.	(only one *l*)
He has **just** come.	He made a **speech** every **week**.

The next four are solid words with only one *l*:

They are **almost** ready.	**Although** he is **almost** sixteen
It is **already** eleven o'clock.	years old and **always** studies
He **always** comes.	hard, he has **already** mis-
I won't, **although** I could.	spelled nineteen words.

Look carefully at the solid words in the following sentences. Learn to write them always as *one* word.

We walked along **together.**	He goes **nowhere** alone.
This is **altogether** too hard.	They cost five cents **apiece.**
She writes **without** thinking.	**Inside** this box is the key.
He does **whatever** he likes.	He ran **outside** the base.
Wherever they go, I will go.	They use beads **instead** of money.
These are, **nevertheless**, hard.	Try to recite **without** "and-uh."

EXERCISE 6. Be prepared to write the following sentences from dictation:

1. We stayed there until he came by in his new car.
2. Wherever you and your friends go, always stick together.
3. Nevertheless, her clothes are altogether too flashy.
4. Nowhere else have I heard such a good speech.
5. Martha copied her theme without misspelling a single word.
6. We always put pencils inside the desks.
7. The lamps are lovely, but they cost fifteen dollars apiece.
8. He is almost sure he left his wagon outside, but it was nowhere in sight when we looked for it.
9. I will wait until he gets here, or he will be disappointed.
10. They almost always disagree about their meals.

Words ending in *ful* and *ous*

The adjective that means "full of awe" is *awful*. The adjective that means "full of pain" is *painful*. Anything that we can use to advantage is *useful*. Such adjectives end in *ful*, with only one *l*.

You know and frequently use in writing several adjectives ending in *ous*, such as *famous, jealous, enormous*. They always have an *o* in the ending. *Bogus, minus,* and *citrus* seem to be the only exceptions.

Notice the *k* sound before *u* in *conspicuous;* the *c* sounds just as it does in *cute* and *cube*.

The *ci* before *ous* has the sound of *sh*—as in *delicious, precious, suspicious, officious, atrocious, ferocious, vicious*. Any such word written without the *i* looks like a face without any nose: the central important feature is lacking. The commonest is *suspicious*. It is the *i* that is necessary to make *c* sound like *sh*.

It is *i* that is necessary to give the right sound to the *g* in *religious*.

A few words have an *s* before the *c*: *con + scious = conscious, unconscious, luscious*.

346

EXERCISE 7. Be prepared to write the following sentences from dictation:

1. The people of the warring nations were hopeful that the awful bloodshed and destruction would soon come to an end.
2. Mr. Crane is very skillful in devising useful gadgets.
3. Everyone was conscious of his officious manner.
4. Though she is conspicuous, she's cute, and I'm jealous.
5. The inn is famous for its delicious meals.
6. The atrocious actions of the vicious enemy shocked the world.
7. Faith has enormous power among the religious.
8. No one was suspicious of the bogus count.
9. Forty-four minus four leaves forty.
10. She seemed unconscious of the enormous value of her precious stones.

Words with *con, ad, re, ness*

A common Latin prefix is *con,* as in **con***ceive,* **con***vict,* **con***spire.* This becomes *com* before an *m,* as in **com***mingle,* **com***merce,* **com***munity,* **com***mend.* Before an *l* it becomes *col,* as in **col***lect,* **col***lide.* A common Latin stem is *mit,* meaning "to send," as in *ad***mit,** o**mit,** *per***mit,** *com-***mit.** Since each of these words ends in a single consonant preceded by a single vowel and is accented on the last syllable, the *t* is doubled before adding *ed* or *ing: ad***mit***ted, ad***mit***ting, o***mit***ted, o***mit***ting, per-***mit***ted, per***mit***ting, com***mit***ted, com***mit***ting.* The *t* is doubled, also, in *com***mit***tee.* The Latin prefix *ad,* as in *ad***mire** and *ad***vise,** often becomes *ac,* as in *ac***quire,** *ac***cuse,** *ac***cept.** There are two *c*'s and two *m*'s in *ac***com***m*o*date.*

A common prefix is *re,* meaning "again" or "back," as in **re***mit,* **re***view,* **re***collect,* **re***fund,* **re***commend.* A careful look at all of these words is *recommended.*

A common suffix is *ness,* meaning "having the condition or quality of." The condition of being busy is *busy* + *ness* = *business;* the quality of being dreary is *dreary* + *ness* = *dreariness;* the condition of being sloppy is *sloppy* + *ness* = *sloppiness.* Of course, if a word ends in *n, ness* is added to it just the same: *sullen* + *ness* = *sullenness,* with two *n*'s; *plain* + *ness* = *plainness,* with two *n*'s; *mean* + *ness* = *meanness,* with two *n*'s.

EXERCISE 8. Be prepared to write the following sentences from dictation:

1. I dislike her sullenness and sloppiness more than her plainness.
2. After the business meeting, the program committee took charge.
3. When they accused the convict of conspiring against the nation, he insisted that he had committed no act of treason.
4. I cannot conceive why she admires him enough to recommend him.
5. She would permit no harshness or meanness in the little community.
6. Collect tickets from all, permitting no one to enter without one.
7. Until we acquire more room, we can accommodate only four people.
8. Though Claude had reviewed carefully, he could recollect nothing.
9. Until he remits the money he owes, he will not be accepted here.
10. He wrote them, asking to be admitted to their school of commerce.

Words with *ly*

The ending *ly* is sometimes added to nouns to make adjectives: a *beastly* cold, a *cowardly* act, the *heavenly* messenger. But much more commonly it is added to adjectives to make adverbs: winter will come *shortly*, speaking *pleasantly*, *evidently* embarrassed, *particularly* hard, *evenly* divided, *queerly* arranged. It will do you no harm to remind yourself again that if an adjective ends in *y*, the *y* is changed to *i* before *ly* is added: *luckily, easily, busily, happily*.

You know the adjective *final*, as in "The umpire's decision is final"; but can you add *ly* to *final*, so as to make *final* + *ly* = *finally*, with two *l*'s, *finally*? Look at another *al* adjective—*usual*. The adverb is *usual* + *ly* = *usually*, with two *l*'s. And do you notice *really*? It is formed by the adjective *real* + the ending *ly* = *really*, with two *l*'s. Here are more examples:

general + ly = generally	special + ly = specially
natural + ly = naturally	practical + ly = practically
accidental + ly = accidentally	grammatical + ly = grammatically

The cue is perfectly simple: "What is the adjective?" Do you mean that something happened "in *former* times"? Then you must write *former* + *ly* = *formerly*. Do you mean that something happened "in an *evident* way"? Then you must write *evident* + *ly* = *evidently*. Do you mean that the polite old man acted "in a *formal* way"? Then you must write *formal* + *ly* = *formally*. Do you mean that the gun

348

was discharged "in an *accidental* way"? Then you must write *accidental* + *ly* = *accidentally*.

Adjectives ending in *ic* add an *al* before taking the *ly*:

artistic + al + ly = artistically
enthusiastic + al + ly = enthusiastically
emphatic + al + ly = emphatically
sarcastic + al + ly = sarcastically

But *ly* is added directly to *public*, forming *publicly*.

EXERCISE 9. Be prepared to write the following sentences from dictation:
1. Generally I greeted her enthusiastically, though I disliked her.
2. Formerly many people worked long hours six days a week.
3. Her work is usually not particularly good.
4. Jones has never spoken publicly before.
5. Artistically the painting is poor.
6. Marie did not dare speak sarcastically to her mother.
7. Luckily I did not scream.
8. He easily overcame these difficulties.
9. Grammatically this construction is all wrong.
10. He accidentally broke one of the priceless goblets.

Words with *i* and *le*

Observe the *i*'s in *divide, divine*. Think of the two together. "Joshua's army was *divided* by *divine* command." With these two words think of *definite*. "Joshua's army was *divided* by a *definite, divine* command." *Originally* is another "*i*" word, made of the adjective *original* + *ly* = *originally*. Another is *delicate,* and another is *disturb*. "The noise *disturbs* the *delicate* invalid." And *medicine* is another. And *similar* has two *i*'s. "This coffee has no effect on me, but a *similar* amount *disturbs* a *delicate* invalid's sleep." *Privilege* has two *i*'s. "We have a *similar privilege*."

The ending *le* is very common for nouns. Three such nouns give much trouble in schools:

There isn't a *particle* of sense in that magazine *article*.
It is a good *principle* to group similar words in your mind.

EXERCISE 10. Be prepared to write the following sentences from dictation:
1. This article on the divine right of kings is well written.
2. I did not find a particle of truth in his statements.
3. I know that hat is hers, but I don't know whose this is.

4. Since the medicine is theirs, you will have to divide it among them.
5. Since her story is a definite copy of yours, I cannot accept it.
6. The tiny bird had broken its delicate wing.
7. It disturbs me that he should assume a privilege that no one else does.
8. Whose did you choose?
9. Originally the estate belonged to a robber baron, but now it is ours.
10. Though their principles are similar to ours, they are not the same.

Words with *ai;* One *s* and two *s*'s; Soft *c* and *g*

You can pronounce *William,* can see that *i* comes before *a,* can hear "yam." If you can see and hear the *y* sound in *brilliant* and *ruffian* (where *i* comes before *a*), what do you suppose is wrong with a person who cannot spell *villain*? Anyone who can spell *lain* (the past participle of *lie*) ought to be able to write about the *villain* of a novel or a play. You can pronounce *Christian;* you can see that *i* before the *a* and can hear "chan." What shall we say of a person who writes *captain* with the letters so arranged that his spelling would have to be pronounced "capchan"? What shall we think of him if he writes *certain* in such a way that it would have to be pronounced "cerchan"?

Your eyes can look at every letter in *decision* and can see only one *s*. Your ears can hear the "zh" sound made by that one *s* before *ion*. In *occasion* you can look upon and listen to precisely the same things: one *s* before *ion* makes a sound like "zhun." But in·*permission* you can see two *s*'s; and you can get the sound of "sh," of "shun." The same observation can be made on *omission* and *mission* and *session* and *cession*. Two *s*'s before *ion* cause the sound of "shun." What, then, shall we think of a student who will write *occasionally* in such a way that it would have to be pronounced "occashunally"?

We have learned to drop the final *e* of a verb before adding *ing*: *write, writing; notice, noticing; change, changing.* The final *e* of verbs and nouns should usually be dropped before *able: love, lovable; desire, desirable; move, immovable.*

But when *c* comes just before the *e* (as in *notice*), the *e* must not be dropped before *able*. Why not? You can readily see if you look at the word *cable*. When *c* comes before *a,* it regularly has a "hard" sound—the sound of *k*:

350

cable sounds like *ƙable*
noticable sounds like *notiƙable*

Why should any young American write about a "notikable differ-ence," a "peakable animal"? In order to "preserve the soft sound" of *c* —the sound of *s*—we retain the *e*. We must write *peaceable, noticeable*.

For the same reason we have to keep the *e* that comes just after a *g;* we must "preserve the soft sound"—the sound of *j*. If we wish to preserve the soft sound of *g* in words like *manage*, we must retain the *e* in *manageable* and *changeable*. Pronounce *revenge;* e must be kept in *vengeance*. Pronounce *vegetable;* the letter after *g* must be an *e*.

The *i* gives the *j* sound to *g* in *religious*. It does exactly the same thing in *allegiance*. Without the *i* the last syllable of these words would have the sound of "gus" and "gance."

Now look carefully at each one of the most important of the words that have been displayed in this section: *villain, captain, certain; decision, occasionally; noticeable, peaceable, changeable, manageable, vengeance, religious, allegiance*. If you pronounce them correctly, you should have no trouble spelling them.

EXERCISE 11. Be prepared to write the following sentences from dictation:
1. Though William, the captain, was brilliant, he was a villain.
2. I was certain that once he had made a decision, he was immovable.
3. On one occasion he asked to be sent on a mission of Christian charity.
4. Forgetting his religious principles, he swore vengeance on his enemy.
5. Though the crew swore their allegiance to his command, William oc-casionally found that the ruffians were not manageable.
6. He hoped for a peaceful solution of the difficulty.
7. Because of the captain's changeable moods, he was hardly a desirable or lovable person.
8. After a stormy session with the crew, he gave three men permission to leave the ship at the next port.
9. His angry mood was so noticeable that the others feared for their lives.
10. The ship, which had lain idle for seven or eight months, was fitted out for a new mission.

Words with *o, u,* and *ou*

You remember "lose, move, and prove." You can remember any one of those easily if you think of it as belonging with the other two. The secret of learning to spell any word that has given you trouble is to "put similar forms together."

There are three common short words spelled with *o* in which the *o* has the sound of *u* in *hunt: done, some, front.* "They have *done something* to the *front* of the house."

Forty is often misspelled. Its principal vowel is an **o**, *forty. Porch* has only one vowel, an **o**, *porch.* "*Forty* people were on the *porch.*"

You can spell *prison,* ending in *on.* You can spell *poison,* ending in *on.* Can you add *er* to *prison* and *ous* to *poison?* "The *prisoner* breathed *poisonous* air."

Notice the *u*'s in the following:

    minute   guard   pursuing   pursuit   accustomed

You know that microbes are very "minute" animals—that is, very "small" ones. The sixtieth part of an hour is a very "minute" portion of time. We do not pronounce the *u* in *guard,* but we have to write it. *Pursuing* has two *u*'s; so has *pursuit.* Think of *accustomed.* "Giving up the *pursuit,* the *guard* returned to his *accustomed* place at the gate."

In words like the following, ending in *nd,* always expect *ou: pound, round, sound, hound, bound, found, mound.* The same is true of words ending in *d: loud, cloud, proud, shroud.* But there is one word as exceptional as it is common—*crowd.* Put the *w* in *crowd.* "The *crowd* grew *rowdy.*"

EXERCISE 12. Be prepared to write the following sentences from dictation:
1. Forty minutes later the guard gave up the pursuit.
2. The round box is filled with poison.
3. We found him bound to a chair on the back porch.
4. The people in front of us pointed to the clouds.
5. His actions prove that he is proud, though he says he is not.
6. Something must be done immediately to protect the crowd from the poisonous gas.
7. The hound crouched behind the mound and waited.
8. From the prison, shrouded in gloom, came a loud wailing sound.

9. I am not accustomed to eating a pound of steak at one meal.
10. If you move that bishop, you will lose the game.

Words with *a; Does* and *goes*

The word *separate* is feared and wondered at in every school in the country. One teacher tries to impress that first *a* by saying, "You should find your father in the word *separate—pa*." Another writes the word on the board with an *a* a foot high— "sepArate." There is the same A whether we say "they were *separated*" or "in three *separate* pieces" or "after a long *separation*."

Study carefully the demons with *a* on this page and the next, noticing once more that there are two *a*'s in *grammar*:

grammar	many	separate
pleasant	sugar	separation
furnace	calendar	prepare
any	secretary	preparation

Bad weather doesn't affect a stationary engine.
Descendants of the Pilgrims no longer wear coarse clothing.
He is affected by the beauty of the altar.
She said it again.

Two common verb forms, very irregular, are *does* and *goes*. "He *goes* where he pleases and *does* as he likes." The contraction of *does not* is *doesn't*.

EXERCISE 13. Be prepared to write the following sentences from dictation:
1. When he goes away, his secretary handles all business matters.
2. She wore a dress of coarse blue linen.
3. It is not pleasant to be separated from those you love.
4. All his descendants were to be affected by what was said that day.
5. Our furnace always needs repairs in the coldest weather.
6. In preparation for the wedding the altar was decked with flowers.
7. In the factory we saw many stationary engines.
8. We must prepare separate meals for them because Jack doesn't like fish and Joe does.
9. Such a long separation is likely to affect her happiness.
10. Again he stressed the importance of a knowledge of grammar.

Words with *e*

The Latin prefix *de* means "about"; *scribo* means "write"; *de* + *scribo* means "write about." Our English words *describe* and *description* have the same *e*. Here is a true story about the difficulty of *describe*: One second-year class in high school had misspelled this word so many times that after three months of constant drilling on it the teacher announced that during the rest of the year any paper—even a long composition—would be marked zero for that one error. Within a month it had been written wrong by three members of the class.

Study attentively these common words with *e*:

describe	enemy	destroy
description	pretty	despair

The Latin word *peto* means "seek"; a teacher who "seeks to make something clear by saying it over and over again" is using *repetition*. *Bene* means "well," as in *bene* + *diction, bene* + *factor, bene* + *volence*. It is the same in *benefit, benefiting* (with one *t*). The noun *effect* is very common, as in "a good *effect*," "had no *effect* on me."

A very common conjunction is *whether,* as in "I don't know *whether* it will rain or not." It begins w-h-e; the only vowels are *e*'s: whe*ther*. "I don't know *whether* his remedy will *benefit* me; the *effect* may *destroy* my health."

People are buried in a *cemetery*. The name for paper, pens, ink, etc., is *stationery*. "We seldom use *stationery* in a *cemetery*. A *cemetery* is a *quiet* place."

The "superlative degree" of adjectives ends in *est: largest, smallest, meanest, prettiest, laziest, busiest*. It is a remarkable fact that some high-school students cannot spell *biggest,* ending in *est.* Note also *great* and *greatest*.

EXERCISE 14. Be prepared to write the following sentences from dictation:
1. They did not despair, though the enemy had destroyed everything in their town from the smallest hut to the greatest church.
2. The repetition of his benediction had an unusual effect on the crowd.
3. Although Constance was the prettiest girl in school, I thought she was one of the meanest.

4. I work after school in the biggest and busiest drug store of our city.
5. I will try to describe my benefactor so that you can understand how much I admire him.
6. He wondered whether to walk through the cemetery or around it.
7. An hour of rest and quiet benefited all of us.
8. He bought three boxes of stationery, the largest one for me.
9. The laziest reporter likes to write a description of a pretty girl.
10. All of us benefited from his benevolence, whether we realized it or not.

Words with *el;* Single letters

The following common nouns, often misspelled, end in *el*:

an angel from heaven	tunnel
nickel	shovel
channel	level

The following words contain only one *m*:

image	imagine	imagination

There is a Greek preposition "apo" which forms the beginning of a great many English words like **apo***plexy*, **apo***stle*, **apo***strophe*, **apo***thecary*. Three very commonly misspelled words begin with the same "apo." Notice that they have only one *p*:

apology	**apo**logies	**apo**logize

There is only one *r* in *around, arouse.* "He is going *around* to *arouse* the people."

EXERCISE 15. Be prepared to write the following sentences from dictation:
1. Briggs brought Jim a shovel and ordered him to dig a tunnel.
2. Crowds gathered around the channel to wait for his return.
3. She kept always before her the shining image of her guardian angel.
4. After a third attack of apoplexy her father became entirely helpless.
5. Imagine, if you can, an old-fashioned apothecary shop selling, without apology, nothing but drugs and medicines.
6. There is no apostrophe in the possessive form of the personal pronouns.
7. In his imagination he became an apostle of the new reform movement.
8. The grocer apologized to Mother for having overcharged her a nickel.
9. Dad was so aroused by this time that he hardly heard her apologies.
10. The flood waters rose to a dangerous level.

Three groups and six marvels

A great many adjectives end in **al**: *real, final, actual, general, usual.* Notice the *al* in *practical* and *principal*:

> a practi**cal** man my princi**pal** reason
> the princi**pal** man his princi**pal** objection

The "principal teacher" in a school is the princi**pal**; the "principal sum of money" is the princip**al**.

To foretell what is going to happen is to *prophesy*. "Jeremiah *prophesied*." "He *prophesies* fair *weather*."

The words that follow are shorter than some people think. Beware of putting extra letters in them.

> **film** trans + late = translate
> an **elm** tree trans + la + tion = translation
> the **helm** of a ship pos + si + bly = possibly
> ath + let + ics = athletics li + brar + y = library

The first three of the following six words seldom occur in high-school compositions that are written about modern topics, but they frequently have to be used in tests on literature. The six words are marvels. If you become familiar with them now, before you form any wrong habits, you will save trouble for yourself later.

> go**dd**ess has two **d**'s com + e + dy = comedy
> nym**ph** ends in **ph** trag + e + dy = tragedy
> **shep** + **herd** = shepherd trag + ic = tragic

Remember that one who herds sheep is a "sheep-herd," which is shortened to *shepherd*. Think of the *e* in *comedy;* it is the *e* that makes the trouble. We have a *g* in *tragic;* that poor *g* is often abused. Give the *g* its place in *tragic* and *tragedy*.

EXERCISE 16. Be prepared to write the following sentences from dictation:
1. As usual, I had to translate the longest sentence in Latin today.
2. Bill is more interested in athletics than in his French translations.
3. Possibly, with Anderson at the helm, the club will reach its goal.
4. In the final act of the comedy the shepherd renounces the goddess and turns again to Marion, his real love.

5. Though Cassandra prophesied disaster, no one believed her.
6. We are to see a film showing the actual scenes of the tragic surrender.
7. She gave us general instructions for using the library.
8. Little Jimmy hoped to find a nymph in the old elm tree behind the deserted house.
9. My principal objection to his scheme is that it is not practical.
10. Caesar's wife fears that her dreams prophesy tragedy.

Composition

Telling about Interesting People

The world is full of interesting people. A few—the stars of television and motion pictures, the champions of various sports, the public figures of politics and government—are known to millions. Their names and faces appear frequently in our magazines. Their faces are seen on our televisions. Their activities are reported in our daily papers. These famous few are interesting because of their accomplishments, which are known to practically everybody.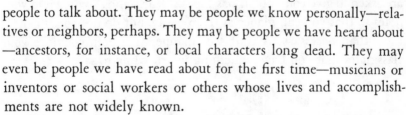

There are a great many other people who are not at all famous. Yet they have done interesting things and led interesting lives and are interesting people to talk about. They may be people we know personally—relatives or neighbors, perhaps. They may be people we have heard about —ancestors, for instance, or local characters long dead. They may even be people we have read about for the first time—musicians or inventors or social workers or others whose lives and accomplishments are not widely known.

What interesting person can you tell your classmates about? Perhaps you have an aunt or a neighbor who is forever winning prizes at county fairs with her unusual quilts or canned fruits or large dahlias. Perhaps you know a man who designs all sorts of strange gadgets or trains homing pigeons or goes prospecting for uranium. Perhaps you have heard exciting stories about one of your ancestors who fought the

Indians or sailed the seven seas or escaped from a prison camp. Perhaps you have recently read about the unusual adventures or amazing discoveries of a person you had never heard of before. Try to find a person that no one else in your class is likely to know.

Once you have selected a person to tell about, you are ready to plan what you will say. Your classmates will probably want to know such things as who the person is, where he lives, what he looks like, how you happen to know about him, and why you consider him interesting. Your problem is to decide how much to tell.

Think carefully about why you consider the person interesting. Is it because of his appearance? If so, you will want to describe in detail what he looks like. Is it because of his work? Then you will want to explain in detail what he does. Is it because of the life he has led? You will surely want to tell several incidents or, perhaps, relate an anecdote about him. Whatever reason you may have for thinking the person interesting, follow that reason in selecting examples for the main part of your talk. Pass over other details quickly. By concentrating on a few related examples, you make clear what the important ideas are.

Prepare your notes carefully, arranging the details in an order of increasing importance. Put the unimportant details first. Save your best example for the last. Then write out your opening sentence, so that you will know how to begin your talk. You will not need a special closing sentence. Simply end with your most important detail.

Practice your talk at least once before coming to class, so that you will know what you are going to say and how you want to say it. If you are asked to give your talk in class, speak clearly and slowly. Hold your notes so that you can glance at them easily, but do not consult them more than necessary. A confident manner will help convince your classmates that you have something worth while to say.

A Glossary of Troublesome Words

Affect and *effect*

Affect, beginning with an *a,* is always a verb, meaning "to influence": "The new ruling did not affect the freshmen." "She was greatly affected by the poverty of their home." *Affect* is sometimes confused with another verb, *effect,* which means "to bring about": "The arbitrator effected a settlement to the strike."

Effect may also be used as a noun, meaning "an influence": "The effect of the stock market crash is still being felt."

EXERCISE 1. Write *affect* or *effect* here the blanks occur:

1. The medicine had a beneficial ——— on him.
2. The music of Beethoven always seems to ——— me powerfully.
3. His speech had quite an ——— on the audience.
4. Let's see how seriously the closing down of the factory will ———
   the economy of the town.
5. Dean Smith plans to ——— many changes in the College's disciplinary
   system.

All right

All right is all right. *Alright* is all wrong. There is no such word as *alright.*

Allusion and illusion

The noun *allusion* means "an indirect reference"; the noun *illusion* means "a misleading appearance" or "a false impression."

> His opening words—"Cowards die many times before their death" —are an *allusion* to Shakespeare's *Julius Caesar*.
>
> By placing a large mirror over the mantel Aunt Marion produced an *illusion* of space.

EXERCISE 2. Write *allusion* or *illusion* where the blanks occur:

1. His beautifully tailored clothes and the rented car created an _____ of wealth.
2. She made no _____ to Martha's refusal to take the job.
3. The shrieking of the many sirens helped produce the _____ of tremendous speed.
4. Luckily Mother did not notice Bob's _____ to our accident, or she would have been worried.

Almost and most

Educated people use *almost*, not *most*, when they mean "nearly." They do not write "He most always calls at five o'clock" or "Most all of us are tired." They write:

> He *almost* always calls at five o'clock.
>
> *Almost* all of us are tired.

When they mean "the greatest number," they use *most*:

> *Most* boys like to hunt and fish.
>
> *Most* of the girls are going to the dance.

EXERCISE 3. Write *almost* or *most* where the blanks occur:

1. We _____ always have an assembly program on Fridays.
2. _____ everyone had forgotten his compass and ruler.
3. Since _____ of the juniors voted for a formal dance, we gave up our plans for a skating party.
4. _____ all of them prefer dancing to skating.

360

Amount and *number*

We use *number* in speaking of persons or things that can be counted; we use *amount* in speaking of quantities.

> She made a *number* of mistakes in the first paragraph.
> Great Britain imports a tremendous *amount* of wheat.

EXERCISE 4. Write *amount* or *number* where the blanks occur:

1. A large _____ of boys are enrolled in our cooking classes.
2. We sent them a _____ of carloads of wheat last Monday.
3. Mrs. Kurtz spends only a small _____ of money on clothes.
4. A prize will be given to the boy selling the largest _____ of tickets.

Anyone else, nobody else, someone else, etc.

The apostrophe and *s* to show possession are added to *else* in expressions like *anyone else, anybody else, someone else, somebody else, nobody else, everybody else.* Expressions like *anyone's else, someone's else,* and *everyone's else* are old-fashioned:

> You must have taken *somebody else's* coat by mistake.
> Has he collected *everyone else's* money?

EXERCISE 5. Write *somebody's* or *else's* where the blanks occur:

1. Can't you borrow someone _____ ticket for Dick?
2. _____ car is blocking the driveway. I can't pull in.
3. Nobody _____ work is as good as hers.
4. Why doesn't he use somebody _____ clubs?
5. She thinks everybody _____ ideas are better than mine.

Beside and *besides*

The preposition *beside* means "by the side of." *Besides*—used as a preposition—means "in addition to" or "except." Educated people do not write "He has a part-time job beside his regular work at Dennison's." Instead, they write:

> He has a part-time job *besides* his regular work at Dennison's.
> No one complained *besides* me.
> Grace sat *beside* me all evening.
> We stationed a guard *beside* the front gate.

EXERCISE 6. Write *beside* or *besides* where the blanks occur:

1. Only five people _____ the officers came to the meeting.
2. _____ being our star football player, he is an excellent student.
3. Standing _____ his uncle was the beautiful girl he had seen on the train that morning.
4. He crouched _____ the crate and waited until they left.
5. Two others _____ you have complained about the poor service.
6. She brought with her three suitcases and a hatbox _____ a large trunk.

Between and *among*

When we are speaking of two persons or things, we use *between;* when we are speaking of more than two persons or things and are thinking of them as a group, we use *among*. We do not say "I divided the money between the three boys." We say:

> I divided the money *among* the three boys.
> Dan planted the tulips *among* the shrubs.
> I divided the money *between* Lee and Mitchell.
> Dan planted the tulips *between* the garage and the house.

But when careful speakers and writers are telling about more than two persons or things and are thinking of them individually, they generally use *between*:

> Do you know the difference *between* flannel, gabardine, and serge?
> The four girls had only one pair of gloves *between* them.

EXERCISE 7. Write *between* or *among* where the blanks occur:

1. _____ the contestants were two boys from Central High.
2. Rita could not decide _____ going to the play and attending the reception.
3. Divide the work _____ the members of the club.
4. The five boys had only ninety-five cents _____ them.
5. Will you explain the difference _____ linen, gingham, and seersucker?

362

Borrow and lend

The verb *borrow* means "get something from another with the understanding that it must be returned"; the verb *lend* means "let another have or use for a time." We do not write "Will you borrow me a pen?" We write:

> Will you *lend* me a pen?
> She *borrowed* my pen and hasn't returned it.

EXERCISE 8. Write *borrow* or *lend* where the blanks occur:

1. She _____ another cup of sugar from me this morning.
2. I hate to _____ my new fountain pen to anybody.
3. Will you _____ me a dollar until Friday?
4. From then on Toby refused to _____ Mac any more money.

Bring and take

We use *bring* when we mean motion toward the speaker; we use *take* when we mean motion away from the speaker. We do not write "Bring this letter to your sister." We write:

> *Take* this letter to your sister.
> *Bring* me an apple, Bob.

EXERCISE 9. Write *bring* or *take* where the blanks occur:

1. Will you please _____ this note to the principal.
2. You will have to _____ these packages to the girl at the front desk.
3. _____ me a chicken sandwich and a glass of milk.
4. _____ Clara to Miss Baron's room on your way out.
5. Nora said you would _____ me the letter tonight.
6. Would you _____ these books to Mr. Quentin for me?

Childish and childlike

Though the adjectives *childish* and *childlike* both mean "like a child," we use *childish* to refer to unpleasant or undesirable characteristics, and *childlike* to refer to desirable characteristics.

> Mary showed a *childish* stubbornness when she refused to play with the others.
> Ernest has always had a *childlike* faith in the future.

EXERCISE 10. Write *childish* or *childlike* where the blanks occur:

1. Aunt Clara has always had a _____ trust in everyone's goodness.
2. Slamming doors to show anger is a _____ thing to do.
3. Maureen answered all their questions with a _____ frankness.

Discover and *invent*

The verb *discover* means "see or learn of for the first time"; the verb *invent* means "make or think out something new."

> Sir Isaac Newton *discovered* the law of gravitation.
> Elias Howe *invented* the sewing machine.

EXERCISE 11. Write *discover* or *invent* where the blanks occur:

1. Do you know who _____ gunpowder?
2. In 1792 Eli Whitney _____ the cotton gin, a machine for separating the seeds from cotton.
3. No one has ever _____ the fountain of youth.
4. I wish someone would _____ an umbrella that doesn't turn inside out in a high wind.

Formerly and *formally*

The adverb *formerly* means "in the past" or "some time ago"; the adverb *formally* means "according to set customs or rules."

> Mr. Zindars was *formerly* president of the firm.
> Miss Catherine Douglas was *formally* presented to the King and Queen at the Court of St. James last year.

EXERCISE 12. Write *formerly* or *formally* where the blanks occur:

1. Many people who _____ earned fifty dollars a week are now making two hundred.
2. The invitations to the reception were _____ worded.
3. Our new superintendent was _____ principal of the Bain School.

364

Hardly and *scarcely*

The adverb *not* is not used in a sentence that contains the adverb *hardly* or *scarcely*. We do not write "He can't hardly walk" or "I couldn't scarcely breathe." We write:

> He *can* hardly walk.
> I *could* scarcely breathe.
> This *is* hardly the time to complain.
> Bobby *is* scarcely able to manage skis.

EXERCISE 13. Write *is, isn't, was, wasn't, can, can't, could, couldn't, had,* or *hadn't* where the blanks occur:

1. I _____ scarcely heard a word, though I sat in the front row.
2. There _____ hardly enough food for six extra guests.
3. The men _____ eaten a thing for days.
4. Jane _____ hardly old enough to go to dances.
5. I _____ scarcely finish this assignment before eight.

Healthy and *healthful*

The adjective *healthy* means "having good health" or "showing good health." The adjective *healthful* means "good for the health." Careful speakers and writers do not confuse the two words. They do not write "Mountain air is healthy" or "That big man looks healthful." Instead, they write:

> Mountain air is *healthful.*
> That big man looks *healthy.*
> He must have rest and *healthful* food.
> We were fooled by his *healthy* appearance.

EXERCISE 14. Write *healthy* or *healthful* where the blanks occur:

1. Swimming is a _____ exercise.
2. Mr. Brownell wants to move to a more _____ climate.
3. Wayne looks _____, but he tires more easily than the others.
4. If you want to be _____, you must have the right food, exercise, and plenty of sleep.
5. A _____ child would not catch cold so easily.

Human and humane

The adjectives *human* and *humane* have entirely different meanings. *Human* means "characteristic of people"; *humane* means "kind" or "merciful."

> Putting things off till later is a *human* weakness.
> By their *humane* treatment of the wounded the conquerors won the respect of the world.

Imply and infer

Careful speakers and writers distinguish between *imply* and *infer*. They use *imply* when they mean "indicate something without saying it outright"; they use *infer* when they mean "reach a conclusion by reasoning."

> His frown *implied* that he was still angry.
> We *inferred* from his frown that he was still angry.

EXERCISE 15. Write *implied* or *inferred* where the blanks occur:

1. She _____ from my opening remarks that I did not approve of her cousin George.
2. Miss Bryant's smile _____ that she did not believe my story.
3. Mr. Clausen's sneer _____ that Ronald was not to be trusted, no matter what he said.

Learn and teach

The verb *learn* means "gain knowledge or skill"; the verb *teach* means "show how to do" or "make understand." We do not write "Roberta learned us a new dance yesterday." We write:

> Roberta *taught* us a new dance yesterday.
> I *learned* how to run the movie projector today.

EXERCISE 16. Write *learn* or *teach* where the blanks occur:

1. We asked Jim to _____ us how to run the tractor.
2. Can you _____ your parts by Friday morning?
3. I could _____ you all I know about diving in a few hours.
4. Though Mr. Ellis tried hard, he didn't _____ Ronald or my brother much French.
5. Will you _____ me how to use this adding machine?

6. My cousin _____ me as much as he could in the short time that we had each evening.

7. Unless Harrison settles down to work, I don't think he can _____ enough shorthand to pass the course.

Leave and *let*

The verb *leave* means "go away" or "go without taking"; the verb *let* means "allow" or "permit." We do not write "Mother wouldn't leave me go to the movies with them" or "Leave me be the pitcher now." Instead, we write:

> Mother *would*n't *let* me go to the movies with them.
> *Let* me be the pitcher now.
> We *will leave* early tomorrow.
> Mrs. Curtis *leaves* the children with me every Saturday.

The contraction of *let us* is *let's*. We do not write "Let's us call Phil" or "Let's us stay home tonight."

> *Let's* call Phil.
> *Let's* stay home tonight.

EXERCISE 17. Write a form of *leave* or *let* where the blanks occur:

1. Aren't you _____ your temper get out of hand?
2. Let's not _____ Madelyn behind.
3. Dave _____ the house without saying a word.
4. _____ her go alone if she wants to.
5. Russell wouldn't _____ us play with his ball.
6. Will you _____ me use your pen next period?

Less and *fewer*

The adjective *less* means "not so much." The adjective *fewer* means "not so many." Educated people use *less* only when they are talking about amounts or quantities. They do not write "There have been less traffic accidents this year than last." They write:

> There have been *fewer* traffic accidents this year than last.
> He earns *less* money than she.

1. Use _____ sugar the next time you make lemonade.
2. From now on we expect _____ complaints about the service.
3. We noticed that Helen took _____ lumps of sugar the next time she came to tea.
4. There has been _____ tardiness this year than last.
5. Can't we do the job with _____ men?

Lie and *lay*

The verb *lie* means "recline" or "remain in a flat position"; the verb *lay* means "place" or "put down." *Lie* never has an object; *lay* may have. Educated people try not to confuse the forms *lay, laid, laid, laying* with the forms *lie, lay, lain, lying*. They do not write "Lay down, Spot" or "Bob laid in the sun all yesterday morning." They say:

> *Lie* down, Spot.
> Bob *lay* in the sun all yesterday morning.
> It *is lying* on the living-room rug.
> *Lay* the baby in the crib.
> She *laid* her glasses on the desk.
> Mother *is laying* out Dad's clothes.

EXERCISE 19. Write a form of *lie* or *lay* where the blanks occur:

1. He has been _____ around the house for days, doing nothing.
2. Who _____ my wet umbrella on this table?
3. The ship has _____ at anchor for several days.
4. Alice _____ the baby in the cradle and tiptoed out of the room.
5. _____ on the davenport and try to get some sleep.
6. Bert and Neal _____ in the shade while the rest of us did the work.
7. For two days the food _____ untouched beside the cot.
8. Has the floor been _____ yet?
9. Tell Elinor to _____ down for an hour or two.
10. The men are _____ the foundation tomorrow.
11. The Barringtons' farm _____ in a secluded valley and is hard to find without a guide.
12. She had just _____ down when the phone rang.

368

Like and *as*

Although *like* is commonly used in everyday speech as a conjunction introducing an adverb clause, many careful speakers and writers prefer *as*. They do not write "Hold your brush like Keith does" or "Fold the paper like I showed you." Instead they write:

> Hold your brush *as* Keith does.
> Fold the paper *as* I showed you.

Like, not *as*, is used as a preposition. We do not say "He held his brush as an expert." We say:

> He held his brush *like* an expert.
> Fold your paper *like* mine.

Most educated people do not substitute *like* for *as if*. They do not write "You acted like you were angry." They write:

> You acted *as if* you were angry.
> It looks *as if* it is going to snow.

EXERCISE 20. Use *like, as,* or *as if* where the blanks occur:

1. His speech sounded _____ he had memorized every sentence.
2. Alan did the work that very afternoon, _____ he had promised.
3. He talked _____ a character from a comic strip.
4. They acted _____ they didn't believe a word we said.
5. You should all point to the picture _____ George is doing.
6. Mrs. Anderson's new hat looks _____ a vegetable garden.
7. Turn the wheel to the right _____ I showed you this morning.
8. He moved slowly and awkwardly, _____ a peasant.

No and *any*

Since *not* and *no* are both negative words, only one of them is needed in a sentence. When *not* is used with a verb in a sentence, the adjective *any* is used instead of the adjective *no*. We do not write "She did not want no food" or "He hasn't no money." We write:

> She did not want *any* food.   OR: She wanted *no* food.
> He hasn't *any* money.   He has *no* money.

EXERCISE 21. Write *no* or *any* where the blanks occur:

1. If we don't hurry, there won't be _____ tickets left.
2. I'm sure she hasn't _____ idea of resigning.
3. Mrs. Crandall certainly has _____ right to complain about other people's children.
4. I won't accept under _____ conditions.
5. Dave has _____ chance to win now.

Precede and *proceed*

The verb *precede* means "go or come before"; the verb *proceed* means "go on" or "move forward." We say:

> Miss Quillan *preceded* Miss Burns as principal.
> After a long pause Gustave *proceeded* with his story.

EXERCISE 22. Write a form of *precede* or *proceed* where the blanks occur:

1. The queen, _____ by two attendants, moved down the aisle.
2. Clement paused a moment to show the guard his permit and then _____ briskly down the hall.
3. Before _____ with her story, Ellen made sure the door was closed.

Since, as, and *because*

We do not use the expressions *being that* or *on account of* in place of *since, as,* or *because* to introduce adverb clauses. We do not write "Being that I was tired, I went to bed at eight-thirty" or "Mother was worried on account of we didn't get home on time." We write:

> *Since* (or *As*) I was tired, I went to bed at eight-thirty.
> Mother was worried *because* we didn't get home on time.
> Mother was worried *on account of* our lateness.

EXERCISE 23. Write *as, since, because,* or *on account of* where the blanks occur:

1. _____ Miss Carson was busy, I took the message.
2. Dale was out two weeks _____ illness.
3. _____ Dick is in charge, you will have to obey his orders.
4. _____ he was the best surgeon in town, he was the busiest.
5. I did not stop, _____ Helen was busy telephoning.

370

Sit and *set*

The verb *sit,* meaning "occupy a seat" or "have a place or position," never has an object. The verb *set,* meaning "put" or "place," may have an object. Educated people do not use forms of *set* for forms of *sit.* They do not write "Grandmother always sets in this chair" or "Those vases have set on that mantel for years." They write:

> Grandmother always *sits* in this chair.
> Those vases *have sat* on that mantel for years.
> Who *set* that crate in the hall?
> Before answering him, I *set* the tray on the table.

EXERCISE 24. Write a form of *sit* or *set* where the blanks occur:

1. Oscar has been _____ there an hour, trying to think of a title for his story.
2. Will you please _____ still and listen to me?
3. May we _____ a while and talk over this matter?
4. Mother prefers to _____ in a straight chair.
5. The men are _____ the posts three feet apart.
6. Dad _____ twiddling his thumbs while I tried on hat after hat.

Them and *those*

The word *them* is a pronoun used as an object. The word *those* is used as a pronoun or as an adjective. Both words mean more than one, but only *those* is used to point out the exact ones meant. Educated people are careful not to confuse these two words. They do not write "Them on the table are mine" or "I like them roses best of all." They write:

> *Those* on the table are mine.　　I put *them* there myself.
> I like *those* roses best of all.　　She bought toys for *them.*

EXERCISE 25. Write *them* or *those* where the blanks occur:

1. Please hand me _____ large books with the red covers.
2. After polishing the shoes, the clerk put _____ in the window.
3. These hats are very nice, but _____ in the window are much prettier.
4. All of _____ dirty dishes on the table should be washed and put away in that cupboard.
5. Motioning the boys to follow him, he spoke to _____ in the hall.
6. There is something familiar about _____ boys in the front seat.

Uninterested and *disinterested*

The adjective *uninterested* means "feeling or showing no interest." The adjective *disinterested* means "free from prejudice or selfish motives." Educated people are careful not to confuse the two words. They do not write "Since her last visit to Hollywood, Irene has been completely disinterested in our Little Theater plays." They write:

> Since her last visit to Hollywood, Irene has been completely *uninterested* in our Little Theater plays.
>
> We can count on Dr. Wagner to give a *disinterested* report of the committee's work.

EXERCISE 26. Write *uninterested* or *disinterested* where the blanks occur:

1. Dr. Gordon surprised us by being completely _____ in our plans to raise money for a new hospital wing.
2. Since Mr. Ellis knows none of the contestants, he will be a _____ judge.
3. You must find a _____ person to arbitrate this dispute.

Where and *how*

Educated people do not use *where* or *how* in place of *that* to introduce a noun clause. They do not write "Did you read in the paper where Joe was high man in his league?" or "I saw how he wasn't paying any attention to my explanation." They write:

> Did you read in the paper *that* Joe was high man in his league?
> I saw *that* he wasn't paying any attention to my explanation.

EXERCISE 27. Write *how* or *where* where the blanks occur.

1. We soon noticed _____ Jim was lagging far behind the others.
2. Do you know _____ Glen put my hat?
3. Marian read in last night's paper _____ Larry had been in an accident.
4. Did you see in this morning's *Herald* _____ Bob was fined for driving without a license?
5. Ben asked me _____ I had answered the first two questions.

Expressing Opinions by Mail

People whose main concern is serving the public are very much interested in the opinions of those they serve. City officials, for example, want to know how the people feel about such local matters as zoning restrictions, tax rates, public health protection, sewage disposal, school budgets. State officials want to hear the people's opinions about such things as parole systems, highway services, state parks, universities, public welfare agencies, state excise taxes, educational services. Federal officials want to know what national legislation the citizens think is necessary or desirable and how best to carry on the affairs of the nation.

You and your classmates have probably discussed many school problems, community questions, and national issues and have expressed opinions about them. But if you want to have your opinion considered by a person who can do something about it, you must see to it that he learns of your views. One way to do this is to write an open letter to the editor of a newspaper, expressing your ideas. A more direct way is to write a letter to the person himself, explaining the situation briefly but clearly, giving your opinion and reasons for it, and ending with a suggestion for the action you hope will be taken. For example:

The Honorable Porter D. Davis
Mayor of the City of Burton
City Hall
Burton, Nevada 89001

My dear Mr. Mayor:

In the April 14 issue of the *Burton News* I read that the annual city budget meeting is to be held at the City Hall on Friday, April 25. In view of this fact, may I take a few minutes of your time to make a plea for something that is of great concern to me and to other teenagers of Burton?

As you probably know, about a year ago a group of Burton High students, under the guidance of our principal and faculty, set up Teen Canteen—a recreational center in the Whitman Building on Main Street. Although we had very little money to work with—chiefly membership dues, donations from interested townspeople, and a profit from the sale of cokes and candy—we have managed to keep the center open for a year. But now we are faced with a serious problem. The Whitman Building has been sold, and we can find no other suitable place at a rental we can pay. Unless we can get more funds, Teen Canteen will have to close.

I feel strongly that the closing of Teen Canteen would be a tragedy —not only for the teen-agers, but for the whole community. It seems to me that the problem is not ours alone, but a community problem. Our city provides funds for beautiful parks with supervised playgrounds for children of grade-school age, but it makes no provision for students of high-school age. I think it would only be fair if some small part of the city funds were allotted to such a worth-while project as Teen Canteen.

I am sure everyone would agree with me that money so spent would be a wise investment, since a center like ours does a great deal of good. It provides a place where teen-agers can meet their friends, discuss hobbies and interests, and keep out of trouble.

Knowing of your great interest in the welfare of this city, I hope that you will be willing to bring up this matter for consideration at the budget meeting. We members of Teen Canteen and our parents would deeply appreciate your help.

Respectfully yours,
Donald Elkins

Notice that though the tone of the letter is generally impersonal, it is friendly. A special mark of courtesy is in the first line of the inside address—the use of the title *The Honorable* before the mayor's name. This title is ordinarily used in the inside address and envelope address of letters to government officials.

For your assignment in this Unit you are to write a letter expressing your opinion on a matter you are concerned about. You might, for example, write to the school superintendent, suggesting the possibility of using school auditoriums for community projects. You might write to your congressman, asking his support for some measure you approve of or urging him to vote against a proposed bill you disapprove of. Or you might write an open letter to the editor of your school or local paper, commenting on some topic you feel strongly about—the traffic situation, the curfew regulations, the city transportation service, vandalism, or anything else you think might interest readers.

Since a letter to the editor is meant for all the readers of the paper, the salutation used may be *To the Editor* or *To whom it may concern,* instead of the *Dear Sir* of the usual business letter. No closing is used, and the signature is often just the writer's initials or a pen name. However, most editors insist that the writer identify himself by giving his full name and address under the signature to appear in the paper.

Before writing the first draft of your letter, make a plan, organizing the details you will use. Revise your first draft carefully, combining sentences in ways you have learned, to make them more effective. Check the spelling of words you know to be personal demons and the punctuation of every part of the letter.

Make your final copy as neat and legible as possible. Since the revised first draft shows clearly how much space the letter takes, you will be able to center the letter on the page.

If you intend to mail your letter, prepare an envelope with your return address on it. If not, rule off a space on the back of the letter about a third of the way down, and write in it the address and your return address, just as you would on an envelope.

If you are asked to read your letter aloud before turning it in, start with the heading and read through to the signature. When others are reading their letters, listen carefully so that you can explain why you think them convincing or how they might be improved.